I0896088

ADVANCE PRAISE FOR

New Readings in American Drama

"Founded in 1990, *American Drama* has consistently attracted innovative and critically astute writings on American plays and playwrights, as this superb sampling, gleaned from the journal's first decade, so amply illustrates. The nineteen essays included in this thought-provoking book illuminate the work of twenty playwrights, from Edward Albee to George Wolfe, and represent cutting-edge analyses by authors both established and emerging. Under the masterful editorial supervision of Norma Jenckes, this book will be welcomed by students and scholars alike and will enhance *American Drama*'s reputation as the preeminent serial in the field dedicated to American dramatic literature and the application of various theoretical methodologies and analytical tools in the exploration of the play text. *New Readings in American Drama* can stand on its own as a testament to the breadth of our drama, offering the reader a feast of ideas and insights by first-rate critics. It is a stunning addition to the critical literature on American drama."

Don B. Wilmeth, Asa Messer Professor, Brown University

"A decade ago, *American Drama* set itself to address the relative disregard for American drama in academe and to provide a forum for the best of dramatic criticism. The evidence for its success is stamped on every page of this book, which not only re-maps that theatre, but brings to bear a whole spectrum of critical approaches in essays that are as perceptive as they are wide ranging."

C. W. E. Bigsby, Director of the Arthur Miller Centre and Professor of American Literature, University of East Anglia

NEW READINGS IN AMERICAN DRAMA

PETER LANG
New York • Washington, D.C./Baltimore • Bern
Frankfurt am Main • Berlin • Brussels • Vienna • Oxford

NEW READINGS IN AMERICAN DRAMA

Something's Happening Here

EDITED BY
Norma Jenckes

WITH THE ASSISTANCE OF
Tricia Hill

PETER LANG
New York • Washington, D.C./Baltimore • Bern
Frankfurt am Main • Berlin • Brussels • Vienna • Oxford

Library of Congress Cataloging-in-Publication Data

New readings in American drama / Norma Jenckes [editor].
p. cm.
Includes bibliographical references and index.
1. American drama—History and criticism. I. Jenckes, Norma Margaret.
PS334 .E87 812.009—dc21 2001038488
ISBN 0-8204-5589-X

Die Deutsche Bibliothek-CIP-Einheitsaufnahme

New readings in American drama / ed. by: Norma Jenckes.
—New York; Washington, D.C./Baltimore; Bern;
Frankfurt am Main; Berlin; Brussels; Vienna; Oxford: Lang.
ISBN 0-8204-5589-X

Cover design by Joni Holst

To:
Margaret Coleman Jenckes (1910-1997)
and
Helen Fleitz Weinberger (1913-2002)

Contents

Acknowledgments xi

Introduction: Something is Happening Here xiii

Chapter One
Staging Hypereloquence: Edward Albee
and the Monologic Voice 1
Deborah R. Geis

Chapter Two
Reconfiguring the Subject/Recuperating Realism:
Susan Glaspell's Unseen Woman 9
Marcia Noe

Chapter Three
Staging a Staged Crisis in Masculinity:
Race and Masculinity in *Six Degrees of Separation* 23
Jennifer Gillan

Chapter Four
Lies That Kill: Lorraine Hansberry's
Answer to *Heart of Darkness* in *Les Blancs* 39
John Gruesser

Chapter Five
From *Birth and After Birth* to *One Shoe Off*:
Tina Howe and the Uses of Feminism 49
Penny Farfan

Chapter Six
Gendermandering: Stereotyping and Gender
Role Reversal in the Major Plays of William Inge 61
Jeff Johnson

Chapter Seven
Arthur Kopit's *Wings* and the Languages of the Theater 73
James Hurt

Chapter Eight
Decoding Cipher Space: David Mamet's
The Cryptogram and America's Dramatic Legacy 87
Janet V. Haedicke

Chapter Nine
"What's the Secret?": Willy Loman as Desiring Machine 101
Granger Babcock

Chapter Ten
Hollywood's Moral Landscape: Clifford Odets's
The Big Knife 119
Albert Wertheim

Chapter Eleven
The Emperor Jones: Naturalistic Tragedy in
Hemispheric Perspective 131
Philip J. Hanson

Chapter Twelve
Collapsing Male Myths: Rabe's Tragicomic
Hurlyburly 147
David Radavich

Chapter Thirteen
Between Two Worlds: Elmer Rice Chairs
the Thirties Debate 159
Barry Witham

Chapter Fourteen
He's Still Falling: Wallace Shawn's Problem of Morality 171
Gaylord Brewer

Chapter Fifteen
The Agoraphobic Imagination: The Protagonist Who Murders and the Critics Who Praise Her 195
Nancy L. Nester

Chapter Sixteen
McLuhan, Perfect People, and the Media Plays of Jean-Claude van Itallie 213
Gene A. Plunka

Chapter Seventeen
Desire, Death and Laughter: Tragicomic Dramaturgy in *A Streetcar Named Desire* 227
Verna Foster

Chapter Eighteen
Ma Rainey's Black Bottom: Singing Wilson's Blues 239
Harry J. Elam, Jr.

Chapter Nineteen
"Any Baggage You Don't Claim, We Trash": Living With(in) History in Wolfe's *The Colored Museum* 255
Marc Silverstein

List of Contributors 275

Index 279

Acknowledgments

This collection is the distillation of ten years of work editing the scholarly journal *American Drama*, which I launched in 1990. Over the years, I have collaborated with hundreds of contributors. With the help of scores of anonymous referees and the members of the editorial board, we publish the journal twice a year. I wish to thank all those people, but particularly I want to mention the help and advice of Edward Albee, Richard Howard, Albert Wertheim, and the late Charles H. Shattuck. Also, I have received marvelous feedback from Dan H. Laurence and from President Joseph A. Steger of the University of Cincinnati.

Within my department I have enjoyed the support of various department heads, especially Fred Milne, who was chairman at the inception of the journal, and Leland Person, the current head, who has encouraged me greatly and added to the practical resources of the journal. I wish to also thank my former graduate assistant Mary Leech, who helped with the initial planning. I reserve my largest professional thanks for Tricia Hill, my current assistant, who had worked for several years as a magazine production director and brought her efficiency and energy to help complete this project. Also, all the essayists, whose work represents the best that we have published, have cooperated fully with the long process of preparing their texts for the press. I owe many thanks as well to Phyllis Korper and Bernadette Alfaro of Peter Lang Publishing, without whom this book would not have been possible.

Personally, I am grateful to my husband, Yashdip S. Bains, for his help and advice, and to my friend, Mary Ellen Lewis, for her enthusiasm, but most of all I wish to express my gratitude to my son, Joseph A. Francis, who has bolstered my confidence about attempting ambitious projects. My largest and last debt of gratitude is to Helen Weinberger (1913–2002) whose philanthropy brought the journal and the Helen Weinberger Center for Study of Drama and Playwriting into existence.

Norma Jenckes

Introduction: Something is Happening Here

Norma Jenckes

Over the past ten years a new way of reading the play texts of American dramatists has emerged in the pages of *American Drama*, a scholarly journal launched in 1990. Scholars of American dramatic literature have employed the methods of such poststructuralist theories as feminism, new historicism, queer theory, and neo-Marxism as well as applying the analytical tools of Lacanian psychology, anthropology, chaos theory, and cultural theory to the works of American playwrights. The late 1980s generated considerable debate about the place of theory in university teaching and scholarly publishing. Some of the older journals did not welcome the incursion of theory into discussions of dramatic texts. Eager to show the ways that new theoretical approaches might illuminate dramatic texts, *American Drama* has been hospitable to all and any theoretical methods.

Although drama and theatre history remain under-theorized and marginalized in the academy by the fierce focus of most critics on fiction as the prominent American genre, *American Drama* has carried forward the significant work of bringing dramatic literature into a more central position in the study of American literature. Making a distinction between theatre and drama, *American Drama* has also focused on the dramatic text, and not the performance, and placed an additional emphasis on playwrights and their development. The proof of the pudding is in the eating, and this anthology is a kind of banquet of the best from the journal's feasting with the panthers of theory. Arranged in alphabetical order by playwright, these essays represent a wide variety of approaches.

The first essay, by Deborah R. Geis, finds postmodernist primacy in the monologues in Edward Albee's work. In her essay "Staging Hypereloquence," she sees Albee's characters as isolated in monologue and seeking dialogue. Using critics like Jean-François Lyotard and Linda Hutcheon, Geis asserts that Albee's work needs to be seen as postmodernist in its "game-playing, fragmentation, and refusal of coherence." In the next essay, Marcia Noe discovers a feminist use of Lacanian psychology and the subject theory of Louis Althusser in Susan Glaspell's device of centering her dramas around the figure of an unseen woman. By so doing, Glaspell, according to Noe, both critiques realism and solves the problem of representing absence.

Jennifer Gillan applies cultural theory to reveal how John Guare explores the tensions in the subjective sense of white heterosexual males being threatened by people of color, women, and gays. She sees *Six Degrees of Separation* as dramatizing the shift of blame for society's decay onto the "deviant" individual. Queer theory and postcolonial theory both contribute to a reading of the play that reveals the hidden soul of American social relations.

John Gruesser brings the tools of postcolonial theory, new historicism, and Africanist discourse to uncover the extent of the playwright Lorraine Hansberry's knowledge and interest in Africa. He credits the writer as one of the first to change the distorted image of that continent. She achieved nothing less than an indictment of colonialism and Africanist thinking while at the same time restoring an oral tradition of African storytelling.

Penny Farfan calls into question the extent and seriousness of Tina Howe's feminism. Taking a committed stance, she warns of a postfeminism in Howe that actually undermines feminist goals. Using gender theory and the work of Althusser, Jeff Johnson examines the plays of William Inge as they participate in the project of creating the national subject and finds in Inge's work "intentional undermining of expected gender roles."

James Hurt credits Arthur Kopit with finding a new theatrical discourse to express the altered world of a stroke victim in his play *Wings*. Hurt enlists the testimony of actual case histories to demonstrate the accuracy of Kopit's dramatic reconstruction. Janet V. Haedicke analyzes David Mamet's play *The Cryptogram* as a kind of defection to the widespread American realist focus on the family, a focus which he had resisted in much of his work.

Bringing to bear an extraordinary range of theorists from Jean-Paul Sartre to Adorno, Lyotard to Hayden White, Granger Babcock examines Willy Loman as a key mover from a tragic hero to a machine whose desiring is an instrument of American capital. In the Clifford Odets movie script *The Big Knife*, Albert Wertheim uncovers a re-inscription of the playwright's personal dilemma and moral ambivalence in Hollywood.

Philip J. Hanson's essay on *The Emperor Jones* provides a welcome change from the critical fascination with Eugene O'Neill's personal life and family problems. In an historicist strategy, Hanson locates O'Neill's play in the realpolitik of U.S. expansionism in the Caribbean and contextualizes Brutus Jones's tragedy in the political tragedy of American intrusions into Haiti. He credits O'Neill with achieving a form of materialist tragedy that the Marxist critic Georg Lukacs had theorized.

Displaying an interest in the questions raised by gender theory, David Radavich places David Rabe's work in the territory of exploring masculine myths already inhabited by the plays of Sam Shepard and Mamet. His analysis of *Hurlyburly* also benefits from applying recent anthropological studies in the exchange of women and the rituals of homosocial bonding.

Using the end of the Cold War and the emergence of post–Cold War openness after 1989, Barry Witham examines a controversial play and its playwright, Elmer Rice. He upholds a bracing tone of free inquiry and gives evidence of the intellectual chilling effect of the Cold War era. Witham's essay is a model of historical revisionism, and he recuperates a work that had been overlooked and undervalued in the ideologically charged period of American intellectual life since 1946.

In analyzing the work of Wallace Shawn, Gaylord Brewer finds in the writer a postmodern moral relativism and a refusal to endorse absolutes that bewilders some audiences and sometimes enrages theatre critics. Fueled by the insights of feminists and the recent feminist critique of psychoanalysis, Nancy L. Nester examines three female playwrights, Susan Glaspell, Sophie Treadwell, and Wendy Kesselman, who create murderous women protagonists whose insanity she reads as their reaction to the debilitating experience of patriarchy. Nester rejects any valorizing of their psychosis and critiques as anti-feminist the presentation of madness as political or cultural revolution.

Gene A. Plunka examines the ways in which the theatrical experiments of Jean-Claude van Itallie with Joseph Chaikin's Open Theatre provided an incubation for his plays that could explore connections between medium and message. He reminds us of the prescience of Marshall McLuhan, whose pronouncements, which were met with some derision when they were first formulated, are now commonplaces of our experience of everyday life. Using genre theory, Verna Foster describes Tennessee Williams's large contribution to the development of tragicomedy. She assesses his achievement in *A Streetcar Named Desire*, which she lauds as his perfecting of the form best suited to portray contemporary life.

With the tools of postcolonial studies and subject theory, Harry J. Elam, Jr. finds in the work of August Wilson a "proactive dramaturgy" that aspires to nothing less than the empowerment of the African American community. Benefiting from African American cultural studies and the history of blues in ethnomusicology, Elam applauds Wilson's achievement in creating in *Ma Rainey's Black Bottom* a vehicle to help African Americans reintegrate with their African roots.

Combining deconstruction, cultural theory and subject theory, Marc Silverstein unpacks George Wolfe's *The Colored Museum* as not only a deconstruction of the clichés of Black representation onstage but also as an attack on the very idea of "museum." He interrogates the role of any museum as always misrepresenting the past, constricting the possibility of new subjectivities, and blocking the development of a cultural politics of difference.

In reviewing the content and approach of these essays, the intellectual and critical project of the journal *American Drama* emerges more clearly. It seems that the journal is itself a post–Cold War project, and the very range and openness of its essays attest to a kind of renewed freedom of inquiry in the area of dramatic criticism. Those of us who study American dramatic literature and its history know that it was the dramatists, the playwrights, and the Hollywood script writers, not the poets or the novelists, who most bore the brunt of McCarthyism in the 1950s and who were most frequently summoned to testify before the House Un-American Activities Committee.

Maybe one of the reasons that American drama is marginalized in the American academy is that it is too popular. It influences public opinion, and it bears witness in an immediate and powerful way to the political twists and turns of our history and the politics of our republic. *American Drama* has been, in its first ten years of existence, a major intellectual conduit for the dissemination of analyses, which demonstrate the connections between the new paradigm of critical theory and the body of American dramatic literature. The essays collected in this anthology display the impact of theory on writing about drama and demonstrate the breaking down of traditional antipathy to theory. Close reading and script analysis are not adequate tools to understand the achievement and direction of the American dramatic genius. The "something" that has been "happening" in American drama has been readings of playtexts that have uncovered new connections, significance and resonances. These essays have enlarged our sense of what drama criticism can achieve. These essayists have helped to bring American drama into the contemporary conversation with theory. The powerful discourses of feminism, postcolonialism, neo-Marxism, new historicism, and postmodernism have helped these writers discover new ways to understand the achievement of American dramatists and raised the intellectual cachet of dramatic literature, criticism, and theory.

Chapter One

Staging Hypereloquence: Edward Albee and the Monologic Voice

Deborah R. Geis

Edward Albee's characters are, above all else, talkers. More than that, they are hypnotic, insufferable, creative, rambling talkers; in short, they are endowed with what one might call the gift of hypereloquence. Sometimes, as with Jerry in *The Zoo Story* and George and Martha in *Who's Afraid of Virginia Woolf?*, the ability to manipulate language is as much a curse as it is a blessing. Often, too, the inability of the speaker to find an audience is what constitutes the curse; this is again Jerry's case, as well as that of the Girl in *Listening*. In modern and postmodern drama, the incomplete or unfulfilled striving for dialogue, particularly in the case of a "hypereloquent" speaker, turns to monologue. The audience is in the paradoxical position of becoming the "listeners," the absent others to whom the monologue is at least partially addressed (even if there are onstage listeners as well), yet remaining unable (except perhaps in experimental theater) to offer the responses that would transform the monologue to dialogue.

This is frequently the situation of Albee's characters who deploy monologues, particularly the lengthy discourses that one might call narrative monologues: Julian's bizarre tale of his first sexual experience in *Tiny Alice* and Tobias's story of the cat in *A Delicate Balance* are only two examples among many. Hypereloquent speech in Albee's work, though, is always two-sided; at the same time that monologic language is shown to have the potential for deception or fraud (a sense that goes back to the "manipulator" characters of Roman comedy or to quack-medicine peddlers both on and off stage), this potential is portrayed by means of Albee's own apparent relishing of and gift for such language. That is, monologue is shown as subversive or somehow "dangerous," yet the structure and pleasure of the plays depends upon it. C. W. E. Bigsby's discussion of the artist's role for Albee helps to articulate this paradox:

> [T]he artist remains a crucial figure, and language a necessary channel of communication, a public symbol of the link between people separated less by experience than fear. And this is the essence of a tension in his work: language as concealment, language as desperate attempt to establish contact;

> fiction as game, retreat, defense against the real, and fiction as moral exemplar, a means to dramatize human need and the possibility of action. (*A Critical Introduction* 300)

The richness of Albee's narrative monologues anticipates or complements Sam Shepard's trademark "arias" in their ability to allow this type of discourse to take over the physical action of the play. A closer look at Albee's speakers, though, reveals that—unlike in Shepard—hypereloquent speech is imbued with distrust, disbelief, and other types of miscommunication for its senders and onstage recipients. Albee thus emphasizes the distinction between the effect of narrative voice *within* the play, and its effect on the theater audience; sometimes the two effects coincide, but more often they are at odds with one another.

A paradigmatic example is the centerpiece monologue of *The Zoo Story*, Jerry's tale about the dog with whom he fails to achieve contact. The narrative itself, as well as the moments of its *énonciation*, mirror Jerry's unsuccessful quest to reach another being. Near the conclusion of the sequence, he says, "If we can so misunderstand, well then, why have we invented the word love in the first place?" When Peter fails to react, Jerry begs him for a response; Peter answers, "I ...don't understand what . . . I don't think I . . . Why did you tell me this?" (*Zoo Story* 36). Peter falls short of realizing that for Jerry, the act of narration embodies an attempt to escape from his isolation; as Jerry says in a frequently cited passage of his dog story:

> Don't you see? A person has to have some way of dealing with SOMETHING. If not with people . . . SOMETHING. With a bed, with a cockroach, with a mirror . . . no, that's too hard, that's one of the last steps. (34)

As long as his monologue has an auditor, Jerry seems to have a chance for an eventual movement into the realm of dialogue. Andrew Kennedy points out that Jerry's insistence on the difficulty of dealing with a mirror is not just that it would force him to face himself (almost literally), but also that doing so "would perpetuate the monologue . . . [and] it is essential for him to provoke a response" (196). If a "response" is available at all, though, it is only partial and ironic, coming as it does at the end of the play when Peter ends up holding the knife upon which Jerry impales himself. Peter's own isolation—rooted in a kind of bourgeois complacency—is of a different nature than Jerry's but it renders him unable to allow Jerry's monologue to succeed in its effort towards dialogue.

In *Who's Afraid of Virginia Woolf*, George and Martha are less existentially isolated than Jerry, yet they, too, are victims of their own facility with language. Just as Jerry can create narratives but to some extent remains imprisoned within his own monologic voice, George and Martha have little else than their storytelling and verbal jousting; even their "son" is a linguistic fabrication. As Bigsby says, "[t]heir elaborate language games are a substitute for real contact" (*A Critical Introduction* 267). The effect is that, even though the two characters engage in dialogue, their narratives constitute, oddly, a type of monologic discourse. They are operating, as Jean-François Lyotard would point out, within a field where deception occurs because the "rules" of their language games are constantly being changed and shifted (61–62). George and Martha manipulate and talk "at" their onstage audience of Nick and Honey, and their narratives themselves are contradicted or destroyed *within* George's and Martha's exchanges (e.g., the "killing off" of their "son"). Anne Paolucci aptly characterizes the "ambiguous explanations, unfinished or incomplete stories, emotional climaxes suddenly deflated into absurdity" as components that underlie the "existential mood" of the play (51). But these failures of language also point to the fragile nature of a world sustained only by the creation of fictions (even as such fictions constitute the framework of the play).

One of the most telling examples of this entrapment within language games and verbal histrionics occurs at the beginning of Act Three, when Martha enters and soliloquizes:

> I cry all the time too, Daddy. I cry allllllll the time; but deep inside, so no one can see me. I cry all the time. And Georgie cries all the time, too. We both cry all the time, and then, what we do, we cry, and we take our tears, and we put 'em in the ice box, in the goddamn ice trays (*Begins to laugh*) until they're all frozen (*laughs even more*) and then . . . we put them . . . in our . . . drinks. (*More laughter, which is something else, too. After a sobering silence.*) Up the drain, down the spout, dead and gone, and forgotten . . . (*Virginia Woolf* 185–86)

Martha's monologue reveals some real emotions, especially in the latter part, yet she is also engaging in a self-conscious parody of a soliloquy. This is evident not only in her laughter, but also in Albee's stage directions at the outset of her speech: "*Goes to the bar, makes herself a drink and amuses herself with the following performance*" (185). Like her tears frozen in the ice trays, the, Martha's ability to express genuine feeling is mostly frozen in her posturing as an "actress"; any sentiment that breaks through toward the end of the soliloquy is promptly returned to the realm of verbal artifice as she clinks the ice cubes into her glass. Albee places the audience in a complex position here, perhaps more so than in *The Zoo Story*. We are aware of Martha's emotions, but we are also aware that she is "acting," particularly as her soliloquy emerges from within a naturalistic context. The crucial distinction here between the perceptions of the spectators and of the characters lies in Martha's failure truly to break out of the "acting" mode; as a result, while she creates a send-up of the soliloquy as a *form* of theatrical discourse, she also travesties the ability of the soliloquy to generate a sustained insight of revelation. Then again, since this is really Albee's (as well as Martha's) travesty, perhaps the joke is on the audience after all. We might even say that Martha's speech is simultaneously a soliloquy, and a parody of a parody of a soliloquy.

With the hypereloquent Julian of *Tiny Alice*, Albee turns toward a more frequent deployment of narrative monologue. The play's most pivotal moments are Julian's three "set" speeches: his story of his real or imagined first sexual encounter, his description (in the scene in which Miss Alice seduces him) of his childhood fantasy of martyrdom, and his dying speech. Bigsby makes a convincing argument for the possibility of seeing the entire piece as a sort of internal monologue:

> [W]hen Albee describes *Tiny Alice* as "something small enclosed in something else," he is not only referring to the central symbol of the castle, but also to the structure of the play, which can be legitimately seen as a monodrama taking place entirely within Julian's own tormented mind. ("Tiny Alice" 133)

In his first two monologues, Julian becomes so immersed in the act of narration that he seems to be reliving the experiences as he describes them. He is, in a sense, seduced by his own language. Miss Alice remarks during his second story that it sounds as if he has recounted it before; he responds that "Articulate men often carry set paragraphs" (*Tiny Alice* 116). There may be some disparity between this view of Julian's discourse and its actual impact, for, as Ruby Cohn reminds us, the three speeches are really too "jagged" to sound like "set paragraphs" (151). Yet insofar as the memories Julian carries exert a powerful force as he embodies them in language, perhaps it is true that for him, they indeed exist *a priori* in the form of narrated "paragraphs." For the hypereloquent speaker, little awareness exists of the changes incurred by the transformation from "text" to "performance."

Miss Alice's moment of focus upon the delivery, the *énonciation*, of Julian's second monologue—rather than its narrative content—points further to the distinction between the spectators' reactions and the onstage auditors' reactions to his hypereloquence. With their highly charged sexual and hypnotic language, Julian's first and second narratives seem designed to have a riveting effect upon the theatrical spectators. In her role as onstage listener, though, Miss Alice refuses to serve as any kind of surrogate audience member in this respect. After Julian's first monologue, rather than responding directly to the narration of his sexual encounter, Miss Alice offers the counterpoint of a curiously detached enumeration of her own qualities: "I . . . am a very beautiful woman . . . [a]nd a very rich one . . . [a]nd I live here, in all these rooms" (62–63). By the end of Julian's second monologue, her verbal seduction becomes a physical one. Alice's discourse and accompanying actions in these two sequences are not entirely insensible to Julian's, yet they deflate and deflect the enunciative impact that the monologues have *inside* the play.

Julian's third monologue, the long confessional speech that marks his death (and the play's conclusion), presents a slightly more complicated case. In the form of a soliloquy, Julian creates multiple inner voices as he addresses both himself and God/Miss Alice. Paolucci characterizes these voices in musical terms, calling the speech

> a magnificent tour de force in which the dying man becomes his own ironic commentator as he moves from impotent fury to despair to bitter exhaustion, taking on simultaneously the roles of pleader and pathetic victim, high priest and Chorus, each emotional leap defined musically in its cadences, its Biblical echoes, its refrains, its rising and falling phrases, its resolutions from tension to tonic. (101–2)

This third speech seems to be different from the two earlier ones because there is no obvious (onstage) auditor physically present to deflate it; his metatheatrical "Exit . . . all" (179) at the beginning of the sequence when the other characters depart suggests a histrionic awareness of his situation similar to that of Martha in the Act Three soliloquy of *Virginia Woolf*. The closing monologue may subsequently, even by the virtuosity required for its delivery, become the most gripping and wrenching—or the most difficult—part of the play for the spectators, as the sheer length of the speech requires an immersion in Julian's consciousness. But Julian is swallowed up—or, as the stage directions indicate, "engulfed" in the sound and shadow of the heartbeat/presence of God/Miss Alice that slowly fills the stage during his monologue, and he must surrender to it, saying, "God, Alice . . . I will accept thy will" (184). The "presence" overwhelming the stage plays a similar role to that of the actual Miss Alice in the earlier monologues, for once again, it forces the collapse of Julian's discourse and causes him to surrender language for feeling. Here, the spectators to some degree share Julian's "engulfment" by the shadowy "presence"—Albee indicates that its sounds in the theater become "deafening" (184). Yet the overpowering image that remains at the end of the play is the highly theatricalized *visual* one of Julian's body spread in the position of a cross, as the lights fade.

The companion plays *Box* and *Quotations from Chairman Mao Tse-Tung* have an even more explicit structural dependence on monologue: in *Box*, a box structure appears on stage (with no characters) and a voice narrates the play; in *Quotations*, three characters (the Long-Winded Lady, Chairman Mao, and the Old Woman) deliver simultaneous monologues, sometimes punctuated by remarks from the Voice of the first play. The only onstage auditor, a minister who does not speak, is intended exclusively for the Long-Winded Lady. Although the monologues of the speakers in *Quotations* occasionally intersect thematically, Albee provides elaborate stage directions to delineate the extent to which each character is aware or unaware of the audience and/or the other speakers.

As in some of Samuel Beckett's late pieces or Robert Wilson's early pieces, the effect of the play is cumulative rather than linear; the narration of *Box* and the monologues of *Quotations* work intuitively and musically for the spectators—who, as with Beckett's *Not I*, must allow an almost unconscious assimilation of the text without having the reader's benefit of going back to reconstruct thematic links. Michael E. Rutenberg offers a helpful interpretation of the way the two works become, in effect, the audience's as well as the playwright's creations (205); I would also emphasize that this is a characteristic of poststructuralist and postmodern work in which the "interpretation" is seen as receiver/reader/spectator-oriented rather than as the sole result of the artist's machinations (Hutcheon 80). It is possible to argue that the audience for these two plays, with their deferment of "accessible" interpretation, is thus in a less "privileged" position than in Albee's earlier works. At the same time, the refusal of the dialogical *within* the works that we saw in the earlier pieces occurs in *Box* and *Quotations* as well. The Long-Winded Lady, whose narrative is the most personal of the three speakers, talks to herself and to the previously-mentioned minister, but he alternates between bored attention, shock, and inattention. The Old Woman "is aware of everybody, but speaks only to the audience" (*Quotations* 14); she receives no response from within the play to the poem she recites, but she does occasionally seem to be listening to the other two characters. And Mao speaks directly to the audience, even though he is unable either to react to others or to receive a response, except for infrequent and tacit ones from the Old Woman. In this respect, then, the audience's advantage of having a cumulative response does indeed place it in a more powerful position vis-à-vis the monologues than the characters themselves are permitted to hold.

While *Box* and *Quotations* seem to represent a brief excursion into Albee's own brand of Beckettian minimalism, they also are less of an anomaly, less of a departure from the stage language of the rest of his *oeuvre*, than one might initially assume. Shortly after these two plays were first produced, Albee said in a *New York Times* interview with Guy Flatley, "There is never any physical action in my plays. Think about it; what *really* happened in *Virginia Woolf?* All the action took place in the spectator" (Kolin 104). Even as early as *The Zoo Story*, Albee relies upon a spare setting and propels the play through verbal rather than visual histrionics; his characters are defined less by what they do than by what they say about what they do. *Listening*, originally performed as a radio play and reconceived (as a "chamber play") for the stage, relies (even in its second form) on sound and language, not visual images, for its narrative; the emphasis of the play itself—the demand to "listen"—mimics the act that the audience must undertake. Yet Albee's characters are unwilling or unable to "listen," to participate in the transformation from monologue to dialogue; in *Listening*, the result of this inattention is that the Girl slashes her wrists. Such failures reflect Albee's own ambivalence about the potential for discursive interactions, in a fragmented postmodern *milieu*, to allow human contact—even as narrative acts, as I have indicated, constitute the plays themselves.

Albee has tended, in recent years, to be defined as one of the twentieth-century playwrights whose works, along with Tennessee Williams and Arthur Miller, marked the flowering and then the closing of the modernist stage's period of poetic realism initiated by O'Neill and others. Perhaps, though, Albee needs to be seen more in the company of Shepard (and other slightly later dramatists) after all. Albee's paradoxical renderings of the monological and the dialogical bring him considerably closer than Williams and Miller to a postmodernist appreciation for game playing, fragmentation, and refusal of coherence. While the achievement of dialogue seemed to create a kind of sanctuary or reprieve from isolation for William's characters and sometimes Miller's, Albee appears to be more skeptical about what dialogue can actually accomplish. His hypereloquent speakers inhabit a postmodern world in which their voices are replicated and disseminated, but their questions are not necessarily answered.

Works Cited

Albee, Edward. *The American Dream and The Zoo Story.* New York: New American Library, 1963.

——. *Box and Quotations from Chairman Mao Tse-Tung.* New York: Atheneum, 1969.

——. *Listening. The Plays*. Vol. 3. New York: Atheneum, 1982. 53–152.
——. *Tiny Alice*. New York: Pocket Books, 1966.
——. *Who's Afraid of Virginia Woolf?* New York: New American Library, 1983.
Bigsby, C. W. E. *A Critical Introduction to Twentieth-Century American Drama*. Vol. 2. Cambridge: Cambridge UP, 1984.
——. "Tiny Alice." *Edward Albee: A Collection of Critical Essays*. Ed. C. W. E. Bigsby. Englewood Cliffs: Prentice-Hall, 1975. 124–34.
Cohn, Ruby. *Dialogue in American Drama*. Bloomngton: Indiana UP, 1971.
Hutcheon, Linda. *A Poetics of Postmodernism*. New York and London: Routledge, 1988.
Kennedy, Andrew. *Dramatic Dialogue: The Dualogue of Personal Encounter*. Cambridge: Cambridge UP, 1983.
Kolin, Philip C., ed. *Conversations with Edward Albee*. Jackson, MS, and London: UP of Mississippi, 1988.
Lyotard, Jean François, and Jean-Loup Thébaud. *Just Gaming*. Trans. Wlad Godzich. Afterword by Samuel Weber. Trans. Brian Massumi. Minneapolis: U of Minnesota P, 1985.
Paolucci, Anne. *From Tension to Tonic: The Plays of Edward Albee*. Carbondale: Southern Illinois UP, 1972.
Rutenberg, Michael E. *Edward Albee: Playwright in Protest*. New York: Drama Book Specialists, 1969.

Chapter Two

Reconfiguring the Subject/Recuperating Realism: Susan Glaspell's Unseen Woman

Marcia Noe

In his introduction to the Cambridge University Press edition of Susan Glaspell's plays, C. W. E. Bigsby says that she wrote "some of the most original plays ever to have come out of America" (30), citing innovations in language, character, and plot in *The Outsiders* and *The Verge*. But Susan Glaspell's most original contribution to American drama—the unseen woman—has nearly gone largely undiscussed in scholarly treatments of her work.[1]

Glaspell uses the unseen woman device in her first solo dramatic effort (*Trifles*, 1916), in the short story based on *Trifles* ("A Jury of Her Peers," 1917), and in her last novel (*Judd Rankin's Daughter*, 1945). Two other plays, *Bernice* (1919) and the Pulitzer Prize–winning *Alison's House* (1930), focus on female characters who never appear on stage. Thus, over a period of twenty-three years, Glaspell refined and developed this unique device until it became one of the hallmarks of her style.

The unseen women of Susan Glaspell's plays—the murderess Minnie Wright of *Trifles*; Bernice, the wronged wife who reaches out from the grave to redeem her husband with a lie; and Alison Stanhope, who broke with tradition in her poetry and in her life—are unconventional women: rebels, innovators, and perpetrators of outrageous acts. This essay argues that building a play around these unseen controversial female figures allows Glaspell to resolve some personal and professional conflicts as well as to represent on stage in a dramatically effective way the realities of women's status in late-nineteenth- and early-twentieth-century American society. Moreover, when viewed within the context of contemporary discussions about the reconstitution of the subject position and the possibility of a feminist mimesis, the unseen woman can be seen to provide a means of reconfiguring the female subject and recuperating realistic representations through feminist stage practice.

"Assuming that women have been excluded from the scene of representation—how to place that experience in representation" is the way Barbara Freedman articulates the dilemma of the feminist playwright (61). In Lacanian terms, the problematics of woman as subject derive from the female's dilemma upon entering the mirror stage when she, unlike her male counterpart, cannot locate herself as subject of discourse and must identify with the male in order to participate in the system of representation (Case, "Split Subject" 130).[2] "In the Lacanian model, woman, as the culturally constructed, as Other, is trapped in man's self-representation, existing only to reflect back his image of reality," writes Jeanie Forte (225).

Feminist playwrights are thus challenged to write plays which allow woman to inhabit the subject position without reinscribing her as the object of male desire, and thus reinforcing the dominant patriarchal ideology. Some have explored alternatives such as the fragmentation of the female subject into a number of roles, as Adrienne Kennedy has done in *The Owl Answers* and *Funnyhouse of a Negro*, transformations of the kind seen in Caryl Churchill's *Cloud Nine* and the separation of body and voice in Hélène Cixous's *Portrait of Dora*. Others have written off traditional theater as a possible site of feminist theater practice, opting instead for media such as performance art and the revue, which to them seem more conducive to feminist alternatives to the traditional theater's patriarchally structured protagonist/antagonist conflict.[3]

However, several decades earlier, Susan Glaspell created a means for woman to inhabit the subject position and at the same time elude the male gaze that objectifies and eroticizes her. In *Trifles*, *Alison's House*, and *Bernice*, the strategy of constructing the play around a central character who never appears on stage simultaneously centers attention on woman and the ways in which the patriarchy marginalizes her and at the same time resolves the problem of representing woman posed by Barbara Freedman. Because she is never seen on stage, Glaspell's unseen woman displaces the male gaze; moreover, her absence refracts the gaze onto the other elements of the play, elements which work in concert to establish her presence through a technique that a critic once described as "the assemblage and coordination, in speech after speech, episode after episode, character upon character, background and foreground, of lines and colors that shall finally coalesce into a vivid, veracious portrait" (*Boston Evening Globe* 27 October 1931).

Glaspell first uses this technique in *Trifles*, whose central character, Minnie Wright, jailed on suspicion of murder before the play begins, is never seen on stage. This one-act play is set in Minnie's kitchen, where she was found by a neighbor rocking and pleating her apron as her husband lay strangled upstairs in their bed. While the sheriff and the county attorney busily investigate the crime scene upstairs, the two farmwives who have accompanied their husbands to the Wright home remain in the kitchen, reminiscing about Minne and speculating about whether she really did kill her husband and what could have provoked her to commit such a heinous crime. Their conversation helps the audience construct a youthful version of Minnie as an attractive young girl who sang in the church choir and enjoyed her friends and pretty clothes as well as a more recent view of Minnie as a withdrawn woman married to a taciturn and stingy farmer, childless, nearly friendless, and completely isolated on an Iowa farmstead.

Minnie's kitchen things also help us to envision her as she was on the day of the murder. The pan of unbaked bread, dirty towels, half-wiped table, and unfinished sewing are signs of an incompetent housekeeper to the officers of the court; to the women and to the audience these props help to establish the presence of a disturbed consciousness.

Almost every action of the farmwives in this tightly compressed play is designed to make Minnie's presence felt. When Mrs. Hale rescues the lone surviving jar of Minnie's cherry preserves; when the women bring in Minnie's dress, skirt, and shoes to take to jail for her; when Mrs. Hale starts to sit in Minnie's rocker and then steps back with a start, setting the chair to rock, we feel as if that third woman is on the stage. Mrs. Hale completes an action begun by Minnie when she takes out Minnie's sewing basket, pulls out the quilt pieces, and finishes a badly sewn piece; later she finds the empty bird cage, and the silk-wrapped dead bird in Minnie's sewing box. These actions enable us to envision Minnie working in her kitchen on the day of the murder and reconstruct the events that precipitated it. Through the technique of piling detail upon detail of setting, dialogue, props, and action, Glaspell makes this unseen woman vividly present on stage.

In *Bernice*, the second of Susan Glaspell's plays to feature an unseen woman character, the title character dies several days before the play begins. Produced by the Provincetown Players three years after the world premiere of *Trifles*, this play in three acts makes use of many of the same techniques used to evoke the presence of the jailed Minnie Wright. Like *Trifles*, Bernice is a one-set play, and, as in *Trifles*, setting and props contribute much to characterization. Stage directions describe the living room of Bernice's country home as "*the house of a woman you would like to know, a woman of sure and beautiful instincts, who lives simply*" (159). To create this effect, Glaspell specifies a set that features an open fire, books, comfortable furnishings, and a wall of windows that open the room to the blazing autumn leaves.

In *Bernice*, Glaspell does considerably more with a device she introduced in *Trifles*: creating several female characters that function as foils to the unseen character and bring out various aspects of her personality. Abbie, the down-to-earth house servant; Laura, Bernice's sister-in-law, who is obsessed with form and correctness; Bernice's best friend, Margaret, the social activist: all of these rather ordinary women evoke, through contrast, the personality of the extraordinary Bernice. As the loved ones who have gathered to mourn and bury her discuss her continually, they create a constantly changing and contradictory picture of the dead Bernice that establishes her as a dynamic presence and the focal point of the play.

This process begins near the end of the first act, when Abbie tells Bernice's philandering husband Craig that Bernice killed herself. In the second act Abbie is revealed to have deceived Craig. Margaret refuses to believe that someone who loved life so passionately could have committed suicide, and Abbie confesses that she is right; Bernice had made her promise to tell Craig this falsehood. But this construction of Bernice—a wronged woman whose last act was a vengeful lie—is even more repugnant to Margaret. In the third act Margaret comes to understand that Bernice's deception was an act of love. Craig has been deeply moved and changed by Abbie's revelation; he now sees that he must have been a very shallow and callous person to have been completely unaware of Bernice's great love for him. This realization has shocked him into a realization that his writing has suffered from the same kind of superficiality and insensitivity. At this time Margaret realizes that Bernice's lie was a gift to Craig of herself, a way of changing him and helping him to live a more fulfilling life.

The unseen woman makes her third appearance in the Glaspell dramatic canon as the deceased poet Alison Stanhope. As in the aforementioned two plays, the *mise en scène* plays a major role in evoking the unseen woman's personality. The breaking up of the family estate on the last day of the nineteenth century requires Alison's family to sort through old newspapers, books, and mementos; in doing so, they reconstruct the ambiance of Alison's past. The conversation about Alison that this project stimulates, as well as the information that comes to light in response to Alison's nephew Ted's questions and to those of a reporter builds to an emotional peak that almost demands Alison's presence; when her niece Elsa walks in at the end of the first act, it is almost as though Alison had returned. In the second act, the appearance of the materialistic Mr. and Mrs. Hodges, who plan to buy the Stanhope home and turn it into a summer boardinghouse, creates a contrast with the genteel serenity with which Alison's unseen presence has suffused the house.

The characters, too, function in making Alison real to the audience, much as they did in *Trifles* and in *Bernice*. Elsa's strong, deep love for the married man she is living with suggests a younger Alison capable of a similar passion. John Stanhope's dedication to duty and his renunciation of his youthful illicit love reflect the more conventional aspect of his sister Alison's personality. Eben Stanhope's thwarted writing talent makes his Aunt Alison's achievement in the same environment seem the work of genius. And Alison's elderly sister Agatha is a picture of what Alison might have become had that genius not been hers. Ann Leslie, the family secretary, falls in love with the reporter and seems likely to fulfill love's promise with him, as Alison longed to do with her Harvard professor. Eben's first wife Louise, cold, haughty, and concerned first and foremost with propriety, functions in contrast to Alison much the way Laura functions with respect to Bernice.

Examined together, *Trifles*, *Bernice*, and *Alison's House* can be seen to share more than an unseen woman character realized by similar techniques; these plays foreground the absence of women from sites of power in pre-suffrage America, exploring issues of power and control that characterize gender relationships, and representing silencing and marginalizing as patterns of interaction through which power is wielded and control is exercised and maintained.

Both the Wrights' and the Norisses' marriages were characterized by power struggles. When Mr. Hale testifies that he discovered John Wright's body accidentally when he went to the Wright farmstead to ask about sharing a party telephone line, he reveals that he had approached Wright with this request before and had been put off (5). His comment that he didn't think Minnie's view on the question would make any difference to her husband, as well as the discovery of the strangled canary and broken bird cage, suggests that Minnie was habitually silenced and dominated by her husband; and that conflict between the Wrights may often have been resolved through violence.

Like the Wrights' marriage, the Norrises' relationship had been defined by the power struggle at its center, the most important issue of which is Craig's unrealized desire to be as important to Bernice as he would have liked to have been. "I never really had Bernice," he tells Margaret, later adding, "I suppose a man's feeling is different. He has to feel that he moves—completely moves—yes, could destroy—not that he would, but that he has the power to reshape the —" (173–74).

Craig's hesitation and inarticulate description of his view of marriage suggest that he would have liked to have been able to control Bernice's feelings for him and thus dominate the marriage. Laura's remark to Margaret that "It's unfortunate that Bernice hadn't the power to hold Craig" (186), ironically foregrounds the power conflict that alienated Bernice from Craig: her withholding of herself from Craig to retain some form of autonomy countered by his philandering as a strategy to make Bernice care more about him. "It's what a wife should want to do," she adds (186), and later suggests that it was appropriate for Craig to want to "dominate the woman he loves" (187). The voice of social correctness and conformity in the play, Laura expresses the traditionally patriarchal notion that the appropriate roles for a man and a woman in a marriage are those of the dominant partner and the submissive partner, respectively. Craig echoes this view in his wish that Bernice's life could have been "made by my life" (174); ironically, it is his life that is made by her death.

The central conflict of *Alison's House*, which builds to a climax when new poems by Alison are discovered which deal with her unrequited love for a married man, also centers on power and control, as members of her family debate how much of Alison's life should be revealed to the world. As a young woman Alison was persuaded by the father figure in the play, John Stanhope, to forswear her married lover and withdraw from active life to preserve the family's good name and uphold the ideals of devotion to duty and the cult of true womanhood; throughout the play, the stifling of Alison is repeatedly enacted by characters who continually silence other characters. When Louise compares her sister-in-law Elsa's elopement with Alison's aborted affair, John Stanhope shuts her up politely but firmly: "Oh, we want to do lots of things we don't do. I might want to ask my daughter-in-law to keep still. In fact, I think I shall" (14). He is more vehement when Ted pesters him for information about Alison to send to his English professor, telling him to be quiet or leave the room (26), and even silences himself when Eben inquires about his allusion to his own extramarital love interest (71). This pattern culminates in John Stanhope's final effort to silence Alison by attempting to burn her newly discovered love poems. Elsa, the Alison figure in the play, convinces her father to save them, and he agrees, reasoning that to do so is to keep Alison alive into the new century. Though some critics and scholars dismiss *Alison's House* as an old-fashioned well-made play, it is more contemporary that it first appears, for Alison, the unseen woman, will ultimately not be silenced. Though Louise, John, and Agatha, representing the patriarchal ideals of the nineteenth century, try to preserve the family image of propriety and adherence to convention, the feminist values of freedom, self-determination, and self-expression, represented by Ted, Ann, and Elsa, prevail: through their efforts the poems are preserved, and through them, Alison will tell her story to the world.

Although *Trifles*, *Bernice*, and *Alison's House* are deeply concerned with the sexual politics of marriage and family life, some critics would question whether they are feminist plays, believing that the feminist playwright must abandon realism, or mimesis, because this mode of theatre makes the social order that it replicates on stage seem right and natural and thus reinforces the patriarchal ideology that undergirds it.[4] Jeanne Forte summarizes the feminist objection to realism when she writes that "classic realism, always a reinscription of the dominant order, could not be useful for feminists interested in the subversion of a patriarchal social structure" (116).

Still, there are scholars who believe that a feminist mimesis is possible. Elin Diamond, arguing for the value of enacting the truth of female experience on stage, discusses Brecht, Irigaray, and Kristeva as sources upon which a feminist mimesis might draw. Patricia Schroeder cites Marsha Norman's *Getting Out* and Wendy Kesselman's *My Sister in This House* as evidence that realism and feminism are not incompatible, showing how innovations such as the divided protagonist, scenes presented out of sequence, and pantomime can be used to adapt realism to feminist ends and concluding that "a flexible realism can depict the values encoded and disseminated by a patriarchal culture, assess the consequences of oppression by powerful cultural agents, and simultaneously support the alternative values—such as autonomy and female community—that feminism espouses." (108)

Like Norman and Kesselman, Susan Glaspell developed an innovative dramatic technique that allowed her to develop a feminist critique within the realistic mode: for Minnie Wright, Bernice Norris, and Alison Stanhope are not only literally unseen on stage but metaphorically unseen in terms of the powerlessness and isolation that mark their lives. Minnie Wright's estrangement from her neighbors becomes apparent when Mrs. Hale tells the county attorney that she hasn't been in Minnie's house in over a year (10), and later emphasizes how isolated Minnie has become as a married woman in contrast to her earlier participation in the life of the community: "Wright was close. I think maybe that's why she kept so much to herself. She didn't even belong to the Ladies' Aid. I suppose she felt she couldn't do her part, and then you don't enjoy those things when you feel shabby" (14).

In a subsequent comment on Minnie's plight, Mrs. Hale describes not only the physical isolation of the Wright farmstead, but the emotional isolation that shaped Minnie's personality and precipitated her act of violence:

> I could've come. I stayed away because it weren't cheerful—and that's why I ought to have come. I—I've never liked this place. Maybe because it's down in a hollow and you don't see the road. I dunno what it is, but it's a

> lonesome place and always was. I wish I had come to see Minnie Foster sometimes. (21)

Alienated from her husband, powerless and silenced by the circumstances of her marriage, and isolated from her neighbors, Minnie is an unseen woman long before she murders John Wright.

Like Minnie Wright, Bernice Norris lived quietly in the solitude of rural life, an unseen woman within both the circumstances of her life and of the play. Nearly every character in the play makes reference to her isolated lifestyle in the country and her aloof, if magnetic personality. People called her "detached," comments her father (162), while Abbie characterizes her as

> loving, and thoughtful, and gay. But always a little of what she is now—[*Faces the closed door*] off by herself. [*With an intensity the present moment does not account for*] You can't expect to understand a person who is "off by herself." (163)

Alison Stanhope shared with Bernice Norris and Minnie Wright their quiet, detached, rural lifestyle. A recluse who immured herself in the family home after having succumbed to family pressure to break off her romance with a married man, she, like them, is doubly unseen.

Moreover, these women are triply invisible. Physically absent from the stage, they are made present through those domestic spaces with which they are most closely associated—Minnie's kitchen, Bernice's living room, and, of course, Alison's *house*. Thus, these settings function metonymically, standing for the unseen woman, who, in return, represents the unseen American woman of her day, relegated to the domestic sphere and excluded from positions of power. The absence of the woman who is central to these spaces defamiliarizes them; making them less hospitable to the characters that we do see. Mrs. Hale and Mrs. Peters reflect this feeling of discomfort with their environment by the slow and hesitating way that they move about and talk in Minnie's kitchen. Stage directions indicate that Mrs. Hale is "*disturbed now and looks fearfully about as she enters*." Both Mrs. Hale and Mrs. Peters "*have come in slowly, and stand close together near the door*" (3).

In *Bernice* the title character is similarly identified with the home and hearth. "Bernice made this house . . . everything is Bernice," states her grieving father, adding "You can't get Bernice out of this room" (160). He then attempts to do just that, moving the tea table into the hall, and in so doing demonstrating his discomfort with the simultaneous presence and absence of his daughter that the furnishings and accessories suggest. Bernice's family and friends echo his distress, restlessly migrating from room to room, trying to simultaneously elude and recapture Bernice's presence in the house, speaking haltingly and in fragments and overlapping utterances that convey their discomfort.

The very title of *Alison's House* makes the same kind of close association between the central character and her domestic environment. In this play the simultaneous presence and absence of Alison destabilizes the *mise en scène*, visually realized through the contrast between the chaotic downstairs living area and the pristine serenity of Alison's upstairs bedroom, preserved just as it was when she was alive, and verbally realized through the dysfunctional communication patterns of the characters. Far from reinscribing and reinforcing the dominant ideology, these works of realism interrogate it. While props, setting, and costumes reproduce the unseen woman's domestic environment in almost photographic detail, her absence disrupts the characters' and thus the audience's comfortable response to the familiar surroundings of everyday life, foregrounds the limitations of this environment and demonstrates its tendency to stifle and constrict the women who inhabit it.

The power of the unseen woman in Glaspell's dramaturgy is demonstrated not only by its effectiveness in reconfiguring the subject and recuperating realism, but also by the way it illuminates the paradoxes of Susan Glaspell's personal life. "Of course I am interested in all progressive movements, whether feminist, social, or economic, but I can take no very active part other than through my writing," states Glaspell in a newspaper interview at the time *The Verge* premiered (Rohe). The mixed message in this statement points to Glaspell's curious ambivalence about feminism and the paradoxical way it functions in her life and work. In her fiction and drama she satirizes the masculine and feminine modes of perception, criticizes the arbitrariness of gendered social roles, and demonstrates the sustaining power of sisterhood. During the early 1920s her expressionist play *The Verge* was embraced and extolled by Greenwich Village feminists; today *Trifles* is frequently taught in women's studies courses.

However, in her personal life, Susan Glaspell was nothing if not traditionally feminine. She lied about her age frequently, giving 1882 as the year of her birth rather than the 1876 date that her appearance in the Scott County, Iowa, census of 1880 suggests (Noe 13). Although she was a popular and successful novelist at the time of her marriage to George Cram Cook, she adopted the role of supportive, self-effacing spouse, quietly earning their living writing short stories so that he could devote himself exclusively to the Provincetown Players. She also relished playing the understanding wife, as this comment suggests, "A woman who has never lived with a man who sometimes 'drinks to excess' has missed one of the satisfactions that is like a gift—taking care of the man she loves when he has this sweetness as of a newborn soul!" (*The Road to the Temple* 324).

When Cook became disenchanted with the Provincetown Players and emigrated to Greece in 1922, Susan Glaspell accompanied him in the spirit of the "whither thou goest" story of Ruth and Naomi, even though doing so meant abandoning her career when her reputation as a dramatist was at its height. After Cook died in Delphi in 1924 and she returned to Provincetown, she devoted herself to keeping his memory alive, publishing his autobiography and a volume of his poems.

Only another man, novelist Norman Matson, was able to distract her from her obsession with her dead husband. During their eight-year relationship, Susan Glaspell supported him financially and mentored him professionally, providing contacts with publishers and writing Sherwood Anderson and Theodore Dreiser, old friends of her Chicago Renaissance days, to suggest that they read Norman's fiction (Noe 54). Nilla Cook wrote that "she subordinated herself, always, to the man of the moment, was *anything* but a feminist, and always sad when work of her own succeeded more than my father's—or after, Norman Matson's."

How can the women who wrote the radically feminist *Trifles* and *The Verge* be the same woman who wrote in *Alison's House* that "when you love, you want to give your man—everything in the world?" (18). How could Susan Glaspell, a charter member of the feminist group Heterodoxy, have explained the genesis of *Trifles* with these words: "I began writing plays because my husband forced me to" (*Here is the piece . . .*).

To answer these questions, we can look to the unseen woman, simultaneously present and absent, who reflects the paradoxes that characterized Glaspell's life and mediates the conflict between her personal life and her intellectual development. By building a play around an unconventional woman, yet never letting the audience see her, Glaspell could reconcile the feminine and the feminist impulses that warred within her. Onto this unseen woman Susan Glaspell could safely project her most radical ideas, emotions, and drives without violating the ideal of the self-effacing, supportive spouse that she tried to exemplify in her relationships with men.

C. W. E. Bigsby has observed that whenever possible, Susan Glaspell works by indirection ("Provincetown" 25) and characterizes *Trifles* as "a play which works by understatement" (26). These methods, the most innovative of which is the character who is both present and absent, allowed Glaspell to simultaneously assert and efface herself. Thus, the unseen woman functioned as a safety valve; through her Glaspell could experiment with feminist ideas and express rebellious impulses, yet balance and temper the effect of the unseen woman's radical ideas and acts with the more conventional female characters who act as foils to her.

Also, the unseen woman provided a way for Glaspell to move from the conventional heroines of her early fiction to the boldly venturesome female characters of her later Provincetown plays. Near the end of her career with Provincetown, Susan Glaspell would make a pioneering horticulturist the protagonist of her most experimental play, *The Verge* (1921), a crusader for free speech the heroine of *Inheritors* (1921), and a birth control activist a major character in her 1922 comedy "Chains of Dew." Thus, unseen women such as Minnie Wright and Bernice Norris can be seen as transitional figures to the radical heroines of her late Provincetown work who do appear on stage.

Finally, through the unseen woman, Susan Glaspell could articulate her own paradoxical position within the Provincetown Players, and, somewhat prophetically, within American theatre history also. Although the second most prolific playwright in the group, she was in many ways the Provincetown's unseen woman, eclipsed by the charismatic leadership of her husband and by the genius of Eugene O'Neill, as she has been in theatre studies ever since. This Pulitzer Prize–winning playwright, who contributed eleven plays to the Provincetown Players, directed the Midwest Play Bureau for the Federal Theatre Project, and wrote one of America's most frequently anthologized and produced one-act plays, was virtually erased from the public memory after her death. By 1975 she had been the subject of only two dissertations, and most of her plays were out of print.

Susan Glaspell and her unseen female characters have much in common: though often silenced and marginalized, they ultimately prevail. Minnie Wright's motives for murder are never discovered by the male investigators, and it is suggested that she will certainly be acquitted, if she is even tried at all. Bernice Norris effects the change in her husband that she had envisioned, and, through her newly discovered poems, Alison Stanhope will finally tell her full story. Like her unseen female characters, and through them, Glaspell prevails, for the unseen woman is a major source of dramatic energy and originality, powerful and multivalent, illuminating the paradoxes that characterize her life and work, as well as the gender relations of her day. Moreover, through the unseen woman, *Trifles*, *Bernice*, and *Alison's House* provide and affirmative answer to Barbara Freedman's question, "Is a feminist theatre possible?" (57) by exemplifying successful attempts to constitute woman in the subject position and enact feminist critiques in plays done in the realistic mode.

Notes

1 Sutherland mentions Glaspell's removal of Minnie Wright from the stage as an example of the kind of accommodation that Glaspell, Zona Gale, and Rachel Crothers made for Progressive–Era audiences whose views on gender roles were widely divergent, and Ben-Zvi briefly discusses this subject, stating that the unseen woman in Glaspell's plays represents woman as void, upon whom the male characters project their own feelings and impose their own words.

2 See Dolan (41–58).

3 See Reinelt; also Forte, "Women's Performance Art: Feminism and Postmodernism."

4 See Case, *Feminism and Theatre* (112–32); also Dolan (83–97).

Works Cited

Benmussa, Simone. *The Singular Life of Albert Nobbs. Benmussa Directs.* London: John Calder, 1979. 75–121.

Ben-Zvi, Linda. "Susan Glaspell's Contributions to Contemporary Women Playwrights." Brater 147–66.

Bigsby, C. W. E., ed. "Introduction." *Plays by Susan Glaspell.* New York: Cambridge UP, 1987. 1–31.

——. "Provincetown: The Birth of Twentieth-Century American Drama." *A Critical Introduction to Twentieth-Century American Drama.* Vol. 1. New York: Cambridge UP, 1982. 1–35.

Boston Evening Globe, 27 October 1931, *Susan Glaspell's Papers*, Henry and Albert Berg Collection, New York Public Library.

Brater, Enoch, ed. *Feminine Focus: The New Women Playwrights.* New York: Oxford UP, 1989.

Case, Sue-Ellen. "From Split Subject to Split Britches." Brater 126–46.

——. *Feminism and Theatre.* New York: Routledge, 1968.

Churchill, Caryl. *Cloud 9. Revised.* American Edition. New York: Methuen, 1984.

Cixous, Hélène. "Portrait of Dora." Trans. Sarah Burd. *Diacritics* 13 (Spring 1983): 2–32.

Cook, Nilla. Letter to author, 10 February 1976.

Diamond, Elin. "Mimesis, Mimicry and the True-Real." *Modern Drama* 32 (March 1989): 58–72.

Dolan, Jill. *The Feminist Spectator as Critic.* Ann Arbor: U of Michigan P, 1988.

Forte, Jeanne. "Realism, Narrative, and the Feminist Playwright—A Problem of Reception." *Modern Drama* 32 (March 1989): 115–27.

——. "Woman's Performance Art: Feminism and Postmodernism." *Performing Feminisms: Feminist Critical Theory and Theatre.* Ed. Sue-Ellen Case. Baltimore: Johns Hopkins UP, 1990. 251–269.

Freedman, Barbara. "Frame-up: Feminism, Psychoanalysis, Theatre." *Performing Feminisms: Feminist Critical Theory and Theatre.* Ed. Sue-Ellen Case. Baltimore: Johns Hopkins UP, 1990. 54–76.

Glaspell, Susan. *Alison's House.* New York: Samuel French, 1930.

——. *Bernice. Plays by Susan Glaspell.* Boston: Small, Maynard and Company, 1920. 157–230.

——. "Chains of Dew." Unpublished typescript, Library of Congress.

——. "Here is the piece. . . . " *Susan Glaspell Papers*, Henry and Albert Berg Collection, New York Public Library.

——. *Inheritors.* Boston: Small, Maynard and Company, 1921.

——. *The Road to the Temple.* New York: Frederick A. Stokes Company, 1927.

——. *Trifles. Plays by Susan Glaspell.* Boston: Small, Maynard and Company, 1920. 1–30.

——. *The Verge.* Boston: Small, Maynard and Company, 1922.

Kennedy, Adrienne. *Funnyhouse of a Negro. Adrienne Kennedy in One Act.* Minneapolis: U of Minnesota P, 1988. 1–23.

——. *The Owl Answers. Adrienne Kennedy in One Act.* Minneapolis: U of Minnesota P, 1988. 25–45.

Noe, Marsha. *Susan Glaspell: Voice from the Heartland.* Western Illinois Monograph Series, No.1. Macomb: Western Illinois U, 1983.

Reinelt, Janelle. "Feminist Theory and the Problem of Performance." *Modern Drama* 32 (March 1989): 48–57.

Rohe, Alice. "The Story of Susan Glaspell." *New York Morning Telegraph* 18 December 1921: 4.

Schroeder, Patricia R. "Locked Beneath the Proscenium: Feminist Strategies in Getting Out and My Sister in this House." *Modern Drama* 32 (March 1989): 104–14.

Sutherland, Cynthia. "American Women Playwrights as Mediators of the 'Woman Problem.'" *Modern Drama* 21 (1978): 319–36.

Chapter Three

Staging a Staged Crisis in Masculinity: Race and Masculinity in *Six Degrees of Separation*

Jennifer Gillan

After four years of Jimmy Carter, American masculinity needed rejuvenation, or so proclaimed Ronald Reagan and the hard-body films such as *Rambo* that coincided with his presidency. This masculinity crisis staged in the 1980s by Washington and Hollywood has been the subject of several recent cultural studies. Susan Jeffords explores how Reagan's speeches and Hollywood films represent the new American man of the 1980s as aggressive, determined, and eminently capable of confronting and defeating enemies of the state.[1] Focusing on how Hollywood scenarios influence Reagan's rhetoric, Michael Rogin claims that the former actor borrowed Hollywood paradigms to cast his enemies as the demons opposite his hero. He split the world evenly into camps of good and evil through "the inflation, stigmatization, and dehumanization of political foes," a "political demonology" that still influences legislation and public opinion and elides the complexities of the United States' role in morally ambiguous international endeavors (xiii).

Drawing on the work of Jeffords and Rogin, among other cultural theorists, Lauren Berlant demonstrates that a binary between iconic and deviant citizenship was established in the 1980s to deflect attention from the realities of contemporary social relations. In this era, formerly unmarked citizens—the representative straight, white, middle-class heterosexual males—claimed that the "American dream" and the "American way of life" had been damaged by the agitation of people of color, women, and gays. Their call for a return to "things deemed normal," to a nostalgic national time when their iconicity was unmarked, diverted attention from the complexities of current social relations. Their logic relied on the claim that "the deviant aspects of the public sphere can be traced and attributed to the deviance of people's private lives [e.g., gay marriage, premarital sex, abortion, welfare dependence]" (Berlant 178). This argument reverses the feminist mantra, "the personal is political," and its original intention to regard intimate relations of domination and submission as a microcosm of the larger inequities of social and economic relations. By transposing the original slogan into "the political is personal," it shifts blame back to the individual, directing attention away from systematic inequality.[2]

John Guare's *Six Degrees of Separation*, first performed in 1990, dramatizes the shifting of blame for social and economic exploitation and general societal decay onto a "deviant" individual.[3] The play centers on the response of a group of wealthy New Yorkers to the discovery that they have been conned by a charming hustler who calls himself Paul and claims to be the son of Sidney Poitier.[4] Most specifically, the reactions of J. Flanders Kittredge, an underground art speculator, and his son Woody to how well Paul assumes their self-proclaimed identities—the self-made, daring speculator and the "fit" and worthy heir, respectively—exemplify what Berlant calls the anxieties of "iconic citizenship." These anxieties are produced in the aftermath of a one-night visit Paul makes to the apartment of Flanders and his wife Ouisa, and then are examined in a series of scenes involving the Kittredges' recounting of the story of that evening to others.

The play's structure makes the audience suspicious of Paul from the outset, at the same time that it demonstrates that the Kittredges overstate the danger Paul poses to them perhaps to deflect attention from their own illegitimate business dealings. The play begins *in medias res* with Flan and Ouisa running around their disheveled apartment, muttering, "We could have been killed." Before we discover by whom and what the Kittredges feel threatened, they relate the story of Paul's evening visit. Through this account the Kittredges, like Guare's audience, are drawn in by Paul's charm, but the hysterics with which the play begins imply that there is another side to this stranger. When Paul appears at their door, he claims to be their children's Harvard classmate who has just been mugged in Central Park. After reciting the addresses of the other old New Yorkers that live around them on Fifth Avenue, he tells them that he turned to them for help because their children said they were "kind." Ouisa is thrilled that her children would compliment her parenting, and Flan is flattered when Paul can point out all of the art objects in the room, most importantly, a double-sided Kandinsky. We soon learn that Flan is an art speculator, not just an art lover. This "evening at home" is really an attempt to gain the confidence of Geoffrey, a white South African gold mine owner, so that he will front two million dollars to buy a Cézanne from a woman who doesn't want her soon-to-be-ex-husband to know she has it. The plan is to resell the painting to a Japanese syndicate. It is apparent from the Kittredges' account that Paul inspires Geoffrey to offer the backing by elevating the evening to more than a simple cash transaction. As Geoffrey puts it, "There's all ways of doing business" (27). The evening ends triumphantly for everyone, and the Kittredges insist that Paul spend the night. The controversy occurs in the morning when Ouisa goes to wake him and finds Paul and a naked hustler having sex in her daughter's bed. She and Flan chase Paul and the hustler around the apartment and out the door. As Flan and Ouisa dash around the apartment checking their valuables, we return to the moment when the play began.

In the second half of the play, as the Kittredges slowly discover that there is no basis to most of Paul's claims, the cracks in the seemingly solid foundation of their own relationship, business, and family life begin to show. The very essence of Flan's identity has been challenged as well. Flan's anxiety that Paul just might be a better speculator and a bigger risk-taker than he is reflects the apprehension Berlant claims is typical of "natal citizens" who fear that those who could not trace their ancestry back to the original Dutch and Anglo-Saxon settlers might start to "extract more wealth and political prerogative than they by birthright should" (196). Berlant characterizes this phenomenon as "birthright anxiety," the fear of the instability of the core definition of an American as a white, heterosexual, risk-taking, self-made man who earned his prestige and wealth. In the 1980s such an assertion of a core image could no longer be made, Berlant contends, in the face of class, gender, and race-based challenges to the supposed natural rights of natal citizens: "Suddenly no narrative seems to flow naturally from the identity people thought was their national birthright" (18).

Guare's play dramatizes several masculine birthright anxieties and fantasies: Woody's anxiety about his literal and symbolic position as Flan's heir, Flan's apprehension about his right to secure for himself the iconic position of self-made American gambler, and Paul's desire to claim that position for his own, since he has demonstrated that he has the luck and pluck to make him a Horatio Alger hero.[5] In the pages that follow, I will explore how the play reflects these birthright anxieties specific to the 1980s, especially in its focus on the reactions of Flan and Woody to Paul. They cannot allow Paul's challenge to go unchecked "because the stability of the core image is the foundation of the narratives that characterize an intimate and secure national society," and as Berlant theorizes, "the nation must at all costs protect this image of a way of life" (175). Woody's and Flan's exaggerated characterization of Paul as a deviant mirrors the practice Berlant associates with the 1980s of vilifying certain groups for "their ill-gotten gains," thereby deflecting attention from the ill-gotten gains of those already in power (176). Berlant calls this deflection of attention from unethical power a "staged crisis in the legitimacy of the most traditional, apolitical, sentimental, patriarchal family values," concocted by the political right. There certainly is a "staged" quality to Woody's outburst over the news that his pink shirt was given to Paul and to Flan's outburst at Ouisa's suggestion that they owe it to Paul to help him. After looking at these two outbursts in detail, I will turn to Paul's own brilliant scripting of himself in the play's first half as a well-adjusted, de-racialized black man, a performance by which he also becomes enthralled. He begins to believe, against his practical experience, that he can lay claim to the rags-to-riches American dream, and then he self-destructively makes decisions in the second half of the play based on that fantasy.

Guare masterfully uses a simple prop—Woody Kittredge's pink shirt—and Flan's simple act of giving it to Paul in place of his own bloodied shirt—to demonstrate the anxiety about heirship that Paul's presence provokes. The pink shirt's significance as a symbol of heirship rights is indicated by the severity of Woody's reaction to the news that Flan gave Paul the shirt that Woody claims his parents purchased in recognition of his new "Soloflex" body. He shouts at them as if they have given away his rightful inheritance: "I treasured that shirt . . . I loved that shirt. The first shirt for my new body. And you gave that shirt away. I can't believe it. I hate it here. I hate this house. I hate you" (42). Woody's extreme reaction exemplifies Berlant's claim that when the "modal form of the citizen" is called into question a crisis is produced and the national future doesn't seem so certain. Woody Kittredge acts as if Paul is the embodiment of the social deviance that has corrupted society and victimized the upper class by undermining the tacit understanding that they are the most legitimate heirs of the nation. That the pink shirt fits Paul as well as Woody indicates a world in which the lines of descent are not as clear as they once were. Paul's acquisition of the shirt also has some figurative national significance since, as Jeffrey Louis Decker points out, when Horatio Alger's "poor boys" acquired a "new suit of clothes" it always symbolized their forthcoming class mobility (xxvi). If Paul "moves up," Woody fears that he will be "squeezed out."

Woody's reaction to Paul suggests that an anxiety is produced when an outsider fits too snugly, as Paul does, into a representative identity. Priscilla Wald explains the opposite phenomenon, theorizing that Americans who conspicuously fail to fit the standard models of American identity produce "anxiety surrounding questions of personhood." In her very insightful study of the impact of ill-fitting selfhood, Wald contends that "misfits" unsettle general assumptions about proper personhood (10). That the same anxiety is produced when Paul, chameleon-like, molds himself to his surroundings and to the cut of the pink shirt can be explained by Homi Bhabha's theory about the complex effect of mimicry: "Even when colonized people imitate the colonizer, the mimesis is never complete, for the specter of that 'not quite, not white' haunts the colonizer, a dis-ease that always contains a specific threat to the colonizer's hegemony" (126). Paul's form-fitting selfhood is a challenge to the natural legitimacy of those who consider themselves the rightful heirs of New Amsterdam.

Because Woody has to "work out" to develop the body that fits the shirt, he becomes the representative of ill-fitting selfhood even though it's Paul as a poor, black, homosexual prostitute, posing first as the son of Poitier, and then Kittredge, who Woody feels should be deemed unsuitable. Because bodybuilding implies that "fit" bodies are not born, but made, Woody's participation in this "work-out" regime indicates that his assumption of his inherited right to success has been disrupted, and he consequently feels the need to shore up his image of personal "fitness." Bodybuilding, argues Decker, can be read as a form of entrepreneurship: "to remake one's body offers an immediate if somewhat superficial and nostalgic gratification of the desire for self-creation," and, in Woody's case, self-legitimization (130). After Paul puts on the shirt, Woody's fears of effeminacy and impotency resurface. Described by Trent Conway, his boarding school classmate and Paul's gay client/lover, as having "barbells for brains," Woody is so unlike his father as to call into question his paternity and certainly seems ill suited to take over this business or manage his wealth. With his charm and skill, Paul, in contrast, slips so easily into the representative pink shirt that he harbors hopes of becoming Flan's surrogate son. Later, he even fabricates a story about being Flan's abandoned love child from his radical sixties youth. The conspicuousness of how well the shirt (and the attached role) fit Paul and not Woody makes explicit the vulnerability of the tacit "birthright assumptions of U.S. nationality" (Berlant 19).

While Woody is anxious because he believes Paul is trying to commandeer his actual position as a legitimate American heir, Flan becomes increasingly fearful about Paul's usurpation of the metaphorical position of heir to the nineteenth-century icon, the self-made American risk-taker. His anxieties are apparent in his outburst in response to Ouisa's suggestion that they should help Paul. Ouisa's stance is that they owe Paul for the transformative experience he provided them. Of course, they are more concretely indebted to him for clinching the deal with Geoffrey, a fact they both acknowledge the night of Paul's visit. Flan admits, "Paul, I should give you a commission" (28). He then offers him fifty dollars, saying, "you saved us a fortune" on dinner. Ouisa adds, "And we picked up two million dollars. One billionth of a percent commission is —." To which Flan chimes in, "Fifty dollars." (29). When Flan thinks Paul is a movie star's son, he can call the money a commission and imply that Paul has potential to be a legitimate businessman and equal contractor. After Paul proves to be a fake—a revelation that does not change the fact that his charm secured the deal with Geoffrey—Flan can only think of him as a hustler, negating his legitimacy as a contractor and faulting him for his failure to be successful at some more legitimate pursuit. If Paul really were Poitier's son, Flan may have been willing to help him gain a foothold in the business world. When he realizes that he is a nobody, Flan must condemn him as a criminal rather than admit that as a poor, urban, black youth, Paul has been systematically shut out from more legitimate pursuits. He may have raw talent and a speculator's instinct, but he could never acquire the Ivy League education and family background necessary for a career in art speculation. In order to efface the complexity of Paul's position and distance himself from any obligation to help him, Flan embellishes the story of his encounter with Paul, making him more villainous each time.

When Ouisa calls Flan's account into question, Flan's melodramatic response suggests just how much a threat Paul has become to Flan's iconic citizenship. Ouisa becomes annoyed that Flan has turned Paul into "an anecdote to dine out on." She questions Flan, "How much of your life can you account for?" His strange answer is, "All! I am a gambler!" The proclamation comes in the final dialogue of the play and seems an overassertion on Flan's part. The vehemence with which Flan makes this declaration indicates that he is actually afraid of losing his sense of himself as the embodiment of an aspect of the National Symbolic. Despite his speculative art deals, Flan does not prove to be much of a gambler in the play. Having grown up in Newport, Rhode Island, and probably graduated from Harvard (How else could his dumb son get in?), Flan has always traveled in the right circles in which he can make the right connections. Most of what Flan would like to attribute to wily risk-taking can be more aptly explained through expert networking. To admit that the circumstances of one's birth do affect one's ability to be an equal contractor undermines Flan's iconic identity as a self-made man. Perhaps it is important to Flan to declare that he is a gambler precisely because his connection with such an iconic identity can no longer be taken for granted.

Because the assumed superiority of their white manhood depends upon the positioning of Paul as "other," Flan and Woody cannot allow Paul to go unpunished. Yet, as the police point out, he has committed no actual crime, except impersonating a preppy student and perhaps "looking back" at those who traditionally were accorded the privilege of the gaze.[6] They later manage to get him arrested for taking money from a young man who actually lent Paul the money. After the young man has his first homosexual experience with Paul, he kills himself; his girlfriend is then willing to claim that Paul stole the money. In the two essays that deal with Guare's play (both rather briefly in the context of a larger discussion of homosexuality in drama), David Roman and John Clum both argue that the Kittredges are most unsettled by Paul's gay sexuality. In his article, Roman focuses more specifically on race, declaring that Paul is a threat to white manhood because he seems to render "white men passive, penetrable" (202) and, as Clum first asserted in his article, "unmanned" (22). Thus, in order to contain Paul, Flan typecasts him as a "spectacle of difference" who is "continually associated with drugs, urban crime, and AIDS" (Roman 201). To use Rogin's terminology, it could be argued that "fearing chaos and secret penetration" Flan needs to transform Paul into a villain "to give shape to his anxieties" (xiii).

Robyn Wiegman's theory of the "negation of masculine sameness" helps illuminate the implications of Flan's vehement assertion of his iconic status as the American gambler as well as his need to cast Paul as the ultimate villain (179).[7] Wiegman contends that in order to reaffirm their superiority, white males need to consign "lack" to black males, thereby negating the disturbing sameness their shared gender implies. When it is revealed that Paul is a hustler, Flan is especially eager to distance himself from him. To maintain his own legitimacy, Flan must overemphasize Paul's illegitimacy. As the play continues, Flan tells stories about Paul that exchange the complexity of his social position for a script in which he is a "phantasm of massive violence or death" (Wiegman 182). The Paul story becomes Flan's "trump card." His clients can't get enough of the "authentic" confidence man story complete with its dime novel dialogue—"We could have been killed. Throats slashed!" Because as an underground art speculator he is involved in some shady business of his own, Flan must resort to melodrama in order to position Paul's villainy in opposition to his own innocence. As Christine Gledhill explains, in melodrama "while the villain is necessary to the production and revelation of innocence, innocence defines the boundaries of the forbidden which the villain breaks" (21).[8] The irony, of course, is that Flan is engaged in breaking the same boundary between legitimate and illegitimate business practices when he makes private, "sensitive" (read "bordering on illegal") art deals for buyers who want to avoid taxes, publicity, or greedy ex-spouses. Despite or perhaps because of his own questionable profession, Flan persists in denying his similarities to Paul, judging him harshly as con man and hustler by standards that he does not apply to his own transactions.

Flan's ability to use melodrama despite the fact that the genre often depicts the contrasts of extreme poverty and unfathomable wealth and waste is consistent with Berlant's claim that the Reagan eighties effected a magical transposition of the victims and the victimizers. Utilizing the political demonology that President Reagan perfected, Flan casts Paul opposite his hero as the embodiment of social deviance and urban decay. Paul becomes part of that "abject population" threatening the "good life" of the rest of the nation (Berlant 175). Flan's melodramatic production mirrors the "staged crisis in the legitimacy of the most traditional, apolitical, sentimental, patriarchal family values," Berlant contends, the political right of the 1980s created to deflect attention from unethical power. The contrast Flan establishes between himself and Paul is similar to that of anti–affirmative action rhetoric. As Thomas Ross explains, an opposition is established in such rhetoric between the "innocent white victim and the undeserving black taker" (556). Commenting on the racist binary, Ross contends, just because "the dominant public ideology has become nonracist," it does not mean that racial thinking has disappeared. It has just been relegated to the unconscious, kept alive by the "manifestations of racial stereotypes that [still] pervade our media and language [and] is reflected in the complex set of individual and collective choices that make our schools, our neighborhoods, our workplaces, and our lives racially segregated" (557). It affects everyone, even those who consider themselves liberals, as is apparent in Guare's play when Dr. Fine, a Jewish man whom he has conned, calls Paul a "fucking black kid crack addict." When another liberal mother calls Paul a "black fraud" and asks Dr. Fine about Paul's drug problem, he backpedals and is embarrassed to admit that he has no evidence of that, "It just leaped out of my mouth. No proof. Oh dear God, no proof" (39, 40). Flan never directly defines Paul racially, but when he repeatedly calls the hustler with whom Ouisa finds Paul a "thing," he is, by association, denying Paul's humanity as well.

Flan's own humanity and legitimacy are strengthened each time he retells Paul's story, just as the white victim can take on a mantle of innocence by pointing a finger at the "black taker." "The idea of innocent victims, particularly when coupled with the specter of those who victimize them," Ross explains, "is a pervasive and potent story in our culture"(555). Certainly, it is a story that helps Flan rejuvenate his potency. His sense of himself as a risk-taking, self-made man is bolstered by his staged confrontation with Paul and his illegitimacy. To shore up his iconic identity, Flan even gets his "friends" at the *New York Times* to run his story about "smart sophisticated tough New Yorkers being boondoggled by a confidence man now wanted by the police" (51). The story, with its proclamation, "Who says New Yorkers don't have a heart?" helps Flan control and circulate his own self-image and reclaim his position as "modal citizen."

Guare carefully undermines Flan's version of the story, not simply in a postmodern sense by casting the whole concept of a single, genuine narrative or stable identity into doubt, but also more subtly by pointing out the similarities between Flan and Paul—so many that he indeed could be his son. While Ouisa is at once frightened and comforted by her connection to Paul, Flan is only disturbed by the proximity of those six degrees of separation. He vigorously denies any responsibility for Paul and scoffs at Ouisa's suggestion that they help him, responding once again in the melodramatic mode: "Help him? He could've killed me." When he adds, "And you," as an afterthought, it becomes clear that all his claims to protection really are a cover for his own self-preservation (61). Ouisa persists, telling him, "He did more for us in a few hours than our children ever did." She reminds Flan, "He wanted to be your child." (61). Guare is careful to depict how Flan's strained relationship with his actual children contrasts with his ease with Paul. When Flan turns Paul into the villain, he uses a technique of Reaganite political demonology, the transferal of malignancies outside one's own borders. In this way, he can claim that the problems aren't with him or his family; they are the fault of deviant citizens like Paul. When Ouisa tries to confront Flan about his tendency to shift the blame, to turn experience into anecdote, he tells her that he is most interested in experience in the abstract: "That's why I love paintings. Cézanne. The problems he brought up are the problems painters are still dealing with. Color. Structure. Those are problems" (62).

Color is a concrete problem for Paul that has affected his ability to secure desirable social and economic contracts; conversely, when he puts on the pink shirt, he imagines that he can leave his own body and personhood behind. To fit the pink shirt is to be the Kittredges' son, that is, to break out of the boundaries of status and hierarchical familial relationships. Woody senses this and fears that by allowing Paul to keep the shirt, Ouisa is symbolically expressing the desire to transfer his father's legacy from him (a blood heir) to a new contractually based partner (28). Tess Kittredge feels similarly dispossessed. When Ouisa explains that Paul has "this wild quality—yet, a real elegance and a real concern and a real consideration," a jealous Tess asks her mother why she didn't just divorce her real kids and "let this dreamboat stay" (38).

For Paul, the evening at the Kittredges starts out as a lark, a way to gatecrash and for one night pretend to be a member of the American elite. As enthralled by the Kittredges as they are with him, Paul fantasizes that he can stay with them and live out the American dream. He becomes quite fond of the pink shirt, forgetting that it is only in a fairy tale that the shirt will instantly make him an equal. When Paul tells Ouisa that she allowed him to be a full person, in his words, "to use all the parts of myself" (i.e., to be more than skin color), he is equating personhood with whiteness and the pink shirt. In that shirt he felt for a fleeting moment "a feeling of genuine membership" in the "utopian 'symbolic' nation" (Berlant 21, 3). Perhaps he feels empowered, as Roland Marchand claims consumers do, by his ability to have the same significant products as the rich (114). Paul seems to imagine himself as part of an advertising *tableau*, like the one featured in a November 1998 Tommy Hilfiger advertisement set on an expansive lawn of a Martha's Vineyard mansion in which a group of models from a variety of racial backgrounds all blend together into one oxford-cloth-shirt-wearing American type. Marchand claims that such "*tableaux* offered Americans an inviting vision of their society as one of incontestable equality" by presenting them a four-color parable of the "democracy of the goods"(112). By depicting equal access to such designer products, advertisers claim that all Americans have the consumer power; what they do not all have, according to Marchand, is political power or control of wealth (113).

Hollywood also helps project this image of a nation of "incontestable inequality" as well, not just because of its many rags to riches plots, but also because its actors seem to be embodiments of the ideal of the self-made, risk-taking individual. Such iconography is useful to the hereditary rich because it keeps hope alive in the promise of class mobility and distracts attention from the core elite who continue to inherit, maintain, and expand their financial empires. Paul avails himself of this Hollywood iconography when shaping himself into the charming young man who enters the Kittredges' apartment. Of course, Paul has an insightful acting coach in Trent Conway, who tells him details of the lives of all the people listed in his address book in exchange for pieces of Paul's clothing. He later acts as Paul's conduct book, introducing him to the precise inflections, activities, and beliefs of the eastern elite. As if he were a character in a Hollywood film, Trent claims that he will transform Paul into "the most eagerly sought after young man in the east" (44). An outsider because of his sexual orientation, Trent also gets caught up in a Hollywood fantasy. Once he helps Paul gain access to all the "right" drawing rooms, Trent imagines he could pretend to meet him accidentally. The community's embracing of Paul would then lead to their acceptance of Trent's sexuality. Then they would both "never not fit in again" (44). If the play were a Hollywood film, it might have such an ending, but Guare is not interested in reconciliations as much as he is in exploring what the demand for seeing them on the screen indicates about the state of American social relations. Indeed, Guare seems to expose such cinematic fantasy scenarios as attempts to untangle in performance the complexities of social and economic realities that have yet to be resolved in real life. Later Ouisa calls Trent "the Henry Higgins of our time," but Guare's play is no *My Fair Lady*. It draws on such rags to riches films, but only to highlight how at odds they are with social and economic realities.

Trent's fantasy is Flan's fear: that one will no longer be able to tell the difference between the legitimate and the illegitimate. Flan's apprehension is not unfounded. Paul might be describing his own performative potential when he explains that the power of an actor like Poitier is that he has "no real identity." Like Poitier, Paul "has no life—he has no memory—only the scripts . . . That's his past" (23). The danger, of course, is that if American icons—the gambler, the self-made man, etc.—are just scripts, then anyone can embody them. For his part, Paul casts himself in several roles throughout the play in an attempt to prove that the cut of the suitable citizen fits him as well as the shirt does. Paul initially presents himself as a rich, articulate, Harvard undergraduate who arrives in New York a day before his father so that he can play a down-and-out Orwellian character for a day (20). With this role-playing Paul positions himself not as one of "them"—those abject others who are perceived to be ruining "the American way of life"—but as one of Them—the elite who are trying to preserve "Our America." He also casts himself as the unthreatening, perfect black young man depicted by Poitier in *Guess Who's Coming to Dinner?* (Cripps 286). He says all the right things about race and the unlimited possibilities for self-making in America. He is a young black man who denies that there is any such thing as white privilege. His audience couldn't agree more. Paul suggests that his ability to rise above race has less to do with circumstances than his own personality and inner resources. Referring to the way that he doesn't feel "color" has impacted his life, he claims, "I suppose that's very lucky for me even though Freud says there's no such thing as luck. Just what you make" (23). By playing these various roles, Paul secures for himself the narrative of the self-made man by implying that race, social class, or the conditions of one's birth can all be overcome with enough initiative.

Of course, like the actor Sidney Poitier, Paul is just trying on all these roles "to see how [they] fit" him (23). What is so disturbing when his fraud is revealed is that they fit so well. Paul's most compelling performance is when he assumes the perspective of white alienation and frustration as represented by his faux Harvard thesis on J. D. Salinger's *The Catcher in the Rye*. The novel explores white fears of loss of power and innocence in a world in which it is unclear what it means to be American. Alan Nadel claims that Salinger's book reflects how in the McCarthy era "rituals of loyalty" replaced any actual grappling with the complexities of a changing America. Instead, people were required to demonstrate publicly that they could convincingly convey "prepared, written, and rehearsed" sentiments (80). Certainly, Paul skillfully pulls off just such a performance. Of course, it is no accident that he chooses a book that chronicles the disillusionment of the modern American and functions as a symbol of anxiety of the loss of white male power and heirship rights. By doing so, Paul counterbalances his threat as a charming, articulate, young black man to such stability.

Paul's stories also help confirm his listeners' belief in the fiction that business transcends race; in other words, any individual regardless of race can be an equal contractor. As they listen to his monologues, admire the Kittredges' double-sided Kandinsky, eat the fabulous dinner Paul concocts, Flan, Ouisa, and Geoffrey feel as if Paul has revealed to them what Kandinsky referred to as "the hidden soul of things" (Leggio 6). More precisely, he has given a transcendent hue to their soulless business transaction. Paul's presence turns the evening into a social gathering and a philosophical discussion, rather than a cash transaction. He appeals to them because he articulates their belief that success is dependent on hard work, risk-taking, and not on birth and networking. Flan, Ouisa, and especially Geoffrey, a South African well acquainted with racial tension, agree with Paul's assertion that there is no luck, "just what you make" and with the "pull-yourself-up-by-your-bootstraps," anti–affirmative action stance such a maxim implies. Paul rejects environmental determinism theory, arguing against the notion that a crummy childhood will affect your adult capabilities. He claims that race has never really affected his life and that he has never been used by or helped by people because of his connections. All of these assertions function to assure the white characters that individuals really are all equally free to make of their lives what they will.

The fictional Paul Poitier can say all these things, of course, because, like his listeners, he is born privileged. The poor black boy who is pretending to be this privileged son may want to believe these things too, but it is obvious from his final conversation with Ouisa in which he makes her promise she will help him if he turns himself in, that he knows that without their help his raw talent really is not enough to allow him to break into and succeed in art speculation. In fact, to gain entry to their world at all has taken an extraordinary amount of risk-taking. The young man the Kittredges know as Paul stabs himself, convinces the doorman to take him to their apartment, and pretends to be their children's friend for no other reason, it seems, than to gain access to their lives. As he has no access to their social or professional circle, he cannot network his way to them, but instead must turn to fraudulent means. His behavior is risky because he could be easily found out, especially since he pulls the same con with two other families. At the end of the play, he even risks calling the Kittredges again, despite the fact that they have already contacted the police. His biggest risk is agreeing during this phone conversation to surrender to the police in exchange for Ouisa's half-hearted promise that the Kittredges will take him on as an apprentice of sorts after he gets out of jail.

Why would Paul, a street kid cognizant of the way the world works, agree to such an utopian plan? First, it seems that he is as enthralled with the Kittredges' stories as they are with his. Like his stories, theirs fall in line with the national narrative of the self-made man. They suggest to him that he has the right personality and natural ability to succeed in the world of art speculation and that he could do so if he studies, works hard, and is willing to take the "grotty" with the glamour. Of course, they don't mention that Flan's class position and his contacts make his position possible. Paul does recognize that success may have less to do with one's paternity than with one's personality, but the right father can provide a forum for the latter.

Unfortunately, Paul falls into the trap of believing his own performance. He starts to think that with enough "pluck" and "imaginative endeavor" he can start a new life for himself as an American speculator in the grand tradition. After Paul helps Flan acquire a fortune by using personality and storytelling ability to secure Geoffrey as a backer for the lucrative art speculation, he assumes that because of his obvious talent at the game that he can speculate as well. He knows better, but he can't help being lured in by the seductive promise of the contract. The United States is supposed to be a contractually organized society in which individuals are free to contract on their own initiative; unfortunately, as Brook Thomas has demonstrated, the equitable social order contract promises has yet to be realized. In the last conversation Paul has with Ouisa before he is arrested and disappears, the lucidity of Paul's declaration, "Mrs. Louisa Kittredge, I am black," stands out (58). With this statement, Paul lays bare the unequal nature of the social contract; they are both bound by their position in the system, positions that both assume a white male center.

With this line, Paul breaks out of rehearsed sentiment and reveals the "hidden soul" of American social relations—that his marked status as a black male is essential for maintaining the white male as the unmarked type.[9] This moment of truth is quickly contained again as the dialogue turns back to the fantasy that Paul can become their apprentice. Paul even tries to impress Ouisa with how much he has learned from her, by telling her that he went to a museum and decided that he liked Philadelphia Chippendale. She "burst out laughing" both at the effeteness of his newly acquired tastes and at the fact that she and her husband actually own two Chippendale chairs. This example suggests that his contact with the Kittredges has cultivated in Paul a desire for material goods that he can never possibly afford. He has absorbed their worldview, obviously repeating Ouisa's sentiment when he says, "I'd rather have one nice piece than a room full of junk"(59). Ouisa fuels his fantasy when she approves his choice, agrees that he can "have it all," and exclaims, "We'll have a wonderful life"(60). This final sentiment mystifies Flan who can't understand why Ouisa wants to include this con man in their family future.

When Paul disappears after that phone call and Ouisa believes that he committed suicide after having been arrested at the spot where she promised to meet him and escort him to the police, Flan tries to assuage her guilt. He still maintains the staged pose of wronged benefactor, assuring his wife that Paul will return: "He'll be back. We haven't heard the last of him" (62). Flan assures Ouisa that they did what they could for Paul, but he failed to live up to his obligations. Rather than demonstrating systematic inequalities, Paul's failures only prove, Flan reasons, that Paul was not equal to the task of making it in America. While he can admit that Paul did have promise, Flan asserts that Paul undermines himself by using it for dishonest purposes; in the process, he betrays the generosity and trust of the Kittredges. As Flan says, reverting to cliché, "Like the papers said. We have hearts." With this sentimental assertion Flan realigns his image of self-righteousness just as earlier in the play Woody shores up his image of personal fitness. Flan has more power over his self-image, though, because he is able to get his version of events circulated by the *New York Times*. Of course, Guare's play intentionally highlights the fact that Flan's is only one of many competing versions of the same story. By spotlighting these struggles for legitimacy, the play is able to "mirror and amplify hypocrisy," to use the words Paul applies to his reading of *The Catcher in the Rye*, in contemporary American culture. More specifically, *Six Degrees of Separation* mirrors and amplifies the hypocrisy of the imagined national community that faults citizens for their failure to realize a promise from which they are already excluded.

Notes

1 See Susan Jeffords, *Hard Bodies*, 245.

2 Berlant also discusses "fetal" and "infantile" citizenship. She argues that the focus on fetuses and other infantile forms of citizenship distracts attention from the problems of adult citizenship. In the play Paul makes the same argument in Ouisa's dream section. He asks why there is so much focus on the beginning and ending of life and not on the years in the middle.

3 The father-son relationships in the film are disastrous before Paul ever arrives, suggesting tensions that have nothing to do with the "deviant other."

4 Poitier specialized in accommodationist roles in films such as *Lilies of the Field* (1963), *To Sir with Love* (1967), and *Guess Who's Coming to Dinner?* (1967). See Bogle.

5 Cohan and Hark contain thirteen important essays that cover representations of masculinity in various cinematic genres. See also Jeffords, *Remasculinization of America*, and Neale.

6 On the dynamics of inter-racial looking, see bell hooks, especially "The Oppositional Gaze," pp. 115–131; and Kaplan.

7 Wiegman develops this argument as well in *American Anatomies*. Her essay in *Unspeakable Images* is also relevant.

8 See Gledhill's introductory essay on melodrama, and Elsaesser.

9 For critiques of whiteness see Richard Dyer and Jane Gaines.

Works Cited

Berlant, Lauren. *The Queen of America Goes to Washington City: Essays on Sex and Citizenship.* Durham: Duke UP, 1997.

Bhabha, Homi K. "Of Mimicry and Man: The Ambivalence of Colonial Discourse." *October* 28 (Spring 1984): 125–133.

Bogle, Donald. *Toms, Coons, Mulattos, Mammies, & Bucks: An Interpretive History of Blacks in American Films.* New York: Continuum, 1996.

Clum, John. *Acting Gay: Male Homosexuality in Modern Drama.* New York: Columbia UP, 1992.

Cohan, Steven, and Ina Rae Hark, eds. *Screening the Male: Exploring Masculinities in Hollywood Cinema.* New York: Routledge, 1993.

Decker, Jeffrey Louis. *Made in America: Self-Styled Success from Horatio Alger to Oprah Winfrey.* Minneapolis: U of Minnesota P, 1997.

Dyer, Richard. "White." *Screen* 29 (4): 45–64.

Elsaesser, Thomas. "Tales of Sound and Fury: Observations on the Family Melodrama." Gledhill 43–69.

Gaines, Jane. "White Privilege and Looking Relations: Race and Gender in Feminist Film Theory." *Screen* 29 (4): 12–27.

Gledhill, Christine, ed. *Home Is Where the Heart Is: Studies in Melodrama and the Women's Film.* London: British Film Institute, 1987.

Guare, John. *Six Degrees of Separation.* New York: Dramatists Play Service, 1992.

hooks, bell. *Black Looks: Race and Representation.* Boston: South End P, 1992.

Jeffords, Susan. *Hard Bodies: Hollywood Masculinity in the Reagan Era.* New Brunswick: Rutgers UP, 1994.

——. *The Remasculinization of America: Gender and the Vietnam War.* Bloomington: Indiana UP, 1989.

Leggio, James, ed. *Kandinsky.* New York: Harry N. Abrams, 1996.

Kaplan, E. Ann. *Looking for the Other: Feminism, Film, and the Imperial Gaze.* New York: Routledge, 1997.

Marchand, Roland. *Advertising the American Dream: Making Way for Modernity, 1920–1940.* Berkeley: U of California P, 1985.

Nadel, Alan. *Containment Culture: American Narratives, Postmodernism, and the Atomic Age.* Durham: Duke UP, 1995.

Neale, Steve. "Masculinity as Spectacle." *Screen* 24 (6): 2–16.

Rogin, Michael. *Ronald Reagan, the Movie: And Other Episodes in Political Demonology.* Berkeley: U of California P, 1987.

Roman, David. "Fierce Love and Fierce Response: Intervening in the Cultural Politics of Race, Sexuality, and AIDS." *Critical Essays: Gay and Lesbian Writers of Color.* Ed. Emmanuel S. Nelson. Haworth, NY: Harrington Park P. 195–219.

Ross, Thomas "Innocence and Affirmative Action." *Critical Race Theory: The Cutting Edge.* Ed. Rich Delgado. Philadelphia: Temple UP, 1995. 551–563.

Stecopoulos, Harry, and Michael Uebel. *Race and the Subject of Masculinities.* Durham: Duke UP, 1997.

Thomas, Brook. *American Literary Realism and the Failed Promise of Contract.* Berkeley: U of California P, 1997.

Wald, Priscilla. *Constituting Americans: Cultural Anxiety and Narrative Form.* Durham: Duke UP, 1995.

Wiegman, Robyn. *American Anatomies: Theorizing Race and Gender.* Durham: Duke UP, 1995.

——. "Black Bodies/American Commodities: Gender, Race, and the Bourgeois Ideal in Contemporary Film." *Unspeakable Images: Ethnicity and the American Cinema.* Ed. Lester D. Friedman. Urbana: U of Illinois P, 1991. 308–28.

——. "Feminism, 'The Boyz,' and Other Matters Regarding the Male." Cohan and Hark 173–193.

Chapter Four

Lies That Kill: Lorraine Hansberry's Answer to *Heart of Darkness* in *Les Blancs*

John Gruesser

> To call a kid an African was an insult. It was calling him savage, uncivilized, naked, something to laugh at. A naked black savage with a spear and war paint. It was equivalent to ugliness. Everything distasteful and painful was associated with Africa. This came from school, from the movies, and from our own people who accepted this. In common talk, the term was always derogatory—"You are acting like a wild African!" This meant heathen, un-Christian. Most children absorbed this and acquired a deep shame of their African past. But I resented the teachers who couldn't give a more positive view. This too was mainly about our own American Negro past. We were very sensitive to such things as how the slavery issue was discussed, even in grade school. I resented all of it. I was very unique in that I extended this [resentment] to the African thing too. The others didn't do this, but I made the connection . . . At the movies when one white man was holding off thousands of Africans with a gun, all the kids were with the hero, but I was with the Africans. When I was thirteen or fourteen I was more sophisticated. I had begun reading Carter Woodson. My brothers and I talked about Hannibal, we had passion, if not information, and we thought Africa was a great thing in the world.
>
> Lorraine Hansberry

The preceding quotation indicates two things about Lorraine Hansberry: first, she was reading and thinking about Africa at a young age; second, early in her life she recognized that the image of Africa dominating Euro-American literature and popular culture was not based in fact but rather a distortion. Recently, literary and cultural critics have reached similar conclusions. From the time of Homer to the present, Westerners have reached out to the least known part of the world and brought it back as language, in the process revealing more about themselves and their culture than about Africans and theirs. "Africanist discourse," a term coined by Christopher Miller, refers to a discourse at odds with itself that projects the West's desires on the perceived blank slate of Africa.

In *Blank Darkness: Africanist Discourse in French*, Miller cites an array of Western and Eastern accounts of Africa to support his assertion that "Africa is conceived of as a void and unformed prior to its investment with shape and being by Christian or Islamic outside" (13). If the Orient is a reverse image in the Euro-American mind (as Edward Said has argued), then Africa, as a third term in the equation, Miller asserts, is virtually nonexistent. Less real than either the West of the East, the continent thus becomes a repository for myriad ambivalent fantasies by the Euro-American imagination: "The blank slate of Africa with no past or future, can be made to fulfill the desires of your own present. From there it is only one step to the fulfillment of your nightmares as well . . . Ambivalence is the controlling force of Africanist discourse" (Miller 248). As a result, Africanist writing produces both favorable and unfavorable depictions of Africa. The positive instances of such writing can thus be defined "as *wishing for something one cannot have*. . . . The negative versions would be *having something one does not wish for*—provided that having is understood as that dubious end-product of a wish, hallucination" (Miller 248–49). In other words, Africanist writing depicts the continent as either a dream or a nightmare.[1] Although Hansberry did not approach the subject theoretically, the means of representing Africa that Miller describes are precisely what she resented.

In *All the Dark and Beautiful Warriors*, *A Raisin in the Sun*, and, most prominently, *Les Blancs*, Hansberry attempts to rewrite the Africanist image of Africa and Africans. Her early novel, a semi-autobiographical work based on her experiences at the University of Wisconsin, depicts a well-spoken, intelligent African student, Monasse from Ethiopia (*To Be Young, Gifted, and Black* 75–85), as does her smash Broadway debut with the Nigerian Asagai.[2] When *A Raisin in the Sun* was first performed, a man in the audience regarded the scenes concerning Africa, particularly the one in which an intoxicated Walter leaps on a table and impersonates an African general, as comic relief from the intense scenes depicting the Younger family's struggle to move into a better, all-white neighborhood. Hansberry, however, took the African theme of her first play extremely seriously. In a 1959 interview with Studs Terkel, she claimed Asagai was her "favorite character," the one who makes the "statement of the play." According to Hansberry, audiences had never seen an African on stage without his "shoes around his neck and a bone in his nose or ears"; thus, she felt it would be "refreshing" to present Asagai as a "true intellectual" ("To Reclaim the African Past"). Moreover, in his recent study of Hansberry's dramatic works, Steven Carter reports that she has researched and projected a work on the ancient Egypt of Aknaton, also known as Amenhotep IV, who ruled from 1375–1357 B.C. and is credited with reforming Egyptian religion (184).

As important as the African theme is to *Raisin* and other works, in *Les Blancs* Hansberry gives it its fullest treatment. The thesis of this paper is that in her final play—which was completed by her former husband and literary executor, Robert Nemiroff, after her death—Hansberry intensifies her efforts to explode the dominant image of Africa by rewriting Joseph Conrad's *Heart of Darkness*, arguably the most influential (and imitated) Africanist text.[3] Moreover, I hope to show that in *Les Blancs* Hansberry tries to pioneer a non-Africanist means of depicting Africa, something rarely accomplished by an outsider, whether Euro-American or African American, and one that has been only infrequently attempted since 1970 by such writers as Alex Haley and William Duggan.

Before analyzing the play, I would like to trace Hansberry's knowledge about and interest in Africa. As the epigraph to this essay indicates, from an early age the author was aware of and reading about the continent. Nemiroff states that Hansberry "remembered vividly seeing newsreels of the Italian conquest of Ethiopia when she was five, and crying over them" (27). At nine, she encountered Africa in the poetry of Countee Cullen, Waring Cuney, and most importantly, Langston Hughes, the only Harlem Renaissance figure to actually visit the continent (Isaacs 334). Moreover, her uncle William Leo Hansberry, one of the greatest African scholars of the century, wrote one of his books about the image of Africa in classical authors, taught Kwame Nkrumah (Ghana's leader after independence), Nnamadi Azikewe (the first president of Nigeria), and other African students at Howard University, and in 1962 had a college at Nsakka in Nigeria named after him in recognition of his contribution to African Studies (Nemiroff 28). In addition to works by Carter Woodson, Anne Cheney reports that Lorraine Hansberry read Jomo Kenyatta's *Facing Mount Kenya*, W. E. B. Du Bois's *Black Folk Then and Now*, and other books on African culture before she went to the University of Wisconsin in 1948. At Wisconsin she continued her reading and met African students.

Harold Isaacs makes much of the fact that Hansberry could not recall having heard about Marcus Garvey before she moved to New York in 1950 at the age of twenty (334). However, this strikes me as less of an "odd fact" than it does Isaacs. The middle-class Hansberry's knowledge of Africa derived mainly from scholarly and literary rather than popular sources. Du Bois almost immediately dissociated himself from Garvey, whose popularity, though vast, was largely concentrated among lower-class blacks, and who was gradually relegated to obscurity after his imprisonment for mail fraud in 1927.

In New York, Hansberry took a year long seminar on Africa with Du Bois, the father of Pan-Africanism, writing a research paper entitled "The Belgian Congo: A Preliminary Report on Its Land, Its History and Its People" (Nemiroff 29). In 1951, she joined the staff of *Freedom* magazine, founded by Paul Robeson, writing three stories devoted to Africa during her five-year association with the Harlem-based publication. Nemiroff reports that during the 1950s Hansberry met many exchange students and exiles from African colonies. In 1961, two years after publishing *A Raisin in the Sun* and a year after starting *Les Blancs*, Hansberry wrote a letter to the editor of the *New York Times Magazine*, apologizing to Patrice Lumumba's widow for the actions of Dr. Ralph Bunche, whose "apologies" for the demonstrations at the United Nations against the murder of the Congo's first and only democratically elected leader "shocked and outraged" African Americans ("Congolese Patriot" 4). Thus, in addition to resenting Africanist distortions of the continent from an early age, Hansberry knew both Africa's history and its contemporary political realities.

In *Les Blancs* American journalist Charlie Morris comes to the isolated hospital cum mission of the "saintly" Torvald Neilson, who for forty years has supposedly been assisting the Kwi tribe in the African colony of Zatembe. Morris makes the journey not only to write about his man "who to millions is Africa" (105) but also to reawaken the spiritual side of himself. What he finds differs greatly from his expectations. The British colony is in a virtual state of war, with a Mau Mau–type native uprising generating such paranoia among the white settlers that even the mission itself turns into a battlefield.

Most of the action surrounds Tshembe Matoseh, who has returned from England to attend his father's funeral. Despite his protestations of neutrality, Tshembe finds himself embroiled in the conflict. He and Morris engage in a number of conversations that force Tshembe to contemplate his allegiances and illustrate the inability of the basically good-natured Morris to fathom the complexities and brutal realities of colonial race relations. Tshembe decides to join the rebellion after learning that his father had been its leader, but his hopes for a peaceful settlement quickly evaporate when the colonial government arrests a prominent African negotiator. The Reverend Neilson is killed in a native revolt, the country erupts in full-scale war complete with colonial aerial attacks on the African population, and Tshembe kills his own brother for betraying a member of the resistance to the police.

Although from this summary the relationship between *Les Blancs* and *Heart of Darkness* may seem remote, specific plot and setting details make the connection clear.[4] Charlie Morris is not only Mr. Charlie but also Charlie Marlow. Both men travel by riverboat in search of a legendary white figure deep in the African bush.[5] The colony's geography and history link it with the Belgian Congo (now Zaire), the setting of *Heart of Darkness*. Like the Congo, Zetembe is one-fourth the size of the United States, and its river leads into the Bremmer (rather than the Stanley, now the Malebo) Pool. Recalling the atrocities of Leopold's Congo Free State in the late nineteenth and early twentieth centuries, Tshembe refers to whites "chopping off the right hands of our young men by the hundred—by the tribe" in the early days of the colony (91). When the paternalistic Belgians abruptly departed from the Congo in 1960 there were no African doctors; similarly, Morris learns that the unnamed colony has no native physicians. Furthermore, American planes carry out the air strikes on the African population in *Les Blancs*, just as United States aircraft were used to airlift Belgian troops to quell a rebellion in the early days of Mobutu's reign following the ouster of Lumumba.

More significant than either Morris's resemblance to Marlow of the links between the unnamed colony and the Congo, the Conradian theme of lying plays a major role in *Les Blancs*. Like Morris, the audience gradually realizes that Neilson's whole life has been a lie. Rather than assisting the Africans, Neilson has actively supported the colonial government, refused to modernize his hospital, and denied treatment of his wife's closest African friend, Tshembe's mother, a married woman raped by a white settler, who consequently dies giving birth to Tshembe's mulatto brother, Eric.

Hansberry has not merely written one more imitation of *Heart of Darkness*, a modernist obsession inspiring such diverse Euro-American artists as T. S. Eliot, André Gide, Louis-Ferdinand Céline, Graham Greene, V. S. Naipaul, and Francis Ford Coppola. Nearly every work by and outsider about Africa, before and since *Les Blancs*, concerns expatriates rather than Africans, almost always assigning to the latter the roles of servants and criminals. Hansberry reverses this firmly established tradition by adopting a radically different focus, emphasis, and method.

First, her protagonist is not a Westerner but rather an educated African, around whom she constructs a *Hamlet*-like plot. While Morris serves an important function, drawing out the protagonist's beliefs and forcing him to confront his dilemma, he lacks Tshembe's stature and acumen. Even more significantly, Neilson, Hansberry's Kurtz figure, never appears on stage. She brilliantly conceives a way of making Neilson's presence, essential to the plot for the lie he represents, felt throughout the play without giving him speaking lines which might distract attention from Tshembe, the hero of the play. In addition, Hansberry deliberately rewrites Conrad's negative portrayal of women. In *Heart of Darkness*, the doubled female characters, the African woman Marlow observes beckoning Kurtz to stay (and with whom the latter has apparently committed unspeakable acts) and the white woman Marlow visits (and lies to) on his return to Europe, Kurtz's Intended, represent corruption and falsehood respectively. Through her mysterious character, The Woman who appears to Tshembe at strategic moments in the play, Hansberry creates a female figure who symbolizes pride, truth, and strength in her African protagonist.

Second, in *Heart of Darkness* and the numerous works it inspired, all of which I have elsewhere described as composing the expatriate (or "going native") tradition, Africa represents a corrupt environment that causes the outside protagonist—whether Kurtz, Greene's Scobie, or Naipaul's Salim—to decay physically, morally, or mentally.[6] Hansberry reverses this, too. Neilson has not, as a result of exposure to the physical corruption of Africa, betrayed the colonial mission by seducing or raping Tshembe's mother as the play initially hints, Morris erroneously supposes, and the expatriate tradition would dictate.[7] Instead, Neilson's corruption, the thing that makes his life a lie, is his Africanist attitude. An extreme example of the paternalism that Hansberry chided Jean Genet and Norman Mailer for in a 1961 *Village Voice* article, the missionary regards Africans as radical other. So long as they act like children, he cares for them, but when the Africans petition for independence, he becomes angry. Likewise, when syncretism presents itself in the flesh and blood form of Tshembe's soon to be born half-brother, Neilson refuses to countenance the possibility, praying for both the child and the mother to die. As the Reverend's wife acknowledges, "Eric was the living denial of everything he [Neilson] stood for: the testament to three centuries of rape and self-acquittal" (125).

However, Hansberry not only reassigns the blame for the falsehood and corruption of Africa to colonialism and Africanist thinking but shows that this is only the first step. As Tshembe tells Morris, merely exposing colonialist sentiments as a lie, as Conrad does in *Heart of Darkness*, is not enough because such falsehoods kill people:

> I am not merely saying that a device is a device, but that it also has consequences: once invented it takes on a life, a reality of its own. So, in one century, men invoke the device of religion to cloak their conquests. In another, race. Now, in both cases you and I may recognize the fraudulence of the device, but the fact remains that a man who has a sword run through him because he refuses to be a Moslem or Christian—or who is shot in Zatembe or Mississippi because he is black—is suffering the utter *reality* of the device. And it is pointless to pretend that it doesn't *exist*—merely because it is a *lie!* (92)

Here I believe Hansberry anticipates one of Chinua Achebe's major objections to *Heart of Darkness* in his influential and controversial essay "Image in Africa."

Lastly, Hansberry attempts to use African methods to tell an African story. In addition to calling for authentic African drums that are "distinct, erratic and varied statements of mood and intent" rather than "movie drums" (41), she employs what she describes as the "tradition of oral folk art" at a strategic juncture in her play.[8] In Act Two scene two, Peter, a docile servant at the mission who is actually a leader in the revolutionary movement where he goes by the name of Ntali, relates the tale of Modingo to convince Tshembe to join the resistance.[9] Modingo was a wise hyena who lived between the other hyenas and the elephants. When the elephants clamor for more room because of their size, the hyenas, who were there first, seek Modingo's advice. As he ponders the problem, the elephants force the hyenas out of the jungle. According to Ntali, this "bitter joke" played upon the hyenas while they "reasoned" explains their "terrible laughter" (95). As Anne Cheney has noted, Hansberry adapted this tale from one she reported on in a December 1952 *Freedom* article entitled "Kenya's Kikuyu: A Peaceful People Wage Struggle Against the British." Like Modingo, Tshembe has been deliberating how the Africans should respond to the demands of the white men. Recited by Ntali near the midpoint of the play, this folk tale convinces Tshembe to take action; moreover, the cry of a hyena that can be heard at key moments in the play underscores the significance of this orally transmitted fable. Steven Carter has noted another use of African oral tradition in *Les Blancs*: as he utters a war cry in Act Two, scene six, the resistance leader Ngago becomes a "poet-warrior invoking the soul of his people" (108).

Thus, by focusing her attention on Africans, associating the corruption and death in Africa with colonialism and Africanist thinking, and using African methods to tell an African story, in *Les Blancs* Hansberry rewrites *Heart of Darkness*, perhaps the most influential work ever written about Africa, in order to explode the standard, distorted Euro-American image of the continent.

In her final play, Hansberry largely succeeds in depicting a non-Africanist Africa, something which very few outsiders before her, black or white, had been able to accomplish. Despite a heightened awareness of the ways in which Euro-American language has been used to subjugate black people, African Americans have often succumbed to the pervasive influence of Africanist discourse. To cite just one example, although Richard Wright actively attempts to acknowledge and overcome his prepossessions about

Africa in *Black Power* (1954), he frequently betrays Africanist attitudes towards the people of what was then the Gold Coast.[10]

Whether Hansberry directly influenced them or not, *Les Blancs* anticipates attempts by recent Western authors to write about Africa in a new, non-Africanist manner. In *Roots* (1976) Alex Haley explodes myths about Africa's past, asserts the value of oral history, and like Hansberry uses its methods to tell an African and an African American story. Meanwhile in *Jacob's Ladder* (1987), John A. Williams provides an innovative, politically progressive story of intrigue set in West Africa that contains fully realized African characters, building upon the precedent established in Hansberry's portrayal of Tshembe.

Like some of their black counterparts, a handful of white authors since 1980 have adopted elements of Hansberry's approach to Africa. In *Antonia Saw the Oryx First* (1987), Maria Thomas creates dual protagonists, a Tanzanian girl and a while American woman, who enjoy a relationship built upon mutual respect; moreover, echoing Hansberry, she indicts Western medicine for perpetuating the outside world's Africanist approach to the continent. Helen Winternitz has followed Hansberry's lead by identifying Western attitudes and Western economic interests as the sources for the corruption and death of contemporary Africa in *East Along the Equator* (1987). In *The Great Thirst* (1985) and *Lovers of the African Night* (1987), William Duggan has gone even further. Emulating Hansberry in the first two books of a projected trilogy, Duggan attempts to use African methods to tell an African story. Complete with genealogies, his novels aspire to be transcriptions of the oral history of the BaNare people of Kalihariland.

This brief look at recent English and American literature about Africa indicates the significance of Hansberry's achievement in *Les Blancs*. She was one of the first Euro-American authors, black or white, to offer a largely non-Africanist depiction of Africa. In an effort to change the distorted image of the continent pervading literature and popular culture, which she had resented since she was a child, Hansberry rewrote *Heart of Darkness*, arguably the most influential Africanist text. In doing so, she shifted the focus, emphasis, and methods of outside writing about Africa, making an educated African her protagonist, designating colonialism and Africanist thinking as the sources for corruption and killing in Africa, and using oral tradition to tell an African story.

Notes

1 V. Y. Mudimbe's *The Invention of Africa* provides numerous insights into the development, scope, and effects of Africanist discourse and should be read in conjunction with *Blank Darkness*.

2 The main character of the novel, Candace, is presumably named for the ancient Ethiopian warrior queen. This supposition is supported by the fact that the preceding section in *To Be Young, Gifted, and Black*, concerning Hansberry's high school years, bears the title "Queen of the Ethiopes" (67–71). In addition, Robert Nemiroff reports that in early drafts of *Les Blancs* the name of the African protagonist was Candace (31).

3 For a description of his role in preparing the final version of *Les Blancs*, see Nemiroff 34–35.

4 In fact, the most extended comparison of *Les Blancs* with another literary work to date has been Steven Carter's elaboration of the connections between Hansberry's play and Hamlet, in which Tshembe resembles the indecisive Danish prince, Major Rice functions as the Claudius figure, the Woman beckons the protagonist to act in a manner reminiscent of the Ghost of Hamlet's father, and Charlie Morris will presumably tell the world of Tshembe's struggle as Horatio does for Hamlet (102–8).

5 In addition to Marlow, it should be noted that in his nationality and profession Morris resembles Henry Morgan Stanley, the man who "found" the "saintly" Livingstone and who opened up the Congo for exploitation by King Leopold II of Belgium.

6 See Gruesser, *White on Black: Contemporary Literature on Africa*.

7 Steven Carter asserts that Hansberry modeled Neilson on Albert Schweitzer, particularly John Gunther's portrayal of the Nobel Peace Prize winner in *Inside Africa* (114–15).

8 Steven Carter discusses the origin and Hansberry's use of the hyena and elephant folk tale at length in his chapter on *Les Blancs* (106–9).

9 In her portrayal of Ntali, the revolutionary who uses subservience and a pidgin English spoken by no other character in the play to disguise his true allegiances, Hansberry may once again have been "signifying" on Conrad, who in *Heart of Darkness* allows his African characters but a single sentence, the ungrammatical "Mistah Kurtz—he dead!" (148).

10 For a discussion of Wright and other African American literary travelers to Africa, see Gruesser, "Afro-American Travel Literature and Africanist Discourse."

Works Cited

Achebe, Chinua. "Image of Africa." *Massachusetts Review* 18 (Winter 1977): 782–94.

Carter, Steven R. *Hansberry's Drama: Commitment Amid Complexity*. Urbana: U of Illinois P, 1991.

Cheney, Anne. *Lorraine Hansberry*. Boston: Twayne, 1984.

Conrad, Joseph. *Heart of Darkness and the Secret Sharer*. New York: Signet, 1950.

Duggan, William. *The Great Thirst*. New York: Dell, 1985.

Gruesser, John. "Afro-American Travel Literature and Africanist Discourse." *Black American Literature Forum* 24.1 (Spring 1990): 5–20.

——. *White on Black: Contemporary Literature About Africa*. Urbana: U of Illinois P, 1992.

Haley, Alex. *Roots*. New York: Dell, 1977.

Hansberry, Lorraine. "Congolese Patriot." *New York Times Magazine* 26 March 1961: 4.

——. "Genet, Mailer and the New Paternalism." *Village Voice* 10 June 1961: 28–31.

——. "Kenya's Kikuyu: A Peaceful People Wage Struggle Against the British." *Freedom* Dec. 1952: 3.

——. *Les Blancs. The Collected Last Plays*. Ed. Robert Nemiroff. New York: NAL, 1983.

——. *To Be Young, Gifted and Black*. Ed. Robert Nemiroff. New York: Signet, 1969.

——. " . . . To Reclaim the African Past." *Lorraine Hansberry Speaks Out: Art and the Black Revolution*. Ed. Robert Nemiroff. Caedmon, TC 1352, 1972.

Isaacs, Harold. "Five Writers and Their African Ancestors." *Phylon* 21 (1960): 243–65, 317–36.

Miller, Christopher. *Blank Darkness*. Chicago: U of Chicago P, 1985.
Mudimbe, V. Y. *The Invention of Africa*. Bloomington: Indiana UP, 1988.
Nemiroff, Robert. "*Les Blancs*: A Critical Background." Lorraine Hansberry. *The Collected Last Plays*. New York: NAL, 1983.
Said, Edward. *Orientalism*. New York: Vintage, 1979.
Thomas, Maria. *Antonia Saw the Oryx First*. New York: Soho, 1987.
Williams, John A. *Jacob's Ladder*. New York: Thunder's Mouth P, 1987.
Winternitz, Helen. *East Along the Equator*. New York: Atlantic Monthly, 1987.
Wright, Richard. *Black Power*. New York: Harper, 1954.

Chapter Five

From *Birth and After Birth* to *One Shoe Off*: Tina Howe and the Uses of Feminism

Penny Farfan

Tony Award–nominated playwright Tina Howe has acquired a reputation as a feminist, as is evidenced through her representation in such publications as *The New Women's Theatre* (1977), *Interviews with Contemporary Women Playwrights* (1987), *Feminine Focus: The New Women Playwrights* (1989), and *Making A Spectacle: Feminist Essays on Contemporary Women's Theatre* (1989). Howe invokes this reputation in the preface to a 1995 anthology that includes three of her less critically acclaimed works, *Birth and After Birth*, *Approaching Zanzibar* and *One Shoe Off*, first stating, "These are the plays that got me in trouble" (ix), and then ascribing the negative reactions that the three plays received to how she conjoined in them feminist content and absurdist form. Howe supports her explanation by maintaining that while her feminist inclinations were apparent in her early play *Birth and After Birth*, she suppressed them in order to achieve commercial and critical success with her next few plays and only allowed her feminism to come "out in the open" again in *Approaching Zanzibar* and *One Shoe Off*, her most recent plays at the time that the anthology was published (x). Howe is vague as to what precisely she means when she calls her plays "feminist," making reference only to female characters and to "ambiguity" (x). As Jill Dolan has suggested, however, "feminism begins with a keen awareness of exclusion from male cultural, social, sexual, political and intellectual discourse" (qtd. in Reinelt 225) and, "ends," as Janelle Reinelt has added, "with a resolve to radically change these circumstances" (225). Considered from this perspective, where feminism implies critical awareness and an intent to transform, Howe's assertions in her 1995 preface are problematic, for while *Birth and After Birth* reads as a feminist play in its representation and critique of the normalizing pressures that the ideal of the heterosexual nuclear family exerts on individual social subjects, particularly women, *One Shoe Off*, which Howe has described as "a continuation of *Birth and After Birth*" (Preface x), is ultimately reactionary in its covert representation of feminism as a hostile force that threatens the institution of marriage and that the two main characters must unite in trying to "hold their ground against" in the final moment of the play (*One Shoe Off* 211). Following a comparative analysis, this paper will propose an alternative to Howe's interpretation of the unfavorable receptions of *Birth and After Birth* and *One Shoe Off* and will account for the shifting attitude towards feminism reflected in the two plays by repositioning Howe as a woman writer whose primary professional identification is not as a feminist but, rather, as a commercial playwright whose orientation to feminism has to a large extent been determined by its marketability on the New York stage.

Written in the early 1970s but not professionally produced until 1995, *Birth and After Birth* is organized around the fourth birthday party of Nicky Apple, as celebrated by his parents Sandy and Bill Apple and their childless friends Mia and Jeffrey Freed, both of whom are anthropologists engaged in research on "children of primitive cultures" (99). Howe has stated that "[when] you deal with childbirth and raising children, you're in a murky, primitive place" and that "family life has been over-romanticized," its "great savagery" insufficiently represented in theatre and movies (Betsko and Koenig 223; qtd. in Moore 101). In *Birth and After Birth*, the presence of the two anthropologist characters at Nicky Apple's birthday party invites consideration of white, middle-class America as a "primitive culture" as Howe brings to light the more "savage" aspects of its child-bearing, child-raising, and family-living practices.

The play begins on the morning of Nicky's birthday, focusing on the internal dynamics of the related institutions of marriage and the nuclear family, as exemplified by Howe's quintessentially American "Apple" family. Within this basic social unit, the husband and father "Bill" has, as his name suggests, been reduced to his breadwinning function and channels his remaining energy into capturing his child's birthday festivities on videotape, an activity he pursues with a zeal that borders on aggression when Nicky does not immediately comply with his directions regarding particular shots (88). Correspondingly, the wife and mother "Sandy" Apple has, as her name suggests, been reduced to her child-bearing function so that, though she is only in her early thirties, she sees herself as old in the sense of "used up" because she has been unable to conceive a second child (86, 100, 138). Given the extent to which Sandy's sense of identity is tied up with her reproductive (dys)function, she not surprisingly delights in recalling her son's birth and in playing baby games with him, yet she is at the same time enraged by his persistent demands upon her, shaking him senseless when he will not accept her refusal to give him grape juice. Paradoxically, then, the four-year-old Nicky Apple is, on the one hand, overindulged by his parents' compulsion to baby him and, on the other hand, expected to curb his childish willfulness or risk physical abuse. Howe's stage direction that Nicky is to be played by an adult actor (80) calls attention to this paradox, while also signifying the degree to which the "small" child dominates and delimits the lives of his parents. As well, Howe's description of the Apples' home as "a surreal space in which the boundaries between the four rooms [kitchen, playroom, dining room, and living room] have long since collapsed" suggests the loss of individual identity within the nuclear family unit (81). Thus, in Act I of *Birth and After Birth*, Howe represents the American ideal of the nuclear family as a coercive structure of relationships that exacts a high personal price from each individual positioned within it.

In the second act of the play, the deadening effects of this model are set into sharp relief when the Freeds arrive for the party and describe their encounter with the Whan See tribe, an obscure, tree-dwelling people perfect in all respects except their practice of "fetal insertion" (127), a harrowing birth ritual whereby the women of the tribe repeatedly re-insert the newborn infant into its mother's womb to be reborn, at enormous risk to both mother and child. In the case of the birth that the Freeds happened to witness, the infant was unable to survive the ordeal and his grief-stricken mother threw herself from the trees to her death below, though she had herself been a willing participant in the re-insertion ritual. Jeffrey Freed interprets the Whan See birthing practice through comparative anthropological analysis:

> You have to remember, these were a highly primitive people who took things literally. When a civilized woman has a baby, she too is possessive, only in more subtle ways. She's possessive of her birth experience and delights in retelling it. She's possessive of her baby and tries to keep him helpless for as long as possible. Well, these Stone Age women were just acting out the same impulse by forcing the baby back into its mother's womb. Through fetal insertion, you see, the primitive mother could experience her moment of motherhood again and again and again. (127)

The Freeds' account of the Whan See birth ritual that results in the death of both mother and child thus functions as a parable through which Howe can alienate or "make strange" the devastating personal and social cost of the reduction of women to their child-bearing function within the correspondingly "primitive" culture that is contemporary America.

Howe implies that it is, ironically, the enormity of the personal cost to individual social subjects positioned within the nuclear family that accounts for the coercive and self-perpetuating power of this unit as a social and moral ideal. Notably, despite Mia Freed's belief that the Whan See ritual of fetal insertion is a "moral defect" or "flaw" in a culture that is otherwise admirable (125), she admits to having actively participated in the ritual herself, initially at the instigation of the older Whan See women, but eventually re-inserting the baby into the birth canal herself (127–28). In her inability to resist the compulsion to take part in a practice that is clearly appalling to her, Mia serves as a parallel to Sandy, who is adamant that her childless friend should have a baby despite the fact that she herself feels so depleted by her reduction to the maternal role that we are told that sand leaks from her head throughout the play and she loses a tooth and a clump of hair. As Janet Brown has noted, the globe-trotting, career-oriented "Freeds" "seem to be in a happier situation than Sandy and Bill in every respect. Only their childlessness enables Sandy to pity them and thus to feel superior. . . . [Only] by Mia becoming a mother would she lose her career and actually be Sandy's equal in situation" (81). The fact that Nicky is "the only attraction" that the Apples "can offer to potential converts" to their lifestyle explains their various efforts to prolong his babyhood (Brown 78), but it also accounts for their need to validate their own lifestyle choice by attempting to impose it on others. Evident in Act I as Sandy fantasizes that the Freeds will change their minds about not having children when they come to Nicky's birthday party and see how happy the Apples are (98–99), this need for self-validation through replication by others reaches its most extreme expression in Act II, when all three members of the Apple family forcibly involve Mia in a grotesquely comic yet horrifically violent enactment of childbirth. This false labor scene follows directly out of the Whan See story and is ironically intercut with Sandy's platitudes about the joys of motherhood as "the most beautiful experience a woman can have" (131).

Notably, Jeffrey Freed, preoccupied with slides of his anthropological research, is initially oblivious to the Apples' assault on his wife. When he does at last come to her defense, his intervention remains at an individual and apolitical level, in no way functioning as a condemnation of the forcible imposition of normative standards of femininity on nonconforming women who have committed themselves to alternative modes of being, as Mia has done through her choice of a career over motherhood. Not surprisingly, therefore, just moments after his intervention on Mia's behalf, Jeffrey supports Nicky's demand that Sandy have more children, maintaining that only children are "more prone to psychosis in later years" and reinforcing Sandy's sense of shame at her inability to conceive a second child by providing information on the negative perception and violent treatment of "barren women" in other cultures (136–37).

Janet Brown has argued that *Birth and After Birth* is not a feminist play, first because it does not "establish a hierarchy in which men are above women" but instead reveals the "limitations of men as well as of women in the nuclear family," and second because "the Apples do not resist their situation" but try "to coerce others into adopting it" (75, 79, 82). Yet while *Birth and After Birth* indeed represents the constraints that the nuclear family unit imposes on all family members, it also calls attention to the relationship between patriarchal dominance and the ideal of the nuclear family,[1] to the particular pressures to comply with normative gender roles that women experience, and to the complicity of women in their own oppression through reduction to their reproductive function. Moreover, while the play's final image of the Apples "[frozen] in an endless embrace" (141) indeed signals their failure to resist the social arrangements that oppress and confine them, it also functions as an open ending that invites critical engagement with the issues that the play has raised but not resolved. In these respects, *Birth and After Birth* reads as a feminist play.

Turning now to *One Shoe Off*, Howe has stated that Dinah and Leonard, the two main characters of her 1993 play, "are the Apples of *Birth and After Birth* twenty years later. Nicky has grown up and left home. It's just the two of them now; the battle lines are more sharply drawn. They're still preparing for a party, but now the fate of their marriage rests on the outcome" (Preface x). Despite these superficial correspondences that Howe identifies and the fact that both plays take place in the domestic arena, there is little other similarity in terms of content, for not only does *One Shoe Off* lack the feminist critical stance of *Birth and After Birth*, but it actually has an anti-feminist subtext, positing feminism as the biggest threat to the traditional values that the play ultimately reaffirms.

One Shoe Off is set in a collapsing, wind-blasted farmhouse that is gradually being overrun by vegetation and that functions as an external sign of the disintegrating relationship of Leonard and Dinah, the long-married couple who own the house. Dinah is a costume designer, and Leonard is an actor who has not worked in the eleven or so years since the couple's old friend and collaborator Parker Bliss sold out as a theatre director and went to Hollywood to make horror movies. At the start of the play, Leonard and Dinah are preparing for a dinner party to which they have invited Parker, whom they have not seen for years, and Clio and Tate, a young couple who live nearby. As the play unfolds, it is revealed that the root of Leonard and Dinah's marital problems is the secret desire that Dinah has for years been harboring for Parker, a compulsive womanizer who uses the same words to proposition Clio at the dinner party that he used on Dinah many years before. When the guests finally leave and Leonard confronts Dinah with his suspicions about her relationship with Parker, she admits that she indeed wanted him but that she has remained faithful to Leonard. In the final moment of the play, husband and wife stand together at the door of their house, and as they shout defiantly into the night in a united attempt to "hold their ground against" the forces that assail them, the wind at last begins to subside (211).

Howe has described *One Shoe Off* as a celebration of the triumph of commitment and fidelity over "the libidinal forces that threaten a marriage," but she has also somewhat contradictorily stated that the play is about "the randomness of life and the catastrophes and how one holds on" and that she sees Dinah and Leonard as "more acted upon by the outside world" (qtd. in Lamont 19; interview with Barlow 276; personal interview). Howe introduces her theme of the random nature of human suffering by means of a story that Parker tells in Act I about a mobile home breaking loose from its trailer and killing five people (153), but the prime threat to Dinah and Leonard's marriage is, of course, Parker himself,[2] and there is nothing random at all about his indiscriminate womanizing. Instead, it is accounted for in an otherwise extraneous bit of exposition about his wife, a successful sculptor called Patsy Cincinnati. During this exposition, Parker refers to himself as "Mr. Patsy Cincinnati," complains that his wife has forgotten his name and that he "could drop off the face of the earth and she wouldn't even notice," and hints through a remark about her poor circulation and "perennial chill" that she is frigid and does not give him the sexual attention that he needs (203–4). Through this exposition, Howe implies that Parker's womanizing is an attempt to compensate for the wound to his ego caused by the fact that his "tiny" and "very feminine" wife is a serious and highly regarded artist who does not devote herself primarily or exclusively to the fulfillment of his needs (203).

Howe has stated that she wrote *One Shoe Off* in response to "events of the eighties and nineties" that she felt were "spinning out of control," including "urban decay and the AIDS epidemic, and just the random suffering that [she saw] people going through: personal, healthwise, economic, whatever" (personal interview). While Howe did not list feminism as one of the forces to which she was responding in *One Shoe Off*, the play's references to Patsy Cincinnati infuse it with an anti-feminist subtext by positing feminism, as exemplified by the real-life feminist visual artist Judy Chicago, whom Patsy Cincinnati is clearly intended to invoke, as the primary threat to the traditional values that the play ultimately reaffirms through its final image of Leonard and Dinah holding fast against an embattling wind. Thus, while *Birth and After Birth* may support Howe's claim to feminism in her 1995 preface, *One Shoe Off* does not.

In addition to her problematic assertion of common feminist content, Howe identifies what she sees as her absurdist style as a further point of continuity between *Birth and After Birth* and *One Shoe Off* (Preface x), and in this point of comparison, she is closer to the mark. However, where form and content coalesce into a unified theatrical vision in *Birth and After Birth*, Howe's style in *One Shoe Off* is labored and inorganic, obscuring rather than clarifying the action and themes and causing the play as a whole to seem tortuously overwritten. Thus, though Howe has described *One Shoe Off* as her *Waiting for Godot*, translating Beckett's "I can't go on/I go on" theme to the marital arena (personal interview), her intended absurdist vision is consistently undermined by a relentless onslaught of tedious absurdities that include such extraneous and heavy-handed gags as Dinah's compulsive intermittent readings of the ingredients of products such as Chap Stick and Worcestershire Sauce (151, 164); Leonard and Dinah's wailed outcries for their married daughter "Po-Po" (150, 197); slips of the tongue such as "cranboobies" instead of "cranberries" (163); and Leonard's pretending he is a crop-duster airplane (162). Howe has further described *One Shoe Off* as being as much "about the theatre" as it is "about survival and the meaning of love" (interview with Barlow) but the play's many theatrical references are inessential and lacking in depth. To cite just one example, though Dinah's exclamation in Act I that she doesn't know who she is (149) would seem to suggest a thematic concern with role-playing and identity, the primary purpose of her continual costume changes appears to be to infuse the play with zaniness, as when she emerges from her closet dressed as a shepherdess and "starts herding imaginary reindeer" (146). A comparative analysis of Howe's use of games in *Birth and After Birth* and *One Shoe Off* clarifies the basic difference in the relationship of form to content in the two plays. In *Birth and After Birth*, the Apples' party game involving barnyard animal sounds (106–7) serves as a comic theatrical expression of Howe's vision of nuclear family living as savage and primitive. In *One Shoe Off*, the game of Concentration focussing on the names of ships (186–92) creates an atmosphere of hilarity but does little to advance the plot, enhance the themes, or illuminate the characters, who are at this point dressed in Chekhovian costumes.

While the combination of feminism and absurdism may account for the lack of commercial interest in *Birth and After Birth,* as Howe contends in her 1995 preface, the critical hostility to *One Shoe Off* derived more from her labored attempts at comic absurdity. In a particularly cruel review, John Simon wrote that *One Shoe Off* "fluctuates between the infuriating and the numbing, and exhibits the kind of strain usually reserved for weight-lifting competitions. You can virtually hear Ms. Howe, effortlessly pursuing ever weirder effects, panting herself into a corner. Any potential laughs drown in the authorial sweat" (84). Similarly, in *Newsday* Jan Stuart wrote that "[rather] than enriching her characters with layers that might lend weight to their disarray, Howe repeatedly opts for another wacky flourish," and that "this time out, Howe's revered eccentricity has become an end unto itself. *One Shoe Off* is a mad-hatter blowout, so enamored of its own topsy-turvy conceits that we too often feel left out of the tea party." Finally, Frank Rich described the tone of *One Shoe Off* as "fey," complained about the "strained ditsiness that clatters so hollowly about the stage," and noted that "Ms. Howe hits most of her characters' calamities and jokes as heavily as the piano chords that punctuate each scene" and that "[when] the time comes to turn sober, the playwright's voice of doom seems as mechanical as her comic conceits." Rich concluded by observing that in *One Shoe Off*, "Howe initially seems eager to reach into more painful and daring territory than in her fine earlier works, yet soon retreats into baroque overwriting that keeps her material and her audience at a distance. You wish she would follow the lead of [set designer Heidi] Landesman's twisted trees and rip through the arch domestic facade that increasingly seems to inhibit her plays."

Shortly after *One Shoe Off* opened in 1993, Howe recalled Rich "using the word 'domestic' with a sort of loathing" in this last sentence of his review and added that a woman playwright

> [takes] her life in her hands when she goes into a domestic arena. I knew after *Birth and After Birth* that I shouldn't do that again and I was unwillingly drawn back into it. And I think in a nutshell that's why the play received the derision that it did—because I'm going into sacred ground and I'm fooling around, and I am altering the normal perception and I am heightening it, and distorting familiar sacred institutions and relationships. And I think that makes certainly male critics very nervous. (Personal interview)

Rich's use of the word "domestic" in his review would thus appear to be Howe's sole basis for asserting that anti-feminist sentiment was at the heart of the negative critical reaction to *One Shoe Off*.[3]

Without diminishing Howe's achievement as a playwright or seeming to assert that she must write feminist plays simply because she is a woman playwright, it should nevertheless be noted that her career has been marked by a certain expediency with respect to feminism. *Birth and After Birth* and an earlier, unpublished work entitled *The Nest* (1970) were in a sense proto-feminist plays, written "out of [Howe's] own experience" at a time when she had not yet been exposed to the feminist movement (Howe, qtd. in Moore).[4] When *The Nest* closed after a single performance and a bad review by Clive Barnes and when *Birth and After Birth* subsequently failed to find a producer, Howe by her own account "made a cold and calculated study of the kinds of plays that were meeting with success," concluded that audiences were "desperate for escape," and consciously decided to switch from writing plays about "courtship and domesticity" to writing plays with unusual settings ("Antic Vision" 12). The feminist tendencies of her earliest works did not disappear entirely from the plays that followed (see Backes; Barlow), but as Howe herself has said, she "[covered] her scent" somewhat by focusing on women as artists ("Antic Vision" 14), with the result that gender issues are generally subsidiary to artistic issues in such popular works as *The Art of Dining* (pr. 1979) and *Painting Churches* (pr. 1984). Notably, Howe's strongest statement of commitment to feminism occurs in her 1985 essay "Antic Vision," which she "jumped at [the] invitation" to write for *American Theatre* (14), which was introduced by critic Jan Stuart, and which coincided roughly with the commercial vogue for women playwrights that Mel Gussow identified in a 1983 *New York Times Sunday Magazine* article in which Howe was mentioned. In "Antic Vision," Howe claimed to be a feminist "—and one of the fiercer ones, to boot" (14). Shortly afterwards, however, in 1987, she received a Tony Award nomination for her play *Coastal Disturbances*, in which she set out "to celebrate the tenderness of men" in order to counteract the brutality of the male characters in works by male authors such as Sam Shepard (personal interview). By the late 1980s, around the time of *Approaching Zanzibar*, she had begun to downplay her feminism altogether so that in a 1989 panel interview published in the *New York Times*, she described herself as "an underdeveloped feminist" and asserted that while her writing is certainly informed by the fact that she is a woman, her "primary interest really has to do with expanding the form, exploring what you can do in the theater" ("Women Playwrights" 42). Finally, by 1993, with the anti-feminist subtext of *One Shoe Off*, Howe was participating in the reaction against feminism that Susan Faludi identified in her 1991 bestseller *Backlash: The Undeclared War Against American Women*[5] and that Jill Dolan has argued is apparent in Wendy Wasserstein's popular 1988 play *The Heidi Chronicles*.[6]

As the above chronology suggests, Howe has been less steadfast in her commitment to feminism than in her commitment to making a living in the commercial theatre. Therefore, while her claim to feminism in her 1995 preface may indeed apply to *Birth and After Birth*, as well as to aspects of such works as *The Art of Dining* and *Painting Churches*, it reads as an expedient attempt to salvage *One Shoe Off*—perhaps her weakest play—from valid criticism by powerful male critics and to market it, despite its anti-feminist subtext, to the feminist readership of such works as *The New Women's Theatre*,

Interviews with Contemporary Women Playwrights, *Feminine Focus*, and *Making A Spectacle*, a readership that must be vigilant of postfeminist texts which, in Tania Modelski's words, "engage in negating the critiques and undermining the goals of feminism—in effect, delivering us back into a prefeminist world" (3).

Notes

1 As Tania Modleski has stated:

feminism has emphasized from the beginning the oppressiveness of the ideology of compulsory heterosexuality and the institution it supports—that of the nuclear family. The family is the structural unit keeping women economically and physically dependent on men; separating women from other women; and, in extreme (though by no means uncommon) cases, providing the space in which men may abuse women with impunity (13).

2 Though Howe is somewhat inconsistent in terms of the chronology of past events (see, for example, 183 and 208), Dinah's aborted encounter with Parker, Parker's abandonment of the theatre, and Leonard's last acting job all appear to have occurred at around the same time.

3 While I do not see evidence of anti-feminist sentiment in the reviews of *One Shoe Off*, I do not intend to suggest that reviews by these critics are never colored by anti-feminist or misogynistic attitudes.

4 See also Howe's essay "Antic Vision," in which she states, "I was a serene innocent who didn't know any better. The feminist rhetoric had barely been articulated, and being such a loner, I wouldn't have heard it anyway. I was simply putting my own antic vision on the stage of what it meant to be a woman" (12).

5 Faludi proposes the following historical overview of the backlash against feminism: "The most recent round of backlash first surfaced in the late '70s on the fringes, among the evangelical right. By the early '80s, the fundamentalist ideology had shouldered its way into the White House. By the mid-'80s, as resistance to women's rights acquired political and social acceptability, it passed into the popular culture" (xix).

6 As Dolan argues: "*The Heidi Chronicles* is a 'postfeminist' mainstream play that distorts the political history of U.S. feminism from the mid-1960s to the late 1980s. The play trivializes radical feminist gains, suppresses feminist rage, and acquiesces to the dominant culture's reading of the end of feminism. The play's traditional realist form helps to preserve its essentially conservative ideology" (49).

Works Cited

Backes, Nancy. "Body Art: Hunger and Satiation in the Plays of Tina Howe." Hart 41–60.

Barlow, Judith. "The Art of Tina Howe." *Feminine Focus: The New Women Playwrights*. Ed. Enoch Brater. New York: Oxford UP, 1989. 241–254.

——. "Interview with Tina Howe." *Speaking on Stage: Interviews with Contemporary American Playwrights*. Ed. Philip C. Kolin and Colby H. Kullman. Tuscaloosa and London: U of Alabama P, 1996. 260–276.

Betsko, Kathleen, and Rachel Koenig. "Interview with Tina Howe." *Interviews with Contemporary Women Playwrights*. New York: Beech Tree Books, 1987. 223–235.

Brater, Enoch, ed. *Feminine Focus: The New Women Playwrights*. New York: Oxford UP, 1989.

Brown, Janet. *Feminist Drama: Definition and Analysis*. Metuchen, NJ: Scarecrow, 1979.

Dolan, Jill. "Personal, Political, Polemical: Feminist Approaches to Politics and Theater." *Presence and Desire: Essays on Gender, Sexuality, Performance.* Ann Arbor: U of Michigan P, 1993. 43–68.

Faludi, Susan. *Backlash: The Undeclared War Against American Women.* New York: Doubleday, 1991.

Gussow, Mel. "Women Playwrights: New Voices in the Theatre." *New York Times Magazine* 1 May 1983: 22+.

Hart, Lynda, ed. *Making a Spectacle: Feminist Essays on Contemporary Women's Theatre.* Ann Arbor: U of Michigan P, 1989.

Howe, Tina. "Antic Vision." *American Theatre* September 1985: 12, 14.

——. *Birth and After Birth. Approaching Zanzibar and Other Plays.* New York: Theatre Communications Group, 1995. 79–141.

——. *One Shoe Off. Approaching Zanzibar and Other Plays.* New York: Theatre Communications Group, 1995. 143–211.

——. Personal interview with Salome Chasnoff and Penny Farfan. 3 May 1993.

——. "Preface." *Approaching Zanzibar and Other Plays.* New York: Theatre Communications Group, 1995. ix–xi.

Lamont, Rosette C. "After Ionesco: The Surrealist Comedy of Tina Howe." *Theater Week* 3 May 1993: 19–20.

Modleski, Tania. *Feminism Without Women: Culture and Criticism in a "Postfeminist" Age.* New York: Routledge, 1991.

Moore, Honor, ed. *The New Women's Theatre.* New York: Vintage, 1977.

Reinelt, Janelle G. Introduction to "Feminism(s)." *Critical Theory and Performance.* Ed. Janelle G. Reinelt and Joseph R. Roach. Ann Arbor: U of Michigan P, 1992. 225–230.

Rich, Frank. "Combine Characters, Toss Madly and Serve." *New York Times* 16 April 1993: C3.

Simon, John. "Unholy Week." *New York* 3 May 1993: 82, 84.

Stuart, Jan. "When Life is Just a Tossed Salad." *New York Newsday* 16 April 1993. *New York Theatre Critics' Reviews* 54.7 (1993): 140.

——. "Women's Work: Tina Howe and Maria Irene Fornes Explore the Woman's Voice in Drama." *American Theatre* September 1985: 11.

"Women Playwrights: Themes and Variations." *New York Times* 7 May 1989, sec. 2: 1, 42.

Chapter Six

Gendermandering: Stereotyping and Gender Role Reversal in the Major Plays of William Inge

Jeff Johnson

After the disruption of the war years, fixed gender-typing was not only desirable, it was required in order to seed the idealism associated with the postwar recovery in America, and the illusion of the well-made family was perpetuated as a necessary condition of social stability at every level of society. The codifying image of Mom, Dad, Buddy, and Sis as the "all-American family" relied as much on religious, political, and business interests as it did on members of the family understanding and sticking to their expected familial roles. Dana Heller, while arguing that the contemporary cliched image of 1950s domesticity represents today a "nostalgia for a lost aesthetics" (2), concedes that the archetype, what she calls "family romance" (3), was "very much alive in post–World War II American culture" (3).

Inge's major plays tend, at first glance, to affirm these commonly accepted gender distinctions. And while it is true that, in his plays, Inge appropriates the gender-determined roles of women expected in the dramatic realism of the 1950s, he also manages, at the same time, to subvert the very stereotypes the public used to reassure itself of its normalcy. This subversion is a technique which might best be defined as "gendermandering," that is, the intentional undermining of expected gender roles for the dramatic purpose of politically destabilizing social norms.

The concept derives from gerrymandering, in which voting districts are manipulated unfairly to gain a voting advantage for one particular party over another. Like gerrymandering, gendermandering can also be culturally subversive, acknowledging and employing stereotypes for dramatic effect while seeming simultaneously to condemn them. It becomes a method used by playwrights and supported by play directors as a means to create what critic Dana Heller calls a "gender-culture realignment" (17), allowing for "a radical de-centering of master narratives" (4) so that gender "boundaries that might have previously served to fix and divide . . . prove to be fluid and dissolvable" (5). It counterbalances "modernity's overinvestment in the gender specificity of separate spheres" (10), exploding what Joanne Meyerowitz describes as "the postwar domestic stereotype and its meanings, how and where it was produced" (2).

Traditionally, gerrymandering suggests "dirty" politics, a tool remnant of New York's Tammany Hall or the Chicago "machine" or Jim Crow laws in the South, employed to "fix" an election by securing a safe seat created for a politician who is able to cull the predictably favorable voters into his or her designated district. Recently, though, gerrymandering has been used by political theorists like Lani Guanier to "correct"—that is, literally to "fix"—voting blocs, many of which were originally rigged by the entrenched incumbent but redrawn to include representatives for minority voters. In gerrymandering, you acknowledge a voting pattern, then manipulate it to guarantee a desired result.

The same is true of gendermandering, in which a stereotype is designated to a character but is then manipulated by the writer to expose the stereotype for what it is. The writer starts with an artificial set of social codes imposed on a character (similar to a voting block), then works to subvert the type by reversing the expected patterns of behavior (as in voting patterns). Just as many people believe that voting districts are not arbitrary but are somehow culturally inherent, "natural," or established by tradition, so too the characters who populate drama are often thought of as neither arbitrary nor free but determined, fixed, their behavior codified by nature and tradition. They cannot escape the pigeonholes into which they are conveniently fitted. Therefore, like gerrymandering, which attempts to redraw political patterns of expected voting behavior, gendermandering attempts to redraw the boundaries of expected social patterns of behavior, giving the lie to "nature" and "tradition" as factors in determining a person's choice of self.

By exploiting these "asymmetries of gender," gendermandering reconstructs the very subjectivity a stereotype denies. It confirms the expected sexual behavior of characters while exposing the pernicious cultural habit of gender-typing. As a dramatic device, it enhances the tension by juxtaposing what is normal against what is abnormal within a social contract of expected behavior. While exposing the stereotypical sexual patterns of the 1950s, Inge's plays were also culturally transitional, preparing the groundwork for the gender-bending so prevalent in contemporary aesthetics.

Gendermandering in Inge is best illustrated by the engaging female characters who exhibit patently male qualities, while prominent male characters display qualities typically female. In *Bus Stop*, for instance, several peripheral characters behave in a reassuringly stereotypical manner, and yet they also act to contrast expected patterns of behavior with the atypical patterns of the other main characters. Will, the sheriff, is a bit prudish but friendly, a typical right-thinking Midwestern pragmatist. Elma is a stereotypical inquisitive young girl, and Carl, the bus driver, comes off as a particularly stereotypical rutting male. Even Lyman, for all his nastiness, is predictably vulgar and pedophilic. More curious, however, are the gendermandered types: Bo and Cherie, Virgil and Grace. The two women are sexually experienced, confident. Cherie feigns innocence, though she readily admits that she's "led a wicked life" (Inge 209) and had "other boyfriends" (209). She is a tough, street-smart, resourceful runaway who quit school at twelve and never looked back. While infused with the feminine qualities of emotional depth, intuition, and passion, she also exhibits unusually strong masculine qualities of contrivance, masking, superficiality, and reason. She is resilient, surviving by her wits as much as her looks. She is capable of playing any role that fits her immediate needs: the helpless victim, the aggressive vamp, the diffident struggling talent naively in search of the career-making gig. Conversely, Bo is plagued by the very qualities he finds most abject in others, qualities he, of course, cannot recognize in himself, those feminine "flaws" of emotional excess, disorder, and inebriation. He claims he never drinks, intoxicated with himself, and is prey to inexplicable destructive urges, giving up much more heat than light. Most important, Bo lacks the one primary quality that defines the masculine: the ability to play, to recognize theatre, to adapt to a role. Bo must be; he is the thing-itself, not a replica; he lacks the luxury of distance from himself which Cherie enjoys. By the end of the play, he learns to act the role of gentleman, is thereby tamed, and fit to assume the role of a normal house-husband.

Virgil and Grace likewise reverse the stereotypical personae of male and female role playing. Grace is the one who is sexually confident, who likes a man with "big hands" (204), who is savvy enough to keep even Carl in line. Virgil prefers a sort of solipsistic, Platonic bunkhouse camaraderie to any active sexual engagement, homo- or heterosexual. Grace, on the other hand, is strong, single, divorced, practical and orderly, able to adapt, to control, and, most importantly, capable of a cool distance from her emotions. When Carl slips into sentimentality, romancing Grace, weakened by his need for her, she rebuffs him with biting irony, undercutting his fumbling attempts at seduction with a dry logic. He quips that his friend "Dobson speaks very highly of you" (164). She responds, "Well . . . he better. Now what you gonna have?" (164). Grace maintains her world, and the diner, on her terms, delegating, advising, taking what she wants, giving what she needs. She is the essence of stability and good judgment. Virgil, however, relies strictly on intuition. At first glance, he seems like a good diplomat: cautious, circumspect, level-headed. But in essence he is moderate in the extreme. He is a loner because he cannot escape his own subjectivity, cannot role-play successfully enough to integrate with society. He cannot project; his individuality collapses into itself.

In addition to exploding stereotypes and gender-typing in typical social contexts of the 1950s, gendermandering in *Bus Stop* allows for a neat pairing off of sexual symmetry and moral balance. From the opening scene, the play version of *Bus Stop* is crackling with sexual tension. Even before everyone is out of the bus, the pairing off begins. Elma, the innocent, goes for the cynical old drunk Lyman (the lying man), impressed that "he wanted to make love to me" (218). The sexually mature Grace hooks up with Carl, the driver (pun intended). Later, as Bo and Cherie stumble through their mating charade, even Virgil and Will couple as diplomats and figures of stability and compromise. But the symmetry of these sexual alignments is more than a mere device to drive the plot: it establishes the central theme of disruption and reconciliation. More importantly, this structural symmetry illustrates the significance in human affairs of an ordering principle, a logic that organizes the inchoate, alogical urges of human emotions.

Grace opens the play by telling Elma that her estranged husband "wasn't much company, 'cept when we were making love" (155). She confesses that she is "a restless sort of woman . . . who has gotta have me a man, just to keep myself from gettin' grouchy" (218). Carl, her one-night stand, comes in with the wind, the violent, passionate wind of March, "like a lion" (162). After immediately making a play for Grace, he tells the sheriff he gets "so damned stiff" (167) that only a walk (in the blizzard) "Freshens a man up" (167) and that "sometimes I walk for hours" (167). Elma, whose budding sexuality is hardly contained but for her ignorance, is "just curious about things" (154) and wonders if she should "Flunk my courses" (155) to attract boyfriends. Lyman, a hedonist philosopher-on-the-lam, connects the gutter to God, so to speak, with his devotion to a failed aesthetics. He claims to "understand everything" (168), he says, but to "despise the way" (168) he says it. Will, the sheriff, embodies judicious behavior, orderliness and common sense. He complains that "A storm like this makes me mad . . . like all the elements had lost their reason" (156). Virgil, too, represents restraint and diplomacy, his integrity reinforced by his name, conjuring both the stern moralist of Dante and the gentle "Virge" of the New Testament. Ironically, however, Virgil's justice, like Will's, is based as much on his sexual neutrality as on his ability to manipulate the heterosexually coded games the others are playing. Disinterested himself, he gives good advice.

These themes of passion and containment, of a necessary human order threatened by natural elements of disruption, are reinforced by Grace's indictment of marriage as a passion-killer. She tells Elma that "makin' love is *one* thing, and being lonesome is another" (155) and that "me and Barton [her estranged husband] was usually fightin'" (155). Finally, she concludes that "all married people aren't like Barton and I" (155) but that she was "just as lonesome when he was here" (155). As a representative of the stable community values, along with the curiously cautious Elma and the responsible, even-tempered sheriff Will, Grace nevertheless is the one who most appreciates the unpredictability inherent in her job, catering to bus loads of strangers habitually arriving and departing, briefly interrupting the routine of her life. When Will complains that the storm makes him "mad" (156) and that he prefers to "see things in order" (156), Grace says, "Let it blow!" (156). And when Elma, still sexually tentative, says, "I'm glad I'm not traveling on the bus tonight" (156), Grace tells her, "Remember, honey, I always serve Carl" (157). The situation in the diner is clear. Will's sanctum of sanity is set against Grace's delight in disorder. And the message is equally clear. The diner, an image of Apollonian order, also houses the potentially subversive "elements" of Dionysian delirium.

The central pairing off in the play is that of the country boy Bo with the city girl Cherie. Ostensibly cast as diametrical opposites—Cherie refined and tender, Bo rough and uncouth—they are actually as similar as they are different, both defined by their masquerades. One reading of the play suggests that Cherie's "decadence" will be "purified" once she is exposed to clean, simple country living; and Bo's saw-toothed edge will be blunted once he understands the difference between roping cattle and charming women. But a different reading suggests that both characters' decadence is based on their masquerade. When Cherie enters the cafe, she is described as "pretty in a fragile, girlish way" (157), and "her lipstick creates a voluptuous pair of lips that aren't her own" (157). When Bo enters, he is described as "rumpledly picturesque" (169) and "could pass" (169) as an "outlaw" (169). Obviously, Bo and Cherie are not what they appear to be; their essences, in Kierkegaard's terms, are divorced from their phenomena. Bo is the ingénue, Cherie the sleazy demimonde Bo thinks is an angel. She is a child/whore, at once a *femme fatale* and Shirley Temple, begging to be protected while inured to being abused. Bo's innocence is equally contradictory. He is a bronco-busting tough guy who cries when his toy is denied him. Just as Cherie projects what she denies, Bo's brashness covers his sensitivity. Bo, who over-identifies himself with the schoolyard bully, conceals the proverbial sheep in wolf's clothing, an idea reinforced by his significantly losing the fight with Will. He appears quick to spark, swaggering and arrogant, but he is also compliant, submissive as a pet. Likewise, Cherie vamps to hide from herself, her tough independence masked by her churlish charm. So their dilemma is this: the more Cherie says no, the more she projects yes; the more Bo says yes, the more he projects no. The only resolution is for each to penetrate the masquerade of the other, to discover, again in Kierkegaard's terms, the essence behind the phenomenon, the face, the truth behind the guise. Bo discovers the woman in the girl; Cherie discovers the boy in the man. After she admits that she has led a "wicked" (209) life, he confesses that he is "kinda' green" (210). Once they remove their masks, their relationship, now honest, can develop in earnest.

Yet all the passengers operate within the same dynamic. Just as Grace (and Elma) are looking forward to the disruption the bus occasions, the passengers are seeking shelter from the storm of unchecked passion raging on the bus. Just as Will is the marker in the diner against which Grace (and Elma) can measure the intensity of her emotions, Virgil emerges from the bus as the one left out, a man whose jaded desire leaves him hungering only for his own music, a "t-backy" (170) image of Midwestern self-reliance. Conversely, Cherie enters disheveled, claiming she needs "protection" (158); but as a torch singer her talent is to provoke and channel passion into expression, to stimulate and control. Bo's job, too, is to bridle the raw animal power of horses and bulls, tapping a source of power and at the same time harnessing it. Of course, in Bo's case self-control is more difficult than busting bulls. When he comes up against the implacable moral imperative of Will, "a very religious man" (190) who has "never lost a fight" (190), and when Cherie sings "That Old Black Magic," Bo's leash on his emotions snaps, and he must be forcibly brought back into line. Finally, regarding Lyman, Will is told by Carl to "keep an eye on *him* too" (167). Lyman expresses his depravity through his ostentatious and patronizing erudition, his perversity internally checked only by his drunken self-loathing, externally checked by the authorities hounding him from state to state. And beyond its function to allow Lyman a dramatic opportunity for self-recognition, the scene from *Romeo and Juliet* reinforces the central themes of the play: disruption and reconciliation, thematic pairing, and unchecked desire as a threat to a traditional stable set of values. The tragic and fatal consequences of Shakespeare's drama, however, are avoided in Inge's comedy by the intervention, this time, of the prudent nurses—Virgil and Will—who successfully minister compromise and discretion to the unruly lovers.

Ironically, given the subversive nature of gendermandering, the conventional morality in the play ensures that aberrant behavior is either corrected or punished. Lyman, clearly branded a monster, fails in his attempt to seduce Elma. Carl and Grace create a marriage of convenience, based on what Inge describes as "animal heat" (204). Cherie tames Bo, he pacifies her fears, and their mutual happiness is all but guaranteed. This perversion, of identifying winners and losers by how well they adapt their instinctual drives to "normal" civilized behavior, creates the most curious dynamic in the play: the pairing off of Bo and Virgil, the replacement of Virgil by Cherie, and the subsequent "punishment" of Virgil for his "unnatural" relationship with Bo. Virgil tells Bo that he "gave up romancin' and decided I was just gonna' take bein' lonesome for granted" (183). He feels "uncomfortable" with women, preferring "the bunkhouse" with his "buddies" (185). Virgil, the paragon of forethought and even-handedness, lacks passion; literally left out in the cold, he exits the play outcast and alone. His role parallels Grace's. He protects and advises Bo the way Grace does Elma; however, Grace's moderated sexuality enjoins her to the community of relations while Virgil's sterility exiles him. Eventually, Cherie assumes the role of mother and wife, displacing Virgil, who stoically accepts his fate by merely commenting "that's what happens to some people" (219), meaning, of course, to those people who have given up the zest for life, whose uneasiness with passion leaves them emotionally anemic.

As in *Bus Stop*, *Picnic* also gendermanders sex roles. Again, the peripheral characters are fairly predictable types. Flo and Mrs. Potts are strong-willed, independent widows, but in essence they remain predictable, their behavior consistent with their circumstances, the one caring for her mother, the other a single mother raising two dynamic daughters. They are solicitous and even-handed, nurturing and protective. Rosemary, the old maid schoolmarm, has a hidden passionate life, but she is no less predictable than the other women around her. She allows her self-loathing to turn first to anger at Hal, then to desperate self-pity, and finally to emotional blackmail against the self-centered business-minded good sport Howard. Millie flirts with sex role reversal, but finally comes off as a typical tomboy who "cusses like a man" (76) and complains when she has to bathe. She is, after all, the archetypal ugly duckling waiting to metamorphose into a nice educated modern young woman who will marry someone like Alan, another bookish brat who, according to Madge, is "the kind of man who doesn't mind if a woman's bossy" (79). And even though Millie and Alan display, respectively, masculine and feminine tendencies that counter their fixed genders, both are well on their way to assuming safe, stereotypical roles. Their cross-dressing is more like optional attire on a window display mannequin, and at any moment they will revert to their expected outfits and settle in.

Hal and Madge, on the other hand, are more spiritually cross-dressed. Hal manages to maintain his masculine surface, his public front. He is a tough athlete, impressing the kids with his diving skills (an easy sexual allusion, the phallic diver penetrating the vaginal pool). A self-proclaimed ladies' man, he claims that he "never had to pay for it" (116), but his pose is a denial. Essentially segregating him from his feminine self, his macho posturing masks his acutely sensitive emotional life, his attempts at assuming the role of career man in control of his life thwarted by his desire to follow his inclinations, to act spontaneously, intuitively, not reasonably, covertly exhibiting Dionysian dissolution. A romantic, an escapist, good at dancing and romancing, for all his masculine guise of control, Hal finds himself most often the victim, not the perpetrator, prey to his libido. For instance, the two women who engage him in a *ménage à trois* also rip him off; his story of the encounter, which at first seems like a fantasy of male sexual prowess, becomes the confession of a man who has been raped and robbed. Likewise, he is attacked by Rosemary, the castrating Medusa. And in an ironic visual twist, at the beginning of the play, Hal, not Madge, acts the passive to-be-looked-at object of desire, the pin-up poster "parading around naked as an Indian" (87). And despite the clearly homoerotic sequence with Alan, which explains as much about Alan's heterosexual inhibitions as it does about Hal's homosexual exuberance, Hal remains the patently heterosexual nexus of desire, to be feared and craved by all the women in the play.

Similarly, Madge is trapped in a surface life of public role playing with which she is less at ease than she might appear. Whereas Hal is feigning his masculinity to mask his feminine urges, Madge has concocted an ultra-feminine demeanor to cover her will to control. Beneath her veneer of femininity, she is calculating, reserved, a master of make-up, of affectation. She is not academic, at least not passionate for the arts, and according to Millie she "cooks and sews and does all the things women do" (99). Her domesticity is ironic, of course, because at first glance Millie is the one set to explode the stereotype. She is aggressive, bookish; she smokes, swears, tries to drink with the men, wants to lead when dancing. But she will conform; after all, she admits she likes Alan. Her female nature is latent, not confused. Madge, on the other hand, must reconcile her public life with her private. She appears as the Dionysian image of the mysterious female, there to be conquered and controlled, but actually Madge knows exactly what's at stake in the game. Where Hal is impetuous, Madge is controlling, weighing the pros and cons of each of her decisions. Even her sexual tryst with Hal is less a momentary lapse of judgment than a perfectly choreographed plot to capture her prey.

As in *Bus Stop* and *Picnic*, *Come Back, Little Sheba* also exposes characters cast into stereotypical roles they cannot maintain. While their superficial life is built around a routine marriage, Lola and Doc find themselves at odds with both their social roles and their private expectations. And just as in the other two plays, the atypical characters—Lola and Doc—are surrounded by conventional types: Turk, the horny dumb jock; Marie, the manipulative vamp-slash-ingenue; Bruce, the "marrying type" (50) cuckold. These characters, comfortable as two-dimensional social types, are the device by which Doc and Lola measure their alienation. This is indicative of how divorced they are from themselves and from the society that defines them. Doc, a dysfunctional Dionysian, craves the masculine world of strength, order, and reason, to which he is culturally entitled. He desperately clings to images, to his mask of decency, as he suffers the dark destructive urges of his desire. He dotes on Marie's pretense of innocence, describing her as "clean and decent" (10), "clean and fresh" (11), one of the "nice girls" (11) who represent, for him, a simple world in which the sordid grit of existence is deferred, and appearance is the only necessary truth. His struggle is to maintain this chimera of convention, where people assume the roles he assigns them according to what he believes are the proper social codes of normality so that he can locate and define himself within this psycho-theatrical *mise en scène*. To maintain an identity, to project clarity and reason and order, he must stay sober, but his inclination is to drink, to destroy his carefully constructed ego-identity, to dissolve the established boundaries of his personality. In a revealing allusion, Doc is entranced by Schubert, the syphilitic Classicist who mastered the technique of structuring the inchoate nature of passion into the geometry of music. Doc envies the composer's ability to arrange and objectify his feelings, but to do so is a trick of the will well beyond Doc's experience. Doc is best at cheap card tricks, using the same sleight-of-hand by which he hoodwinks himself, half-believing in a world of his own projection.

Perversely, Lola is the one who represents ideals of common sense, sobriety, and restraint, but she longs to release herself to her passions. In a significant contrast to Doc's appreciation of Schubert, Lola prefers the radio show "Ta-boo" (22) which offers its listeners "temptation" and enjoins them to "leave behind your routine . . . day-to-day existence . . . and follow me where pagan spirits hold sway . . . a moon-enchanted isle" (22). "Ta-boo" is a paean to Bacchus, celebrating the primitive rhythms of the deep unconscious. She wants what Doc fears. For all her posing, all her frantic, pathetic attempts to order the potential chaos in her marriage, Lola is repressing an intense desire to escape the rigid routine of her mundane life. A former beauty queen, according to Inge, "She is by nature coy and kittenish" (14). But she is also no longer capable of having children. Thus divorced from her nature, as both an object of adulation and as a procreative mother, Lola craves a return to her mythical essence, to surrender to her dreams, to dissolve her fabricated identity in a delirium of desire. Desperate for sensual stimulation to counter her stoic optimism, her sterility, her forced moral fortitude, she flirts with the postman, the milkman, Turk. She resorts to vicarious voyeuristic fantasies by spying on Marie, and is so intense, so "dazed" (23) with Turk that, when he's posing in his track suit, "all his muscles in place" (23), he complains that "she makes me feel naked" (24). If Doc wants to transcend his desire, Lola wants to give herself over to it.

Inge's last major play, *The Dark at the Top of the Stairs*, is more problematic. In the context of gendermandering, his attempt to delineate the conflicted natures of his characters is less successful, and the fact that the characters as types do not reveal any opposite movement against themselves might explain the lack of dramatic tension in the play. The motivation for the mother at the center of the family drives her not to escape typified behavior but to enter into it, to conform to it. She thinks her salvation, and that of the family, lies not in subverting stereotypes but in being one, aspiring to become a white, mid-America, Norman Rockwell archetype. Aside from the faulty structure of the play, in which most of the dramatic action, like Reenie's trauma at the dance and Sammy's suicide and Rubin's being fired, occurs offstage, the ironic desire of the mother to displace her existential individuality with a representation and to enter the symbolic as a sanctuary from the contingencies of life may be the primary reason for the play's sentimentality. It sags through set bits of moralizing speeches, replete with lines like "There are all kinds of people in the world" (294) and "Times are changin'" (298).

Set in the 1920s, the play nevertheless conforms to the typical gender behavior codified by the 1950s social milieu prevalent in Inge's other plays. In fact, the date of *The Dark at the Top of the Stairs* seems artificial. Prohibition, the transition from horse-based to automobile-based jobs, and the Midwestern bigotry toward Jews inform the psychological dilemmas facing the characters as they make choices that actually shape the action of the play. The types the characters represent were as established in the collective cultural imagination of the time of the play as they were in the 1950s when it was written and produced. Rubin is "the traveling salesman," happier on the road visiting the Mavis Pruitts along his route than he is at home offering the order and stability around which his family will thrive. Cora is "the doting mother" left home alone, less a wife than the mother of Rubin's children, who, from her own insecurity, has created children ill equipped to confront the world. Reenie, "the introverted daughter," too shy to go to the dance, would rather study in the library or play Chopin alone. Brother-in-law Morris plays the "hen-pecked husband," Lottie the "nagging wife." The only curious character, Sonny, typifies an effeminate "sensitive male child" who prefers reciting poetry, going to movies and filling scrapbooks with photographs of movie stars rather than playing with the neighborhood boys his own age. With characters as tightly type-cast as these, the moments of madness are few, as the characters cling to their masks and conform to expected patterns of behavior. Even Rubin's slapping his wife seems predictable, and her forgiving him equally so. The suicide of Sammy, the "nice Jewish boy," intended to shock, has such weak psychological grounding, seems so forced and abrupt, that the effect of the action merely highlights the contrivance.

Nevertheless, one scene in the play demonstrates a gendermandering that allows for strong dramatic tension while threatening to unravel the carefully constructed stereotypical tapestry on which the family weaves its drama. It occurs when Sammy, Flirt and Punky have arrived to pick up Reenie for the party, and they are waiting downstairs for her as she frets in a nervous panic upstairs. Punky and Flirt dance at the back of the room, and Sammy asks Sonny if he wants a "wild West ride" (266). Sammy "kneels on the floor" (266) and lets Sonny sit on his back, then romps like a horse around the room. To underscore the subtext of the scene, Sammy then gives Sonny his sword, which Sonny feigns to stick into himself. Further emphasizing the impact of the action, after being told he cannot go to the party with Sammy as his date, Sonny lashes out in a tantrum as intense as any lover's. The juxtaposition of the heterosexual couple who "indulge in a little private lovemaking" (267) with the overtly homosexual action of Sonny riding Sammy and then swapping the phallic sword tears away the convenient social conventions. In the moral context of the play, Sonny's latent homosexuality, a sign of the normative breakdown in the family, results from the father's absence. Significantly, Aunt Lottie, more concerned about Flirt and Punky, ignores the much more subversive implications of Sammy and Sonny "horsing around." As she is accustomed to seeing only what she expects to see, she affirms the stereotypes of the nice Jewish boy and the peculiar child, while the sense of the gendermandered action reveals exactly the opposite: a breakdown of stereotypical behavior completed outside her experiential reality.

The play, however, does not sustain such moments, as the other three major plays of Inge manage to do. The action reverts to a normative payoff in which the return of the father means the reestablishment of the family unit; the family becomes "normal," comfortable in its stereotypical sanctity. Sonny is "cured" in the end of being a so-called mamma's boy, or a sissy (231, 294), by simply reverting to another stereotype. He is the son who triumphantly breaks from his mother. Cora forbids him to sleep with her anymore, then his father returns to displace him from his mother's bed. As if to compensate his son, Rubin sets Sonny up with a girl who is an accomplished whistler, and the son, comfortable in his sudden new role, rejects the final proffered embrace of his mother. Reenie, too, from the suicide of Sammy, has emerged from her emotional shell, shedding both her introversion and her bitterness toward her brother. Their final action is to go off to see a movie together, like best friends. Rubin apologizes for slapping Cora and promises to get new work on his own terms. As the man of the house, he asserts his prerogatives, reminding his wife that she can't "talk to a man like that" (296). Both attempt to affirm their moral rectitude by succumbing to their culturally determined roles, husband and wife. Still, Cora's final sexual innuendo, "I'm coming, Rubin. I'm coming" (304), is hardly satisfying as she strains to provide some climatic closure to her sense of restoration. If she is "coming," her satisfaction is all too neat to be either plausible or convincing. Yet, perversely, that is her achievement: to become predictable.

In his foreword to *Four Plays*, Inge stresses that he "never sought to write plays that primarily tell a story" (vii), preferring instead to create "extensions of meaning beyond the immediate setting" (viii). He acknowledges that "a play's merits can exist, not in the dramatization . . . but in the over-all pattern and texture of the play" (viii). It is this moral imposition, his attempt to order passion, to marry design to desire, that secures Inge his significance and perennial value as an American playwright. But beyond his interest in writing plays to "dramatiz[e] something of the dynamism . . . in human motivations and behavior" (vii), his remarks underscore the playwright's concern with action and character, or, in more modern terms, plot and psychology. Even though Inge manages to create strong dramatic tension through the dynamics of story and situation, he engineers or gendermanders his characters to challenge and subvert the stereotypes so ingrained in the culture of the 1950s. He creates a deeper current below the surface of his plays, an existential subtext of people divorced from their essential mythical and cultural roots. This elevates Inge's work from mere popular theatre to the arena of sexual politics.

Works Cited

Heller, Dana. "Introduction: Plotting the Family." *Family Plots: The De-Oedipalization of Popular Culture.* Philadelphia: U of Pennsylvania P, 1995.

Inge, William. *Four Plays by William Inge.* New York: Random House, 1958.

Meyerowitz, Joanne. "Introduction." *Not June Cleaver: Women and Gender in Postwar America, 1945-1960.* Ed. Joanne Meyerowitz. Philadelphia: Temple UP, 1994.

Chapter Seven

Arthur Kopit's *Wings* and the Languages of the Theater

James Hurt

In the closing years of the twentieth-century theater, there seems to be an increasing impulse to create new theatrical idioms, a "tradition of the new" (to quote Harold Rosenberg's famous phrase) that charges the playwright with the imperative not just to tell new stories or engage new themes but to find theatrical discourses adequate to the expression of new visions. The formal models of Ibsen, Artaud, Brecht, and Beckett are still potent, but increasingly audiences seem to feel that new sensibilities call for new languages of the stage. Tom Stoppard, Brian Friel, and Maria Irene Fornes come to mind as examples (from three national English-language theaters) of playwrights who have restlessly and continually reinvented the dramatic language of the stage. In their most characteristic plays, the only convention is that there are no conventions; the stage is constantly redefined to embody the playwrights' visions.

One constant element in Arthur Kopit's prolific and varied career has been this sort of self-consciousness and inventiveness about his medium. Even the undergraduate plays of his Harvard years (1955–59) show the urge to use the stage in new ways. Parody, pastiche, and clashing juxtapositions of tones and genres mark these plays, as they do *Oh Dad, Poor Dad* and (more successfully) *Indians*, in which the mingling of realistic narrative and a Wild West show concretizes rather than merely states Kopit's revisionist history. But nowhere is Kopit's ability to forge ad hoc theatrical idioms for his work more successful than in *Wings* (1978).

Wings has been contextualized in a number of ways. Doris Auerbach has read it against Roman Jacobson's studies of similarity and contiguity disorders in aphasia through which he established his critical distinction between metaphor and metonymy. Her reading is heavily metaphorical, emphasizing the play's universality rather than its particularity. Suzanne Burgoyne Dieckman and Richard Brayshaw, in an illuminating essay, have placed it in the context of Kopit's other plays; and Margot Anne Kelley, in an equally fine study, has located it in relation to postmodernism, information theory, and chaos theory. I would like to take a slightly different tack by contextualizing the play against other literary representations of stroke, especially two explicit sources for the play, and by examining the theatrical language that Kopit has devised to capture the inner reality of this horrifying experience.

In his preface to the play, Kopit traces its origins to a major stroke his father suffered in 1976 and to his resultant visits to a rehabilitation clinic in upstate New York. Although *Wings* is a tribute to his father (who later died from the results of the stroke), Kopit realized that his father could not be the model for the protagonist of the play, because Kopit could not establish the emotional distance he needed and because his father's case was "too severe, too grim" (viii). Accordingly, the models for the composite figure of Emily Stilson were three women he met at the rehabilitation clinic. Two were patients, a woman in her late seventies who had been an aviatrix and wing-walker in her youth and a woman in her late twenties who had escaped the worst ravages of her left-brain stroke because she was left-handed. The other was their therapist, Jacqueline Doolittle, who had herself experienced temporary aphasia as a result of brain damage in an automobile accident (viii–xv).

Kopit describes the play as an attempt to answer the question about stroke victims "What was it like inside?" (vii), and he goes on to say of the play that it is a blending of fact and speculation. On the one hand, he aspired, he says, to "an absolutely solid clinical accuracy" (xii). On the other, he recognizes that "any attempt to render a person's consciousness through words, even autobiography, must be speculative" (xv). Kopit's distinction between fact and speculation suggests the twin achievements of the play: the tough realism of its unflinching representation of the devastation caused by a serious stroke and the creation of a language of the stage to convey the inner experience of the stroke victim. Any reading that stays close to the actual experience of the play must do justice to both dimensions of it: the reality of stroke and the dramatic discourse by which that reality is conveyed to the audience.

This tension, of course, is present in any literary work, but it takes on some special features in literary representations of stroke or other brain injury. There are many such representations, ranging from personal narratives by survivors, such as May Sarton's *After the Stroke* (1988), Eric Hodgins' *Episode* (1967), Charles Clay Dahlberg and Joseph Jaffe's *Stroke: A Doctor's Personal Story of His Recovery* (1977), and Robert McCrum's "My Old and New Lives" (1996), to such more overtly literary treatments as Samuel Beckett's *Not I* (1972) and Alan Ayckbourn's *Woman in Mind: December Bee* (1986).[1] The simple dichotomy between the real and the imaginary is radically undercut in such works by the nature of brain damage, which often renders problematical the nature of the "real," the reliability of the perceiving self, and the stability of such presumably human attributes as the sense of personal identity, the ability to communicate with others, and the continuity of perceived experience. These difficulties are bypassed in retrospective narratives, which report stroke experiences from the vantage point of recovered health, but they often become central in accounts which try to capture the contemporary nature of the stroke experience.

Kopit is quite explicit about his sources for the clinical dimensions of his play. They include, besides his interaction with Jacqueline Doolittle and her two patients, two books on brain damage: Howard Gardner's *The Shattered Mind* and A. R. Luria's *The Man With a Shattered World* (see Preface xvi). These two books clearly made a major contribution to the play, supplying everything from short passages quoted verbatim to general points which appear in paraphrase and a general model for the design of the play.

Howard Gardner's *The Shattered Mind: The Person After Brain Damage* (1975) is a sophisticated book of medical reportage written for a general audience by a neuropsychologist who had been based at the Aphasia Research Center of the Boston University School of Medicine and the Boston Veterans Administration Hospital. *The Shattered Mind* is a substantial survey, almost 500 pages long, of the state of knowledge of the brain in 1975. In it, Gardner is interested both in the often surprising results of brain injury and in the insights they open into the functioning of the uninjured brain, as the title of his opening chapter indicates: "Brain Injury as an Avenue to the Mind." Subsequent chapters deal with aphasia (disturbance of language function), alexia (loss of reading ability), recognition, memory, cognition, and the relation of brain injury to art. A close reading of *The Shattered Mind* and *Wings* together reveals a pervasive indebtedness of the play to the book. For example, it is clear that Emily Stilson suffers from a condition called "Wernicke's aphasia," which is characterized by verbal fluency and a good command of syntax, but an inability to extract meanings from verbal materials and to encode ideas into meaningful units. A Wernicke's aphasic, then, produces speech that is fairly smooth and syntactically correct but is a meaningless babble of neologisms and inappropriate word choices. Gardner develops his description of Wernicke's aphasia through a case study of a patient he calls Philip Gorgan (67–75). Gorgan provided the model for Emily Stilson's speech, along with the younger of the two patients Kopit met at the rehabilitation center, whereas the older patient who was the major model for Emily suffered from a different form of aphasia called "Broca's aphasia," characterized by a monotonous speech made up almost entirely of "content" words and lacking melody and syntactic richness (Gardner 63).

The other written source that Kopit names for the play is Aleksandr Romanovich Luria's extraordinary *The Man with a Shattered World: The History of a Brain Wound* (1972). Luria (1902–1977), one of the major neurologists of the twentieth century, wrote a number of standard neurological texts, including notably *Higher Cortical Functions in Man* (1962), but he also wrote two examples of what he called "Romantic Science"—*The Mind of a Mnemonist* (1968) and *The Man with a Shattered World*—books in which he aspired not only to present accurate science but also to characterize their subjects as entire human beings, in a blending of science and literature, "neurological novels," as he called them.

The Man with a Shattered World is largely made up of passages from the diary of L. Zasetsky, a twenty-three-year-old Russian soldier who was wounded at the battle of Smolensk in 1943. Shrapnel destroyed much of the left parietal-occipital area of his head, a loss that left him blind in his right visual field, unable to read or write, and unable to grasp such simple sequences as the primary numbers or the progress of the seasons. He retained, however, the function of his frontal lobes: his will, his desires, and the abilities to perceive his situation, make plans, and monitor his progress in carrying them out. Luria saw the young soldier about three months after he was wounded and continued to see him as a patient for twenty-five years. Zasetsky eventually learned how to read, though slowly and laboriously, and to write, somewhat more easily, by relying on automatic writing of whole words and sentences rather than syllable-by-syllable writing. As part of his effort to recover part of what he had lost, he kept a journal for twenty-five years, which eventually stretched to an amazing three thousand pages. Luria reprints short excerpts from this diary, interpolating paragraphs of his own, commenting on and interpreting Zasetsky's narrative. *The Man with a Shattered World* is in many respects a devastating book, involving as it does the cruel irony of a man who has lost almost everything but the capacity to perceive his own pain. And yet, finally, it is in many ways an heroic and inspiring book. As Oliver Sacks writes in his foreword to a 1987 reissue of the English version:

> And perhaps there is a universal here which applies to us all, even if we learn it anew from Zasetsky—the lesson also taught by Socrates, Freud, Proust—that a life, a human life, is not a life until it is examined; that it is not a life until it is truly remembered and appropriated; and that such a remembrance is not something passive, but active, the active and creative construction of one's life. (xvii)

Kopit's debt to *The Man with a Shattered World* appears to be somewhat different from that to *The Shattered Mind.* He seems to have derived from Zasetsky-Luria not so much verbal passages and specific details about brain damage as, first, the crucial idea of presenting the experience of brain damage from within, in the patient's own language rather than mediated by "normal" observers and caregivers, and, second, the idea, as explicit in the book as in Sacks's eloquent description, that the extreme experience of brain damage can have some relevance beyond the clinical. Kopit may even have derived some inspiration for his play, with its complex manipulation of subjectivity, from the peculiar double voice of *The Man with a Shattered World*, the alternating voices, undifferentiated by typography in the American edition, of Zasetsky and Luria, the "inner" and "outer" voices, the sufferer and the observer of the suffering.

Kopit's achievement in *Wings* is to create a stage discourse that can suggest the inner, lived experience of a victim of stroke while also remaining true to the clinical facts of the condition. As he writes in the preface: "[I]f *Wings* was to be effective, it would have to deal specifically with its central character and not with some general condition called stroke; at the same time, to be effective, it would have to possess an absolutely solid clinical accuracy" (xii). He does this by creating an open, fluid stage space that can generally represent Emily Stilson's field of consciousness, while at the same time occasionally shifting the subject position represented by the stage picture to include other views of her condition. Thus the audience is sometimes placed within Emily Stilson's consciousness, sometimes within the consciousness of another character, and sometimes located in a position that allows access to both her inner world and the outer world from which she is perceived by others.

Kopit's dramaturgy in *Wings* draws upon the dream-play tradition of modern drama, from Strindberg through the Surrealists and Expressionists to Beckett. The key to his highly original intervention in this tradition of the representation of subjectivity on the stage is its fluidity and flexibility. Whereas Strindberg in his dream plays placed the audience in the consistent subject position of "the dreamer," and the German Expressionists, for example, controlled the audience's subjectivity through such devices as the roving spotlight, Kopit moves the audience rapidly and without transitions from outer to inner and from Emily Stilson to those who attend her, radically decentering its perceptions in a way that replicates not only the experience of the outsider trying to understand what is happening to the stroke victim but also, perhaps, the unstable and contradictory experience of the victim herself.

Wings has a fluid four-part structure: a brief "Prelude" followed by a somewhat longer "Catastrophe" and two extended sections called "Awakening" and "Explorations." Kopit directs that it be performed without intermission.

In "Prelude," we see Emily sitting in an armchair, reading a book. She, a floor lamp, and a table with a clock are each illuminated by a pin-spot in the midst of engulfing darkness. First the floor lamp disappears, its spotlight snapped off, followed by the table and clock, which continues to tick loudly. The clock skips a beat, resumes ticking, and then stops, as Emily "STARES OUT IN TERROR" (8).

This simple representation of the onset of the stroke effectively defines the nature of the stage space and announces some of the major concerns of the play. At first we are invited to view the simple scene realistically, from the point of view of outside observers, placed in the space of conventional audienceship ("objective," stable, unreflective, implicitly powerful and voyeuristic). As the stroke begins, and Emily's senses begin to fail with the disappearance of the lamp and table with a clock and the distortion of the regular ticking of the clock, we must rapidly revise our subject position and realize that we are seeing the stage space and hearing its sounds as Emily perceives them. This is only the first of the play's frequent and fluid remappings of subjectivity.

Since perception of the lamp, table, and clock depend on sight and the perception of the ticking of the clock depends on hearing, the scene also introduces the play's concern with the disordering of such basic dimensions of the world as space and time, the "shattered world" of Luria's title. This disordering is complicated by the introduction in the next scene of an equally disordered language, and the progress of the play will be toward the partial and temporary reordering of the world so simply shattered in "Prelude."

The apparent simplicity of unselfconscious health is followed by the perceptual complexity of a storm in the brain in "Catastrophe." Here the full resources of the setting stipulated by Kopit in his production notes come into play:

> The stage as a void.
> System of black scrim panels that can move silently and easily, creating the impression of featureless, labyrinthine corridors.
> Some panels mirrored so that they can fracture light, create the impression of endlessness, even airiness, multiply and confuse images, confound one's sense of space. ("Notes on the production of this play," n.p.)

An elaborate sound system is called for, with speakers all around the theatre.

Kopit arranges the text of this section in three parallel columns: one that gives the images the audience sees on stage, a second that lists the sounds it hears, and a third that gives the lines spoken by Mrs. Stilson. This scene plunges the audience suddenly and shockingly into Mrs. Stilson's damaged consciousness. Later in the play, we briefly leave her mind and see the world as outside observers see it, but here we are trapped inside the stroke victim's world. Consequently we can experience, if not necessarily analyze, the lines along which her world has shattered. The most immediately obvious are fragmentations of visual and aural perceptions. The first sight is of whiteness: "*Dazzling, blinding.*" Occasionally, the whiteness throbs with "brief rhombs" of color, principally red. Gradually, brief images emerge from the whiteness, "*like apparitions*"—doctors, nurses, doors opening and closing, fragments of hospital equipment—all nightmarishly multiplied by reflection in the mirrored curtain. Sound is similarly shattered. The first sounds are nonverbal—wind, labored breathing, a sound which alternately seems to be a siren and a woman screaming; gradually verbal sounds emerge—garbled, incomprehensible voices: "Just relax. No one's going to hurt you," etc. Distorted visual and aural perception in "Catastrophe" reflect the shattering of space and time that Kopit sees as one of the basic components of his somewhat generalized representation of stroke. Space and time are similarly distorted in Mrs. Stilson's verbalizations in this scene. Panic-stricken reactions to her present situation are blended with an abruptly resurrected memory, or possibly fantasy, of flying a plane in a storm:

> *Oh my God oh my God oh my God—trees clouds houses mostly planes flashing past, images without words, utter disarray disbelief, never seen this kind of thing before! Where am I? How'd I get here?* ("Catastrophe," n.p.)

Mrs. Stilson's words are as problematic as her sight and hearing, since stage action represents her perception of her speech rather than speech itself. As Kopit notes, "Since we are perceiving the world through Mrs. Stilson's senses, there is no sure way for us to know whether she is actually saying any of these words aloud" (9–10). Kopit's dramatic discourse here—a rough theatrical parallel to "stream of consciousness" in fiction—leads the audience to experience Mrs. Stilson's stroke firsthand, as it were, but with a further twist: to Mrs. Stilson's uncertainty over the "real" is added the audience's uncertainty over its theatrical representation. Mrs. Stilson cannot distinguish between external action and her internal experience; we cannot distinguish between theatrical representations of the objective and subjective.

In "Awakening," the storm inside Mrs. Stilson's head has subsided, and we can begin to assess the damage it has done. Even more than in "Catastrophe," Kopit employs his fairly simple theatrical means to convey complex psychological experiences, moving the audience figuratively in and out of Mrs. Stilson's perceptions to communicate both her frightening experience and the difficulties her doctors and nurses have in understanding her exact condition. Like Mrs. Stilson, the audience cannot rely on accustomed ways of hearing and seeing but must learn new vocabularies of both. For example, Mrs. Stilson spends most of the long scene sitting quietly in a chair downstage; yet we gradually realize from the context that her body is often elsewhere, in a hospital bed, for example, or on an examination table or being rolled down hallways on a gurney. Kopit explains this feature of the play in his opening production notes:

> It is posited by this play that the woman we see in the center of the void is the intact inner self of Mrs. Stilson. This inner self does not need to move physically when her external body (which we cannot see) moves. Thus, we infer movement from the context; from whatever clues we can obtain. It is the same for her, of course. She learns as best she can. ("Notes on the production of this play," n.p.)

To this we should add that the audience, too, can only do the best it can. Despite clues from the context, it is often unclear where Mrs. Stilson literally is, as her "inner self" sits quietly downstage.

"Awakening" (and the rest of the play) raises the question (among many others) that Gardner calls the "question of pivotal psychological interest" in brain-injury cases: "[W]hat is the relation between impairments of language and disorders of thought?" (28). As a sufferer from Wernicke's aphasia, Mrs. Stilson's language is fluent but bizarre:

> *Hapst aporkshop fleetish yes of course it's yes the good ol' times when we would mollis I mean collis all around still what my son's name is cannot for the life of me yet face gleams smiles as he tells them what I did but what his name is cannot see it pleasant anyway yes palms now ocean sea breeze wafting floating up and lifting holding weightless and goes swooooping down with me least I . . . think it's me.* (25)

Even from this word salad, it is possible to extract some meaning, mainly in the form of visual images: a memory of her son's childhood face, an image of a day on the beach perhaps blending with a memory of flying. The question, though, is whether these jumbled words accurately mirror Mrs. Stilson's damaged thought processes or not. Has she lost the capacity for sequential thought or is she thinking clearly but is unable to express her thought? Is Wernicke's aphasia a disorder of thought, language, or both? These difficult-to-answer questions raise other far-reaching ones, which Gardner articulates:

> What is the relation between language and other sign systems such as sign language, Morse code, and musical notation? Is aphasia inevitably accompanied by personality change? What is the relationship between language and thought? Can a person deprived of his or her ability to communicate via language still retain the capacity to think? (53–54)

Mrs. Stilson's progress in recovery is marked off in explanatory stage directions in "Awakening." But no attempt is made to resolve the basic mysteries of her condition, whether she has lost the capacity to think or merely the temporary ability to verbalize her thoughts. These mysteries are suggested by the audience's continual uncertainty as to the ontological status of what they see and hear.

As "Awakening" begins, a doctor in the background repeatedly calls her name, with no response, whereupon the doctor says, "IT'S POSSIBLE SHE MAY HEAR US BUT BE UNABLE TO RESPOND" (23). As Mrs. Stilson begins to speak, we are predisposed to believe that she is actually unable to speak and that we are occupying her inner world, privy to her unspoken thoughts: "*Still . . . sun moon too or . . . three times happened maybe globbidged rubbidged uff and firded-forded me to nothing there try again*" (23). (In the printed text, speeches "actually" spoken are in Roman type, inner speech is in italics, a clarification of course unavailable to the audience at a performance.)

After a time, "OUTSIDE SOUNDS BEGIN TO IMPINGE" (24), notably a loud floor polisher which, unable to interpret, she hears as a fierce animal's growl. This inaugurates a sequence in which Mrs. Stilson is gradually able to hear and see the world around her, without, however, being able to interpret it. Her struggles to make sense of her impressions lead to a series of misinterpretations: the floor polisher is an animal, a change of light and a slight breeze catapult her into a memory of wing-walking.

In the next stage of her recovery, Mrs. Stilson becomes able to recognize the presence of hospital staff around her and to hear them speak. The doctors and nurses move from the background and surround her downstage chair for the first time. "HER INNER AND OUTER WORLDS ARE BEGINNING TO COME TOGETHER" (30). For the first time, Mrs. Stilson actually speaks: "What?" (30). But though she can hear, she cannot interpret what the doctors say:

SECOND DOCTOR: Ahwill.
FIRST DOCTOR: Pollycadjis.
SECOND DOCTOR: Sewyladda?
FIRST DOCTOR (WITH A NOD): Hm-hm. (31)

At this point in the scene, the audience's subject position is abruptly redefined. To this point, the audience has been both outside and inside Mrs. Stilson's mind, able to hear both outside voices, the doctors calling her name, for instance, and her interior, unheard voice, "*Still . . . sun moon too or,*" and so on. But at this point, we are confined to Mrs. Stilson's inner world, hearing outside voices only as she hears them.

But this perception is untrustworthy. As Mrs. Stilson gradually recovers her ability to understand what is said to her and to reply, she thinks, coherently, she cannot be confident (nor can we) that what she hears herself say is what others hear:

NURSE [WARMLY]: Would you like some pudding?
MRS. STILSON: No.
NURSE: Good, I'll go get you some. (33)

In her confusion, Mrs. Stilson continues to generate fallacious theories about her situation, here, a conviction that her plane has crashed and she has been captured and brought to a farmhouse disguised as a farmhouse by enemy agents, who are interrogating her (34).

In the third major segment of "Awakening," Mrs. Stilson continues to narrow the gap between her inner perceptual world and the outer one. "THE SPACE MRS. STILSON NOW IS IN APPEARS MUCH MORE 'REAL' AND LESS FRAGMENTARY THAN WHAT WE HAVE SO FAR BEEN OBSERVING. WE SEE MRS. STILSON HERE AS OTHERS SEE HER" (34–35). It is less certain what perceptual space the audience occupies. We hear the doctor's undistorted speech as well as Mrs. Stilson's jumbled replies, as in the opening segment, but here Mrs. Stilson apparently hears the doctor clearly, too, but may be hearing her own incoherent replies as logical. We seem to have moved outside Mrs. Stilson's mind for the first time and see and hear her only from the outside, as Kopit's note that we see her here "as others see her" suggests.

This examination scene is heavily indebted to Gardner and Luria, as well as, undoubtedly, to scenes Kopit witnessed in the hospital. A doctor questions her about simple facts ("Where were you born?" "Are there seven days in a week?" etc.) and about the names and uses of simple objects, as Gardner does Philip Gorgan (Gardner 70–71) and Luria does Zasetsky (Luria 17–20). The requests to cough and to identify and use a toothbrush echo passages in Gardner's examination of David Ford and Philip Gorgan (Gardner 66, 73).

The gradual improvement in Mrs. Stilson's condition we have been witnessing through the previous part of "Awakening" slows and almost halts in this third segment. She does badly in the examination, unable to understand the request to cough and to identify and name a toothbrush, managing finally only to call it a "tooovebram, tooove-britch, bratch brush bridge, two-bridge" and to hold it to her lips, without motion. In a momentary fit of anger over her food, she is able to speak clearly: "Out! Get out! Take this shit away, I don't want it! Someone get me out of here!" (41), but when she calms down she cannot sustain her coherence. Kopit comments on this sequence:

> SHE IS DESPERATELY TRYING TO PIECE HER SHATTERED WORLD TOGETHER. UNDOUBTEDLY, IT IS THE DOMINANT MOTIF IN HER MIND. BUT IT IS A MOTIF PROBABLY MORE ABSENT FROM HER CONSCIOUSNESS THAN PRESENT, AND THE QUEST IT INSPIRES IS INTERMITTENT AT BEST. HER MENTAL ABILITIES HAVE NOT ONLY BEEN SEVERELY ALTERED, THEY HAVE BEEN DIMINISHED: THAT IS THE TERRIBLE FACT ONE CANNOT DENY. (38–39)

At this point when progress has slowed and we begin to realize that full recovery will not be possible, Mrs. Stilson reaches the deepest point in her inner life and reexperiences the death of her mother:

> *Mother! . . . didn't say as she usually . . .* PAUSE
> *And I thought late enough or early rather first light coming so when didn't move I poked her then with shoving but she didn't even eyes or giggle when I tickled.* (39)

We as an audience have left the outside world again and are back in Mrs. Stilson's consciousness, experiencing what the hospital staff has no access to: memory images that herald, by association, Mrs. Stilson's own movement toward death.

"Awakening" ends with a series of short scenes that introduce Amy, the gentle therapist who is to preside over Mrs. Stilson's final days. In the last, Mrs. Stilson makes one small, final link between her perceptions and the external world. She feels "Something . . . wet," realizes that they are tears, and recognizes, with Amy's prodding, that they mean that she is sad (47).

The last section of *Wings*, "Explorations," is structured in four sequences, each in a specific setting, with fluid transitional material between them. The audience is assigned throughout this section what in fiction would be called a first-person point of view. They are privy to Mrs. Stilson's unspoken thoughts (again represented by italics in the printed text) and see and hear other characters only as Mrs. Stilson perceives them.

Again, Mrs. Stilson's degree of recovery is described explicitly in Kopit's stage directions. In the opening sequence, in the hospital's recreation room, we are told that the room

> SHOWS MORE DETAIL AND COLOR THAN ANY SPACE WE'VE SO FAR SEEN. PERHAPS A VASE OF FLOWERS HELPS TO SIGNAL THAT MRS. STILSON'S WORLD IS BECOMING FULLER, MORE INTEGRATED. . . . NEW TIME SENSE HERE, A LANGUOR ALMOST. THE DREAD MRS. STILSON FELT HAS BEEN REPLACED BY AN ACKNOWLEDGMENT OF HER CONDITION, THOUGH NOT AN UNDERSTANDING. (52)

The scene confirms what has been suggested earlier: that in the neurological debate over whether aphasia is merely a linguistic impairment or involves also a cognitive deficit, Mrs. Stilson exemplifies the latter position. Behind the jumbled speech lies the "terrible fact" that her mental abilities have been diminished.

At the beginning of the scene, Mrs. Stilson has reached what is to be her highest level of recovery. Her linguistic skills are fairly normal, except for frequent difficulty in remembering words, and significantly she is aware of other people with names and individual personalities, for the first time in the play (except for the therapist Amy, who appeared near the end of "Awakening"). She has partially regained her sense of time and space, though she still has difficulty integrating her inner and outer worlds:

> MRS. STILSON IS UNABLE TO KEEP OUTSIDE IMAGES AND INNER THOUGHTS GOING SIMULTANEOUSLY. WHEN SHE'S WITH HER THOUGHTS, THE OUTSIDE WORLD FADES AWAY. WHEN THE OUTSIDE WORLD IS WITH HER, HER THOUGHTS FADE AWAY. (53)

As she leaves the confusing tumult of the recreation room, she wanders through the gauze panels and mirrors that have been used to represent her isolated, fragmented perceptions, and there is a brief return to the bombardment of random voices of "Catastrophe." In this sequence (56–58), she hears "blocks of sound" in random order which express the clinical view of her condition. These short snatches of text are quoted or paraphrased from Gardner's *The Shattered Mind* (23, 24, and 446ff.).

In the last three segments of "Explorations," a group therapy session, a tape-recorded lecture on stroke, an individual therapy session, and a walk in the snow, Amy gradually emerges as the presiding angel over Mrs. Stilson's final explorations of her past, her stroke, and her present condition. (Amy's name is perhaps intended to suggest "love.") In the last sequence, the fragmentation and abrupt shifts in the audience's subject position fade away, and the semblance of a return to the conventions of realistic drama signal the partial reintegration of Mrs. Stilson's consciousness. The conversation is halting and full of memory lapses, but the question of whether we are experiencing the scene from "inside" or "outside" Mrs. Stilson's mind becomes irrelevant, since the two coincide.

There is one last shift in our perceptions, however, to match a shift in Mrs. Stilson's. Amy gradually fades, and Mrs. Stilson's speeches again become interior ones (again signaled by italics in the printed text). She is having a second and apparently fatal stroke:

> *It comes now without my asking . . . Amy is still beside me but I am somewhere else. I'm not scared. It has taken me, and it's clear again. Something is about to happen.* (73)

The external world gradually fades until Mrs. Stilson is left alone in a pool of light in the midst of encircling darkness. She has one final, soaring fantasy of flying and wing-walking and dies: "MUSIC. HINT OF BELLS. LIGHTS TO BLACK. SILENCE" (78).

In *Wings*, Kopit devised a fluid, poetic language of the stage to achieve his twin aims of creating a vivid individual rather than "some general condition called stroke" and maintaining "an absolutely solid clinical accuracy." Original as his achievement is, it is not without antecedents. The various theatrical transformations of expressionism lie in the background, as do his own earlier excursions into representations of subjective experience on the stage. Samuel Beckett is a precursor if not a source, not so much the plays, perhaps, as the fiction, with its extended monologues ambiguously poised between interior and exterior, its abrupt stylistic shifts between the eloquent and the terse and incoherent, and its concern with such "unliterary" areas of experience as powerlessness, uncertainty, and emptiness. The ending of *Wings*, especially, evokes the final page of *Malone Dies*, with its startling subjective representation of death.

But another, and perhaps even more important, background for *Wings* is the literature of stroke, in which he found not only the basis for the clinical accuracy he sought but formal models as well. Howard Gardner's case studies of stroke patients struggling to pull together the fragments of their shattered minds and, especially, the maimed, heroic Zasetsky, trying to re-create himself as he creates a book, stand in the background of Kopit's quest to find a theatrical language to represent "brain injury as an avenue to the mind."

Notes

This essay is dedicated to the memory of my father and to my brother, both of whom endured multiple strokes with courage and resilience.

1 Gardner includes a survey of stroke narratives in *The Shattered Mind*, 397–422.

Works Cited

Auerbach, Doris. *Sam Shepard, Arthur Kopit, and the Off Broadway Theater.* Boston: Twayne, 1982. 103–10.

Dieckman, Suzanne Burgoyne, and Richard Brayshaw. "*Wings*, Watchers, and Windows: Imprisonment in the Plays of Arthur Kopit." *Theatre Journal* 35.2 (May 1983): 195–211.

Gardner, Howard. *The Shattered Mind: The Person After Brain Damage.* New York: Knopf, 1975.

Kelly, Margot Anne. "Order Within Fragmentation: Postmodernism and the Stroke Victim's World." *Modern Drama* 34 (1991): 383–91.

Kopit, Arthur. *Wings.* New York: Hill and Wang, 1978.

Luria, A. R. *The Man with a Shattered World: The History of a Brain Wound.* Trans. by Lynn Solotaroff. With a foreword by Oliver Sacks. Cambridge: Harvard UP, 1972.

Chapter Eight

Decoding Cipher Space: David Mamet's *The Cryptogram* and America's Dramatic Legacy

Janet V. Haedicke

My private silence
to your public guilt
is all i got

"Admonitions," Lucille Green

Ever the stepchild in theatre scholarship, American drama suffers extra-familial status because of its focus on the familial. The irrepressible strain of domestic realism which runs through our theatre putatively upholds a foundationalist ideology of linearity, transparency of language, and stability. Consequently, feminist critics have waged the most vitriolic of attacks on the genre as validating the closure of an objective reality through the realistic form and of a gendered family system through the domestic content. Yet this tradition in American drama continues to lure even those playwrights initially derisive of it. Most recent to succumb is David Mamet, who, like Eugene O'Neill and Sam Shepard before him, flouted critical praise of his resistance to the American theatre's "(over) reliance on the primal family unit usually embittered and embattled within the living room" (Roudané 6). But this shift from workplace to living room with *The Cryptogram* in 1995, prophesied by *Reunion* in 1979 and confirmed by *The Old Neighborhood* in 1997,[1] should neither surprise nor dismay. Consistent with the playwright's avowed intent to demystify the American dream, Mamet's defection to domestic realism signals a subversive and transformative ethic in American drama which constitutes its most significant legacy.

Mamet exposes the mythologized, politically capitalized Family as a system providing a prototype for the economic system. Since business is "what America is about" (Mamet "David Mamet" 137) and the subtext of business is power, Mamet predicts ever-worsening polarization in a country which has always constituted his subject. To bare the "national unconscious" (qtd. in Bigsby, *Beyond Broadway* 274), the plays dramatize our sanctified separation of the personal and the professional (a founding target of feminism) that exonerates criminality and even violence. In this corrosive, hierarchical system, it is legitimate for "those in power . . . to act unethically" ("An Interview," Roudané 74). Cherished all-American values of individualism, self-reliance, and persistence are summoned to the service of success, which comes only at the expense of another. Mamet's denunciation of the American dream as a dead end of "basically raping and pillage" (qtd. in Savran 133) foregrounds the gendered nature of power: "American capitalism comes down to one thing. . . . The operative axiom is 'Hurrah for me and fuck you.' Anything else is a lie" (qtd. in Dean 190).

In his focus on this "fucking," whose literal as well as figurative manifestation is embodied in the iconic Family, Mamet has consistently, if tacitly, conflated the business and familial systems, the public and private realms, exposing a landscape of spiritual bankruptcy as the illusionary borders between the two dissolve. In the grip of a "terrorism" as much ontological as it is commercial (Savran 134), Mamet's characters fight for a piece of a disintegrated dream, struggling hopelessly to define themselves by performing media-shaped American roles. "Entropic figures" (Bigsby, *Beyond Broadway* 253), they are confined by spaces emptied of meaning, an emptiness hardly mitigated by a diarrhetic language that echoes the hollow myths paralyzing them. With an internalized "fuck you" ethos, Mamet's males unleash disjointed fragments, sound-bites which aim not to communicate but to dominate, "not to speak the desire but to speak that which is most likely to bring about the desire" (Mamet "David Mamet" 137). The desire is for place, for power, for an identity defined against a vanquished Other; ironically, the words of these competitors only circumscribe them, reflecting Mamet's perception of subjectivity as mediated by language: "'Our rhythms describe our actions—no, our rhythms prescribe our actions'" (qtd. in Wetzsteon 39).

As with the language, so with the dramatic form, since Mamet's realism, like much in the American canon, cracks under its own excess. Dismissing his early plays as immature, "episodic glimpses" (Harriot "Interview," 78), Mamet defends the well-made play as the structure which imitates human perception's ordering of experience. It is, however, the illusory nature of perception itself, hence of linearity and classical realism, which provides the focus. His concern ultimately more epistemological than social, Mamet dramatizes "the fiction which is America" (Bigsby, *Beyond Broadway* 275), the country and its Dream revealed as purely perceptual and truth as provisional; the power struggles which characterize contemporary relationships emerge as performances to enthrone one version of reality.

The mediation of subjectivity by language, the complication of causality by chaos, and the undermining of the autonomous Cognitive self by irrational selves—these create a relentless tension or, in the terms of chaos theory, a bifurcation point in the system.[2] The more Mamet's characters push to define their place in an ordered universe, the more their worlds are exposed as fictional and entropic; an America of fruited plains will emerge only upon abdication of the quest for a fixed identity and evacuation of the barren Dream:

> The solution—which is to say solution which will enable us to function happily in the midst of rational uncertainty to a personal and seemingly unresolvable psychological problem—is the dream; the solution to a seemingly unresolvable social (ethic) problems the drama (poem). (*Writing* 9)

The liminality of Mamet's realism extricates it from the Cartesian logic of classical realism and betokens a fissure in dominant ideology. Beneath the surface hopelessness of the plays arise possibilities for both the country and its theatre; on the dissolving border between order and chaos, at the point of "rational uncertainty" where binarism implodes, Mamet locates transformation:

> the theatre affords an opportunity uniquely suited for communicating and inspiring ethical behavior. . . . In a morally bankrupt time we can help to change the habit of coercive and frightened action and substitute for it the habit of trust, self-reliance, and cooperation. (*Writing* 26–27).

There thus emanates from Mamet's stage that transformative ethic which perpetuates an American tradition of liminal realism. Emphasis on the communal yearnings of the soul and the communal function of theatre permeates the metadramatic aspects of a drama wherein characters attempting to perform themselves into being against an Other thwart community. Mamet regards this perversion of the theatrical impulse as tainting any system which resorts to hierarchy for its order:

> In the family, as in the theater, the urge to control only benefits the controller. Blind obedience saves him the onerous duty of examining his preconceptions, his own wisdom, and, finally, his own worth. (*Writing* 32).

This linking of the economic, theatrical, and familial systems illuminates the lure of domestic drama as an excavation of the originary site of binarism, that gendering which denies communal possibilities. To posit in the American tradition this feminist impulse obviously smacks of heresy, and to do so in Mamet's dramaturgy risks banishment from the ranks since women are not merely marginalized but often completely excluded. In this realm of the "Phallus in Wonderland" (Zeifman 125):

> The subject of [males'] complaints is often a woman, or that more forward, buxom, and aggressive woman, America, who has bestowed upon them a dream, the Great American Dream, only to prove a prick-teaser, or that other woman, more mammary, plump, and vigorous yet, Mother Nature, a female God, rancorous and vindictive, who fucks up every single thing and every single man. (Almansi 193)

Invariably, the plays give rise to an equation of playwright and character, notably Lakeboat's Stan, who defines women as "Soft things with a hole in the middle" (59). Yet Mamet notes that a byproduct of the failed American dream is that "the people it has sustained—the white males—are going nuts" ("David Mamet" 134) and mocks rampant misogyny: "But if you look around the United States of America you will see that we do have a certain amount of misogynistic men. For example, all of them" ("Interview," Harriott 84). Though exposure of the emptiness, impotence, and violence of the male realm does not in itself counter its hegemony, domestic realism like Mamet's can sound a transgressive note through the "fucked," feminized Others at the margins of world and stage.

The Cryptogram brings to center stage both the margins and the ghosts who inhabit them. In a parodic Oedipal triangle, the characters here are all feminized Others—a child, a mother, a gay man—in a "Waiting for Daddy" scenario. Mamet's Beckettian focus on consciousness in an entropic, hermetic landscape belies the "narrowness" (Roudané 7) of the domestic play space, exposing the capitalized Family as a gendered system producing and reproducing the hierarchy of the economic system. The play strikes at the rotten core of the American Dream and its epistemological roots in self-definition against a (M)other. Thus the stage set, "Donny's living room in 1959," centers the wife-mother, who, white and middle-class, would indeed have been confined to the private realm; in fact, recalling Linda Loman and her like, Donny is off-stage when the play opens and perceived initially as a disembodied voice. The on-stage position is occupied by Del, the "seeming paterfamilias" (Simon 76), whose fatherhood is only provisional since he is eventually revealed as gay.

Though in 1959 the homosexual was as closeted as the housewife-mother was privatized, Del assumes with Donny's son, who descends from upstairs in his pajamas, a patriarchal stance in dealing with "Issues of sleep" (3). Ten-year-old John is the only character to use the stairs, which in production "dominate the static, neutral set" (McCue 21) and suggest a tension, not only in the family between the child's world upstairs and the adult world downstairs, but also in consciousness between the flux above and the stasis below. *The Cryptogram*, like all plays according to Mamet, is about "the ends of a situation which has achieved itself fully" (*Writing* 111); its set and blocking, therefore, immediately signal a family which is a casualty of Family, that illusion of a static and closed system at its apogee in the 50s.[3] The opening line of the play, John's "I couldn't find 'em" (1), refers literally to his slippers but figuratively to those referents which, in giving meaning to his world and fixity to his identity, will enable him to sleep. His repeated descents to seek explanation from the adults serve only to reveal that they, too, suffer the anxiety of an uncertain reality, since their answers are relentlessly cryptic and contradictory.

As the three characters provide a parodic representation of Family, the myth itself emerges as a coded representation designed to engender and gender identity. For these, the requisite Others in such a system, identity as well as reality remains a "cryptogram": "something written in code or cipher." The latter term, referring to "the mathematical symbol (0) denoting absence of quantity" or "a person or thing without influence or value," describes precisely the three characters on Mamet's stage. Because the father, Robert, is an absent presence who pervades this space, his wife, his son, and his friend are present absences who seek definition through him. Their cryptic language is a code, as packed as John's slippers of which Del says, "I wondered that you'd take them with" (2). Desiring above all full presence, the three engage in a three-act conversation which belies the adult pretense of communication and truth in its pauses, fragments, arbitrary emphases, and non sequiturs.[4] The physical absence of the father in a phallogocentric culture renders each of these as psychic absences, a fact which the child persistently underscores.

Expecting "to go in the Woods . . . ?" (4) the next day with his father, John deflates Del's rationale that excitement is the "natural" cause of his insomnia and insistently questions: "Why isn't he home?" (5). Ignoring Del's "We don't know" (5), John resists his belatedly appearing mother's demand that he sleep and asks again his father's whereabouts. Donny's perfunctory and contradictory "I don't know. Yes, I do, yes. He's at the Office. And he'll be home soon" (11) apparently repeats a nightly ritual, the mystically capitalized Office in the male public realm failing to squelch the child's yearning. John's fixation on objects (to the point that Simon terms the play's form "dramatic fetishism" [79]) reflects a desperation for referents of a stable, objective reality in which presence can be secured—hence his anxiety about tearing a blanket found in the attic. Unpersuaded by Donny's advice to "absolve yourself" (30), John awaits the "Third Misfortune," the inevitability of which he has inferred from a childhood book. Listing the first misfortune as the teapot which his mother broke in the kitchen, John stubbornly insists on the torn blanket as the second misfortune since "I thought I tore it now" (30). Though Del refutes this blurring of perception and reality, it is he who suggests to John a game of observation to play with his father on the trip: objects oberved by day are to be recollected in writing at night to "sharpen your skills" (32) and "orient yourself" (34). John dismisses the pond as object for this game "Because it's changing" (36), but his attempts to fixate reality are as feeble as the mother's assurances about the father's coming home: "He'll be here when he gets here, I think" (38).

Practicing "The Game" (49), John picks up from the mantelpiece as he ascends the stairs a letter that confirms an observer-influenced reality and his prescience of the third misfortune. A note informing Donny that "My husband's leaving me" (51) verifies the tear in the fabric of the family that has so terrified the child. By the next night, the sleepless John has lost hope for certainty, opening Act II with a tormented reflection to his mother that foregrounds the epistemological focus of the play:

> We don't know what's real. And all we do is say things. (*Pause.*) Where do we get them from? And, or that things, go on forever. (*Pause.*) Or that we're born. Or that dead people moan. Or that, or that there's hell. And maybe we are there. Maybe there are people who've been there. Or, or else why should we think it? That's what I don't know. And maybe everything is true. Maybe it's true that I'm sitting here. (54)

Himself suffering at age ten from his parents' divorce and at age twelve (in 1959) from an abusive stepfather,[5] Mamet, with a "great longing to belong," shares John's torment:

> But the world of the outsider . . . is based on observation. The habit of constant acute awareness can be seen in animals with no recourse . . . It is the habit of the young child. Historically, it is the habit of the Jew. (*Writing* 73)

It is also, of course, the habit of the homosexual and of the woman, similarly scripted in a masculinist economy as sexual and social outsiders. Del's stance as logician, a detective of truth as in his assertion of a "'clue'" (39) to John's problem, is as specious as his patriarchal posture. Logic and power are purely performative, belied by Del's frustration over a prewar photograph, which Donny has retrieved from the attic. Advising John on an object for the observation game, Del undermines his own premise: "Something that doesn't change. (*Of photo*). Who, who, what is this?" (36). Del puzzles over this lost history, himself in Robert's shirt for reasons as obscure as the identity of the photographer. Though he finally fixates on the latter mystery as the cause of his memory lapse, another emerges in Donny's apology for having sex with Robert under a blanket, oblivious to Del's presence: "But I wondered. Did you hear us; and, if you did. If it upset you. (*Pause*.)" (42).

Pushed to the borders in a heterosexual realm, Del cannot locate himself in their history, since his own narrative has been suppressed. The perennial family friend who futilely searches for the missing father, he toasts the constancy of friendship but stumbles over such substitutes for the word "unified" as "be. be. be. be-nighted" or "be-trothed" (61). Del's trouble with the "be's" of causality and being subverts his performance of an inscribed male epistemology; the abnegation of even illusory control reflects the position of an excluded, disempowered Other, who apparently shares Donny's desire for Robert. Having denied knowledge of Robert's intent though he must have planted the letter, Del is trapped in his lie by another of the play's objects, a German pilot's knife which Robert supposedly gave him on a camping trip. Although she has interpreted "the Odd Gesture" (64) as Robert's severing his ties, Donny negates this specific "Meaning" (64) of a parachutist's knife in recalling that she saw the knife in the attic while putting away Robert's equipment.

When challenged, Del founders again on his favored shoals of logic and causality:

> DEL: Be, because, be . . . what are you saying to me? Am, am I to be accused of this!
> DONNY: Of what?
> DEL: Well, that's my point. (72)

This meaninglessness of meaning reveals the treachery of that objective reality which Del has postulated to John; likewise, the knife exposes the treachery in Del's bestowing the Wizard's "blessings on your House" (14), words which the mother has tellingly forgotten. Unable to grant to the child that stable place which he himself has never found, Del confronts Donny with not only his own betrayal but also her family's complicity in his exclusion:

> What do you think? He'd traipse off in the wilds . . . with me . . . ? To talk about life? Are you stupid? Are you blind? He wouldn't spend a moment with me. Some poor geek . . . 'Here's my Old Friend Del . . . (74)

The geek finally confesses that he lent Robert his room to be with a woman, having spent the week in his library "nook" in fishing clothes.

Del's confession, however, does not constitute the moment of truth of Oedipal narrative nor does the play provide classical realism's assurance of that objective reality which the characters seek in totemic objects and words. Although Del feebly attempts expiation by bringing John the father's knife and Donny a purloined copy of the Wizard's book, Donny decimates the objects' significance. The precious knife can hardly be "a 'combat' trophy" (84) since Robert was a flier: "Could he get it in the Air? You 'fairy'?" (86). Overcome by the betrayal even of objects, Del cries: "Excuse me, that the souvenir that he gave me, as a War Memento, with 'associations,' that it had no meaning for him. And what would I know about the war? I live in a Hotel. (*Pause.*)" (87). This non sequitur spotlights Del's position outside of history with its closed narrative and outside of homes with their closed nuclei. When he inveighs against his own failure, in keeping her book, to achieve the freedom of "truth," Donny again devalues his object of propitiation in pointing out that the book is his copy and his deception in this case only perceptual.

Mamet here dramatizes his conviction that "to discover a truth is to have it come out of your own mind. It's not an objective reality. . . . It's a matter of perception" ("Two Gentlemen" 12). Aristotle's and Stanislavsky's theories of "true action" ("Interview," Harriott 93) being based on human perception's connection of random elements, the dramatic action is the quest of the protagonist for a single goal; however, the protagonist may be split as in a dream and the goal be unrealizable. As the quest in *The Cryptogram* is for the Truth posited by Oedipal narrative and classical realism, the play answers feminist theorist Teresa de Lauretis's call for work that is "narrative and Oedipal with a vengeance, for it seeks to stress the duplicity of that scenario and the specific contradiction of the female subject in it" (157). In subverting the form, the play subverts the ideology as the protagonist, here split into three, finds only an encrypted reality and truth. And, finally, it is the mother among these Others, who most evokes a consciousness of the performative nature of the quest, the illusory nature of linearity and meaning, and the observer-influenced nature of reality. As Act I is arguably John's and Act II Del's, so Act III is Donny's.

Coded as family center, Donny is obviously off-center as she is offstage at play's beginning when she breaks the teapot and twice asserts "I'm alright . . ." (7). Hardly "alright," this server of tea is expected to fill the emptiness and bestow presence to the other two present absences, to make the males "alright," a term that, uttered some fifty times, becomes a leitmotif in the play. But just as Donny had originally resisted her husband's "'let the child cry'" (39) approach to John's insomnia, so she resists Del's logical explanations, insisting that "It's all such a mystery. . . . All our good intentions . . ." (21). Faced with a child desperate for a stability that she cannot grant, this exhausted mother haunts the narrative of the first two acts with her perception that meaning is encrypted. For her "fantasy of rest" (24) while John is camping with his father, she is "consumed with guilt" (40), conflicted in that excruciating way which most mothers will recognize. Even when deserted and crying herself, Donny must comfort John, who has imagined phantom voices in his room and comes downstairs to write, "'I'm perfectly alone'" (76). In the face of this mantra intended for reassurance but terrifying in its implications for both of them, the mother "cradles" the child, although she cannot assure him that he "was right" (76).

As they prepare to move a month later in Act III, Donny attempts to school her child on the uncertainty of existence: "John: Things occur. In our lives. And the meaning of them . . . the meaning of them . . . is not clear. . . . But we assume they have a meaning. We must. And we don't know what it is" (79). Displaced physically and psychically by her husband's always defining, now actual absence, this single mother, performing a role not even verified by this term in the 1950s, is left with a child yearning for both a father, who has yet to appear, and for the normative stability of the family, which she is coded to provide. Though longing to succor this son forced from the mythic innocence of childhood and dwelling on death, Donny cannot resanctify the Family with its stable hierarchies and identities:

> What do you want me to do? John? I am no God. I don't control the World. If you could think what it is I could do for you. John, everyone has a story. Did you know that? In their lives. This is yours. And finally . . . finally . . . you are going to have to learn how you will deal with it. You understand? I'm going to speak to you as an adult: At some point . . . At some point, we have to learn to face ourselves. (80)

Despite reviewers' consensus that John is "stonewalled" (Lahr 71) by his mother, I see Donny as urging John to navigate the inevitability of chaos and to create his own narrative as a decentered subject.

Accordingly, Donny rejects Del's narrative of happiness through the forgiveness of "Some poor Queen" (94). Refusing the sentimental equation of womanhood and sacrifice, this (M)other realizes that not only the dominant male but also this othered male have defined themselves against her:

> No, look here: don't tell me I'm going to make a sacrifice for you, and it's for my own good. Do you see? Because every man I ever met in this shithole . . . Don't you dare come in my house and do that. You faggot. (94)

Donny's language signals her transgression of mythic mother/monster boundaries as her name signals that transgression of male/female boundaries necessitated by her role as mother and father. Erased as object by husband as well as friend and son, Donny struggles for an identity through "Othering" the "faggot," who, himself straddling prescribed male/female boundaries, retaliates with the claim that the pattern of male betrayal is not "chance" or "mystery" but something "you provoke" (94). Into this (M)other-blaming scenario enters John, who exasperates Donny into an admission that "No. It isn't alright" (99).

Having performed the "alrightness" of order and stability for the sake of her child, the depleted mother finally confronts the son, whose prescribed Oedipal trajectory is to script her as Other:

> What must I do that you treat me like an animal? . . . Don't stand there so innocently. I've asked you a question. Do you want me to go mad? . . . Can't you see that I need comfort? Are you blind? (99)

John Lahr, I suspect, reflects the audience in disparaging Donny's "aria of victimization" and perceiving her outburst as "emotional abuse" (73), a reaction attributable not only to an inevitable sympathy for the child but also to the tenacity of the mother/monster binary code. Despite devastating betrayals, the mother is expected unequivocally to signify the nurturance of Woman. Deprived of the Oedipally requisite identification with the father but still possessing a feminine Other for negative mimesis, John indeed is blind to his mother (recalling Donny's self-confessed blindness to the homosexual). It is a blindness which has driven many mothers to the threshold of madness and monsterhood.[6] Experiencing the self becoming Other in a child, the mother is ultimately positioned in a binary logic as a castrated object-other by the very agent of her own transformation beyond this perceptual limit.

Donny, then, can only concur with John, who hears voices calling to him, voices which he has associated with her calling from the dead. Her final "Yes I'm sure they are" (100) affirms that she is to her son, as to all the male world, the disembodied voice in the kitchen—an absence against which to define presence, a death against which to define life. Unprotesting when Del resumes his pseudo-patriarchy and gives the boy the father's instrument of castration ("Take the knife and go" [101]), the mother abandons her normative "What would your father say?" (27) role. She leaves unanswered John's and the play's final appeal—an appeal, of course, to her: "They're calling my name. (*Pause.*) Mother. They're calling my name" (101).

The father's phony knife having castrated all of them into feminized Others, it now becomes a means of suicide for the fatherless child with presumably no access to manhood. Though reviewers unanimously attach this closure to the play, the curtain falls with John poised on the stair landing, at the threshold between upstairs and down and life and death. Donny's silence, it seems to me, in a play in which silences speak, haunts the stage at the final moment, suggesting another narrative. Recognizing the death of John's childhood, which she was powerless to prevent, Donny abdicates the position of defining Other, confirming that "Finally, each of us. . . . Is alone" (90). At the threshold of adolescence, John may use the knife on himself, finishing the job that his father has begun, or on the box in the attic, retrieving the torn blanket and redeeming the past. Donny has urged her child to construct his narrative according to a truth which can only be provisional. Her refusal now to provide a voice to echo her child's internalized ones leaves him and the audience on the border between the hegemonic order that the hierarchical Family represents and the intrinsic chaos that the actual family embodies, between a stability desperately sought and an instability vainly denied.

Despite the bleakness of the play, this ending on the border signals an emergence from the entropy of the family living room. Forced out of the home, this family in flux can evolve into a higher complexity than a gendered order. Oedipal narrative has been disrupted as the mother invalidates her object position within it, providing for her son instead the possibility of transformation through the telling of his own story.[7] A nascent feminist ethic, Donny's echoes Mamet's own: "It's not our job to change the world. It's our job to act according to precepts we perceive to be right" ("Two Gentlemen" 12). If these outsiders can break the chains of betrayal in ideology's perceptual prison and celebrate the performance of perception, they may perturb the order of masculinized hegemony with the chaos of feminized Otherness. As Mamet notes in a theatre-as-family metaphor, "in any situation of unhappy tyranny, the oppressed must free the oppressor" (*Writing* 33).

In transgressing paradigmatic boundaries engendered within the gendered Family, these border dwellers, urged by the (M)other of Others, can negotiate the cryptogram of reality and, in changing themselves, may indeed change the world. And in transgressing boundaries drawn by classical dynamics and classical realism, Mamet sounds "the essential celebratory element of theatre. That what we celebrate with the audience is the capacity for strife, the capacity for revelation, and the capacity for self-knowledge" ("Celebrating" 93). It is a note which has reverberated in the legacy of American drama—in the turbulence of its families and in the liminalities of its realism. It celebrates the potential of the butterfly to complicate causality, the power of the ghost (M)other to speak her "private silence" and exit the crypt, and the promise of the feminized cipher to emerge as feminist code-breaker and deliver America from its rapacious Dream.

Notes

Clifton's poem captures the voice of a "mama," speaking here to her "boys" and reflecting the sexual, if not racial, marginalization staged in *The Cryptogram*.

1 Mamet, moreover, insists that *American Buffalo* "sneakily enough is really a tragedy about life in the family—so that is really the play which is closest to *Death of a Salesman*" ("Celebrating" 93).

2 Nobel Laureate Ilya Prigogine concludes that "bifurcations can be considered the source of diversification and innovation" (70) and encourages interdisciplinary application of this concept. If "dissipative structures" arise beyond the bifurcation point, then an unstable system such as family can emerge from entropy and "choose" its state.

3 Talcott Parsons's concept of "structural functionalism" dominated family theory in the 1950s, prescribing for women an "expressive" role in the family.

4 Kroll discovers in the play the source of "Mamet-speak," which is "at bottom a child's lingo, the trial-and-error, stop-and-start nonresponsive speech tactic of kids. It's the sound of tainted innocence" (72). All emphases and ellipses in quoted passages are original unless otherwise indicated.

5 Mamet remembers that "we children, and I especially, felt ourselves less than full members of this new, cobbled-together family" (*The Cabin* 4). Within their literally "model house," the mythologized kitchen table came to be associated "with the notion of blood" (4) since the stepfather's rages regularly resulted in the shattering of its glass top.

6 At the *David Mamet at 50 Celebration*, actor Felicity Huffman, in response to my query about her portrayal of Donny, observed: "She is horrible, and she is us."

7 Of Mamet's previous plays, Bigsby observes: "The process of his plays is one . . . which in its assumption of the minimum community constituted by the storyteller and the listener begins the urgent business of reconstruction" ("David Mamet" 136).

Works Cited

Almansi, Guido. "David Mamet, a Virtuoso of Invective." *Critical Angles: European Views of Contemporary American Literature*. Ed. Marc Chenetier. Carbondale: Southern Illinois UP, 1986. 191–207.

Bigsby, C. W. E. *A Critical Introduction to Twentieth-Century American Drama*. Beyond Broadway. Vol 3. Cambridge: Cambridge UP, 1985.

——. "David Mamet." *Contemporary Writers*. Eds. Malcolm Bradbury and Christopher Bigsby. London: Methuen, 1985.

"Cipher." *American Heritage Dictionary*. New College ed. 1976.

Clifton, Lucille. "Admonitions." *Contemporary American Poetry*. Ed. A. Poulin. 4th ed. Boston: Houghton, 1985. 75.

"Cryptogram." *American Heritage Dictionary*. New College ed. 1976.

Dean, Ann. *David Mamet: Language as Dramatic Action.* Rutherford: Associated University Presses, 1990.

De Lauretis, Teresa. *Alice Doesn't.* Bloomington: Indiana UP, 1984.

Harriot, Esther. "Interview with David Mamet." *American Voices: Five Contemporary Playwrights in Essays and Interviews.* Jefferson, NC: McFarland, 1988. 77–97.

Huffman, Felicity. Address given at David Mamet at 50: A Conference and Celebration. Las Vegas, 1 November 1997.

Kane, Leslie. *David Mamet: A Casebook.* New York: Garland, 1992.

Kroll, Jack. "Phantoms in the Dark." Rev. of *The Cryptogram*, by David Mamet. *Newsweek* 20 Feb. 1995: 72.

Lahr, John. "Betrayals." Rev. of *The Cryptogram*, by David Mamet. *New Yorker* 1 Aug. 1994: 70–73.

Mamet, David. *The Cabin.* New York: Turtle Bay, 1992.

———. "Celebrating the Capacity for Self-Knowledge." *New Theatre Quarterly* 4 (Feb. 1988): 89–96.

———. *The Cryptogram.* New York: Vintage, 1995.

———. "David Mamet." *Savran* 132–44.

———. *Lakeboat.* New York: Grove, 1981.

———. "Two Gentlemen of Chicago: David Mamet and Stuart Gordon." With Hank Nuwer. *South Carolina Review* 17 (Spr. 1985): 9–20.

———. *Writing in Restaurants.* New York: Viking, 1986.

McCue, Jim. "Will Somebody Please Tell Him?" Rev. of *A Whore's Profession* and *The Cryptogram*, by David Mamet. *Times Literary Supplement* 15 July 1994: 21.

Prigogine, Ilya. *The End of Certainty: Time, Chaos, and the New Laws of Nature.* New York: Free Press, 1996.

Roudané, Matthew C. "Mamet's Mimetics." Kane 3–32.

———. "An Interview with David Mamet." *Studies in American Drama, 1945–Present* 1 (1986): 3–81.

Savran, David. *In Their Own Words: Contemporary American Playwrights.* New York: Theatre Communications Group, 1988.

Simon, John. "Broadway Goes Off." Rev. of *London Suite*, by Neil Simon and *The Cryptogram*, by David Mamet. *New York* 24 April 1995: 76+.

Wetzsteon, Ross. "New York Letter." *Plays and Players* 23.12 (Sept. 1976): 39+.

Zeifman, Hersh. "Phallus in Wonderland: Machismo and Business in David Mamet's *American Buffalo* and *Glengarry Glen Ross*." Kane 123–35.

Chapter Nine

"What's the Secret?": Willy Loman as Desiring Machine

Granger Babcock

Arthur Miller's *Death of a Salesman* (1949) conveys its critique of American capital in a more complex and subtle manner than critics have thus far recognized. Most criticism of the play, as Sheila Huftel points out, is "governed by the need . . . to know and understand Willy Loman" (103). Unfortunately, much of the energy expended to understand Willy has been too narrowly focused on analyzing the individuated character traits of the protagonist and the attendant issue of tragic stature. The play, in fact, suggests just the opposite—that Willy is not autonomous, self-generated, or self-made (even in "failure") but that he is completely other to himself; he is more puppet than person, more machine than man, and as such he announces the death, or disappearance, of the subject, the death of the tragic hero, and the birth of "the desiring machine."

Most critics recognize that Arthur Miller intends Willy Loman as a victim of "society." But Willy's construction as a victim is interpreted within the parameters of a self-generated individual and is used as the main reason conservative critics deny *Salesman* tragic status. As a victim, the argument runs, Willy has no understanding of his situation; he is, in the words of Dan Vogel, "too commonplace and too limited" (91). Unlike *Oedipus*, *Hamlet*, or *Lear*, Willy is incapable of self-knowledge and is, therefore, not tragic but pathetic: "He cannot summon the intelligence and strength to scrutinize his situation and come to some understanding of it" (Jacobson 247). Even liberal critics like Thomas Adler and Ruby Cohn, who are generally sympathetic towards Willy, tend to judge his character harshly; in their estimation, he is either a "victim of himself and his choices," or he "has achieved neither popularity nor success as a salesman, and has failed as a gardener, carpenter, and father" (Adler 102; Cohn 44). Willy's problem (or part of his problem), then, according to these critics, is that he accepts his fate; he does not possess the vision, volition, capacity, strength, knowledge, or pluck to fight against the cultural forces that shape his life.

The underlying assumption of these arguments is that Willy *can* change his life—with a little hard work, perhaps—but that he *will* not. Behind these judgments is a model: the national subject, or what I will call the masculine unconscious. This model can also be described as the autonomous, active male subject that determines and makes itself, as well as the liberal subject, the rugged individual, or the exceptional American. Whatever linguistic sign the masculine unconscious uses to communicate itself, it is wholly other to the subject, and it is given to the subject by the publicity apparatus of capital. Miller calls this other the "law of success":

> The confusion of some critics viewing *Death of a Salesman* . . . is that they do not see that Willy Loman has broken a law without whose protection life is insupportable, if not incomprehensible to him and to many others; it is a law which says a failure in society and in business has no right to live. Unlike the law against incest, the law of success is not administered by statute or church, but it is very nearly as powerful in its grip upon men." (*Collected Plays* 35; hereafter referred to as *CP*)

In *Dialectic of Enlightenment* (1947), Max Horkheimer and Theodor Adorno identity the "law of success" as an effect of the "technological rationale" which dominates the cultural and economic institutions of modern industrial nations:

> Through the countless agencies of mass production and its culture the conventionalized modes of behavior are impressed upon the individual as the only natural, respectable and rational ones. He defines himself as a thing, as a static element, as success or failure. (28)

That is, under what Horkheimer and Adorno call late capitalism, individual behavior is reduced to a series of "protocols" or stereotypical responses found on the job, on the radio, in the movies, and in the then-emerging television industry. For Adorno, these standardized models of behavior signal the end of the liberal subject, since "motivation in the old, liberal sense" was being appropriated and "systematically controlled and absorbed by social mechanisms which are directed from above" ("Freudian Theory") 136. In other words, the subject's desire for success (e.g., for material wealth, to "get ahead"), which the subject believes is self-generated, is, in fact, his identification with the rationale of the apparatus, which has programmed individual consumption as spontaneous thought or reason or the assertion of individual will.

Viewed in light of Horkheimer and Adorno's discovery, the operations of Willy Loman's mind reflect this change in subjectivity. Specifically, Willy assumes that his desire is spontaneous, when in fact, as Miller suggests in

Timebends (1987), it has been "hammered into its strange shape by society, the business life Willy has lived and believed in" (1982). Willy's desire does not make him autonomous; it makes him "common," since that desire is what motivates all the men in the play and indeed most men in our culture. In constructing Willy, Miller exposes the liberal subject as a fiction, as part of a structure of value that is an effect of the economy. To dismiss Willy as "pathetic" because he does not have the strength of character to understand his situation or because he has made the wrong choices is to recode the play according to the protocols of the apparatus (i.e., a man is either a success or he is a failure). Willy chooses nothing; he merely follows a blueprint. Like a machine, he operates according to plan. The publicity apparatus tells Willy that if he works hard like Edison, that if he perseveres like Goodrich, that, if he is "well liked" like Dave Singleman, then he will rise like Charley and become rich and powerful like J. P. Morgan. The blueprint also tells Willy that if he does not become "a success," that if he does not become like a Gene Tunney or a Red Grange, then he is a failure—and that it is his fault. Willy's question to Ben and to Bernard—"What's the secret?"—is therefore by design. Willy cannot see that there is no secret—that success or status is largely determined by extrinsic factors.

Conservative critics do not recognize Willy as an effect of the economy because the critical field in which they operate does not permit this. For them, he is a problem, not a cultural symptom. Critics from the left, such as Raymond Williams, Michael Spindler, and John Orr, while they see Willy as a symptom of capitalistic culture, have focused more on Willy's objectification than on his relationship to the apparatus that produced him. Williams, for instance, argues that "Willy Loman is a man who from selling things has passed to selling himself, and has become, in effect, a commodity which like other commodities will at a certain point be discarded by the laws of the economy" (104). While Williams's argument concerning Willy is certainly accurate, given Willy's desire to "make an appearance in the business world (*CP* 146), I would like to suggest a different way to read Willy, which is more in keeping with the model of subjectivity theorized by Horkheimer and Adorno in *Dialectic of Enlightenment*, and which, I believe, more fully represents the rationalization of consciousness brought about by the symbolic apparatus of late capitalism.

In their book *Anti-Oedipus: Capitalism and Schizophrenia* (1983), Gilles Deleuze and Felix Guattari problematize previous models of subjectivity by eliminating the opposition around which the subject is constructed: "there is no such thing as either man or nature now, only a process that produces the one within the other and couples the machines together. Producing-machines, desiring-machines . . . the self and the non-self, outside and inside, no longer have any meaning whatsoever" (2). According to Deleuze and Guattari, the cognitive subject no longer exists, since the subject-object split on which its identity is based has collapsed. The boundary between subject and object collapses, they argue, under the weight of the publicity apparatus of late capitalistic cultures, which colonized the subject from without by pouring its narratives inward. They replace the cognitive model with a quasi-cybernetic model, the desiring machine. The desiring machine runs on information from the outside; its goals, writes Jean-François Lyotard, are "programmed into it" and therefore it cannot "correct in the course of its functioning" (16). The man/machine is programmed to fit the body of capital, to adjust to the demands of efficiency of the larger system. Deleuze and Guattari stress that the identity produced by the system is "a producing/product identity" (7). That is, the machine produces, or in Willy's case, reproduces, not only biologically but also ideologically, for the system at the same time that it is produced or constructed by the system.

A more effective way to interpret Deleuze and Guattari's "producing/product identity," especially when we consider Willy Loman and the other men in *Salesman*, is to see it as a producing/consuming identity. The male subject desires to reproduce itself (pass itself on) at the same time it desires to consume success narratives, cheese, Chevrolets, Studebakers, aspirin, women, refrigerators, etc. The male subject reproduces itself by having children and acting as a model for those children. Willy, for instance, wants his sons to learn the law of success embodied by his brother Ben: " . . . when I walked into the jungle, I was seventeen. When I walked out I was twenty-one. And, by God, I was rich" (*CP* 159–60). The male subject consumes by buying products. Listen to Happy:

> . . . suppose I get to be merchandise manager? He's a good friend of mine, and he just built a terrific estate on Long Island. And he lived there about two months and sold it, and now he's building another one. He can't enjoy it once it's finished. And I know that's just what I would do. I don't know what the hell I'm workin' for. (*CP* 139)

Or listen to Howard Wagner talk about his wire recorder: "I tell you . . . I'm gonna take my camera, and my bandsaw, and all my hobbies, and out they go. This is the most fascinating relaxation I've ever found" (*CP* 178). Willy's desire has also been programmed; just listen to Linda tell us why he bought a Hastings refrigerator: "They got the biggest ads of any of them!" (*CP* 148).

The three passages suggest that Miller is aware that (re)production and consumption are programmed. Desire is mediated by an other, by the publicity apparatus of capital. The "subject" merely occupies a circuit or an outlet, or, to use Lyotard's word, a "post," through which messages or units of information pass (15). Willy (or Happy or Howard Wagner) is reduced to the function of a receptacle/transmitter; information travels through him and in him. In this process, memory (the site of the other) becomes a depository for and a transmitter of the masterprograms or "masternarratives" of the system in which the desiring machine operates. The machine's program can thus be viewed as a metanarrative that is used to reinscribe or recode reality into a pattern that the larger system finds acceptable. The metanarrative acts like the unconscious because it is wholly other to the subject and because it works through the subject to structure social life. This operation is seen in Happy's description of the merchandise manager's mindless consumption, in his building of houses which he soon deserts only to build new houses; his desire spins metonymically out of control, seeking difference or fulfillment in what is essentially the same. Neither man understands why he buys things or why he works, yet they both buy and work without question. Presumably they work to "get ahead," to "accomplish something," but in reality they are, like Willy, programmed for the body of capital; it doesn't matter if they get ahead, if they succeed, or even if they become "number-one man." What does matter, however, is that everybody desire to work so that everybody can afford to consume. Desire, to used Sartre's term, has been "massified."

At this point, we turn out attention to Willy Loman and explore how the dreams of capital have programmed his "life." Throughout the play, Willy consumes and then reproduces models and axioms that are part of the masculine unconscious:

> Be liked and you will never want. (*CP* 146)
> A man oughta come in with a few words. (*CP* 149)
> I gotta overcome it. I know I gotta overcome it. I'm not dressing to advantage, maybe. (*CP* 149)
> Everybody likes a kidder, but nobody lends him money. (*CP* 168)
> But remember, start big and you'll end up big. (*CP* 168)
> Start off with a couple of your good stories to lighten things up. It's not what you say, it's how you say it—because personality always wins the day. (*CP* 169)

These axioms (and the model they represent) appear in the text as isolated linguistic events, as the recitations of a lone idiolect, but they are in fact "splinters" or units (traces) of the metanarrative of national subject that speak through the subject. Willy consumes these bits of information just as he consumes aspirins and cheese. Their presence indicates that Willy's subjectivity has been "interpellated" by the ideological apparatus.[1] Another indication of Willy's interpellation are his numerous contradictory statements. Early in the play, for instance, Willy calls Biff a "lazy bum" because Biff does not have a steady job. Three lines later, however, after Linda tells Willy that Biff is "lost," Willy replies incredulously, "Biff Loman is lost. In the greatest country in the world a young man with such—personal attractiveness, gets lost. There's one thing about Biff—he's not lazy" (*CP* 134). Willy then reminds Linda that "Certain men just don't get started till later in life. Like Thomas Edison, I think, or B. F. Goodrich" (*CP* 135).

In this instance, the masterprogram operates to allegorize the experience of the "subject" by making the subject part of the national narrative of progress; the process is therefore synecdochical (e pluribus unum). The process reveals itself as a fusion or syndesis of narratives, modes of masculinity from different historical periods, that cover over the reality of the present and mystify history. This fusion is first discovered in the practices of late-nineteenth-century advertising, where the consumer ideology is bound together with eighteenth- and nineteenth-century conceptions of masculinity. The adjusted or emergent narrative is deposited on the hegemonic narrative, which in turn lends the newer representation its legitimacy or authority.

However, the crucial thing to note about the masterprogram is the way in which Miller suggests it operates through Willy to reinscribe his family history as part of the success narrative of the national subject. Willy desires to be the same as his father or his brother Ben; he desires to be other than he is, to inhabit earlier periods of capital through an other's body, which is essentialized or universal. By banishing *differance*, Willy hopes to construct a stable subjectivity. He no longer wishes to feel "temporary" (*CP* 159) about himself. He no longer wants to be part of the body of capital, which is always (magically) transforming itself, adjusting itself, expanding itself—like the neighborhood in which he lives. The desire to be successful, then, is the desire to connect himself to a transcendental masculinity that erases the reality of his present social position. This erasure is achieved, however, at a cost. The subject is restored to fullness by transforming extrinsic social factors into personal failure. Willy performs this function to empower himself, to restore the independence of the subject, which has been irretrievably lost. In the process, however, he learns to misrecognize himself (and Brooklyn). At the same time, Willy also learns to marginalize other masculinities, the alternative men he might represent, in favor of the dominant models advocated by the culture industry (i.e., Edison, Goodrich, etc.).

As C. W. E. Bigsby notes, "Willy Loman's life is rooted in America's past" (184). More precisely, his identity is rooted in models from two different periods of American capital, which are conflated in his mind. Willy's father represents the unfettered and unalienated labor of mercantile capital. His brother Ben represents the accumulative processes of monopoly capital. Both figures are mythic; that is, both figures embody an heroic past that is disseminated by the symbolic practices of capital and reproduced in individual men. Together, Miller suggests, they represent the (his)tory (not an history) of the (white) race in America. Or, as Irving Jacobson suggests,

> What Willy Loman wants, and what success means in *Death of a Salesman*, is intimately related to his own, and the playwright's, sense of the family. Family dreams extend backward in time to interpret the past, reach forward in time to project images of the future, and pressure reality in the present to conform to memory [ideology] and imagination. (248)

The flute 'melody' that marks the beginning and the ending of the play, and which is heard periodically throughout, is the emblem or signature of Willy's lost father. According to the stage directions, "It is small and fine, telling of grass and trees and the horizon" (*CP* 130). It is, as numerous critics point out, the aural symbol of his "pioneer virtues" (Parker 33). It is the sound of the unalienated commodity, which later returns (transformed) as the mass-produced "golden" pen that Biff steals. It is the sound of the past in the present, the still active residual model which operates to marginalize the present. It represent the desire for opportunity and mobility associated with westward expansion. Willy's father, as Ben tells him, was a small entrepreneur whose life was determined by the structures of a mercantile economy:

> Father was a very great and very wild-hearted man. We would start in Boston, and he'd toss the whole family into the wagon, and then he'd drive the whole team right across the country, through Ohio, and Indiana, Michigan, Illinois, and all the Western states. (*CP* 157)

Willy's father was a "great inventor" who would "stop in the towns and sell the flutes he'd made on the way" (*CP* 157). "With one gadget," Ben tells Willy, "he made more in a week than a man like you could make in a lifetime" (*CP* 157).

Ben's last statement seems unlikely, and its hyperbole marks a confusion in Willy's mind produced, or mediated, by the other's desire. Willy desires to be like his father because his father is like other successful men, other "great" inventors; his father is a model citizen—he has amassed a fortune.

His father is like America's first model citizen, Ben Franklin, who "invented" electricity and the lightning rod. His father is like Thomas Edison and B. F. Goodrich, both rich and famous because of their inventions. Nevertheless, given the mercantile economy in which Miller locates Willy's father, it is unlikely that he could have produced a "gadget" that earned him more in a week than Willy earned in his lifetime. This type of event was more common (but still relatively isolated) in the period of capital Ben represents (monopoly capital) when "great" inventors like Edison and Goodrich did earn more money in a week (by producing technology for an emergent industrial economy) than a salesman could in thirty-five years. The figure of Willy's father exists simultaneously in Willy's "mind" with the figures of Edison and Goodrich. The simultaneity of the Franklin-Edison-Goodrich-father Loman narrative produces a fusion of the individual figures by marginalizing their differences; this fusion, again, is produced by the publicity apparatus of capital. Through the other, that is, Willy plugs himself into the success narrative as he rereads his family history.

A more elaborate example of this type of conflation is found when we examine Ben Loman. On one level, Miller uses the figure of Ben to link the formation of the national subject to the founding of the Republic—that is, Miller clearly chooses the name Ben to remind his readers of Ben Franklin's paradigmatic American masculinity. Ben's continual repetition of the rags to riches story—"Why, boys, when I walked into the jungle, I was seventeen. When I walked out I was twenty-one. And by God, I was rich" (*CP* 157)—is a deliberate echo of Franklin's *Autobiography*, in which Franklin tells his readers that he walked into Philadelphia with the clothes on his back and within a few years became rich and famous. Notably, Miller conflates the Franklin myth with another version of masculinity from a later stage of American capital, not to differentiate the two but to suggest that they are both operative and that the latter version is just a rearticulation of the former. The phrase "acres of diamonds," which Ben continually uses, alludes to a series of lectures and books written by the evangelist Russell Conwell in the 1890s "to spread the gospel of material wealth" (Innes 64–65; Porter 24–27). Conwell's writings, which included *The Safe and Sure Way to Amass a Fortune and Be a Benefactor*, and *Achieve Greatness*, were typical of the "success cult" that dominated American magazine and popular book culture around the turn of the century (Green 111).

The assumptions about masculinity at the core of Franklin's *Autobiography* are present in Conwell's writings as well. Both writers construct masculinity in very ahistoric ways by insisting that "success" is the result of personal agency or character. Miller uses Ben's speech, which Willy is remembering, to illustrate that language has a history. The traces of Franklin's and Conwell's stories survive as moments of the past in the present, and because they have been decontextualized by the operations of the publicity apparatus, they exist only as ideology within memory (i.e. devoid of their cultural context, they become part of the same moment, the typology of American maleness—no products of specific historical periods and circumstances). These representations do, however, bear the mark of their history and, as such, their difference can only be recognized when their history is restored. The conflation of Franklin and Conwell in Ben's speech is recognized when we try to account for the fact that Ben Loman and Russell Conwell inhabit an America radically different from Franklin's. Ben's ascendancy to what Willy calls "success incarnate" (*CP* 152) takes place in the late 1880s, a period marked by intense imperial expansion and expropriation of native labor and resources. As what Ruby Cohn calls a "ruthless adventurer" (41), Ben represents the accumulative processes of monopoly capital (roughly 1880 to 1910).

Further, the mode of masculinity that Ben represents is radically out of place in the America of the late 1940s (as is Willy's father's "pioneer" masculinity). Willy's desire to be like Ben and like his father manifests itself as a nostalgia that seals him off from the present. As a result, Willy cannot recognize "reality," and he therefore engages in the success fantasy given to him by the other. In addition, Miller also suggests that the nostalgia for previous models or paradigms is constituted by their ability to provide ready-made (read: reductive) interpretations of the world; this operation, however, as Hayden White suggests, is disabling (and therefore destructive) because it prevents individuals and societies from imaginatively confronting the problems of the present (39).

One result of Willy's interpellation is that he cannot see Brooklyn as it is—that is, he is not satisfied with seeing it the way it is; he desires to see it as other, as the Old West or the frontier. As he tells Ben, "It's Brooklyn, I know, but we hunt too" (*CP* 158). Willy's desire to see Brooklyn as other is also a symptom of the machine in crisis. The flute melody that represents the fiction of infinite space and unfettered masculine autonomy of the frontier (i.e., the mobility that most Americans expect and desire) is an ideological formation directly at odds with Willy's "reality." Willy can see the "towering angular shapes" that surround his house "on all sides" (*CP* 130), and he is aware the changes in his neighborhood:

> The way they box us here. Bricks and windows, windows and bricks. . . . The street is lined with cars. There's not a breath of fresh air in the neigh-

> borhood. The grass don't grow anymore, you can't raise a carrot in the backyard. They should've had a law against apartment houses. Remember those two beautiful elm trees out there? When I and Biff hung the swing between them. . . . They should've arrested the builder for cutting those down. They massacred the neighborhood. . . . (*CP* 134–5)

Yet the cultural processes that allow the "they" to box him in, to massacre the neighborhood, go unrecognized because his models program him for "oversight." In other words, his knowledge of the world is produced by models that act to exclude or screen out disruptive bits of information. Willy's knowledge of his world represents a desire for older models that reduce his understanding of his social position.

His models also prevent him from seeing the history of his present (ultimately they push his vision inward, which leads to annihilation). His question to Linda that concludes the diatribe about the neighborhood—"How can they whip cheese?"—outlines the contour or boundary of his knowledge about the operations of capital; this question marks the limits of his awareness, outside (or inside) of which he cannot see or transgress. The question represents his limit as a subject. The salesman, ironically, does not understand how products are made. They appear to him, as they sometimes did to Marx, "as autonomous figures endowed with a life of their own" (165). Willy's seemingly trivial question reveals how effective the publicity apparatus (with its fetishization of consumption) is in marginalizing the effects of technological change. As William T. Brucher points out, Willy's "unexpected, marvellingly innocent question about whipping cheese reveals an ambivalence toward technology livelier and more interesting . . . than a simple dichotomy between farm and factory, past and present" (83–84). Willy's "marvellingly innocent question" reveals a complete ignorance of the cultural processes that affect his life, that cause him to lose his job. Willy's life is, in fact, a denial of the transformative powers of capital. Any recognition of change is subverted by the transcendent (fetishized) models that he worships, which do not record or reflect any change. Celebrity—the lives of B. F. Goodrich and Thomas A. Edison and Dave Singleman—has replaced history. The consumption of technological "progress," as Willy's broken cars, refrigerators, fanbelts, and leaky shower and roof attest, has replaced "real" social relations.

A second result of Willy's interpellation is that he "embues" his sons with the values of the other, what he calls "the spirit of the jungle." These values are mediated through the figure of Ben Loman. "There was the only man I ever met who knew the answers," says Willy (*CP* 155). "There was a man started with the clothes on his back and ended up with diamond mines" (*CP* 152). How does Ben achieve this goal? According to Willy, "The man knew what he wanted and went out and got it. Walked into the jungle, and comes out, the age of twenty-one, and he's rich!" (*CP* 152). And this triumph is just what Willy wants for his boys; when Ben comes to visit, Willy brags to him that "That's just the spirit I want to embue them with! To walk into the jungle!" (*CP* 160). He's bringing them up to be "rugged, well-liked, all around" (*CP* 157). Ben, of course, approves: "Outstanding, manly chaps!" (*CP* 159). Willy's desire is therefore reproduced through and in Biff and Happy; because of Willy's pedagogy, they become carriers of the program. Willy wants them, as Ben advises him, to "Screw on your fists and . . . fight for a fortune . . . " (*CP* 183). He doesn't want them to be "worms," like Bernard (*CP* 151). But as Brian Parker points out, the aggressive practices Ben represents while "admirable in combatting raw nature [become] immoral when turned against one's fellow man" (33).

I suggest above that Ben's aggressiveness represents a brutality that Miller equates with American imperialism. Another way to read Ben's aggressiveness—this time, within the boundaries of the nation—is as competition. Historically, as C. Wright Mills notes, "for men in the era of classical liberalism, competition was never merely an impersonal mechanism regulating the economy of capitalism, or only a guarantee of political freedom. Competition was a means of producing free individuals, a testing field for heroes; in its terms men lived the legend of the self-reliant individual" (11). Whether or not what Mills argues is historically representative, it is safe to assume that in a decentralized economy (an economy without the hierarchy of industrialized structures), individual competition through labor was a way for many to create mobility and wealth. However, as the economy became more centralized and hierarchical, competition, as Willy says, became "maddening" because it did not yield the same results (imagined or otherwise) as it did for men of Willy's father's and Ben's generations.

In Willy's time, in fact, competition has become warlike. After returning from a selling trip, for instance, Willy tells his family he "Knocked 'em cold in Providence, slaughtered 'em in Boston" (*CP* 146). Willy's gift to his sons on his return from this same trip is a punching bag with "Gene Tunney's signature on it." "[I]t's the finest thing for the timing," he tells his apprentices (*CP* 144). Elsewhere, Willy describes business as "murderous" (*CP* 159). When Biff goes to ask Bill Oliver for a loan, Willy's advice is "Knock him dead, boy" (*CP* 170). The violence of Willy's language echoes the ruthlessness of his model, Ben—the same man who attacks Biff—"Never fight fair with a stranger, boy. You'll never get out of the jungle that way" (*CP*

158). Willy's desire to emulate Ben's power thus leads him to bring "the spirit of the jungle" into his home, where it reveals itself in what Sartre calls the "counter-finality." His positive intention of providing his boys with a model for success results in the negative legitimation of theft and fantasy.

Miller problematizes Willy's pedagogy by suggesting that even sanctioned expressions of masculinity involve theft. In the scene which follows Ben's fight with Biff, for example, Willy has his sons start to rebuild the front steps because Willy doesn't want Ben to think he is just a salesman; he wants to show Ben that Brooklyn is not Brooklyn ("we hunt too" [*CP* 158]); he wants to show Ben what kind of stock his sons come from: "Why, Biff can fell any one of these trees in no time!" (*CP* 158). Instead of providing the materials to rebuild the front stoop, however, Willy directs his sons to "Go right over where they're building the apartment house and get some sand" (*CP* 158). Charley warns Willy that "if they steal any more from that building the watchman'll put the cops on them" (*CP* 158). Willy responds, addressing Ben, "You shoulda seen the lumber they brought home last week. At least a dozen six-by-tens worth all kinds of money" (*CP* 158). This, of course, is a parody of Ben's logging operations in Alaska, but it also suggests that the individualism that the success ideology sanctions legitimates theft, just as that ideology legitimates the expropriation of foreign land and mineral resources. This is made even clearer in the following lines, when Willy excuses his sons' behavior because as he says, "I got a couple of fearless characters there" (*CP* 158). Charley counters: "Willy, the jails are full of fearless characters (*CP* 158), and Ben responds, "And the stock exchange, friend!" (*CP* 158). Again, these lines suggest that Miller recognizes that even legitimized expressions of masculine behavior, practices, and beliefs that the American publicity apparatus valorizes involve theft.

A further example of Miller transforming the success ideology into theft is found in the scene where Biff "borrows" a football from his high school locker room so that he can practice with a "regulation ball" (*CP* 144). Willy, predictably, laughs with Biff at the theft and rewards the action by saying "Coach'll probably congratulate you on your initiative!" (*CP* 144). Initiative, even in Franklin's day, is one of the key elements of masculine autonomy, and here, Miller insists that initiative is a form of theft. Later in the same scene, Biff tells his father, "This Saturday, Pop, this Saturday—just for you, I'm going to break through for a touchdown" (*CP* 145). Happy then reminds Biff he is "supposed to pass" (*CP* 145). Biff ignores Happy's warning and says, "I'm *taking* one play for Pop" (*CP* 145; italics mine). This taking is a pattern that will eventually take over Biff's life, for as Biff tells Willy at the end of the play, "I stole a suit in Kansas City and I was in jail. . . . I stole myself out of every good job since high school!" (*CP* 216). More important for Miller, however, is that this one moment of taking represents a typical moment in the dominant version of American masculinity. Biff's "theft" of the play is another instance of his initiative, another example drawn from the headlines which celebrate individual achievement. For a moment in Willy's mind, Biff is like Red Grange or Gene Tunney. As he tells Charley, "When this game is over . . . you'll be laughing out the other side of your face. They'll be calling him another Red Grange. Twenty-five thousand a year" (*CP* 186). What is lost in Biff's taking, however, is the team. Biff's initiative, and his desire to place himself above the goal of the team, jeopardizes the collective goal of the team—to win the City Championship.

Miller addresses the counter-finality of fantasy in the climax of the play, which is organized around Biff's trip to Bill Oliver's office, where he plans to ask Oliver to stake him in a new business venture, "The Loman Brothers," a line of sporting goods. This fiction has been created as a way to deflect Willy's fury at learning that Biff plans to "[s]crew the business world!" and return to the West, because in the West he can do as he pleases. That is, he can swim in the middle of the day, and, working as a carpenter, can whistle on the job; he also tells Happy that "we don't belong in this nuthouse of a city! We belong mixing cement on some open plain . . . " (*CP* 166). At the same time, Biff expresses his hatred of the business world because "They've laughed at Dad for years . . . " (*CP* 166). Willy responds in a characteristic manner: "Go to Filene's, go to the Hub, go to Slattery's, Boston. Call out the name Willy Loman and see what happens!" (*CP* 166). At this point, to quell Willy's anger, optimistic Happy starts the familiar story ("He's going to see Bill Oliver, Pop" [*CP* 167]) that quickly develops into a success fantasy before the fact: Happy's "feasible idea" is to borrow money from Bill Oliver to start a line of sporting goods (*CP* 167). Of course, Happy's idea is neither feasible nor sensible; it is, in fact, absurd that Biff believes he can borrow ten thousand dollars from a man he has not seen in fifteen years and from whom he stole merchandise.

At the end of the second act, however, Happy's pipe dream comes apart as Biff begins to insist on the truth; Biff tells Willy that he "was never a salesman for Bill Oliver," that he was a shipping clerk. Willy insists that Biff was a salesman for Oliver, and when Biff tries to correct Willy by asking him to "hold on to the facts," Willy says he's not interested in the facts (*CP* 198–99). What he is interested in is another story, and Willy and Happy begin to work to reimpose the success fantasy they have constructed at the end of the first act, but the fantasy is interrupted by Biff's announcing that he has stolen Bill Oliver's fountain pen.

The final confrontation occurs two scenes later when Biff tells Willy "you're going to hear the truth—what you are and what I am" (*CP* 216). Biff rejects Willy's "phony dream" because

> I ran down eleven flights with a pen in my hand today. And suddenly I stopped. . . . I saw the things that I love in this world. The work and the food and time to sit and smoke. And I looked at the pen and said to myself, what the hell am I grabbing this for? Why am I trying to become what I don't want to be? What am I doing in an office, making a contemptuous, begging fool of myself, when all I want is out there, waiting for me the minute I say I know who I am! (*CP* 217)

This is an assertion of Biff's desire against Willy's desire and the fantasy that Willy's desire constructs. Because Biff recognizes that his father's dream is false, that his father has been positioned by the law of success to believe in the autonomous male, he is in a position to resist (at least partially) the ideology. Biff does not believe in the version of universal citizenship that Willy believes in. Biff recognizes that he is "a dime a dozen" (*CP* 217), that he will never be B. F. Goodrich or Thomas Edison or Red Grange or J. P. Morgan or Gene Tunney. He attempts to resist the ideology of the success narrative because he doesn't want to be other; he doesn't want to be number one: "I am not a leader of men, Willy, and neither are you. . . . I'm a dollar an hour, Willy. . . . A buck an hour" (*CP* 217). Willy, a believer to the bitter end, insists that he is exceptional: "I am Willy Loman, and you are Biff Loman" (*CP* 217). At this point there is a complete repudiation of the success fantasy: Biff screams, "Pop, I'm nothing! I'm nothing, Pop!" (*CP* 217), and he begins to hug his father and cry.

Commenting on this scene, Miller writes that Biff embodies "an opposing system which . . . is in a race for Willy's faith, and it is the system of love which is the opposite of the law of success" (*CP* 36). However, Miller claims that "by the time Willy can perceive [Biff's] love, it can serve only as an ironic comment upon the life he sacrificed for power, and for success and its tokens" (*CP* 36). Biff rejects the law that makes men compete with each other and steal from each other in order for them to be successful. Instead, through his characterization of Bernard, Charley, and, (at the end of the play) Biff, Miller seems to offer the possibility of a system where men love each other and try to help one another, rather than exploit one another. His solution to the problem of individualism is moral rather than revolutionary, for as he points out, the "most decent man" in the play "is the capitalist (Charley) whose aims are not different from Willy Loman's" (*CP* 37). The difference between Willy and Charley "is that Charley is not a fanatic": "he has learned how to live without that frenzy, that ecstasy of spirit which Willy chases to the end" (*CP* 37). Likewise, "Bernard . . . works hard, attends to his studies, and attains a worthwhile objective" (*CP* 37). Miller also notes that these people all come from the same social class (*CP* 37), yet Charley and Bernard do not succumb to the frenzy because, in Miller's view, they manage to resist the law of success and can act like decent men. What makes their resistance possible? Miller offers no specific answer. The play suggests that some men are able to do this while others are not; it offers hope, but no specific program: "What theory lies behind this double view? None whatever. It is simply that I knew and know that I feel better when my work is reflecting a balance of the truth as it exists" (*CP* 37).

Nevertheless, because the play is organized around the consciousness of Willy Loman, the play does not reflect the balance that Miller seems to have intended. Because Willy is such a strong presence, he pushes Bernard and Charley to the margins of the play. Willy's is the dominant voice, and it is through this voice that Miller maps the discourse of national identity as it interpellates the "low man." Through this process, Miller attempts to construct a counter-discourse by exposing the contradictions within the dominant understanding of the social world. The power of the dominant discourse lies in the ability of its codes and protocols to regulate understanding of the social world; they allow individuals to interpret their experience only in previously elaborated paradigms. In *Salesman*, Miller shows how these codes and protocols are reproduced through memory as they are recirculated and repeated in the texts and representations of the publicity apparatus. The epilogue of the play also suggests that we are free of these representations only in death. When Linda says "We're free. . . . We're free" (*CP* 222), Miller is not just ironically commenting on the paid-up mortgage; he is also suggesting that Willy is free from the law of success only in death.

D. L. Hoeveler suggests that Linda's lines are ironic for another reason. Reading the drama as a "psychomachia," Hoeveler stresses that the *Requiem* functions as a final comment on Willy's dream: "All the characters who had preciously functioned as parts of Willy's dream or nightmare are now supposedly free of him. . . . But each of the characters continues to embody the values that Willy demanded of them" (80). These "parts," however, to revise Hoeveler, not only embody the values that Willy demands of them, but also they embody the values of the dominant mode of production and the cultural apparatus which reproduces that mode by reproducing its values. Willy is a part of the body of capital, just as are Happy, Biff, Charley, Bernard, Howard Wagner, and Linda; and as Mark Poster writes, the capitalist mode of production forces human being not only to become "things . . . in appearance," but also "They undergo . . . a profound interior alteration" (53). They become desiring machines, or as Sartre stresses in *Critique of Dialectical Reason*, they become other to themselves. They embody the value of the Other (the publicity apparatus) that programs them to see others as rivals. The irony of this operation, as Sartre points out, is that in attempting to be different (in attempting to be number one, to earn the most money, to conquer the world) everyone's desire is the same. Desire, therefore, organizes individuals so that it can isolate them. Sartre calls this formation serial, or unified, alterity.

Ultimately, all the men in the play labor at alterity programmed by the other (or others) as parts of the machine of capital. Their desire and their isolations are expressions of the larger machine. Their "prefabricated being" (being as other-than-itself) is fixated on consumption by the publicity apparatus of capital (Sartre 227). The system of value that the play represents permits no true relationship between men; it permits only isolation through competition. The dissatisfaction of the desiring machine can therefore only express itself through nostalgia, an eternal return to previous models and their (pre)determining goals. The consequence of this interpellation is that solidarity is nullified by the desire of the other, thereby ensuring that men will continue to be exploited by their desire. As Deleuze and Guattari point out, "Desire can never be deceived. . . . It happens that one desires against one's own interests: capitalism profits from this . . . " (257). In the end, then "attention must be . . . paid" (*CP* 162) to Willy Loman not because he is somehow exceptional (by being an aberration) but because his repression is paradigmatic. Willy has not, as Michael Spindler points out, "seized upon the notion of success as a substitute for genuine identity" (206). Willy, again, seizes nothing; his gods are not given to him. Attention must be given to such a man by readers of *Salesman* who would fetishize masculine autonomy, since Miller powerfully suggests that masculine desire is an instrument used by the publicity apparatus of American capital to organize and to regulate social relations and the economy.

Notes

1 In the work of Louis Althusser (162–70), interpellation denotes the process by which human subjects come to recognize themselves as such by identifying themselves with the subjects referred to by an impersonal "apparatus" of ideological statements. For instance, as the free and the brave in the phrase "the land of the free and the home of the brave."

Works Cited

Adler, Thomas. *Mirror on the Stage: The Pulitzer Plays as an Approach to American Drama.* West Lafayette: Purdue UP, 1987.

Adorno, Theodor. "Freudian Theory and the Pattern of Fascist Propaganda." *The Essential Frankfurt School Reader.* Ed. Andrew Arato and Eike Gebhardt. New York: Continuum, 1985. 118–37.

Althusser, Louis. *Lenin and Philosophy and Other Essays.* Trans. Ben Brewster. London: NLB, 1971.

Bigsby, C. W. E. *A Critical Introduction to Twentieth-Century American Drama.* Vol. 2. Cambridge: Cambridge UP, 1984.

Bloom, Harold. ed. *Arthur Miller's Death of a Salesman.* New York: Chelsea House, 1988.

Brucher, Richard T. "Willy Loman and the Soul of the New Machine: Technology and the Common Man." *Journal of American Studies* 17 (1983): 325–46.

Cohn, Ruby. "The Articulate Victims of Arthur Miller." Bloom 39–46.

Deleuze, Gilles, and Felix Guattari. *Anti-Oedipus: Capitalism and Schizophrenia.* Minneapolis: U of Minnesota P, 1983.

Green, Theodore P. *America' Heroes: The Changing Modes of Success in American Magazine.* New York: Oxford UP. 1970.

Hoeveler, D. L. "*Death of a Salesman* as Psychomachia." Bloom 77–82.

Horkheimer, Max, and Theodor Adorno. *Dialectic of Enlightenment.* 1947. London: Allen Lane, 1973.

Huftel, Sheila. *Arthur Miller: The Burning Glass.* New York: The Citadel P, 1965.

Innes, Christopher. "The Salesman on the Stage: A Study in the Social Influence of Drama." Bloom 59–75.

Jacobson, Irving. "Family Dreams in *Death of a Salesman.*" *American Literature* 47 (1975): 247–58.

Lyotard, Jean-François. *The Postmodern Condition: A Report on Knowledge.* Minneapolis: U of Minnesota P, 1984.

Marx, Karl. *Capital.* Vol. 1. New York: Vintage, 1977.

Miller, Arthur. *Arthur Miller's Collected Plays.* New York: Viking, 1957.

——. *Timebends: A Life.* New York: Grove, 1987.

Mills, C. Wright. *White Collar: The American Middle Classes.* New York: Oxford UP, 1951.

Orr, John. *Tragic Drama and Modern Society: Studies in the Social and Literary Theory of Drama from 1870 to the Present.* London: Macmillan, 1981.

Parker, Brian. "Point of View in Arthur Miller's *Death of a Salesman.*" Bloom 25–38.

Porter, Thomas. "'Acres of Diamonds': *Death of a Salesman.*" *Critical Essays on Arthur Miller.* Ed. James J. Martine. Boston: G. K. Hall, 1979. 24–43.

Poster, Mark. *Sartre's Marxism.* London: Pluto, 1979.

Sartre, Jean-Paul. *Critique of Dialectical Reason.* London: New Left Books, 1976.

Spindler, Michael. *American Literature and Social Change: William Dean Howells to Arthur Miller.* London: Macmillan, 1983.

Vogel, Dan. *The Three Masters of American Tragedy.* Baton Rouge: Louisiana State UP, 1974.

White, Hayden. *Tropics of Discourse: Essays in Cultural Criticism.* Baltimore: Johns Hopkins UP, 1978.

Williams, Raymond. *Modern Tragedy.* London: Verso, 1979.

Chapter Ten

Hollywood's Moral Landscape: Clifford Odets's *The Big Knife*

Albert Wertheim

No name is more associated with New York agitprop theatre of the 1930s than that of Clifford Odets. As Odets confronted a "me first," acquisitive capitalism that left a generation of workers starving, unemployed, and shattered, his anger was both profound and dramatic. And particularly during 1935, which marked at once the nadir of the Great Depression and Odets's *annus mirabilis* as a playwright, that anger found its voice. In that year Odets had four major works produced in New York: *Waiting for Lefty*, *Awake and Sing!*, *Paradise Lost,* and *Till the Day I Die*, each of them inscribed with Odets's hard-hitting vision and impassioned language meant to open the eyes of Americans so that they would see something larger than their immediate and personal distress. For Odets, society was a moral landscape, and the Depression an event that rendered men and women actors in a modern morality play. In his dramas, appetite and lupine greed were encountered by modern Everymen, the Joes and Ednas, the Ralphies, who were driven into their roles and sometimes to their enlightenment by the direness of the times. Odets was a playwright who discovered in the Depression a dramatic occasion to teach people how to become better, an occasion for moral and political education.

What must it have been like for Odets, so imbued with the Marxist idealism and political ideology espoused by his beloved 1930s Group Theatre, for a man so much a product of the hard-bitten New York and Philadelphia he knew so well and where he had grown up and where he had come of age as a playwright, to fall headlong, during the subsequent decade, into the soft, seductive, West Coast arms of the motion picture industry; into a Hollywood environment itself as alluring and erotic as Jean Harlow or Frances Farmer beckoning amorously to millions of enthralled viewers seated in the fantasy land and darkness of local movie palaces?

In many ways, it could be said that Hollywood as Siren, as Pacific Coast Lorelei, shipwrecked Odets; and if it did not altogether destroy his talent as a creative writer, it doubtless blighted it. In Hollywood and after Hollywood, he was never again to capture anything close to the success he had enjoyed during the 1930s. Certainly Odets himself had intimations of this, and his consequent love-hate relationship with Hollywood was an open secret during the 1940s. He recognized Hollywood as the Tinsel Town it was and still is. He saw beneath its shallowness, and he knew and understood it as an incarnation of corporate capitalism in its most glamorous and seductive form.

Not surprisingly when, in 1948, Odets's *The Big Knife*, a drama set in Hollywood, hit the stage, critics understandably saw it—and continue to see it—as Odets's intensely personal dramatization of his own tragic situation in America's movie capital. After seeing a preview performance of *The Big Knife*, Allan Lewis wrote Odets an enthusiastic letter (*Odets Papers*, box 14, February 1949), in which he warmly extolled Odets's play for using Hollywood as a bellwether of American life:

> As to the play—it is written with dynamite, words explode with fury and hate. The play has the power of deep personal experience, the cry of a man that must be heard, that has got to be said, and stridently. And this is good, for the passion and venom must out and if it can do so with the fuming rage that this play has it makes strong theatre. It is nonsense to talk of the writer being removed, preserving objectivity, for he can better keep his balance in the heat of an honest fight. Objectivity can lead to a sterile liberalism. You have created a violent attack on a corrupt and corrosive industry, and through what you say of Hollywood comes the picture of an American scene where cultural decency and honest artistry are submerged in the greed and inhumanity of a movie magnate or the preservation of a bank balance. . . . The one adverse comment would be that the audience may not make the transition from Hollywood to themselves, may not see that values being torn to shreds here are the same forces that destroy their own creative needs . . .

Yet in his book (Lewis 112), published twenty-one years later, Lewis ungenerously and, I believe, short-sightedly changed his attitude, asserting the more common assessment of the play:

> When Odets returned to Broadway with *The Big Knife*, his first play after many years of financial success in Hollywood, he retreated to the personal drama. Charley Castle seeks to escape from Hollywood's erosion of his artistic integrity, but he really wants the physical comfort that Hollywood offers. The drama never reaches beyond Odets's own dilemma. Everyone attacks Hollywood, particularly those who have been its best-paid hirelings. No one has yet made the attack significant. Satire would be a more effective weapon.

Lewis here forgets his initial and well-founded enthusiasm for the play, and shows that he has neither read Nathaniel West's *Day of the Locust* nor properly understood what Odets was saying in *The Big Knife*. Similarly, John Mason Brown's vitriolic review of the play saw *The Big Knife* as nothing more than Odets'ss mean-spirited attack on Hollywood (Brown, 34–35).

To regard Odets's play merely as a castigation of Hollywood is to misunderstand it, to see it as less than it is, to reduce it to a melodrama penned by a man bent on biting the hand that generously fed him, a man at odds with himself for having "sold out" (Murray 162, and Miller 80). To be sure, *The Big Knife* and its main character, Charlie Castle, are not completely separable from Odets's personal situation. Like his infamous relationships with women, Odets's love affair with Hollywood was filled with an admixture of passion and ardor, anger and disgust. It was an alloy comprised at once of great amorous energy and of revulsion. In a similar way, his letters to his wife, Bette, are filled with warm solicitude and words of genuine affection which alternate with vitriolic charges about her insufferable infringement upon his creative energy and talent. As with Bette, Odets loved Hollywood even as he saw the sacrifice of his talents to her seemingly all-consuming needs. But finally *The Big Knife* is not about Hollywood, or Odets, or even Charlie Cass the idealist actor who came to Hollywood admiring FDR and who becomes Charlie Castle, the sybaritic, politically disengaged, Hollywood matinee idol. What the critics seem determined not to see is that in *The Big Knife*, Hollywood was simply a cipher figuring larger moral and existential issues.

For Odets, Hollywood, that city of movie sets, was itself an appropriate setting; not so much for film as for a morality drama of Elizabethan stage grandeur. Long before he even thought of writing *The Big Knife*, Odets kept a file of personal observations about Hollywood. Among the notes he wrote during the 1940s is a sardonic one that reads, "Hollywood, like carbon monoxide, is colorless, odorless gas; and like carbon monoxide has 100 times the affinity to blood that oxygen has" (*Odets Papers*, box 10). In Hollywood, moreover, he saw as well the several familiar types and parasites of the film industry in much the way that seventeenth-century allegorist John Bunyan saw the creatures and caricatures who populate his *Primrose Path* and *Vanity Fair*. Caricaturing the Hollywood agent, for example, Odets writes in his notes:

> The agent is sinister because, as in certain Hitchcock movie scenes, you think you are talking to a friend working on your side until you discover

> with horror that he is all the time working for "them." The agent's principal job is to keep you in line for the studio. This is understood by everyone concerned, except the client. What a client can really get is previously understood, too.

That sense of Hollywood as a landscape or backdrop for a modern morality play is also there when, in a letter to his most trusted friend, the producer, director, critic Harold Clurman, Odets outlines some play ideas. The letter, dated 5 August 1947, well before Odets set pen to paper and eighteen months before the opening of *The Big Knife*, nicely reveals the zygote that Odets would develop into a full-length stage play:

> . . . a more recent idea about a public figure of a man (most likely a Hollywood star) who kills a child as a hit & run driver and reveals the whole sickness of modern life in the struggle to reach a decision as to confess or not his guilt. (*Odets Papers*, box 3)

And three weeks later (27 August 1947), in a fifteen-page letter to Clurman, one can recognize the rapidly developing embryo taking shape:

> I want this play to be Elizabethan in brutal, excited feel. For many years now capitalism at its extreme, and Hollywood in particular, have been as ghastly murderous and terrorizing as anything Shakespeare or Webster wrote. That sinister feeling, that total disregard of human life, I want to get in this play. So what I want to write is an Elizabethan tragedy and if my luck holds, and the quality of my talent is intense enough, that is what will come out. (*Odets Papers*, box 3)

Rather than write a nasty insider tragedy about Hollywood, Odets clearly wished to use the Hollywood setting, much the way Jonson and Webster used Italy or Shakespeare used Denmark and Scotland, as an image of the rank world that corrupts and tests its inhabitants. Indeed, Odets's protagonist, Charlie Castle, comes to see himself as Macbeth, "in blood / Steeped in so far that, should [he] wade no more / Returning were as tedious as go o'er." And that Shakespearean connection is made absolute when Charlie Castle views his plight and exclaims, "I can't go on, covering one crime with another. That's Macbeth" (70)[1] Castle sees himself as well as a Hamlet who, in the midst of his despair, asks his friend Hank, "Why don't you stay here, Hank—be my Horatio?" (59).

Even more, Charlie reminds one of a Faustus who has already made his fatal choice prior to the play's first act. And as in Marlowe's *Doctor Faustus* or late medieval moral temptation plays, *The Big Knife* provides a corrupt, satanic tempter-antagonist for its modern-day Everyman. At the moral—or rather immoral—center of Odets's Hollywood is Marcus Hoff, the Mephistophelian movie mogul, whose histrionics and blandishments bring out the worst in susceptible men like Charlie Castle. Marcus Hoff is every bit as witty, shrewd, comic and manipulative as any Mephistopheles. And reminiscent of Faustus' signing his pact with Mephistopheles, Charlie Castle signs his Hollywood contract with Hoff Federated Studios. Marcus's satanic henchman and general factotum wryly and aptly comments to Charlie, "Just keep in mind that the day you first scheme . . . you marry the scheme and the scheme's children" (61). These words could as easily have come from the pen of Christopher Marlowe as from that of Clifford Odets. Furthermore, like the world of *Doctor Faustus* (or the world of morality drama from which Marlowe liberally drew), Hollywood seemed for Odets populated not merely by archetypes such as "the agent" he described in his notes, but also by classic physiognomies that go with those archetypes. Indeed Odets, from the 1930s until his death, kept a clipping file of Hollywood photos and classic faces that included the profiles of female and male models and performers as well as of producers and directors. That file, which Odets labeled "Hollywood Types," contains facial shots of Laurence Harvey, Milton Berle, Warren Beatty, Charles Laughton; and mug shots from *Operation Bikini*, including the posed faces of Tab Hunter, Frankie Avalon, Scott Brady, Jim Backus, Gary Crosby, Michael Dante, and Jody McCrea. There are likewise in Odets's file photos of Shirley MacLaine as Gittel in *Two for the Seesaw* as well as of Edie Adams, Paul Newman, several Hollywood producers, Burt Lancaster, Fay Spain, Jane Fonda, and Fay Wray and her ex-husband John Monk Saunders clipped from Saunders's obituary (*Odets Papers*, box 10, 11 March 1940). During his Hollywood years, moreover, Odets produced paintings as well as movie scripts and plays. His canvases titled *Diva*, *Italian Movie Star* (Sophia Loren), *Smoker*, *Burlesque Girl*, *Actress*, and *Straight Man* similarly display his admirable talent for caricature (Odets, "In Hell + Why," 8, 24–25, 28–29; Weales, 56–57).

In *The Big Knife*, Charlie Castle is a character reaching for Elizabethan tragic dimension, a Faustus or Macbeth who has made irremediable choices, has essentially sealed his fate, yet wishes to retrieve his moral rectitude. It is important that this play set in Hollywood never shows Charlie Castle acting on a movie set or making deals in the business offices of a film studio. To pun on the medieval theatre term, *The Big Knife*'s only mansion is the one in Beverly Hills owned by Charlie Castle; and all of the play's action takes place in its single set, the so-called "Playroom" of Charlie's mansion. It is in that appropriately named playroom, which features a much-used bar, that Charlie, like a morality play protagonist, is visited by the grotesques and demons of Hollywood: Patty Benedict, the insidious conflation of Hedda Hopper and Louella Parsons; Dixie Evans, the blowzy would-be starlet; Connie Bliss, the lustful wife of the man who went to jail in Charlie's stead for the hit-and-run fatality; Nat Danziger, Charlie's agent, who is really working for the studio; and of course those incarnations of unvarnished Evil, Marcus and Coy.[2] There Charlie is also visited by the play's incarnations of Good: his wife, Marion, whom he frequently calls "angel," and by Hank Teagle, his friend and better self, of whom he asks, "But where the hell do you stash your angel wings?" (38). And at the rear center of the set there is a prominent iron spiral staircase leading to the upper regions of the house. Those private and unseen upstairs areas seem to be the areas of grace from which Charlie has fallen. It is theatrically appropriate that it is there he commits suicide by slashing his wrists while running the water in his bathtub. And it is appropriate, too, that the first sign of Charlie's suicide death is marked by the bathwater dripping from upstairs through the ceiling and down into the playroom.

What *The Big Knife* is meant to be is not a castigation of Hollywood but Odets's powerful portrait of the American post–World War II wasteland, devoid of the ethics and ideals that had sent Americans to the battlefields of Europe a few years before. And it is a wasteland replete with untrammeled acquisitiveness. What has happened to Charlie Castle in Hollywood is Odets's terrible image of the sickness besetting American life. A heartsick Hamlet-like Charlie seeing what is rotten in the state of California and in America, feelingly laments to his Horatio friend, Hank: "When I came home from Germany . . . I saw most of the war dead were here, not in Africa and Italy. And Roosevelt was dead . . . and the war was only last week's snowball fight . . . and we plunged ourselves, all of us, into the noble work of making the buck reproduce itself!" (58).

Hollywood offers a particularly apt linguistic atmosphere for Odets's purposes. Edward Murray suggests that there is an undertone of homosexuality noting the vocative uses of "darling," "lovely," and "boyfriend" for the male figures in the play or of Smiley Coy's calling Charlie "Ella" (Murray169–70). Murray notices as well the feminine, subaltern imagery of lines like Charlie's "I'm like a girl in a summer-time canoe—I can't say no!" (26) that recur throughout the play. Yet Odets's aim in writing such language seems not at all meant to imply homosexuality but to deepen his portrait of a world structured, as is its representative language, to emasculate its denizens. It is the studio bosses like Hoff and, ironically, the women—

Marion, Patty Benedict and Dixie Evans—who wield power, who are the doers. Without wishing to exaggerate the importance of Odets's title, one could argue that the Hollywood of studio producers like Hoff is the Hollywood phallically represented in the play's title. Certainly the play suggests that men like Charlie, powerful male figures in on-screen cinematic fictions, are off-screen ironically courted, seduced, and overpowered like women.

Charlie loses his virginity and is whored in Hollywood, and that kind of passivity or disempowered masculinity is very much in keeping with morality play and post–morality play structure. A passive Everyman or Human Genus, or the archetypal figure of emasculated man, Samson in Milton's *Samson Agonistes*, is fixed on stage in one spot to be visited by the men and women who wield power over him. In Milton's drama this is particularly clear as a bound Samson is faced with the power of Harapha and of Dalila. R. Baird Shuman, in criticizing *The Big Knife*, says the play "revolves around Charlie Castle, who, peculiarly enough, is probably the weakest character in the play"; and in so saying, Shuman unwittingly touches the plays structural essence (Shuman 122, Miller 80).[3]

What transpires in plays structured like *The Castle of Perseverance* or *Samson Agonistes* is also what Odets allows to transpire in *The Big Knife*: the central and emasculated character reclaims, heroically and sometimes tragically, his masculine power by moving from a passive to an active state. For Odets, the emasculation of the central character by Hollywood is a sign of the times. It is what has happened to the American public after the anger of the thirties and the war of the forties. Speaking of Hank Teagle's novel about American society, Charlie says, "You're right, Hank. Your hero's half a man, neither here nor there, dead from the gizzard up. Stick him with a pin and see, psst! No feelings!" (58). Obviously, Charlie is that moribund, desensitized half-man; and he has become so because in postwar America, the captains of industry threaten the spirit of American individualism and of the classic American Everyman, who is reduced to a receptive female role. And for Odets, Hollywood movie moguls are just one glaring example of those satanic captains of contemporary industry; and Charlie Castle is just one victim, one example of oppressed American individualism. Odets uses Hollywood almost metonymically. It is his shorthand for a more general American postwar fall from grace. When Charlie Castle makes his one exit from the stage and the play, he ascends the staircase not merely to his death but to what is the only way he can reclaim grace.

It was Odets's closest friends, Harold Clurman, and director Jean Renoir, who perceived what Odets meant to dramatize in *The Big Knife*. After reading a first draft of the script, Clurman wrote in a letter to Odets (15 October 1947):

> The core of your play is a bitterness which people today want to gloss over in platitudes, in sentimental evasion, or in the subterfuge of calling such bitterness "confusion," "neurosis," and "craziness." In other words they will try to suggest that you are writing about special people, whereas you are really writing about everybody. You are writing about the fundamental base of middle-class America. (*Odets Papers*, box 3)[4]

And reading a later draft, Jean Renoir wrote (15 November 1948):

> Your Hollywood background becomes as rich as the court of Denmark or Venice in the 15th century. And your hero is the brother of all those kings, generals, great lovers, who talk in the latin or greek verses we had to translate in school. (*Odets Papers*, box 4)

Likewise, critic John Gassner recognized the flaws of *The Big Knife*, but also recognized its strength, when he wrote of Odets that he "deliberately chose Hollywood as a symbol for everything deteriorative and unscrupulous in our society: he returned to the 'Golden Boy' theme of how a materialistic, success-worshipping world corrupts the soul" (Gassner 26).

Most important, we have among Odets's papers his own words about *The Big Knife*. In a seven-page letter of rebuttal (24 March 1949) to critic John Mason Brown, who had written caustically and deprecatingly of *The Big Knife* in *The Saturday Review of Literature* (Brown, 34–35), Odets defends his play against the charge that continues to dog it, that it is an anti-Hollywood play written by a man who, as Lewis Allen was to say, had been all too willing to become one of its best-paid hirelings. Odets must have been particularly stung by Brown's high-handed, savage, and personal attack, for Odets's letter is dated just five days after the Brown diatribe appeared. In his unpublished letter, Odets passionately writes:

> As for intention, "The Big Knife" is not about an actor and it is not about Hollywood. It is a morality play about a certain kind of modern Prince of Success and some of the human problems which come in the wake of his elevation. The Hollywood background was chosen because the author knew it from more than hearsay; and because, secondly, Hollywood is the very glass and symbol of high success the wide world over. . . .

> The better part of Charlie Castle is represented in my play by his wife, Marion, a woman who, as he says, is "the iron hoop that keeps my rotten staves together."
>
> Well, in conclusion, I must tell you that I wrote "The Big Knife," not because I have personal pains, but exactly because so many people in Hollywood (and in the other high places of the land) are so utterly "realistic" about their work and so unmoved morally by the rotten fruit of that work. Much of the work is demeaning and degrading to themselves and to the millions who later view it. Hollywood is purveying a steady diet of bon-bons to a great people who are hungering for the simple bread of a spiritual life, that's all.
>
> Forced from time to time to make a living from Hollywood (and giving honest, skilled work in return), I am unable to remain "realistic" about the enormous abuse there of human possibilities. Let me lose my writing hand when I stop writing out against the abuse of human talent and aspiration in any shape or form, in this, my native land! (*Odets Papers*, box 4)

Odets's eloquent but unpublished response lucidly suggests the tenor of his thinking as he wrote *The Big Knife*.

Odets's reply can also serve for the later criticism leveled at *The Big Knife* by Gerald Rabkin, who argues:

> The Marxist eschatology provided the dramatist with a structural referent, for implicit in the dialectical struggle is an essential drama, the vanquishing of the old class by the new . . . The structural failure of *The Big Knife* lies in Odets's inability, after the loss of political commitment, to substitute a suitable unifying dramatic metaphor. (Rabkin 199)

What Odets makes clear in his letter to Brown is that fifteen years and a world war have created new issues for America, for which the Marxist rhetoric and vision of the Depression era are no longer apt. It is, moreover, precisely the loss of that ideological and social clarity in American life that Odets is writing about in *The Big Knife*. In the world of 1930s New York oppressed taxi drivers challenging corrupt unions in *Waiting for Lefty*, it was "us against them." But in the new, late 1940s world, a world epitomized by a Hollywood replete with seductive and duplicitous euphemistic language, with luxury, and with sweetheart deals, the issues and the lines of combat are blurred, even as the characters' thinking is blurred by the alcohol they imbibe from the centrally placed bar, itself euphemistically referred to as "the lemonade stand" (7). In 1935, people were starving, children were stricken with rickets, lives were shattered by the economic hard times. The times were tough and the issues clear. In 1949, however, times were good. Postwar affluence had come to the United States, and, consequently, social issues and moral decisions were both less pressing and less clearly delineated.

In a world of oppression, heroism is relatively easy. But how, Odets ponders through the figure of Charlie Castle, can one retain the hard edge of heroism and moral rectitude in a soft world of near sybaritic ease? Castle's malaise stems from his failure to name an enemy. As in *Waiting For Lefty*, it is natural to shout "Strike!" in the face of the indigence and human indignity unleashed in the 1930s. But, as Charlie Castle finds and as Odets knew, it is far less easy to challenge a world of swimming pools, parties, beautiful people, million-dollar contracts, elegant clothes, beach houses and expensive cars. It is precisely the loss of much-needed political involvement in the United States, in Hollywood, and in Charlie Castle's life that comprises the central issue of *The Big Knife*. Classic tragic character that he is, Charlie is so corrupted, "in blood steeped so far," that when he has his moment of tragic insight, his Aristotelian *anagnorisis*, it is already too late for him to reform, and suicide is his only way out. It is, however, for the other characters, for Odets's Macduffs and Horatios, for Marion and Teagle, and of course for the audience, to learn from Charlie's tragedy, to see the moral issues behind the seductive facade of the new American postwar affluence, to recognize filth in a silk stocking, and to act so that commitment to social and political ideals in America does not die a death induced by a surfeit of riches.

The shrewd and jaded characters of Odets's play understand Charlie Castle and in so doing understand America as Odets saw it after the war. Charlie's agent, Nat, explains, "Everybody has a delusion that you're very tough—they mix you up with the parts you play. But I know you better. You're a special, idealistic type. The only thing—business and idealism don't mix—it's oil and water. Darling, you expect too much from yourself" (20). Nat's comment is as much an image of America as of Charlie Castle. Hank Teagle, a writer and Charlie's best friend, speaking Charlie of the book he is completing, says, "I still try to write out of Pascal's remark: 'I admire most those writers who tell, with tears in their eyes, what men do to other men.' This book is about a man like you . . . It's a fable about moral values and success" (57). *The Big Knife*, too, using Hollywood as its backdrop and symbol, is a fable about moral values and success.

Notes

1 Parentheses after references refer to the Dramatists Play Service 1949 edition of *The Big Knife*.

2 Brooks Atkinson curiously put his finger on the morality play texture when he wrote in his review of *The Big Knife*, "Always a vivid writer, he [Odets] has put together a whole company of authentic individual people, characterizing them brilliantly and displaying them in a series of scenes." *The New York Times*, 25 February 1949, 28.

3 Miller recognizes Charlie as the person who is continually on stage and at the center of the action but who never leaves his playroom. "It as if," Miller says, "everyone has access to the world outside the stage except Charlie, who is confined to the Hollywood castle that his own name betokens." Miller goes on to compare the play to Ibsen's *A Doll's House*.

4 One can only wonder what Odets must have felt when he read his friend Clurman's essentially negative review of the play in *The New Republic* (14 March 1949), 28–29. There Clurman writes, "As a mechanism for conveying a definite theme, idea or emotion, '*The Big Knife*' is misbegotten. . . . The ostensible point of this is that a good person in our society becomes the prisoner of forces that will manipulate him as a commodity. Unless he is a saint or a revolutionary he can live only by dying. Apart from any judgment as to the validity of this thesis, the play fails to demonstrate it."

Works Cited

Brown, John Mason. "The Biting Hand." *Saturday Review of Literature* 19 Mar. 1949: 34–35.

Clurman, Harold. "The Big Knife." *New Republic* 14 Mar. 1949: 28–29.

Gassner, John. "The Big Knife." *Theatre Arts* 33 (July 1949).

Lewis, Allan. *American Plays and Playwrights of the Contemporary Theatre.* New York: Crown, 1970.

Miller, Gabriel. *Clifford Odets.* New York: Continuum, 1989.

Murray, Edward. *Clifford Odets: The Thirties and After.* New York: Ungar, 1968.

Odets, Clifford. *The Big Knife.* New York: Dramatists Play Service, 1949.

Odets, Clifford. *Clifford Odets Papers.* The Lilly Library, Indiana University, Bloomington.

Odets, Clifford. *"In Hell + Why": Paintings on Paper from the 1940's and 1950's.* New York: Michael Rosenfeld Gallery, 1996.

Rabkin, Gerald. *Drama and Commitment.* Bloomington: Indiana UP, 1964

Shuman, R. Baird. *Clifford Odets.* New York: Twayne, 1962.

Weales, Gerald. "Awake and Paint." *American Theatre* 13 (September 1996): 56–57.

Chapter Eleven

The Emperor Jones: Naturalistic Tragedy in Hemispheric Perspective

Philip J. Hanson

In little more than the two decades preceding the first production of *The Emperor Jones*, U.S. expansionism built up steam. In 1898 Spain ceded Puerto Rico to the United States. The same year American troops occupied Cuba. In 1903 Theodore Roosevelt took Panama and in 1905 established a customs receivership in the Dominican Republic. The United States occupied Nicaragua in 1909 and purchased the Virgin Islands in 1916. In 1915 U.S. marines took Haiti and remained there until 1934.[1] The announced reason for occupying Haiti was the violent overthrow of Haitian president Guillaume Vilbrun Sam, one of the Haitian presidents cited by Eugene O'Neill as a model for the title character in his play, *The Emperor Jones*.[2] In 1920, the year the Provincetown Players put on *The Emperor Jones*, O'Neill's theater group was enacting much the same logic that was being played out, and historically had been played out, in the political theater of Western Hemispheric relations.

The contiguous relationship between the tragedy of Brutus Jones and Haitian political history materializes at the very outset of the play in the politically charged language of O'Neill's stage directions, which read, "The action of the play takes place on an island in the West Indies as yet not self-determined by white Marines. The form of native government is, for the time being, an empire."

O'Neill's language is loaded with political irony and pessimism. The fragility of self-rule and native government are conveyed by the ominous phrases "as yet not self-determined" and "for the time being." His choice of an island in the West Indies as the setting reminds us of a hemispheric history of imperialism which began with Columbus's landing and the subsequent initiation of an Indian slave colony. The phrase "white Marines" refers to specific and recent events in U.S.-Haitian relations. Reading *The Emperor Jones* in the context of this hemispheric history alerts us that the play is a particular sort of African tragedy. Treated by O'Neill with the deterministic logic of naturalism, Jones' tragedy emerges as the collision of centuries of accumulated tragic African American experience with the local experience of the black descendants of slaves from the era of Dessalines and Toussaint L'Ouverture.[3] Reading the play within a context of such hemispheric history leads to both a redefinition of its tragedy and to a reconsideration (or an expanded definition) of the complexity of the relationship between twentieth-century American drama and definitions of naturalist tragedy.

In 1914, writing about the state of drama of the period and about what he took to be the fundamental changes that had occurred in drama, George Lukacs wrote that in traditional tragedy, "in Greek and even in Shakespearean drama we can still easily distinguish between man and his environment, or speaking from the viewpoint of drama, between the hero and his destiny." Raising the question of what made tragedy in dramas of the period, Lukacs concludes that drama, because it had become "more novelistic," resulted in "the maintenance of personality [being] threatened by the totality of external data" (436–37). That is, tragedy was becoming less a result of a bad decision made by a character (or a character's father, as in the case of Oedipus) or of a flaw in the character's personality (as in the case of Lear) than the consequence of larger external forces beyond the character's control. In Lukacs's words, "What we are discussing here is the increased complexity which determines dramatic character" (427). This poses a problem for Lukacs as he seems to imagine the end of tragedy or at least the threat of such an end. He remarks, "The threat to it is indisputably great, and in naturalism, for instance, we can see that it virtually ceases to be dramatic." Lukacs finds his way out of this problem by coming to two conclusions. First, man grows dramatic by virtue of the intensity of his will. And second, since "the heroes of the new drama—in comparison to the old—are more passive than active; they are acted upon more than they act for themselves; they defend rather than attack; their heroism is mostly is mostly a heroism of anguish, of despair." By this logic, the determinism of naturalism means that the hero "must engage in the struggle; something drives him into it which he cannot resist; it is not his to decide whether he even wishes to resist" (429–30). Ultimately, Lukacs concludes, "It is not so important that the problem be thought through to its end . . . in the new tragedies the tragedy is asserted as primary; the various particular phenomena of man, life, and the events of drama are all regarded as tragic; here the tragedy is *a priori* to life" (438). If one historicizes Lukacs's conclusions and considers *The Emperor Jones* in the context of such reasoning, it becomes possible to consider Jones's tragedy as arising from a hemispheric history which, for the most part, preceded his birth.

In 1925, in a letter to Arthur Hobson Quinn, O'Neill referred to seeing

> the transfiguring nobility of tragedy, in as near the Greek sense as one can grasp it, in seemingly the most ignoble, debased lives. . . . I'm always acutely conscious of the Force behind—(Fate, god, our biological past creating our present, whatever one calls it—Mystery certainly)—and of the one eternal tragedy of Man in his glorious, self-destructive struggle to make the force express him instead of being, as an animal is, an infinitesimal incident in its expression. (*Letters* 195)

The connection of particular importance to *The Emperor Jones*, which O'Neill makes here, concerns the relationship of an "ignoble, debased" life to the forces "behind" it which create, for Jones, his temporal present and the sociological conditions in which he must live. In the same letter O'Neill goes on to say that the purpose of such tragedy is to "bring home to members of a modern audience their ennobling identity with the tragic figures on the stage." O'Neill's concept of tragedy as he explains it here is, partly, at least, Aeschylean. The tragedy is to bring forth some sort of knowledge through suffering. The focus of O'Neill's remarks is the audience. They are to be ennobled through an identification with the tragic subject.[4] Most of the suffering Jones does in the play takes place in the forest, as he is pursued by locals who have rebelled against his exploitive rule as emperor. Yet the play provides enough information about Jones's past to reveal that his past suffering and his exploitive reasoning arise from the same set of conditions (to use Lukacs's term, *a priori* conditions). Nothing prevents a contemporary audience from gaining a knowledge, along the lines of O'Neill's remarks, of the historical situation of Jones's tragedy.

References in the play to Jones's American experiences suggest the connection O'Neill strives to make between the exploitive character Jones evinces on the island and his shaping American past. One irony of Jones's experience on the island emerges when he explains to Smithers, the English capitalist entrepreneur (who serves as a reminder of a European history of exploitation in the West Indies), why he struggled to become emperor:[5]

> You didn't s'pose I was holdin' down dis Emperor job for de glory in it, did you? Sho'! De fuss and glory part of it, dat's only to turn de heads o' de low-flung, bush niggers dats here. Dey wants de big circus for deir money. I gives it to 'em an' I gits de money [With a grin] De long green, dats me every time! (O'Neill's brackets 7)

Jones tells Smithers that there are two kinds of stealing: the little stealing Smithers does and the big stealing Jones does on the island. He explains the environment in which he absorbed such a philosophy: "If dey's one thing

I learns in ten years on de Pullman ca's listenin' to de white quality talk, it's dat same fact. And when I gits a chance to use it I winds up Emperor in two years" (8). In an abstract and historically ironic sense, Jones has learned his business ethics and methods from the very class whose ancestors, socioeconomically speaking (south of the Mason-Dixon line), would have enslaved Jones's ancestors. Jones's profit incentive matches the logic of the period in which the play was written. Of the U.S. occupation of Haiti Hans Schmidt reports that

> Anti-imperialists argued that imperialism profited a privileged minority of American businessmen, while the expenses of conquest and military occupation were borne by all people. . . . James Weldon Johnson [and others] charged that the marines invaded Haiti as bill collectors for the National City Bank of New York. (17)

Ironically, the marines introduced a form of slavery, a corvée, in which native Haitians were forced to work on the roads (the same work done by chain gangs in the United States during this period). This quasi-slavery system, resembling as it did nineteenth-century slavery in the United States and occurring in an area of the hemisphere where Columbus had enslaved Tainos to gather gold and where African slaves eventually replaced the Tainos on sugar plantations, further enraged critics of the marine action.[6] The intervention in Haiti took place within the context of the larger U.S. claims to a liberal-progressive foreign policy, which had as its declared goal introducing democratic liberalism to technologically "deprived" peoples. But racism complicated the U.S. approach to Haiti. Marines shocked the mulatto elite of Haiti by referring to Haitians as "niggers." In 1920, the year *The Emperor Jones* was first produced, an atrocity story published in the *New York Times* provided an evocative connection between U.S. race history, the race history that was unfolding in Haiti, and the events of O'Neill's theatrical tragedy. That paper reported "how American marines, largely made up of and officered by Southerners, opened fire with machine guns from airplanes upon defenseless Haitian villages, killing men, women, and children in the open market places; how natives were slain for 'sport' by a hoodlum element among the same Southerners."[7] What *The Emperor Jones* reveals is that as these old racial hatreds, which arose from a shared hemispheric history of racial oppression, were being renewed and played out in Haiti, they were almost at the same moment being played out on the American stage. Ironically, Jones, a product of Jim Crow and circumscribed opportunity, practices the methods of his own oppressors upon his fellow blacks on the island. Jones, though black, exercises a logic strongly resembling that of the exploiters of Haiti.

At points in the play it becomes quite apparent that Jones has been marked by vestiges of the American slave system. In an attempt to intimidate Jones, Smithers reminds him of race practices in the United States. Smithers remarks, "I've 'eard it ain't 'ealthy for a black to kill a white man in the States. They burns 'em in oil, don't they?" Jones responds, "You mean lynchin' 'd scare me?" Jones adds that his jail time may have resulted from killing a black man. He suggests, "Maybe I gits twenty years when dat colored man die" (11). The different treatment accorded blacks in the United States for crimes against other blacks, as opposed to crimes against whites, is apparently only a small point in the play—at least in plot or thematic terms, until one considers how historically it carries great emotional, legal, and political meaning. A former sharecropper, Mississippi born Viethel Wills, recalls what it was like to grow up in the Jim Crow South in the early part of the twentieth century: "You [a black person] could steal a white man's hog and get life or ten years for it. And you could kill a black man and go free. That's just the way the South was at that time" (interviewed in *The Promised Land*). Explaining the societal stake white lynchers and enforcers of Jim Crow laws had in their actions, historian Neil R. McMillen remarks, "lynching was deemed necessary because black[s] could not be otherwise trained to subordination" (237) Jones's remarks suggest he has committed crimes. But the play argues his crimes cannot be separated from his racially based experience—and his race's history—in America. That the flow of what Stephen Greenblatt calls "social energy" was not merely one way (that is into the play) is illustrated by the effect it had in the South (12). O'Neill recalled that when the company performing *The Emperor Jones* ventured into the "South proper" they were "warned by the Ku Klux Klan jackasses not to venture further" (*Letters* 170).

This point is one of several which ultimately connects American and Haitian history. Judging by the play, O'Neill's interest in Guillaume Vilbrun Sam arose out of three apparent factors: Sam's vicious methods for maintaining power, the violence of his overthrow, and the pretext made by the U.S. of intervening to keep order in Haiti because of the unrest caused by Sam's overthrow. In the words of Hans Schmidt,

> The overthrow of Sam was exceptionally bloody and repugnant to public opinion both within Haiti and in the United States. Sam, in office less than five months, was implicated in the massacre of 167 political prisoners. . . . After the massacre of the prisoners . . . Sam took refuge in the French

> legation. . . . Enraged mobs violated the legations and killed both Sam and Etienne. Sam was dragged from the French legation and publicly dismembered. Portions of his body were then paraded around the streets of Port-au-Prince in a grotesque spectacle accompanied by vindictive cries of the mob. (65)

Sam's overthrow took place in July of 1915. While U.S. officials claimed to be shocked by the sadism of the treatment accorded Sam, a little more than a year earlier the *Boston Guardian* had reported that in Marshall, Texas, "Charles Fisher, a negro youth, was recently badly mutilated by a mob near here. . . . the mob sheared off the youth's ears, slit his lips and mutilated him in other ways below the belt." The *Cleveland Gazette* reported in December of 1914 the story of a mob in Shreveport, Louisiana, of "200 white men" who took Watkins Lewis, a black man accused of murdering a white, and bound him to a tree trunk. "Fallen trees and branches were heaped about him. . . . 'I didn't do it' [Lewis] screamed as the flames leaped about him." In the U.S. the sort of violence accorded Sam was being vented on black American citizens with startling regularity. In 1915, just months before Sam's overthrow, the *Chicago Defender* connected widespread race violence at home to expansionist desires abroad:

> The United States is sending missionaries to teach the heathen . . . ministers preach on the good to humanity, but here in the South the same dastardly crimes are committed. . . . Today the businessmen are trying their hardest to get into South America, and the Latin countries are only going to allow them in under certain conditions. Race discrimination and lynchings will be no upholders there. The people there brand Americans as lynchers, and it will be hard for the Americans to convince them otherwise.[8]

One ironic component of Jones's personal tragedy relevant to the account in the *Chicago Defender* is that he does not comprehend the historical connection between the lynchings with which Smithers attempts to intimidate him and the exploitive—and intimidating—tactics he employs to profit from the natives of the West Indies island who share his ancestry.

Just as the references to lynching are charged with historical meaning, so the image of the black man on a chain gang being whipped by a white carries its own particular historical significance. It connects to the efforts in the United States in the immediate postbellum period by the ex-slaveowners of the South to retain their former hold over their ex-bondsmen and bondswomen.[9] In the same conversation, Jones tells Smithers, "Maybe I gits in 'nother argument wid de prison guard was overseer ovah us when we're wukin' de roads. Maybe he hits me wid a whip and I splits his head wid a shovel and runs away and files de chain off my leg and gits away safe" (11).[10] Connecting Jones to the existing Southern chain gangs deepens the play's sense of the historical marks Jones carries with him to the island, since chain gangs have a particularly ugly connection to black history and slavery in America. At the close of the Civil War, A. Philips, a future warden of a Mississippi penitentiary made an ominous prediction: "Emancipating the negroes will require a system of penitentiaries."[11] His connection, rather than addressing the needs or potential of ex-slaves, focuses on control. Seeking to reassert power over its newly freed work force, the dominant class of ex-slaveholders experimented with several methods of labor control. In addition to the labor gangs of the immediate postbellum period and the more successful resort to sharecropping, former masters benefited from the convict-lease system, which gave way to chain gang labor of convicts. Frequently the racial nature of chain gangs made the connection to slavery all the more troublesome.

Edward L. Ayers remarks, "To planters used to managing slaves, the bound labor of convicts must have seemed a welcome opportunity to return to accustomed ways. . . . Obviously the roots of such forced labor reached into slavery" (191). Jones's connection to the chain gang, with its image of whipping, echoes the complicated reality of blacks imprisoned in the South in the half century following the Civil War. Whatever their crimes, the factor of race continuously challenged the concept of legal justice and contributed to the accumulating racial problems that resulted. Rather than recognizing the meaning of his own history, Jones repeats the exploitive acts of his oppressors.

The irony of Jones's historical blindness is borne home by the image of a local black woman attempting to steal from the emperor near the beginning of the play. The old and cheaply dressed black woman is discovered by Smithers sneaking around the opulent emperor's palace. Smithers threatens her with his riding whip and she denies stealing. But the image conveys a great deal about the circumstances of Jones's having stolen from the natives. The people he is supposed to protect have been reduced to thieves and beggars by his misrule. His failure to decipher the potential constructiveness that his rule might do for his own people is later compounded by his being revealed as spiritually and ethically deficient. Using logic as old at least as the Crusades, Jones tells Smithers, "Doesn't you know dey's got to do wid a man was member in good standin' o' de Baptist Church? . . . Let dem try deir heathern tricks. De Baptist church done pertect me and land dem in hell" (15). Jones, like many of the actual Haitian emperors, discounted the value of the African-based Vodoun (or Voodoo) religion. Vodoun was, for much of Haiti's history, primarily a religion of the peasant, a religion which helped peasants cope with many of their social afflictions. Jones discards their religion on the basis of his belief that their non-Westerness makes them ignorant and heathen. His action recalls the suppression of African religion and customs by Southern plantation owners. On a point suggestively relevant, plantation owners also banned the use of drums by slaves who had come from African societies where drums were part of the culture.[12] When the Marines took Haiti, one of the things they forbade was the use of drums.[13] Referring to the split between the traditional ruling class of Haiti (up to Duvalier), with its emphasis on lighter colored skin, Harold Courlander writes,

> For the elite, Vodoun has often been an embarrassment and a tribulation. They have felt the need to apologize for its existence. . . . They have tended to equate it with the darkness of race, without really perceiving that it helps to satisfy essential social needs for which the elite, so often in political power, have never been able to supply more than superficial answers. (23)

In the play, the constant beating of the drum suggests Jones's state of being severed from his cultural heritage. He is cut off from his religious, historical, and cultural roots. The drum, a symbol of the connections between African and Haitian religion, stalks Jones with its constant thumping. Notably, Haitian soldiers had made Vodoun charms to use in battle against the marines during the U.S. intervention. When Jones asks, "What's dat drum beatin' fo'?" Smithers replies, "That means the bleedin' ceremony 'as started." Smithers adds, "And they're there 'olden their 'eathern religious service—makin' no end of devil spells. . . . Ternight when it's pitch black in the forest, they'll 'ave their pet devils and ghosts 'oundin after you" (14–15).

In *The Emperor Jones* O'Neill wanted the drum beat to start slowly and intensify until it matched the frenzied pulse of the terrified Jones. O'Neill explains, "One day I was reading of the religious feasts in the Congo and the uses to which the drum is put there; how it starts at a normal pulse-beat and is slowly intensified until the heart beat of everyone present corresponds to the frenzied beat of the drum" (Estrin 58). In the Haitian version of African religion the *loa*, gods which are often the same as those worshipped in Africa (but which may arise from the meeting of Catholicism and Vodoun), communicate with worshippers in dreams or when the worshipper is in a trance state induced by ritualized dance and drum music. In effect the votary is possessed by the gods, who then communicate with him or her through the possession. This concept—given the central place of the tom-tom in this play—is worked out in the drum-driven convulsive flight of Jones. Within the context of the Vodoun trance the worshipper often receives some message in the form of dreams or visions. In the play, the drum drives Jones to his series of visions, which in racial and historical terms provide him with a kind of African-centered epiphany.[14] Jones's pain, which intensifies throughout his flight, is tragic in that the gods who pursue him through the drum music and the series of trances he experiences are the gods of his own ancestors. Alfred Metraux suggests that

> in Haiti gods, like men are extremely touchy and any trifle can give offense. Simply forgetting to dance the number of *rondes* to which they believe themselves entitled . . . makes them ready to pounce. . . . They may even resent imprudent words uttered by their worshippers in a temper, and it is not unusual for the *loa* to visit upon children the sins of their parents. (67)

The point is not whether or not O'Neill believed in the *loa*. He likely did not. Rather the question he raises by the particular ethnic iconography he offers for Jones's tragedy concerns what he meant when he referred to "the Force behind" lives that were "ignoble and debased." With respect to the sins of the parents being visited upon the children, Jones becomes an ironic target for tragic vengeance since, in historical terms, his own parents or ancestors are not to blame for his sins. Paradoxically, he has absorbed the ethics of the oppressors of his ancestors, and for this, in the terms of the play, he must be sacrificed. Taken altogether the visions offer a rationale for such a sacrifice. To understand this rationale, it helps to evaluate another aspect of the naturalistic reasoning O'Neill presents in this play. Writing about naturalism in the theater, Emile Zola made a central distinction between pre-naturalistic drama and the drama of naturalism:

> In effect, the great naturalistic evolution, which comes down directly from the fifteenth century to ours has everything to do with the gradual substitution of physiological man for metaphysical man. In tragedy metaphysical man, according to dogma and logic, reigned absolutely. The body did not count; the soul was regarded as the only interesting piece of human machinery; drama took place in the air, in pure mind. Consequently, what use was the tangible world? Why worry about the place where the action was located? . . . Why notice that Queen Dido was a boy whose budding beard forced him to wear a mask? None of that mattered. . . . the play was heard. . . . on a higher plane than man, in the world of ideas. . . . The whole history of our theatre is in this conquest by the physiological man.

> [Playwrights of the past] have had only one task. . . . to progress towards truth, to sift out more of the natural man and impose him on the public. (367–68)

By the reasoning of naturalism, physiological man is subject to physical forces, especially, in the language of naturalism, to environmental forces which decide his fate (notably Lukacs uses the word "destiny"). That many of these forces existed "*a priori*" to the events of the play only intensifies the character's tragedy. The order of the visions Jones is made to experience and the particular choices O'Neill makes in selecting subject matter for the visions emphasizes the deterministic nature of Jones's tragedy and points to the role of hemispheric history in the making of tragedy.

Though the visions begin relatively late in the play, they work to pose a characteristic naturalistic question, then they offer an explanation which is also characteristic of naturalistic theory of the period. The first vision presents Jeff, the black man Jones has murdered. Jones sees him playing craps. Apparently, Jones's argument with Jeff occurred during a craps game, and Jones killed Jeff. Questions coherent with the naturalist enterprise arise over Jeff's activity. In socioeconomic terms, what is the status of playing craps in 1920? Who engages in the game? Booth Tarkington's 1921 novel, *Alice Adams*, portrays a social-climbing woman who has the bad luck of coming across her good-for-nothing brother playing craps with some black men. She quickly attempts to cover her apparent shame by explaining that he is "literary," studying the blacks for sociological reasons. Decent people don't play craps. So for an audience of the twenties, the series of visions for Jones begins with a clear portrait: he is at the bottom. The ensuing visions attempt to get behind this first image, to explain it and to evaluate what it means.

Notably, after having fired his gun—which makes the image of Jeff disappear—Jones returns to the question of his religion, the same question he debated with Smithers. In a suggestive comment, he remarks, "Dat Emperor's job sure is hard to shake." His conclusion points to his predicament. His past is unshakable; it's what has made him; and by the reasoning of this play, it extends back to points far in advance of his birth. Trying to contend with the vision of Jeff by resorting to his Christian religion, Jones says, "Ha'nts! You fool nigger, dey ain't no such things! Don't de Baptist parson tell you dat many times? Is you civilized, or is you like dese ign'ernt black niggers heah?" (24). This last question gets at one of the central issues of the play. Is Jones like the African religionists or is he a Christian Baptist? What exactly does it mean to be "civilized"? He looks like the people on the island. But he claims to be superior. And his superiority derives from his sense of being civilized. One of the puzzles the ensuing visions will attempt to put into context is why Jones feels he must separate himself from the island's natives.

His second vision, that of the chain gang, conflates American race history with Jones's punishment for killing Jeff. If Jones deserves to be punished, he does not deserve to be whipped without reason. The chain gang adds a racial element to his punishment. The image of the whip itself, in the hand of a white guard, used on a black man on a chain gang, is so loaded that it cannot help but evoke the complicated history of black crime and efforts of the dominant class to achieve containment. The first image of Jones killing Jeff is now compounded by contingent American history. Lukacs points out that the drama of the naturalistic period represents "a web of complex interactions." He adds, "Investigation of a man suited for drama coincides with an investigation of the problem of man's relation to other men" (441). O'Neill pointedly referred to some of his tragic characters as having "ignoble" lives; he was anticipating comparisons to the traditional central characters of Greek and Shakespearean tragedy. Jones's tragedy is large when viewed as representative of the tragedy of a people, whose particular history is evoked by the setting and the choice of events meant to recall recent U.S. intervention in the West Indies.

The emotionally charged vision of the slave auction block reinforces these possibilities and intensifies claims for a historically grounded reading of the tragedy. The vision also raises the question, what system has been instrumental in the making of Brutus Jones. "Young belles and dandies . . . come to the slave-market for diversion." Their lack of empathy for the black men and women, one of whom is nursing a baby, heightens the horror of the vision. Terrible things happen to oppressed people without even any particular emotional involvement on the part of their oppressors. The dandies make witty remarks; the belles twitter. Jones "screams and leaps madly to the top of the stump. . . . paralyzed with horror" (27). Jones cries, "What you all doin', white folks? What's all dis?" (28) The movement of the vision reflects the sociological approach of W. E. B. Du Bois in *Souls of Black Folk,* which begins with images of degraded blacks but probes until he finds the causes for the degradation.

The double meaning of the word "haunts," which recurs throughout Jones's vision clarifies as he approaches his next vision. What does it mean to be haunted by one's racial history? Partly it means that in some sense that history remains present, in front of one. The images of the visions supplied by O'Neill keep that history in front of Jones. Doing so reminds an audience—or a reader—that Jones's earlier exploitive acts occurred when he was ignorant of that history, a factor in the making of his tragedy. By this point in the play, Jones' flight has reduced his trousers to a breechcloth. His tattered appearance enables him to fit in coherently with the slaves in the hold of the slave ship which he encounters in his next vision. The effect of merging Jones—visually—with the African slaves is to solidify the connection that the auction vision introduced. Jones is not separate from the "heathen" Africans. He is of them. He suffers from a history he shares with them. By "some uncanny compulsion" Jones's voice merges with the despairing "wail" of the enslaved "chorus" of Africans. The wail of the slaves goes on "to the rhythmic beat of the tom-tom" (30). Placed in a "trance" by the tom-tom, Jones comes to a Vodoun altar; "as if in obedience to some obscure impulse, he sinks into a kneeling, devotional posture before the altar" (30). The distance Jones has attempted to place between himself and the local blacks has been collapsed by this act. Up to this point Jones has differentiated himself from the locals by claiming to possess a superior religion. His claim, ironically, is presented as separating him from his own people and from understanding the implications of his own history. This failure to comprehend himself in historical terms—or in the larger context of a shared hemispheric history—has contributed to his rapacious actions as emperor.

The African imagery of this vision increases with the entrance of the Congo Witch Doctor in African costume. Significantly, the Witch Doctor commands the velocity of the beating of the tom-tom. He speeds it up. The effect on Jones is to bring him into participation in the dance. For the first time, he joins in the religion of his people. The stage directions read, "The whole spirit and meaning of the dance has entered into him, has become his spirit" (32). The effect is that "there is salvation." But the salvation can only come through sacrifice, the sacrifice of Jones's life. The lesson Jones has had to learn is that he must give himself for his people. Up to this point in the play, in the context of the religious logic of this vision, Jones has been sinning against history. The sacrifice is completed when Lem and the other locals shoot Jones. The lesson for exploiters echoes that of other Haitian overthrows of despotic rulers who have adapted the exploitive tactics of the oppressors of their ancestors.

The *a priori* history, which both explains Jones and effectively makes this a tragic play, has been unravelled in the visions. Jones exists as part of a "complex web" of hemispheric racial experience. Separated from that web, the play loses its claims to tragedy. Jones's life is ignoble only as part of that web. The concept that Jones's American experience and claims to Western gods somehow sets him above or apart from his people has been proven to be illusory and a factor in Jones's destructiveness, an element in the making of his tragedy. In his methods Jones resembles the Haitian rulers of the period leading up to the U.S. intervention. In Schmidt's words, "From 1898 to 1915 no Haitian president served a complete term and only one died a natural death while in office; the other ten were either killed or overthrown, seven of them during the chaotic period after 1911" (42).

Jones's sacrifice in the play emblematizes the sacrifice of his potential. Smithers acknowledges Jones's talents, but readers of the play recognize that those talents have gone to waste. The Haitian elite of this period had "looked to Europe and especially France for inspiration and disavowed all African and black associations, while the masses were involved in a unique acculturation of African and European heritages" (Schmidt 22). In its effort to "get behind" the history and circumstances of Jones's tragedy, the play, through its naturalistic methodology of probing into the near past and the distant past, evokes a larger hemispheric tragedy that continues into our own time.

Notes

1 For details, see Schmidt, 4–6.

2 See Arthur and Barbara Gelb, 438–39. O'Neill also engaged material from the lives of Henri Christophe (who made himself king in 1811, ruled brutally, established a corvée, and eventually shot himself in the head), and on that of Jean-Jacques Dessalines. Dessalines was the first black leader of Haiti to have himself proclamed emperor (thereafter going by the title Emperor Jacques I). Dessalines based his actions on accurate rumors circulating in Haiti that Napoleon was about to have himself proclaimed emperor of France. Dessalines, a former slave, built the opulent Haitian palace that was to house his successors until 1912. With his fellow revolutionary Toussaint L'Ouverture, Dessalines orchestrated the first successful slave rebellion in the Western Hemisphere.

3 In this article, I have benefited from the theoretical insights on tragedy of Brereton, Sewall, and Williams. I have also benefited from the general account of how tragedy works in O'Neill's plays from a reading of Ahuja. For readings either directly or indirectly concerned with *The Emperor Jones* which are of some relevance to my own views, see Bigsby, 133–44, Moleski, 37–52, and Pawley, 137–49.

4 For a discussion of this point, see Sewall, 1–8.

5 On British involvement on Saint Dominique and elsewhere in the West Indies, see Geggus, passim, and Logan, 52–57, 64–65, 69–70, 81, 392–96. For British involvement in Jamaica at the time of the U.S. intervention in Haiti, see Schmidt, 9.

6 Schmidt comments that "the roping together of workers was especially upsetting to the peasants, since it recalled legends of French colonial slave gangs" (101).

7 Quoted in Schmidt, 119.

8 One change in Haitian government forced on Haiti by the U.S. occupation was that outsiders—notably whites—be allowed to own land in Haiti. Since Dessalines's time, whites had been prohibited from owning land out of Haitian fears of a return to slavery. See Heinl and Gordon, 135, Schmidt, 10–11, and Plummer, 102, 112–13. The three newspaper articles were reprinted in Ginzburg, 90, 93, 96.

9 Interestingly enough, in May of 1995 the state of Alabama reinitiated chain gangs. Blacks responded by charging their action recalled slave practices; the A.C.L.U. has vowed to sue.

10 Jones's tentativeness about the events he describes ("Maybe I does all dat and maybe I don't") is swept away at the end of the play when the series of visions he experiences demonstrate he is haunted by the occurrence of the events he describes.

11 Quoted in Ayers, 187.

12 On this point, see Plummer, 33, 36–39.

13 See Courlander, Drum and Hoe, 190.

14 On the uses of the drum in Vodoun, see Courlander, 189–203; Courlander and Bastien, passim; Metraux, 58–100.

Works Cited

Ahuja, Chaman. *Tragedy, Modern Temper, and O'Neill.* Atlantic Highlands, NJ: Humanities P, 1984.

Ayers, Edward. *Vengeance and Justice.* New York: Oxford UP, 1984.

Bentley, Eric, ed. *The Theory of the Modern Stage.* New York: Penguin, 1992.

Bigsby, C. W. E. "Four Early Plays." *Modern Critical Views: Eugene O'Neill.* Ed. Harold Bloom. New York: Chelsea House, 1987. 133–44.

Brereton, Geoffrey. *Principles of Tragedy.* Coral Gables: U of Miami P, 1968.

Courlander, Harold. *The Drum and the Hoe: Life and Lore of the Haitian People.* Berkeley: U of California P, 1960.

Courlander, Harold, and Remy Bastien. *Religion and Politics in Haiti.* Washington, DC: Institute for Cross-Cultural Research, 1966.

Estrin, Mark W., ed. *Conversations with Eugene O'Neill.* Jackson: U of Mississippi P, 1990.

Geggus, David Patrick. *Slavery, War, and Revolution: The British Occupation of Saint Dominique, 1793–1798.* Oxford: Clarendon P, 1982.

Gelb, Arthur, and Barbara. *O'Neill.* New York: Harper, 1962.

Ginzburg, Ralph, Compiler. *100 Years of Lynchings.* Baltimore: Black Classic P, 1988.

Greenblatt, Stephen. *Shakespearean Negotiations.* Berkeley: U of California P, 1988.

Heinl, Robert Debs, and Nancy Gordon. *Written in Blood: The Story of the Haitian People, 1492–1971.* Boston: Houghton, 1978.

Logan, Rayford W. *The Diplomatic Relations of the United States with Haiti, 1776–1891.* Chapel Hill: U of North Carolina P, 1941.

Lukacs, George. "The Sociology of Modern Drama." 1914. Trans. Lee Baxandall. Bentley 425–50.

Metraux, Alfred. *Haiti, Black Peasants, and Voodoo.* New York: Universe Publishers, 1960.

Moleski, Joseph J. "Eugene O'Neill and the Cruelty of Theater." *Critical Approaches to O'Neill.* Ed. John H. Stroupe. New York: AMS P, 1988. 37–52.

O'Neill, Eugene. *Selected Letters of Eugene O'Neill.* Ed. Travis Bogard and Jackson Bryer. New Haven: Yale UP, 1988.

——. *The Emperor Jones.* 1920. *Nine Plays by Eugene O'Neill.* New York: Random, 1932.

Pawley, Thomas D. "The Black World of Eugene O'Neill." *Eugene O'Neill in China: An International Centenary Celebration.* Ed. Haiping Liu and Lowell Swortzell. New York: Greenwood P, 1992. 137–48.

Plummer, Brenda Gayle. *Haiti and the United States: The Psychological Moment.* Athens: U of Georgia P, 1992.

The Promised Land. Dir. Edmund Coulthard. Part 1. Prod. Discovery/BBC. Documentary. 1995.

Schmidt, Hans. *The United States Occupation of Haiti, 1915–1934*. New Brunswick, NJ: Rutgers UP, 1971.
Sewall, Richard B. *The Vision of Tragedy*. New Haven: Yale UP, 1959.
Williams, Raymond. *Modern Tragedy*. London: Chatto and Windus, 1979.
Zola, Emile. "From Naturalism in the Theatre." Trans. Albert Bermel. Bentley 351–72.

Chapter Twelve

Collapsing Male Myths: Rabe's Tragicomic *Hurlyburly*

David Radavich

Dramatic narratives of decadent, confused patriarchy under siege have dominated American theatre of the 1970s and 80s. David Mamet's stage works document the struggle of men to maintain close ties against a backdrop of mutual competitiveness, fear of and hostility toward women, and distrust of intimacy longed for but incapable of being acknowledged. Sam Shepard and Dave Rabe have mined the same area, with concentrated focus on the shifting tectonics of masculine longing, fear, and distrust. Rabe's *Hurlyburly*, one of the richest of these plays, anatomizes the homosocial quest for lasting male friendship in a world of fractured relations with women, corrupting work demands, and confused fraternal loyalties. What distinguishes this play from others of its kind is the singular linking of elegiac emotion with a tragicomic structure signifying promise and denial, arousal and defeat. On another level, *Hurlyburly* enacts what Raphael has called a "freestyle" initiation involving the "death of the boy" (4, 50–51): an inarticulate ritual of pain without clarification, of primitive emotion without adequate myth.

The central struggle for manhood in the play involves Eddie's attempts to retain and solidify his friendship with Phil over the objections of Mickey, the entrenched roommate with prior loyalty claims of his own. Mickey is necessarily displeased at the attention Eddie lavishes on Phil, as is Artie, who demands at one point, "so could you give me a hint as to the precise nature of the delusion with which you hype yourself about this guy . . . that you desert me for this fucking guy all the time" (100). The intense closeness of Eddie and Phil is only indirectly acknowledged in much of the play, as the hilarious antics and frequent comings and goings of the Gang of Four obscure the central dynamics. Yet at the end, Eddie's grief about Phil's death seems palpable as he struggles to articulate the intimacy he has lost: first by refusing Mickey's offer of consolation, then by exploding with a torrent of displaced pain at an unflappable, distant Johnny Carson, and finally, by pouring out his grief to Donna, who can only respond with irrelevant concerns of her own. Eddie remains alone with his loss, both psychologically and emotionally, as the strictures of his environment provide no intelligible context for his experience. The play thus takes on symbolic overtones of a confused, post-adolescent initiation during which Phil, the "boy," is sacrificed for the development, however flawed, of Eddie.

The maturation pattern involving the "death of the boy" also requires the exclusion or demonization of women, traditionally seen in primitive initiation rituals (Van Gennep, qtd. in Raphael 4–5). Females, particularly mothers or mother figures, are prohibited from participating in a process through which makes solidify their bonds. In *Hurlyburly*, male exclusionary tactics include both de-humanizing treatment and verbal abuse of women: "Critics [have] emphasized that the three women in the play were the victims, pawns, or temporary playmates of the men" (Kolin 90). The male characters repeatedly refer to women as "ghouls" who "eat men alive" or "bitches" who "hate men," who "nitpick," "undermine," or "get their hooks into" men (20, 22, 66, 150). At one point, Phil demands of Donna, "What are you, a chair? . . . Don't you have any self-respect?" (57).

Audiences of *Hurlyburly* have been less disturbed by the verbal barbs directed against women, however, than by their treatment as willing sexual and emotional commodities. All three females—Donna, Darlene, and Bonnie—seem embarrassingly available for the men's sexual gratification, only occasionally raising objections to egregious male behavior. Summoned by Eddie with no clear indication of her "purpose" (servicing Phil's sexual and psychological needs), Bonnie raises modest objections: "Is this particular guy just being ceremonial here with me, Eddie, or does he want to dick me?" (95). Only after Phil has pushed her out of her own moving car does Bonnie seriously object to the outrageous affronts to her dignity: "See . . . I am a form of human being, just like any other" (111). Throughout the scene, Eddie worries primarily about Phil's fragile emotional state, as he assumes that Bonnie is available for any man on demand and therefore has, at best, only modest grounds for complaint: "Don't you fuck everybody you meet?" (112).

At the same time, much of the play is deliciously comic, attacking fundamentally sexist attitudes in contemporary American males, whom Rabe pillories in a powerful deconstruction of male fantasy of the eternally available woman. Both Donna and Bonnie exhibit a conspicuous, highly stylized willingness to be passed from one man to another without discrimination in either desire or result: both products, and victims, of conventional masculine degradation of women. Elsewhere, misogynist barbs arise out of contexts of male bravado, exaggeration, and myth-making, all clearly intended as satire.

The quintessence of male comedy occurs at the end of Act II, as the four men hold forth about the delicate presence of Phil's infant daughter:

> EDDIE: This really makes me hate my ex-wife . . . I mean, really hate my ex-wife.
> ARTIE: And this little innocent thing here, this sweet little innocent thing is a broad of the future.
> MICKEY: Hard to believe, huh?
> EDDIE: Awesome.
> ARTIE: Depressing. (122)

Here, Rabe takes deliberate aim at male attitudes more exaggerated and stylized than in Mamet, where the authorial perspective less clearly distances itself from the sexist values of the characters.

While the women in *Hurlyburly* serve as convenient commodities for male reassurance and gratification, the primary emotions revolve around the feelings the men have for each other. Indeed, their relative indifference to women except for ready, socially sanctioned access to sexual intercourse is conspicuous. Eddie confesses that he hasn't "been interested in a woman for years, seriously, I have this horror show of a marriage in my background and everybody knows it . . . " (31–32). The self-dramatizing context of this confession leaves its seriousness open to question, but the pattern of tragicomic deflation is clear. Eddie's wonderfully comic half-seduction of Darlene in Act I later declines to infrequent encounters and his frank confession, in Act II, that "She doesn't love me . . . my girlfriend doesn't love me" (119). Eddie's repetitious "suck my dick" in the same sequence functions partly as displaced frustration, partly as mocking self-pity, and partly as comic mantra. Initially, Phil's response to Eddie's summoning of Bonnie for his benefit is lukewarm: "So call her" (88). In the context of male banter, Phil manages to work up a desperate, comic need for Bonnie's services, only to throw her out of the car later for no clear reason except "she smiled" (110). Apart from the off-stage pregnancy of his wife and its implied intimacy, Phil remains noticeably unsexual throughout the play. Mickey and Artie both participate in brief, essentially meaningless one-night stands on which little emotion is wasted.

The real emotion in *Hurlyburly* centers not on women but on Eddie, the status male of the group with whom the others seeks to ally and thereby define themselves. Prior to the arrival of Phil, Mickey has had the greatest claims on Eddie, who maintains early on that Mickey is "my roommate, my best friend" (31). Mickey, however, is disturbed by Eddie and Phil's developing camaraderie: "Didn't I beg you to let me have some goddamn quiet this morning? Eddie, I begged you!" (23). Mickey seeks to "prevent Phil from being taken seriously by anyone," while Eddie, in turn, begins to cast doubt on his prior relationship with Mickey: "See! And you'd know it, too, if you were my goddamn friend like you think you are" (24). As status male, Eddie has the power to dispense favors and friendship; the installation of Phil as clear "favorite" later leads Artie to lament Eddie's "delusion" about Phil and Mickey to mock them as "two guys in love" (89, 100). Phil symbolically assumes the power of Eddie's patronage in Act I by asking to sleep in his bed, to which Eddie responds, "We'll do something later" (30). Mickey senses a "conspiracy" early on, which only intensifies as the play develops. Thus Eddie's friendship with Phil unfolds in a context of considerable jealousy and discontent in the other two men.

The relationship between Eddie and Phil corresponds to a long line of masculine friendships, dating in American literature from at least Cooper's *Leatherstocking Tales*, in which a male "couple" composed of a higher-status male and lower-status male embark on a mutual adventure apart from the restrictive demands of women. Leslie Fiedler has admirably detailed the American male desire for a "holy marriage" to another man in the absence of women and sex:

> In our native mythology, the tie between male and male is not only considered innocent, it is taken for the very symbol of innocence itself; for it is imagined as the only institutional bond in a paradise world in which there are no (heterosexual) marriages or giving in marriage. (350)

Hurlyburly falls obliquely in this literary tradition, which finds its American quintessence in *Huckleberry Finn*. The friendship between Eddie and Phil enacts itself in the liminal space of the men's apartment, unmoored from the social demands of work, family, hygiene, and communal responsibility. As the status male, Eddie serves as patron/mentor of the conspicuously younger and less experienced Phil, who seems "at sea" in maneuvering his way through life. Unmarked by the more conventional signifiers of race or class difference, their relationship embodies a tense dynamic between the self-destructive male psyche out of control and the masculine desire for a validating connection with other men.

Compared with the engaging innocence of *Huckleberry Finn* and other earlier narratives, recently treatments of homosocial desire have turned conspicuously decadent. The friendship between Bob and Don, his boss and mentor in Mamet's *American Buffalo*, is marked not only by violence and the infliction of pain but also by a confused inarticulateness at odds with feeling and desire. Male friendships in the work of playwrights like Shepard, Mamet, and Rabe generally seem defensive and tired, obscured by verbal gamesmanship and studied bravado, operating in a dark, nightmarish world situated in the underbelly of American society. Only rarely does emotional seriousness peek its head above the surface, as when Mickey, the commentator in crucial sections of *Hurlyburly*, accuses Eddie and Phil of being "in a fucking frenzy" (24).

Given the socio-sexual dynamics of the past several decades, it would be easy to read such comments as signifying latent sexual jealousy on Mickey's part and unacknowledged homosexuality on the parts of Eddie and Phil. In *Hurlyburly*, the context suggests superannuated adolescence in its dotage. The setting in a "clubhouse" or "power-center" for "the bachelor life," where aging males in a "mid-life crisis" can indulge in all the accoutrements of masculine living at its unrestricted, if decadent, best; moldy food, alcohol, TV, stereo, and plenty of high-grade drugs (Löffler 24; Rabe 48, 146). While the three women arrive on call to perform sexual favors—a male fantasy of long standing—wives are banished from the scene altogether. They only appear indirectly, through the unheard voices of Agnes in Eddie's telephone conversation or through the presence of Phil's infant daughter at the end of Act II.

Otherwise, women's conventional expectations of men for companionship, fatherhood, and financial support are kept uneasily at bay offstage, allowing the apartment to remain a bastion of male freedom and desire. Unlike the picaresque partners of Cervantes and Twain, however, the males in David Rabe's adventures go nowhere, as Phil drives his car around and around: ". . . I'm spendin' days on the freeways . . . I been the last three days without seeing another form of human being in his entirety except gas station attendants" (71). Even Donna, who mimics the easy transience of the men, arrives from nowhere in particular, hitchhikes to places she doesn't know, rides for hours up and down a hotel elevator, and finally arrives back at the apartment for no clear reason. Phil's suicidal journey takes him to "a brief but unsustainable orbit . . . to land in a tree on the side of a cliff-like incline" (144). Rabe's "adventure" is one of confusion and self-destruction, of lack of direction and purpose. As Bonnie puts it, "It's a rough century all the way around . . . who does anybody know who's okay?" (110).

While the picaresque impulses of the central characters remain frustratingly unfulfilled, Eddie becomes increasingly caught up in the self-destructive excesses of Phil. The latter has in fact been married twice, his earlier marriage resulting in three children who he hasn't seen "since I went to prison": "I don't want any more kids out there, you know, rollin' around their beds at night with this sick fucking hatred of me. I can't stand it" (65). The friendship between Eddie and Phil, like other male partnerships in the American novel tradition, seems to thrive on social inequality. Eddie comes across as noticeably more nature and sophisticated than Phil, a suitable mentor for a man who has somehow destroyed two marriages and served time in jail, who moves through life in a "useless fucking orbit" (80). Phil values Eddie's talent for proffering advice: "This is our friendship—this conversation—these very exchanges. We are in our friendship. What could be more important?" (68).

Against this foundation of struggle for masculine validation and affection, overt sexuality in the play is expressed through females serving as "coins of the realm"—tokens of displaced intimacy exchanged among the men. All three women become involved in sexual, if not necessarily coital, ways with more than one of the four males: Donna has sex with Artie, is fondled by Mickey, and finally sleeps with Eddie; Darlene makes love with both Mickey and Eddie; and Bonnie, known to have slept with many men, is sent off to have sex with Phil and asked by Eddie to "suck his dick" (119). In addition to this ready interchange of women, largely without penalty of jealousy or undue complication, two of the men "pimp" for the others, as Eddie offers Darlene to Mickey and Bonnie to Phil, and Artie offers Donna to the other three men, having already enjoyed her himself. The men thus not only share but seek to share the women, who become communal sexual property of the *locus virilis*. Significantly, the wives remain offstage and unavailable for an exchange that serves to solidify relations among the men.

The masculine sharing of women can be said to manifest itself as displaced gratification for a more direct sexual act considered socially taboo or psychologically unacceptable. Eve Sedgwick has laid out the underlying dynamics of such sharing as it appears in English literature, whereby men obviate a forbidden intimacy between themselves by sleeping with the same woman:

> "To cuckold" is by definition a sexual act, performed on a man, by another man. Its central position . . . emphasizes heterosexual love chiefly as a strategy of homosocial desire . . . by which men may attempt to arrive at satisfying relationships with other men. (49–50)

Mickey's one-night stand with Darlene evidently began as an exchange for which he received permission: "the main point is, I asked" (32). In the opening scene, However, his grandiose offer to give her back to Eddie with a caveat—"maybe she's not as dynamic as you might think"—reveals no small amount of hostility and a breakdown in the relationship between the two men (34). The immediate cause is Phil, whose presence disrupts the intended intimacy between Mickey and Eddie achieved through Darlene. Periodically, Mickey's broken involvement with Darlene surfaces as a painful reminded or Eddie's vulnerability. Her reference to two rival lovers in Act III pricks Eddie into recalling, with some irritation, his own sexual rivalry with Mickey.

By contrast, the intimacy achieved when Eddie summons Bonnie to have intercourse with Phil, to soothe and refresh him, promises nothing but mutual enjoyment. Eddie even sells the arrangement ". . . you're gonna love her. This bitch who dances naked artistically in this club. That's her trip" (89). The interaction between Eddie and Darlene in Act I features hilarious use of psychobabble to mask sexual strategies, but their involvement takes a conspicuous nosedive once Phil returns to his wife Suzie, a decision Eddie opposes as "carnage . . . gore on the highway . . . insane . . . fucking nuts" (66–67). In Act II, Eddie confesses to Bonnie that Darlene "doesn't love me" (119), and by Act III, Darlene complains about their difficulty connecting:

> I don't think there's a lot more we ought to, with any, you know, honesty, allow ourselves in the way of bullshit about our backgrounds to exonerate what is out just plain mean behavior to one another. (129)

The problem arises from Eddie's preoccupation with the missing Phil, for whom he wants to "just hang around a little in case he calls." Darlene serves as the primary means through which the two men solidify their masculine intimacy; once their friendship falters, the relationship with her cannot be maintained.

Like Darlene, Mickey feels increasingly detached from and frustrated with Eddie's behavior: "Could this be destiny in fact at work, Artie, and we are witnessing it?—the pattern in the randomness, so that we see it . . . from this apparent mess, two guys fall in love" (89). His real motive—to displace Phil as favorite and return to Eddie's singular graces—becomes clearer in Act III, Scene 3, when the men return from Phil's funeral. After Artie has headed home to sleep, Mickey crosses "*behind Eddie, pats him on the back,*" and asks, "How you doin' Edward?" The formality of his address is striking as is the ferocity of Eddie's subsequent rejection of Mickey's attempt at reinstatement: "Fuck you about him, Mickey . . . I mean, where do you get the goddamn scorn to speak his name . . . And you never loved him either" (151). Disgusted, Mickey departs in defeat:

EDDIE: you don't have any feelings at all.
MICKEY: I don't have your feelings, Eddie; that's all. I have my own. They get me by.
EDDIE: So what kind of friendship is this?
MICKEY: Adequate. Good night. (152)

This final scene is conspicuous for the difficulty all the characters have in naming the source of Eddie's grief. After a series of outpourings that prompts Mickey to call Eddie "a mess," Mickey utters an astonishingly misdirected opinion: "I mean, to whatever extent THIS FUCKING TORMENT OF YOURS is over whatshername, Darlene, believe me, she isn't worth it" (152). Darlene's name has not been mentioned once in the prior dialogue, and her name promptly disappears again in the speech following. Later, as Eddie rails against Johnny Carson, the untouchable icon on inanimate TV, he can only try, unsuccessfully, to make a morbid joke about a guy who died, and astronaut who "went around the moon and ended up in Congress and had surgery for a malignancy in his nose, then passed away six months later" (154). Only in the presence of Donna can he begin to voice his pain by describing the lone singer at the funeral:

> But then this guy from way in the back of the church would sing, and you couldn't hear the words even, just this high, beautiful, sad sound, this human sound, and we would all start to cry along with him. (*He gasps, tries to breathe*). (159)

This is as close as Eddie comes to communicating his sadness, but Donna can only respond by redirecting the conversation toward the geographic origins of her attire, which are, in any case, false. Having found no sympathetic outlet for his grief, Eddie lies down in Donna's arms—symbolically, without any sexual motives—in a final desperate attempt at human connection.

Thus the quest for close male friendship ends in failure and, even worse, in Eddie's inability to find anyone to share or even listen to his lament. A significant difficulty in communicating underlies the remarkable welter of words in this play, as the characters themselves don't understand what they are saying, let alone what they mean to say:

MICKEY: I know what you think you're saying, but you're not saying it.
EDDIE: I do. I do. I know what I'm saying. I don't know what I mean, but I know what I'm saying. Is that what you mean? (150)

The self-protectively distant Mickey declares his friendship with Eddie "adequate," departing with a final outburst of sarcasm: "Wait up for Phil, why don't you? Wouldn't that be great if Phil came by? To keep you company. I'm sure he will. He always did" (153). But Eddie cannot hear this outburst because he has the TV blaring, "set for life" (153). Johnny Carson cannot hear Eddie's monologue, and Donna cannot understand Eddie's tangled web of verbal associations. The resulting isolation is mitigated only by sleep and the nonverbal, impersonal sympathy of "pleasant dreams."

This collapse at the end of *Hurlyburly* represents not only the deflation of desire typical of tragicomedy but also the breakdown of patriarchal order. The comic quest of a "men's temple," where superannuated boys can play with no financial worries and no women to demand, limit, or condemn (Löffler 24), cannot forestall the insistent demands of the larger world and, ultimately, death. No mention is ever made of money or expenses, and work responsibilities play a decidedly limited role in this drama of male irresponsibility. Although Artie is said to have a career and attend meetings, Phil's professional potential seems distinctly limited, and Eddie's indifference to a required meeting in Act I indicates a cavalier attitude, at best, towards the demands of work. Most of the dramatic action takes place at night, without the restrictions of work-a-day reality. In both Act I scenes that take place during the day, characters lounge, take drugs, watch TV, and otherwise idle away their time. To the extent that work emerges as a subsidiary theme, it is summarily dismissed as corrupt and silly. Two major bosses are derided as "scumbag faggot who likes to jerk tough guys like you around" and a "known anaconda" (28, 42). Both TV and film are denigrated as "total shit," as Eddie includes himself with "every other whore in this town" (29, 30), recalling Mamet's Fox and Gould in *Speed-the-Plow*. Eddie and Phil revel in frequent orgies of obliteration, which, under normal circumstances, would torpedo any career chances.

Rabe's play can be said to operate outside the strictures of work, career, money, and family, not unlike the fabled journey on the raft by Twain's famous duo. But the comic premise, the desire for escape and adventure, is not realized, leading *Hurlyburly* toward its essentially tragic conclusion. Rabe's play is not a "confused comedy," as Beaufort would have it, but a tragicomedy of the central self-defeating male fantasy of our time. The comic elements arise from both the extremity of the men's situation—like that in Neil Simon's *Odd Couple*, adrift from the social moorings of wives and families—and from the blatant exaggerations and half-truths uttered in an atmosphere of ritualized linguistic license. Much of the play delightfully parodies an extreme form of rootlessness, addiction, and chauvinism current in masculine mythology since the rise of feminism. The seriousness of Phil's decline into suicide, however, signals both the breakdown of male friendship as a viable bond that can be sustained either apart from or in opposition to women, and the silencing of the need for male intimacy which has come to be seen as either "debased" (i.e., homosexual) or impossible. That the central characters view work as a "systematic scam" indicates their alienation from the previously cohesive patriarchal order, which has so broken down that men cannot help or mentor each other, but instead use or undermine other males to advance themselves in that Eddie calls the "reptilian hall of Hollywood fucking hall of fame" (43).

Unlike the principal characters in *Sexual Perversity in Chicago*, *American Buffalo*, and *Speed-the-Plow*, Rabe's male "couple" is not reunited at the end of *Hurlyburly*. Mickey does not represent an adequate replacement for the lost Phil, and Donna only offers momentary solace for a man many years her elder. Eddie's descent into inexpressible isolation represents, on one level, the kind of masculine grief which Robert Bly attributes to the industrial displacement of the father as a significant force in the upbringing of young men. Attempting to fill the psychological gap, adult males seek other compensations to counteract an essential isolation they have difficulty even naming. Like the plays of Mamet and Shepard, Rabe's anatomized the masculine sense of loss in recent decades—of the father (*Sticks and Bones*) as of the friend or brother (*Streamers*). Underneath a shrewdly comic exterior, Rabe's *Hurlyburly* provides an even more extreme and elegiac variation on this theme of the American male losing an intimacy he knows not how to articulate. More than *Streamers*, with its multivalent plot, the later play focuses on the primary relationship between Eddie and Phil and the consequences of its demise on the surrounding social fabric.

The atmosphere of *Hurlyburly* is one of exuberant decadence, confusion, and pain, accompanied by an inability to define and come to terms with experience. What differentiates Rabe's articulation of the homosocial quest is his successful reliance on comedy and satire, both realized and half-realized, as a means of revealing the dynamics of male intimacy and of masking the implications. Unlike Shepard and Mamet, whose work *Hurlyburly* mimics and parodies with gleeful abandon (Mickey blowing smoke into Donna's mouth, Eddie and Mickey's sex-conquest stories), Rabe consistently relies on crisply articulated satire as an important component of his playwriting repertoire. His women, while oppressed by the males on stage, nonetheless voice their own desires: ". . . you should certainly be told that in my opinion you are totally, one hundred percent, you know, with your head up your ass about me" (Darlene in Act II, 111). The "gender gap" which so concerned Frank

Rich manifests itself in the men's "archaic sexual attitudes' (B4), while Rabe's satire points at something beyond: a genuine friendship lost, a potential sharing with women on something other than a sexual basis, with need finally exposed and acknowledged.

Viewed in a somewhat broader context, *Hurlyburly* represents yet another recent articulation of misguided initiation. According to Raphael, the contemporary absence of socially sanctioned rituals to demarcate the passage from boyhood to the more responsible arena of adult masculinity results in "freestyle variations" and "makeshift males' (50, 190). Not surprisingly, this often leads to misdirected violence and fails to prepare males psychologically for their essential place in society. In *Hurlyburly*, middle-aged males who still have not come to grips with their passage into manhood attempt to enact retrograde fantasies that can no more than halfway satisfy their cravings for escape, adventure, and fulfillment. In the absence of any clear mentoring by older males—who, like Artie, are ridiculed for devotion and hard work—the men in this play remain fundamentally unable to direct their energies constructively into work, marriage, family, or society.

Works Cited

Barnes, Clive. "Rabe's *Hurlyburly* Pins Hollywood to the Wall." *New York Post* 22 June 1984: 43.

Beaufort, John. "*Hurlyburly* Is Confused Comedy." *Christian Science Monitor* 3 July 1984: 27.

Bly, Robert. "A Gathering of Men." With Bill Moyers. PBS Interview. WILL, Champagne-Urbana. 8 Jan. 1990.

Fiedler, Leslie. *Love and Death in the American Novel.* New York: Stein and Day, 1966.

Kolin, Philip. *David Rabe: A Stage History and A Primary and Secondary Bibliography.* New York: Garland, 1988.

Löffler, Sigrid. "Das herrliche Geschlecht." *Die Zeit* 27 April 1990: 24.

Mamet, David. *American Buffalo.* New York: Grove, 1976.

——. *Sexual Perversity in Chicago. With The Duck Variations.* New York; Grove, 1981.

——. *Speed-the-Plow.* New York; Grove, 1987.

Rabe, David. *Hurlyburly.* New York: Grove, 1985.

——. *In the Boom Boom Room.* New York: Knopf, 1975.

——. *Sticks and Bones. In The Basic Training of Pavlo Hummel and Sticks and Bones.* New York: Viking, 1976.

——. *Streamers.* New York: Knopf, 1977.

Raphael, Ray. *The Man from the Boys: Rites of Passage in Male America.* Lincoln: U of Nebraska P, 1989.

Rich, Frank. "Theatre's Gender Gap Is a Chasm." *New York Times* 30 Sept. 1984: B1, 4.

Sedgwick, Eve Kosofsky. *Between Men: English Literature and Male Homosexual Desire.* New York; Columbia UP, 1985.

Chapter Thirteen

Between Two Worlds: Elmer Rice Chairs the Thirties Debate

Barry Witham

In one of the most celebrated cases of the Cold War, Alger Hiss was sentenced to prison in 1950 for committing perjury in his testimony regarding the Communist Party before the United States Congress. Hiss, who has maintained his innocence for the past half century, became a symbol for the Cold War years in the United States much as Sacco and Vanzetti had become a symbol for the anti-foreign hysteria of a previous decade. Hiss argued eloquently (*In the Court of Public Opinion*, 1957) for a frame-up engineered by his nemesis, Whittaker Chambers, but his equally eloquent accusers—including the future president of the United States, Richard Nixon—maintained that Hiss was guilty.

Following the "conclusion" of the Cold War, the Hiss hunters and defenders refueled their fight with both sides convinced that the newly accessible files of the KGB and other agencies would provide evidence for their long debated charges. Both sides found additional support, and the enigma of the case continues. In a 1993 issue of the *National Review*, "new" information relating to Hiss's guilt was trumpeted, and later that year, an interrogation document from the Hungarian Secret Police set off a furious debate in the pages of the *New Republic*, *Nation*, and *Commentary*, illustrating perhaps the futility of ever resolving the conflict.[1]

The fascination with the Hiss case persists in the United States because it is one of the most visible landmarks in the Capitalist/Communist ideological war which historian Irving Howe has called the most fundamental issue of the twentieth century (qtd. in Kakutani C21). The war was played out on various fields: the Palmer raids, labor battles, the HUAC hearings, the Lincoln Brigade, Scottsboro, etc. And it led to huge personal battles which reduced the conflict to a size that many Americans could understand: Lillian Hellman and Mary McCarthy, Elia Kazan and Arthur Miller, Dave Beck and Harry Bridges.[2]

The theatre in the United States participated in this conflict of course, sometimes overtly as in the productions of the New Playwrights Theatre in the twenties and sometimes more covertly as in Arthur Miller's political allegory about witch trials in Salem, Massachusetts. Lillian Hellman's *Watch on the Rhine* (1941) repudiated isolationism and argued for a Popular Front alliance against Nazi Germany. And Robert Sherwood's *There Shall Be No Night* (1940) rejected his long articulated and passionate isolationism in favor of opposing the Russian invasion of Finland.

There are countless other examples and no need to belabor the point here, but what is particularly fascinating is how the reexamination of the Cold War may affect critical and historical views of the theatre during and before these turbulent years. As new histories and memoirs of the American Communist Party appear, it is clear that aesthetic doctrine and practice were important to the Comintern and that American liberals and progressives often supported Soviet policy while never becoming members of the party.[3] It is especially intriguing to recall how the American playwright Elmer Rice positioned himself in the Socialist discourse and how he tried—particularly in his 1934 production of *Between Two Worlds*—to actually chair the debate between Capitalism and Communism, to present in effect both sides of the question and see what conclusions might be drawn. That debate—and its subsequent controversy among theatre critics—became so heated that Rice abandoned the Broadway stage for nearly three years at the height of his career.

Rice was not a minor figure. One of America's most-produced dramatists, his plays ranged across a landscape from the naturalistic *Street Scene* (1929) to the experimental and expressionistic *Adding Machine* (1923) and included popular courtroom melodramas and extended paeans and critiques of the American way of life. He also directed many of his own works, owned a Broadway theatre and was Hallie Flanagan's first choice to direct the important New York unit of the Federal Theatre Project in 1935. He promoted the career of the woman scene designer, Aline Bernstein, subsidized lagging productions with his own money and was a co-founder of the important Playwrights Company in 1938. He was also passionate about civil rights, deeply opposed to censorship of any kind and an active member of the American Civil Liberties Union.

By the early 1930s, Rice, like so many of his colleagues, was deeply perplexed by the implications of the Wall Street collapse and the apparent failure of the Capitalist system. His 1933 production of *We, the People* is a virtual catalogue of American ills churned out of the Depression: closed factories, lost jobs, labor conflict, police injustice and homicide. A proclaimed Socialist, Rice was also deeply intrigued by the emerging political experiment in the Soviet Union where the apparent economic success of the first Five-Year Plan contrasted vividly with the economic despair in his own country.

Thus in 1932, Rice, like other Americans before and after—John Reed, Lincoln Steffens, Hallie Flanagan, etc.—set sail for Russia determined to see the aftermath of the revolution first hand. Although he would later claim little sympathy for the notion of a dictatorship of the proletariat, Rice was enormously moved by the experience, by the sheer audacity and idealism of transforming an entire society. Over a ten-week period, Rice and his son, Robert, visited Moscow and Leningrad as well as a variety of other cities and villages. The record of the trip—which was to become significant in his dramaturgy—is preserved in the pages of Rice's autobiography, *Minority Report,* which was published in 1963. It is a fascinating account, rich in detail about the theatre, their travels, and philosophical debates with Intourist guides. The purpose of this paper is to examine briefly that narrative and then discuss how it resonates in Rice's dramaturgy, particularly in his ill-fated 1934 production of *Between Two Worlds.*

Rice appears to have two major projects in his published record. First, he wants to dispel some "myths" about the Soviet system. This was a popular strategy for American intellectuals in the thirties because information was so conflicting and confusing. As the angst of the Show Trials and the discrediting of Trotsky grew, many Americans were unable to distinguish between the actual events and the Stalinist propaganda. So that, for example, there is this description of Rice's visit to a women's prison:

> The prison was organized as a shawl manufactory. The women worked in large, airy rooms equipped with radios; they were locked up only at night. We saw the nursery and playroom for the inmates children, the "club" where movies were shown, and the schoolroom. By the time a prisoner was discharged, she was literate, had been taught a trade, and was eligible for trade union membership, which meant job security. (293–94)

Of living conditions Rice notes that they visited an apartment house "which though jerry built, was up to date. Each two room unit had cooking facilities; there was at least one bathroom on each floor. On the ground floor was a large auditorium suitable for concerts, movies, and meetings" (293). And of religion: "After all that I had heard about suppression . . . I was amazed to find the church packed to the point of suffocation" (302). Of course, he was not blind to more troubling aspects and interrogated his hosts about censorship, civil liberties, and political "crimes." But he also stresses the "my strictures, though sharply combated, were not resented; I spoke my mind freely but was never chided for doing so" (297).

Second, Rice spends a considerable amount of time comparing the American and Soviet systems in a balanced way which is apparently intended to create a sense of objective analysis. Several of these moments are quoted here to give a sense of his "project" and to suggest how he returns this "reading" in *Between Two Worlds*.

On the simplicity of divorce in Russia Rice notes that "it was mechanical and cold-blooded, yet more realistic and honest than the collusion, perjury and legal hypocrisy that characterize American divorce procedures" (293). Of the charge that Russians only allow visitors to see certain things, he writes, "Of course we do not go out of our way to show foreigners our Skid Rows, segregated schools, tenant farms and death houses" (292). On the Soviet concern for prison rehabilitation: "In short, the emphasis was upon rehabilitation rather than upon punishment, a policy for whose advocacy my friend Judge Ben Lindsey of Denver had been denounced as an impractical idealist and a softy" (294). And of his discussions with his guide from Intourist: "We both ardently wanted a world in which peace, equal justice and security for the individual prevailed. It was about methods that we disagreed. The same may be said today of millions on both sides of the Iron Curtain." (313).

Of course the comparative "ease" with which Rice moved through the Soviet visit is important in considering his observations. After all, he was a distinguished visitor, a famous playwright and someone sympathetic to the system. And this figures into the narrative in a number of ways. At Lenin's tomb hundreds of people were waiting to get in, "But as tourists we went to the head of the line" (291). He travelled frequently by first-class rail accommodations, and on a boat trip along the Volga "our cabins were comfortable, there was a promenade deck, and a combination dining room/lounge with a sweeping view" (306). At a trial of some gypsies, "the police, assuming from our Lincoln limousines that we were important officials, opened a lane through the shouting, gesticulating crowd" (318).

This does not mean that these perks influenced Rice's perceptions unduly, because there were many times when he had to travel in uncomfortable circumstances and endure bad food and drink. But at the same time his pilgrimage was certainly a privileged passage in the classless society.

And his final estimation? Although he sees much that he admires, Rice is cautious about censorship, dogmatism, and the impression that civil rights are not primary in an "evolving" society. In an interesting passage he compares the Soviet system to organized religion and concluded that "it was as indifferent to the true principles of socialism as many religious bodies were to the true principles of Christianity" (305).

Still the trip had a huge impact on him and his need to see what was good and positive in the society. In a vivid paragraph Rice reveals the depths to which the Russian experiment had touched him and reminds us of the idealism and enthusiasm with which so many young Americans embraced the "idea" of the Soviet Union:

> Robert and I went back to Negoreloye to meet my wife and daughter. On the trip back to Moscow, I had a strong psychological reaction. My wife was, of course, full of news about the activities and personal problems of our friends in America, in which, ordinarily, I would have been greatly interested. Yet now it all seemed remote, alien and unimportant. Then it dawned upon me that during the seven weeks I had been in the Soviet Union, my attention, thoughts and conversation had centered almost entirely upon social, cultural and political matters. Personalities and the private concerns of individuals had been completely overshadowed by broad social movements and conflicting philosophies. It took a great deal of effort to get back into the old orbit. (318)

That orbit included the theatre and an active confrontation with the ills that confronted America in the Depression-driven days of 1932. Roosevelt was running for president against the incumbent, Herbert Hoover, and the Communist Party was presenting a slate of William Z. Foster and the black union leader James Ford. Although Rice claimed little patience with the American Communist Party and felt that the dictatorship of the proletariat was "nonsense" (328), he did vote for them rather than Norman Thomas's Socialist Party. Times were desperate and Rice believed that a meaningful protest was better than a vote for any of the traditional parties' strategies.

His European journey and contemporary American politics led to three plays, the first of which, *We, the People*, opened in 1933 to controversial notices and audience enthusiasm. Set in America, the play follows the fortunes of a representative group of citizens as the Depression destroys their lives. And while Rice was probably not a member of the Communist Party, *We, the People* is in some ways a model of "third period" doctrine which the Comintern had imposed on CPUSA in 1933. Under this directive, Capitalism was supposedly entering its notorious third period of existence, and the obligation of party artists was to show it in as poor a light as possible. Rice targets every painful aspect of Depression-ridden America as his young, middle-class hero is finally radicalized by the injustices of Capitalism. It is a powerful indictment of American politics, and audiences greeted it with cheers and boos depending upon their political beliefs.

Brooks Atkinson observed that if it comes to "a question of choices, Mr. Rice is a revolutionary" (*New York Times* 23 Jan. 1933).

In 1934 Rice composed *Judgement Day*, a passionate anti-fascist courtroom melodrama based on the Nazi Leipzig trial of Communists charged with the Reichstag fire. Although the oppressors in the play are identified as "Slavs" rather than Germans and the play is set in an imaginary Balkan country, it is clear that the regime and the characters are based on Nazi models. Rice travelled through Berlin on his way home from Moscow and was disturbed by the gathering war clouds there. In *Minority Report*, he mentions that specific characters in *Judgement Day* were based on Hitler and Goering (334). It is also interesting that this anti-fascist play appeared at a time when the Comintern was beginning its Popular Front campaign to turn away from heavy indictments of Capitalism in favor of vilifying Fascism, which was the backbone of most party doctrine until the Stalin-Hitler pact in 1939.

The reviews of *Judgement Day* were vociferous and mixed, praising Rice for his passion but condemning his melodrama and histrionics. He became increasingly disturbed about the power of the newspaper critics and questioned their qualifications and function. At night he witnessed enthusiastic responses—pro and con—to *Judgement Day*, but audiences remained small. Rice contributed his own money to keep the play running and grumbled about the hostility of the press. This chafed his sense of fairness and prepared him for the rupture that occurred after the production of *Between Two Worlds*.

Between Two Worlds (1934) was a conscious attempt on Rice's part to dramatize the Soviet and American systems. He believed that such an examination would allow people to evaluate the strengths and weaknesses and thus avoid the dogmatism and chauvinism that often characterized such discourse. While we cannot know what private dreams Rice may have had for the success of the production, it is clear that he undertook it with a passionate desire to address questions which were being fiercely debated in American politics and which were frequently leading to hysterical charges of "fellow travelling" and traitorous behavior.

In order to underscore the play's title, Rice set the action aboard an ocean-going liner, the SS *Farragut*, on an Atlantic crossing from New York to Cherbourg. The design by Aline Bernstein depicts the two upper decks of the ship along with a veranda café and allows for a variety of simultaneous scenes as well as large and small group arrangements. The set was both functionally imaginative and reflective of a privileged existence where the passengers are waited upon by busy servants. More than one critic referred to the play as "Ship Scene" because it evoked the busy shipboard life in the same manner that Rice's *Street Scene* had evoked urban existence in New York.

The principal action of the play is a love triangle among a young socialite (Margaret) and two suitors. Edward is a wealthy New York public relations type with reservations about the course of American capitalism, and Kovolev is a Bolshevik film director who is returning to the Soviet Union after a sojourn in Hollywood. Each of the suitors causes Margaret to re-evaluate her own goals and motives, thus helping to effect the resolution of the piece. There are also a variety of subplots, including the revelation that Kovolev was responsible for the deaths of the family of a "White" Russian, Princess Golytsin, who is also a passenger on the crossing. There are forty-two characters in the play, and the action takes place over a week's time.

One of Rice's primary strategies is to present Kovolev in a "balanced" manner. Thus early in the play we are drawn to him because he speaks to, and is subsequently kind to, the black maid (Rose) of a decadent film star. Kovolev's kindness to her not only resonates with the widely publicized civil rights planks of the American Communist Party but stands in stark contrast to the way that most of the white people treat her. However, we also see the brutal side of the Russian revolutionary when he strikes the Princess and shows no remorse in admitting to having ordered her family's deaths. At moments like this he seems firmly entrenched in the ideology of class justice and the superiority of his party doctrine.

Rice teases out this balanced portrait through the play much as he does in his account of his Soviet trip. Kovolev does not indulge in the drinking bouts which characterize much of the shipboard behavior, but his is boorish and rude with little provocation. He claims not to be moved by the sentimentality of moonlight and romance but admits to Margaret that the jazz does stimulate him sexually.

And it is with his seduction of Margaret that Rice attempts to corner the elusive Bolshevik and reach some conclusions in this ocean-going ideological debate. Margaret shares many of the excesses and contradictions of her class and race. She is waited on by a maid, doted on by a wealthy family, has no idea how many dresses she owns, and seems destined to a privileged life. She has a college education but apparently few analytical skills; she recognizes the plight of the poor but has no real idea of what she might do about it. She is engaged to a man for whom she seems to have little interest but who is socially right for her.

However, unlike other passengers on the SS *Farragut*, Margaret comes to recognize the limitation of her world view, and she is earnest in trying to understand the Bolshevik critique of her privileged position. She also is challenged by Kovolev to confront her womanhood and their attraction to each other:

> This is a biological impulse over which we have no control. I am a man and you are a woman and it is a law of nature that men and women shall be attracted to each other. When this impulse seizes us we do not stop to reason about it. We act according to our sense and desire. But you are afraid of even this. You do not have even the courage to fulfill your biological function. (259)

Kovolev's seduction is successful, but its aftermath, in which both he and Margaret attempt to deal with this experience, allows Rice to focus on his final response. Kovolev tries to pass off the fact of their evening together as just that—a one-time thing. Margaret, however, confronts him with the fact of his having manipulated her and urges in him a recognition of decency in behavior towards other human beings. And it is this plea for decency which seems to be at the heart of Rice's passion and the distinguishing trope between the two systems. Ultimately, Margaret prevails although Rice gives Kovolev a final speech which justifies his behavior and illuminates the harshness of the Soviet experiment.

> MARGARET: You hurt me terribly.
> KOVOLEV: Yes, I know that. I was thinking about it afterwards. And I said to myself: "Why?" I will give you an explanation, but I'm not sure it is the correct one. Life in Russia is very difficult, very severe. We have been fighting now, for nearly twenty years: the war, the revolution, the civil war and now the counter revolutionists and the wreckers. Everything is really very difficult. We have much to do, very many obstacles to overcome. We have many powerful enemies, both without and within. The revolution is not yet entirely won. And so each of us is a fighter, a soldier. We have suffered much; we are not willing to give up what we fought for. It makes us determined. It makes us fierce. We cannot allow ourselves to deviate. We cannot afford to become weak. (298)

They part, both changed by the seeming wisdom of Margaret's appeal to decency and respect. In his attempt to be fair, however, Rice cannot avoid one final tribute to Kovolev. As he is about to disembark he re-encounters the black maid, Rose, who thanks him for his earlier kindness. He addresses her as "comrade" as the play ends.

Kovolev is modeled very much on the idea of the new Soviet man that Rice sympathizes with in his memoirs, and *Between Two Worlds* works hard to present a balanced view of the political debate. Many of Rice's Americans are boorish, corrupt, impotent, and crude. But with Margaret the author finally comes down on the side of Capitalism. With all its faults, it still provides a place for civility, decency, and respect for individual rights. He will not concede—even with his admiration for the Soviet system—what the *Daily Worker* was quick to point out: "He [Rice] doesn't stop to consider that these qualities are practically nonexistent in a world in which the philosophy of dog eat dog prevails" (30 Oct 1934).

Between Two Worlds arrived in New York at a propitious moment. The Comintern was instructing the American Communist Party to moderate its anti-Capitalistic stance in favor of a more balanced view that could achieve the Popular Front. Rice had cast the magnetic Joseph Schildkraut as Kovolev and the talented and attractive Rachel Hartzell as Margaret. And audiences were aware of the controversial nature of Rice's two previous productions. In spite of some ideological reservations, the *Daily Worker* called *Between Two Worlds* his finest play to date, "faultlessly cast, beautifully acted and smoothly directed, Mr. Rice has never yet written so incisively, with such fresh observation, nor drawn his characters so fully in all their facets" (30 Oct 1934).

The Capitalist papers were less impressed. While Rice had hoped that the play would suggest "the possibility of a compromise between the apparently irreconcilable extremes" (341), some critics saw only "red." Richard Lockridge in the *Sun* defined a "fellow traveller" and then announced to his readers that "the Communists consider Elmer Rice to be one" (26 Oct. 1934). Burns Mantle opined that he met "so few bolsheviks" that he wouldn't know how to judge Mr. Schildkraut (*Daily News* 26 Oct. 1934). John Mason Brown decided that "Americans will apparently lead better lives if they see pink and not red" (*Evening Post* 26 Oct. 1934). And Robert Garland recognized the strategy of "Communist pros and cons" but concluded that "I haven't the least idea what Mr. Rice is getting at" (*World Telegram* 26 Oct. 1934).

While some critics did grasp the intent and praised the result—Brooks Atkinson, for example—the general response was indifference and confusion. And some was just silly. In the *New York American*, Gilbert Gabriel confided that "upon the testimony of at least two women in the audience Joseph Schildkraut kisses as heroically as he declaims" (26 Oct 1934). Rice was furious. *Between Two Worlds* sank with almost no trace. It ran for thirty-two performances.

Shortly after the play opened, Rice spoke to a class at Columbia University and denounced the critics. He complained about the power that they exercised in the American theatre and in a pique of anger threatened to resign from the stage. The speech was reported in the press, and the resulting uproar in the New York papers—where he was chided for whining rather than expressing a sincere complaint—further provoked him. On November 11, 1934, he wrote a farewell speech and made good on his threat. Stung by the reception of *Between Two Worlds*, Rice attacked the Broadway stage, where "as everywhere in our civilization, the profit system stifles the creative impulse . . . controlled by businessmen, real estate operators and entrepreneurs whose chief interest is to capitalize creative talents . . . and turn them into dollars and cents" (*New York Times* 11 Nov. 1934). But he reserved his greatest scorn for theatre critics whom he called the "bulwarks of commercial theatre" and characterized them as men "without intellect, perception, sensitivity or background who pander to the taste of the bored, insensitive and complacent" (*New York Times* 11 Nov. 1934). Rice, one of America's most prolific writers, abandoned the theatre for three years. His serious attempt to examine in dramatic form the ideological war that was threatening to divide the country was taken seriously only by the *Daily Worker*, further tarring him with a red brush.

Rice eventually came back to Broadway with *American Landscape* (1938), in which he continued the attack on fascism and was effusive about American democracy. He even invoked ghostly characters from the past to remind his audience of the power and potential of the United States. Harriet Beecher Stowe and soldiers from previous wars people the stage and stir patriotic sensibilities. *Between Two Worlds* was forgotten, even by its author. In his thick autobiography of some 475 pages, Rice granted it seven lines. He pronounced it a failure in every way.

Today, however, as revisionist historians take a new look at those long years leading up to and away from the Cold War, it may be helpful for theatre scholars to review their conceptions and preconceptions about that time, especially in view of the plays and companies that have been canonized and passed along for posterity. Have we in the United States ignored the drama of the infamous "third period" such as Paul Sifton's *The Belt* or Rice's *We, the People* because critics then and some historians later were uncomfortable with their anti-Capitalistic critique or with Stalin's manipulation of the Comintern and the American Communist Party? Have we reserved the bulk of our critical writing for those plays which passed the magical 100-performance marker and thus deprived students of a broader picture of our cultural history? And more importantly, in the paranoia of the red-baiting years, with their attendant name calling, have we failed to take into account the very real Communist influences which infused and invigorated the American theatre? Elmer Rice was almost certainly not a member of the party, but the three plays that he wrote and produced after his trip to Russia in 1932 substantially reflect Comintern policy in the shift from "third period" to the Popular Front. And even though he considered his attempt to chair the Communist debate in *Between Two Worlds* a failure, the play makes vivid that "foreign country" that we call "the thirties."

Notes

1 See Cohen, Tanenhaus, Schmidt, and Klingsberg.

2 Soviet spy master Pavel Sudoplatov has recently stirred this pot again with charges that J. Robert Openheimer was indeed a valuable agent and that the Rosenbergs were idealistic, minor figures in acquiring the atom bomb secrets.

3 See, for example, Klehr and Haynes.

Works Cited

Atkinson, Brooks. "Review: *We, the People.*" *New York Times* 23 January 1933.
Brown, John Mason. "Review: *Between Two Worlds.*" *New York Evening Post* 26 October 1934.
Cohen, Jacob. "Innocent After All?" *National Review*, 18 January 1993, 26–33
Gabriel, Gilbert. "Review: *Between Two Worlds.*" *New York American* 26 October 1934.
Garland, Robert. "Review: *Between Two Worlds.*" *World Telegram* 26 October 1934.
Hiss, Alger. *In the Court of Public Opinion*. New York: Knopf, 1957.
Kakutani, Michiko. "Hellman-McCarthy Libel Suit Stirs Old Antagonisms." *New York Times* 19 March 1980: C21.
Klehr, Harvey and Haynes, John Earl. *The American Communist Movement: Storming Heaven Itself*, New York: Twayne, 1992.
Klingsberg, Ethan. "Case Closed on Alger Hiss," *Nation*, 8 November 1993, 528–32.
Lockridge, Richard. "Review: *Between Two Worlds.*" *New York Sun* 26 October 1934.
Mantle, Burns. "Review: *Between Two Worlds.*" *New York Daily News* 26 October 1934.
"Review: *Between Two Worlds.*" *Daily Worker* 30 October 1934.
Rice, Elmer. *Between Two Worlds*. New York: Coward McCann, 1935.
——. "Farewell Speech." *New York Times* 11 November 1934.
——. *Minority Report*. New York: Harper, 1963.
Schmidt, Maria. "The Hiss Dossier," *The New Republic*, 8 November 1993, 17–18
Sudoplatov, Pavel. *Special Tasks*. Boston: Little, Brown, 1994.
Tanenhaus, Sam. "Hiss, Guilty as Charged," *Commentary*, July, 1993, 2

Chapter Fourteen

He's Still Falling: Wallace Shawn's Problem of Morality

Gaylord Brewer

Critics are radically divided over the merit of Wallace Shawn's work. John Simon attacks *Aunt Dan and Lemon* as offending "against taste, intelligence, and basic hygiene as it waits for someone to step on it and put it and its captive audience . . . out of their misery" ("Real Lemon" 129). Jack Kroll, a Shawn enthusiast, insists the playwright is "extraordinary . . . a voice to rank with David Mamet and Sam Shepard" and of the three "is the most disturbing to our cozy assumptions." *Aunt Dan and Lemon*, he continues, is full of "savage, sorrowing humor . . . how decent, cultivated people rationalize corruption, murder, and terror" ("That Nice Mr. Hitler" 90). To an earlier Shawn work Simon also responds venomously, that "nothing in the world could save *Marie and Bruce*. . . . The play is performed without intermission or any other mercy, and could have been worse only with Shawn in it" ("Harold and Maude" 85–86). Kroll counters that the play "sees, hears, smells and tells more about the way we really live now than any American play in years" and describes its author as "one of the most deeply seeing, sharply writing playwrights we have" ("I Love You" 117). Such opposed responses are typical; one reacts to Shaw with either a conspicuously personal abhorrence or an endorsement of almost religious ferocity. Actor-activist Jim Luken, for example, embraces the playwright's most recent effort, *The Fever*, as "social gospel" (Warrick B1) and has accepted its postscript invitation to perform the monologue in living rooms of acquaintances, penetrating the very privileged class the play criticizes. Shawn's work consistently confronts and, more disturbing, by implication accuses its audience of social and political culpability. He is by profession, writes Ross Wetzsteon, "a passionate provocateur" (36).

One remarkable effect of Shawn's plays is that, despite a decisive change of focus, purpose, and temperament in recent works, they have continued, indeed with increased force, to generate controversy. Earlier offerings examine through ruthless snapshots the individual exposed to hostile social circumstances. The cast is often large: The La Mama production of *The Hotel Play*, "the all-time epic play" (Kroll "Cast of Thousands" 81), boasted seventy-six actors, the setting frequently a bar, party, or vacation gathering. The contents are scatological and sexually explicit. Later plays and the nature of their controversy are seemingly different. *My Dinner with André* is a necessary bridge to *Aunt Dan and Lemon* and the beginning of an interrogating introspection which culminates in *The Fever*. These three works are primarily monologues. Dramatic conflict remains in the dialogue and debate of interior voices. The plays are political in the broadest sense: human action, thought, and choice inescapably bound with a global morality. Peculiarly, Shawn's early plays tend to make public secrets of sexuality and daily deceit; the last decade's works, however, increasingly privatize public notions of self and nation.

The two types of plays are of course not as disparate as they first appear. Even Shawn's earliest work contains themes which will permeate his later drama. The author notes: "I knew—I knew—that beneath my work's primeval, hysterical facade there was a calm little writer in an armchair just waiting to burst forth . . ." (*André*, 13). Conversely, his work beginning with *My Dinner with André* recasts earlier concerns. "In our society all those most interesting things are hidden," comments the writer (Shewey and Shacter 223). His goal, the unearthing of such cultural secrets, particularly those American, has remained constant regardless of approach. Reading his early plays one is struck by the number of recurring motifs, most of which only now suggest their full implications. *Our Late Night*, Shawn's first production, is the work after which "something went wrong" with its director André Gregory. Shawn recalls, "He dropped out of the theatre" (*André*, 18). If the play was not solely responsible, it somehow crystallized for Gregory his uncertainty as to how to proceed. Clive Barnes considers *Our Late Night* "the sickest of jokes . . . it is about a party—a horrendous party" (Barnes L20+). Such epithets could be applied to all the early plays. In *The Hotel Play*, for example, one again sees the public illness and nausea commonplace in Shawn. A girl whose vacation is over laments, "I feel sick! I'm sick, sick, I'm so sick—My stomach hurts so much!" (10). A wife feels "so dizzy" (16); a young man moans "I'm really feeling sick to my stomach" (34); a psychiatrist who acquires the illness of his patients vomits when seeing an attractive woman. In *The Hotel Play*, nausea and vertigo are associated with frustrated sexuality—frequently betrayal, desertion, or a simple inability to converse. Stomach illness is bound up with a distaste for food, a further disaffection of the leisure class. "I'm so tired of eating. . . . Three meals a day, day after day . . . " (23).

The Hotel Play is a malicious work. Shawn eschews conventional plot and character development, offering instead a flow of humanity; its undisguised hatefulness undercuts a facade of vacation enjoyment. Fragile health, exposing a debilitating interior malaise, anticipates the metaphoric illness in *The Fever*. Overseeing and vaguely directing action is the clerk, the play's only continuous character. His adhesive function over diverse moments, as well as his voyeurism and detachment, identify him as a prototype of Lemon. Stage directions become significant: "From his tall chair behind the bar, the clerk can watch what's going on" (13). He presides with an odd equanimity over what the author describes as "a kind of strange dream . . . of strange human beings" (6), not unlike the dream of the mind constituting Lemon's embrace of evil. Vacationers are all in various degrees unable to escape their neuroses; pleasure comes from sadistic degradation. Through all of this, the clerk remains cryptically convivial.

Frank Rich argues that some moments of *The Hotel Play* are "too convincing and excruciating to be safely categorized under the distancing rubric of black comedy" (C3). The play is surprisingly painful, considering its sketchiness and the brief lives of its characters. Guests continually refer to each other as pigs, a dehumanization appropriate to their attempts to devour one another emotionally, tying again the themes of food, nausea, and the rotting body. This latter image is put to powerful use in *Aunt Dan and Lemon*:

> But my father was a kind of caged animal, he'd been deprived of everything that would keep him healthy. His life was unsanitary in every way. His entire environment—his cage . . . was unclean. He was never given a thorough washing. So no wonder . . . his fur was falling out, he was growing thinner every day. His teeth were rotten, his shit was rotten, and of course he stank. He stank to hell. (14–15)

This description supposes the interrelatedness of bestiality and decaying moral values. *The Hotel Play*, while lacking the later play's resonance, already addresses its cardinal themes.

Similarly, the tropical setting is important, anticipating *Summer Evening* (the first third of *A Thought in Three Parts*) and, most significantly, *The Fever*. Nearly lost amid *The Hotel Play*'s manic pace are instances of the ravaging of local culture for the casual recreation of the wealthy. Both native and visitor are exploited by faceless owner-imperialists. The clerk refuses to tell a guest the cost of his room, responding with uneasy and ominous laughter: "But well—that's the tropics, you know! Ha ha! You'd better get used to it!" (11). A moment later, his offhand explanation to another guest, concerning a lost reservation implies violent native unrest. A cavalier tone of dismissal renders the situation more troubling: "We haven't had mail service here for two years now—there's a religious dispute among the local people, you see—what a trouble for us Ha! Ha!" (11). The clerk's continually exclamatory delivery, regardless of subject, soon seems demented, even demonic. This isolated tropical paradise is the hell of other people that Sartre might appreciate. "I wish there were some dogs and cats staying in this God-damned hotel," reacts a single man. "I'm so sick of people, I could just throw up" (22). The guests are dizzy, nauseated, alternately cold and overheated, and plagued by flies "as big as birds" (21); they seem uniformly miserable. One comments: "And I thought this would be such a peaceful place! A restful vacation! Aha ha ha ha!" (21). The play's frenzied laughter grows increasingly horrifying.

Summer Evening not only resembles recent work thematically but develops Shawn's technique of narrative monologue laced with volatile dramatic fragments. This method is central to the characters of *Marie and Bruce* and later evolves into a conflicted internal voice. The setting of *Summer Evening* is immediately recognizable: "A pleasant hotel room in a foreign country" (1). In the simple trappings of such a locale, Shawn's speakers wage their inner and outer wars. Bed, night table, window, bathroom—these are the same around the world and sufficient for Shawn's basic conflicts. Only windows spoil the scene, allowing outside intrusion of poverty and torture. The dialogue in *Summer Evening* is delivered "very fast, much faster than people really speak" (31). The young couple talk at, rather than to, each other. Monologues are delivered while the other spouse is offstage; when physically onstage together, David and Sarah speak in disjointed fragments; they end by slipping into grandiose stream-of-consciousness fantasies. Such stylistic contrasts, as well as a "specter of brutal sexuality" beneath the couple's trivial dialogue (Chaillet 479), foreshadow Shawn's most cogent statement on contemporary relations, *Marie and Bruce*. David, like Bruce, is fussy, exasperatingly imperturbable, and overly intellectual. His first line, which begins the play, typically qualifies its syntax: "Well dinner was not so bad, in fact" (31). David is rigidly articulate yet crippled by uncertainty; he is determines to create an illusion of enjoyment even at the expense of truth. His complaint, the difficulty of removing "those little bones" (31) from his hare, identifies him as a pampered and aloof tourist. Sarah's first soliloquy, after her husband departs for more food, is equally revealing: "I must say sometimes I rather would like to lie in bed all day and all night and just have tea and toast and jam, if a maid would bring them, I mean" (32). Like her husband's lines, Sarah's lengthy speech illustrates the ennui of their life together, an existence of bed, service, rich foods, books, and a slow, barely endurable passage of time.

Only when the partner is out of the room does the other confess his or her need. David reveals fearful loneliness to a closed door: "Stay with me. Stay with me. Don't stop me. I love you. I—" (35). Sarah's needs are more passionate and more violent; she is the blasé young wife in search of dangers to bring herself and her husband back to life: "there's nothing, there isn't anything I wouldn't, I wouldn't, I wouldn't, I wouldn't do for pleasure. I'd stick a hot poker up my ass if I thought I would like it" (35). David and Sarah are reminiscent of Hemingway's young expatriates not only in their emptiness but in their simple, suggestive language. Sarah's unconvincing ease recalls a story such as "Hills Like White Elephants"; her indirect desperation invokes a number of doomed Hemingway couples: "Really? Really? But you see you don't need to stay awake just for me. I'm fine. I'm fine" (37). This spareness and the dark subtext of disjointed exchanges make *Summer Evening* the Shawn play most suggestive of the work of Harold Pinter. Consider David's coerced explanation of love:

> DAVID: Well it's quite like hatred—
> SARAH: Yes—
> DAVID: But slightly different—
> SARAH: Yes—
> DAVID: We don't really want to kill each other.— . . .
> SARAH: Love's not killing—
> DAVID: No.
> SARAH: Or beating?—
> DAVID: No. We want to—
> SARAH: —putting your penis in my mouth?—
> DAVID: Well yes—it could be.
> SARAH: Good. Do you love me? David?
> DAVID: Oh yes. Oh yes. (40)

The exchange ends with humorless comedy and reinitiates the violent sex fantasies which conclude the piece. Although Sarah is disgusted with her husband's coldness, her ominous repetitions and periodic explosions:—"Are you actually only a little piece of shit, who's learned how to talk about feelings?" (40)—combine with an inverted desire to be tortured to disclose a barely suppressed rage which, typical in Shawn's work, is inseparable from love.

The most significant feature of *Summer Evening* in terms of later plays is, like *The Hotel Play*, its unidentified foreign setting. Paradoxically, the locale both raises the stakes of the couple's unrest and undermines it. David is "afraid of the bugs" (35) in the hallway; in the bathroom Sarah is disturbed by an insect "as big as my hand" (37); such innocuous details of infestation assume important symbolic functions in *Aunt Dan and Lemon* and *The Fever*. Also, like so many Shawn characters, Sarah experiences "a kind of dizziness" 939) indicative of her instability. Meanwhile, a native festival continues outside the hotel room. Sarah's anxiousness to participate in it alone is frustrated by David's congenial and restricting desire to accompany her, an extension of his fear of being alone. Unlike the narrator of *The Fever*, David has a companion in this foreign place, and he will not relinquish her.

The fantasy at the piece's conclusion merges with the festival, the latter still the more threatening: "God, do you hear those sounds? They never get tired?" (41). The couple finally generate a moment of sensuality when David intellectually reduces himself to a savage; "Now, it's night, there are stars, there are clouds, and they're racing in the sky, and I'm dragging your body by the feet, dirty feet. Your head gets bloody. I'm running" (41). Sarah is aroused. The flowers on the dress she will buy symbolize a sexuality illuminated by the outside:

> SARAH: Red flowers. White flowers on the white—
> DAVID: —stems—pale leaves—
> SARAH: —just the light from outside. (*He touches a switch on the night table, and the lights of the room go out.*) Yes. (*They touch.*) Yes. (*They touch.*) Yes.
> DAVID: May I?
> SARAH: Yes. (41)

Sarah is able to escape, in the play's closing moment into a concocted primitivism she has affirmed throughout, although David's last politeness weakens the moment's legitimacy. What is undeniable is the call of the festival, an economically poor but physically enticing culture just beyond the window.

Marie and Bruce is the most fully realized of Shawn's earlier plays. Like *The Hotel Play*, it spans a single day, during which the bitter Marie plans to leave her husband and grows increasingly ill at the impossibility of doing so. Settings are as usual: bedroom, party, restaurant. Robert Brustein recalls the work as an "appalling, traumatizing play" which "teetered precariously for a few weeks, making audiences miserable and enraging critics. . . . *Marie and Bruce* is one of the most savage assaults yet on the failure of the American promise" ("Two Couples" 28). The play thoroughly articulated the alienation, frustration, and angst of contemporary urban relationships. As does *Summer Evening*, with which it shares much, *Marie and Bruce* opens with a monologue. Shawn is close to the technique of *Aunt Dan and Lemon*. Marie frames the play with lengthy expositions, while short, dramatized scenes with Bruce are juxtaposed with overhead snatches of banal party dialogue that remain beyond her control. This issue of control presents a crucial difference in the recollections of Lemon. Nevertheless, Kroll correctly assesses the play's effectiveness within a "double focus" which reveals the "terrifying implications of the smallest, most ordinary events" ("I Love You" 117). Marie is a storyteller, and her voice contains a shocking range of tone, from the ferociously profane to the lyrical and dreamlike. She is a more developed Sarah from *Summer Evening*; her problem, an imperturbable husband, is the same; Marie, however fails to cause Bruce to hear, so to speak, the native dance. In the end she falls into resignation, "a sort of Manhattan Molly Bloom . . . wifelike and motherlike, over her little Bruce. . . . There is a sadness in the innumerable 'little's that big Marie has uttered; the marriage is terrible and will last forever" (Gill 65).

In *Marie and Bruce* the bed serves not merely as place of repose and leisure but as the squalid vantage point of the invalid. Marie screams the entire first scene at her husband: "Now do you have to lie there in that disgusting heap?" (3). After Bruce departs, she reflects that the apartment, dishes, and bed are all "filthy" and that she is "sick." The bed and small apartment symbolize for Marie the isolation and impossibility of every aspect of her life. Curiously, even events such as stripping the bed are told to the audience rather than enacted physically. *Marie and Bruce* denies dramatic performance; Bruce is a solicitous coward and indifferent to action, and Marie is forced to share his dysfunctional prison of words. She mocks Bruce's preciousness and contrived syntax, revealing both the depths of her hostility and the deficiency of his complacence:

> "I think I'll just slip on my clothes, actually"—how cute, what a cute little fellow—"I think I'll just slip on my clothes, actually"—"I think I'll just slip on my clothes, actually"—"I think I'll just slip on my clothes, actually"—It was a miserable summer. It was hot. We didn't have jobs. We were running out of money. We didn't have anything to read that was good, it was all worthless shit. I had the flu the whole time—I was sick, I was weak, I felt dizzy—
>
> *He returns, dressed.*
>
> You God damned fucking son of a bitch, you pig, you shit, you revolting turd— (5–6)

A desperately hateful tone and shocking transitions are typical of the play. Shawn experiments with echoed dialogue at the conclusion of *Youth Hostel*, but in *Marie and Bruce* he forces an absurd, harrowing exaggeration. Marie's later denial of her affection for Bruce contains both the vehemence of a spell to cast him away and the pathos of trying to prove to herself an impossible truth: "Do you know that I never loved you, Bruce? I never loved you. I never loved you" (47). Shawn's dramatic strategy, contends David Savran, "relies on repetition rather than development. Characters do not change but constantly repeat themselves. . . . What changes is the spectator's response, which passes from amusement to disgust to understanding—insofar as the enigma of human cruelty can be understood" (208).

An exhaustive discussion of *Marie and Bruce* could explain the play's many peculiar themes: the association of scholarship and history with excrement, Bruce's homoeroticism, Marie's psychosexual dream life. However, of particular importance to Shawn's nagging moral dilemma is Marie's symptomatic physical illness. At the party, Bruce notices his wife's cold hands. Her response is both derisive and alarmed: "Am I sick? Cancer? What? Bruce? Some serious illness? Do you think—" (20). From that point her condition worsens. She dozes drunkenly on the couch as a swirl of speakers babble of illiteracy, poverty, and education, subjects trivialized and undercut by context. Words seem largely the cause of Marie's sickness. She dreams of a world where every person was "somehow extremely complex and interesting, but at the same time terribly relaxed" (29), implying by contrast the reality of the party: strained, tense, shallow. At the ensuing dinner, Bruce's language smothers her. "Bruce, I can't talk. I don't feel well. I feel very dizzy" (56). She is uncertain, lost, stripped of even the torrent of obscenities which sustained her earlier. Bruce, meanwhile, links illness and nausea with insanity, recalling, "a time when vomiting was induced in patients whom today we would classify as mentally ill. Then the vomit itself was kept in containers . . . " (40). As the audience's tolerance of Bruce diminishes, sympathy for Marie increases. Amid the barrenness of the social gathering, she is ravaged, ill, and alone. Like the narrator of *The Fever*, her loathing of self and others induces not only physical illness but fantasies of confinement and brutality: "I thought it would be a murderer. . . . I thought it would be a torturer who was coming to strip me and strap me down and beat me with his fists and then rape me. . . . I was feeling very sick" (45). The play's climax fails to release Marie from her marriage duress, yet she pronounces Bruce's sentence:

> No—you see, Bruce, you see, Bruce, you're not alive. You're not a person. You are not a person, you are only meat. I am telling you the truth now,

> Bruce, and I'm telling you that you are dead. You're a horrible dead piece of meat. . . . You may say things, but I don't have to listen, because you are death. You are filth, You are only meat. You are filth. You are only filth. (57–58)

This final expulsion exhausts her spiritually and physically, allowing the unexpected gentleness of the taxi ride home, the clean sheets, the acceptance, apparently, of her commitment to a faceless "nothing." In the original Public Theatre production, Marie's condemnation of her husband is accompanied by a bodily assault which also fails to arouse him; during the party, mannequins filled stage space between living celebrants, implying scant difference. Marie recognizes her place in the society of the dead discussed in *My Dinner with André*:

> WALLY: But if they're rich and live in the city and have a thousand things to play with, then they always seem to be bored, and it's impossible to find anything to interest them.
> ANDRE: Well, the word "spoiled" isn't a chance word, it's a strong word.
> WALLY: Yeah.
> ANDRE: To be spoiled.
> WALLY: Right. In other words, they're just—they're lost, in that sense. I mean, "spoiled" means, you know—I mean, a piece of meat that's been spoiled can't be unspoiled. It's doomed. (91)

Without question, *My Dinner with André* is the crucial work dividing Shawn's ouevre. He had "been working as a playwright for ten years. My plays had been intense, extreme, even maniacal. That was fine, but now I wanted to do something else . . ." (13). The project allowed Shawn to escape continual self-scrutinizing interiority, through an interrogation of André to approach an "exterior life as a mediocre human being and dilettante of normal intelligence" which had "remained unchronicled" (13). *My Dinner with André* is a clever, complex exploration of reality and artifice which Richard Schickel argues is actually "less stagy, more authentic, than life" (94). Its drama originates from clashing ideas, rather than character, a technique Shawn continues to use superbly. Gregory recently noted that he and Shawn remain "bizarre reflections of each other" (Falk 20); in a sense, they represent dual sides of one conflicted personality, much as *Aunt Dan and Lemon* and *The Fever* elaborate single voices. The men are cast not merely as themselves, but as purified ideological foils, realized, writes Kroll, "out of their passion, their foolishness, their absurd humanity" ("Conversation Piece" 78).

Shawn's self-creation owes much to his quotidian male characters. Bruce describes himself as "a nice guy" (3); David, in *Summer Evening*, feels he is "known as a nice—as a good chap, actually" (31). Wally as character acknowledges he is "a perfectly nice guy" within " the small circle of the people I know as friends" (82–83). These trite defenses ignore larger social and moral realities, and Shawn as author elaborated this deficiency: "I'm giving a conscious performance as a terribly obtuse and self-righteous bourgeois" (Atlas D15). In the voice-over beginning the script, he defines himself as a member of a spoiled class, enjoying a life in the arts and a background of isolating wealth: "When I was ten years old I was rich, I was an aristocrat, riding around in taxis, surrounded in comfort, and all I thought about was art and music" (17). Affluence has passed; yet, in the context of the film, the taste and standards of an aesthete remain. In early scenes Wally is nervous, uncomfortable, incredulous, and vaguely contentious. "By the end," he explains, "I'm thinking about myself, about life, and taking André very seriously. That's the story of the film" (Atlas D15). In this sense *My Dinner with André* posits more potential for growth beyond cycles of repetition than any earlier work.

Shawn confesses his "secret profession . . . is that I'm a private investigator, a detective. I always want to ask questions" (21). Gregory, in his preface, defines *My Dinner with André* as a "work which is made up entirely of questions" (11), a sophisticated third stage in the maturation of the artist achieved after learning craft and the telling "with passion and conviction everything that you think you know about your life and your art" (11). Gregory's own equation places Shawn at a point where the younger artist admits an exhaustion of interior material. Shawn, recalls Gregory,

> felt that either I had had a complete nervous breakdown . . . or else a creative block, or a spiritual awakening, or a combination of all three, but whatever it was, when he reached my age (Wally is ten years younger than I am) he didn't want to go through the same thing. (10)

For Shawn, asking questions is not merely an artistic method but a way to ease anxiety and connect with his friend.

The men in *My Dinner with André* are touched by art more than life; this idea is complicated by life lived as theatre and vice versa. Stanislavski's questions for the actor to "constantly ask himself as a character, Who am I? Why am I here? Where do I come from? and Where am I going?" (26) grow indistinguishable from Shawn and Gregory's self-interrogation as humans. "I don't know about you, Wally, but I just had to put myself into a kind of training program to learn how to be a human being" (108). André continues, "Or maybe what we're really afraid of is thinking about a kind of existence that we've lost, which if we were to remember would make us give up everything" (110). This is the political and moral challenge realized in *The Fever*, where the damage of certain questions to self-conception can be unalterable: "And a voice says—Why not all of it? Why not give her all you have? Be careful, that's a question that could poison your life" (38). Shawn's struggle to return to the human, to compassion, courage, and clear vision manifests in *My Dinner with André* as the questions of the maturing artist, while André's self-damnation could easily come from *The Fever*: "I really feel I'm just washed up, wiped out—I've just squandered my life" (60).

As much as it anticipated Shawn's recent work, *My Dinner with André* echoes themes of early plays. André labels society "an insane dream world" (61) of robots and sleepwalkers. They discuss the indirect manner in which Americans deal with emotion. Tragic events are disguised by manic laughter—"Aha ha ha ehee hee hee oho oho! Wo-ho ho ho!" (67)—and odd linguistic symbols. For example, the foreigners in *The Hotel Play* punctuate a conversation of gibberish with raucous guffaws, as if each thought must be accompanied by a punch line. Wally discusses the party as confused social spectacle, a scene enacted in each of his works:

> I mean, that's the only way anything is expressed—through these inane jokes. That may be why I never understand what's going on at a party, and I'm always completely confused. . . . Everything passes in a kind of trance. (68–69)

Shawn's narration of the film is a mixture of early and later tendencies. *My Dinner with André* represents a fluidity distinct from his fragmented, consciously abrupt plays. Still, fragments are included in, rather than replaced by, Gregory's recollections, which are recalled by a single voice, in leisure, as in both of Shawn's subsequent plays. No dramatic action remains except that re-created and interpreted by a character. Gregory precedes Lemon in this way, but curiously so does Shawn. Shawn's voice frames the script and, within his comments, Gregory's words are lodged, stored, and retrieved. At the beginning and end of their conversation, the men's voices overlap Shawn's voice-over, suggesting concurrent realities: the dinner and the dinner recollected. By what he selects to present, Shawn directs the piece; but also, like the audience, he is drawn to André's expensive table to enjoy a performance.

The playwright casts himself as curmudgeon to André's mystic; his comments, until nearly the end, are more intrusions than meaningful additions. They are almost always theatrical references emphasizing a sheltered life:

> WALLY: God—incredible—(*Long pause.*) By the way, did you ever see that play *The Violets Are Blue?*
> ANDRE: No.
> WALLY: Oh, well when you mentioned the violets it reminded me of that. (*Pause.*) It was about—er—people being strangled on a submarine.
> ANDRE: uh-huh.
> *Silence. Close-up of WALLY's face perspiring.*
> WALLY: Well, so that was Christmas. What happened after that? (45–46)

The scene is uncomfortable, typical of Wally's difficulties through early stages of the conversation. He continually attempts to illustrate Gregory's adventures from his participation in *The Master and Margarita* or *The Mandrake*; the film argues whether theatrical experience may be as legitimate as, indeed inextricable from, any other. Pauline Kael calls the film a "story of the search beyond theatre turned into theatre" (83); still, Wally seems deficient and consequently, defiant. Within André's critique of the stage's ability to provoke an entranced age is an attack on the sort of plays Shawn himself has written:

> Or how does it affect them to see a play that shows that our world is full of nothing but shocking sexual events and violence and terror? Does that help wake up a sleeping audience? . . . So the play simply tells them that their impression of the world is correct, and there's absolutely no way out, there's nothing they can do. They end up feeling passive and impotent. (87–88)

Shawn apparently agrees with such an implied dismissal of his loud, directly indicting early work; afterwards he will adopt a quieter, more cunning voice, the voice of an Aunt Dan presented without contrary argument. Rather than continuing to write plays which scream out the world's avarice and cruelty, he begins to present evil calmly, through his narrators, as natural, proper, and embraced.

The irony undercutting the film's insights is André's economic security. André, as one critic states it, "has the leisure of terror" (Hatch 484). Shawn's character notes this early, resentfully acknowledging his friend's "got some money hidden away somewhere—I mean, how the hell could he have been flying off to Asia or wherever he went and sill have been supporting his family?" (19). In watching the film, more than in reading the script, one realizes the crucial significance of its economic and class subtext. Wally gawks at the fleshy, jabbering faces filling the posh restaurant, senses their strained conviviality. Amid white wine and tablecloths, enjoying quail and fish pâté, over the delicate notes of a string quartet, the men confer on the deadening effects of luxury. André is at home in this world; to Wally, it constitutes a strange and not unpleasant dream of youth.

An unnamed waiter plays a largely silent but important role. Occasionally, as Wally and André indulge in mutual performance, discussing artifice and reality, only their reflections speak from mirrors above the table; cameras subtly reveal the prosaic business of the restaurant. Unobtrusively, a bartender fills orders; the waiter uncovers dishes. Except for a rare oblique glance, diners are oblivious to the excellent service upon which even the flow of their discussion depends. The waiter and his white-coats, faceless boys who remove plates and fill water glasses, keep courses precisely moving. Often the waiter's entrance will undermine the moment's topic. Following André's impassioned recollection of being stripped, run naked through the woods, and buried alive, the waiter arrives with their exquisitely prepared quail. Later, interrupting André's criticism of "absolutely abnormal behavior" (67) in America, the inability to directly express sorrow, the waiter brings salad to cleanse the palate, refills wine glasses, and inquires, "Is everything all right, gentlemen?" They reply in unison: "Fine, thank you . . ." (67). They seem unaware of a discrepancy increasingly obvious to viewers; the efficacy of the waiter's actions, his talent, grace, and simple, silent dignity in contrast to self-indulgent talk. The waiter's place is to serve. He is described as "in his seventies. His face shows that he has seen and experienced the suffering of the world" (20). Wally and André's conversation continues interminably, until the restaurant is empty. The men find themselves out of words for a moment, and Wally looks up as if coming abruptly out of a trance. He sees waiters smoking and talking together, white-coats spreading fresh tablecloths for the next day's clientele. Somehow, the moment is pivotal. Wally seems dazed. Silence, after so many words, is shocking and potent. The waiter approaches the table with the bill; Wally sees him for the first time. For a moment, their looks hold. The music is slow, sad, melancholic, "Erik Satie's Gymnopedie #1" (113).

Dinner is over. Wally's voice-over resumes. He splurges for a taxi, a return to his wealthy heritage, and for the duration of his trip home feels an unusual community with his surroundings. "There wasn't a street—there wasn't a building—that wasn't connected to some memory in my mind. There, I was buying a suit with my father. There, I was having an ice cream soda after school" (113). Such hypersensitivity, experienced in a surreal moment, is impossible to maintain. Already the scene is in the categorized past; Wally returns home and anxiously relays to his girlfriend "everything about *My Dinner with André*" (113). That is, even as one watches the passing city, the closing credits, events have already transpired twice; the dinner has been nostalgically re-created through memory and language.

André recounts a similar hyperawareness earlier in the evening: "But I really felt as if I were floating above the ground, not walking. . . . It was a feeling of recognizing everything, of being able to be aware of the reality and the specialness of even the most ordinary things" (38). The feeling fades. His experience and Wally's, coupled with numerous moments from earlier plays, foreshadow the "fetishism of commodities" (20) which haunts *The Fever*'s narrator. What is the true value of objects? What are the intricate relationships implied by economic exchange?

> The cup of coffee contains the history of the peasants who picked the beans, how some of them fainted in the heat of the sun, some were beaten, some were kicked.
>
> For two days I could see the fetishism of commodities everywhere around me. I was a strange feeling. Then on the third day I lost it, it was gone, I couldn't see it any more. (21)

Coffee in the morning, throughout Shawn's work representative of simple values, reveals its darker meaning. Like André, Shawn's later narrator is float-ing in space" (2), vertiginous with surfeit emotion. André adds that "if we allowed ourselves to see what we're doing every day, we might find it just too nauseating" (81). Commodities, materialism, economic inequities—in general, the political themes central to Shawn's subsequent work—are repeatedly voiced in *My Dinner with André.* Charmed by polished automobiles, buried alive with his valuables, André elaborates, for Shawn's later exploration, a "world totalitarian government based on money," where those bored to sleep "will not say no" (92).

My Dinner with André anticipated *Aunt Dan and Lemon* in the saturation of André's language with the Nazi references. The group trance induced by André's beehive is "something like Hitler's Nuremberg rallies" (30). He later approaches a conspicuously Aryan flag maker; the Tibetan swastika the man weaves into André's flag indicts, again, passivity, meditation, art. The line between one swastika and another is thin, and the flag is haunted. Such references are too numerous to catalog. André sees himself as a Nazi persecutor, Hitler's architect Albert Speer, who "was a very cultivated man, an architect, an artist, so he thought ordinary rules of life didn't apply to him. . . . I really feel that everything I've done is horrific" (57–58); but he is also victim, "flashing on death camps and secret police. . . . I started to cry uncontrollably" (54). This paradox, a self-loathing of oneself as both torturer and prisoner, is realized by New York City, "the new model for the new concentration camp, where the camp has been built by the inmates themselves, and the inmates are the guards, and they have this pride in this thing that they've built . . . so they exist in a state of schizophrenia . . . " (93). A last analogy is particularly telling: "Nazi demons that were released in the thirties in Germany were probably a reaction against a certain oppressive kind of knowledge and culture and rational thinking""(103). In these words are seeds of revisionist history, the potent half-truths employed so searingly in the genocidal speeches of Aunt Dan and her apostle.

Aunt Dan and Lemon is Wallace Shawn's longest play, his most stylistically challenging. Scenes of exploitation and sexuality are integrated into a monologue on the nature of evil. Aunt Dan's tutelage includes lessons on the necessity of violence and on justifying homicide. Brustein contends that the play is "impossible to evaluate . . . in dramatic terms" ("Hostile Audience" 26). *Aunt Dan and Lemon* contains little internal tension, not even ideological conflicts that drive *My Dinner with André*. Aunt Dan's ideas reign. Lemon's mother is the some advocate of compassion, of "a heart which is capable of weighing" actions (48), public as well as private. Her quiet voice is easily extinguished beneath Dan's charisma and energy. Gerald Weales isolates the play's true source of drama "The Tension in *Aunt Dan and Lemon* is between audience and characters. There is no one on stage to say an effective no to Lemon" ("Bobbing and Invading" 180). Fragments interrupting Lemon's monologue amplify political motifs rather than develop character or plot. Shawn rejects any theatrically contrived defeat of Lemon as "a form of lying" that "would have given the audience the impression that in my opinion those thoughts had been safely buried at least for the evening and everyone could go home and sleep in peace, whereas I actually don't believe that" ("Notes in Justification" 193).

Aunt Dan and Lemon is about ideas: their relationship to action, their "unlimited destructive power" ("Notes in Justification" 193). Host for the evening is Lemon. Her inability to eat recalls earlier characters' distaste for food, sickness, nausea, and dizziness. The world of the play is one of rot, decay, and decrepitude, where mind and body have failed, like those of Kafka's hunger artist, to find sustaining food. Lemon's first words introduce the active yet subordinate role one will be forced to play: "Hello, dear audience, dear good people who have taken yourselves out for a special treat, a night at the theatre. Hello, little children. How sweet you are, how innocent" (1). The audience is incriminated by its presence. Shawn's translation of *The Mandrake* begins similarly; "Good evening, everyone. And if you're glad to be here, well then let me say, God bless you!" (11).[1] The audience participated in a society which has ceased to nourish life. "My parents both died in their early fifties, and it wouldn't surprise me if I were to die even younger than that," explains Lemon (1).

Lemon essentially lives without a body, a life of memories based not on physical experience but "things I was told" (5). She is the ideal student, a receptacle for Dan and her friends (these latter, whom the girl has never met, visit like phantoms and address her directly). Aunt Dan is recollected as a magical storyteller. Lemon's ability to listen makes her a rare figure for Shawn; previous characters often merely wait to speak. If in *My Dinner with André* dialogic exchange is experience, then *Aunt Dan and Lemon* presents listening as a kind of life. A fairy-tale quality pervades Lemon and Dan's nocturnal meetings: "by six o'clock I'd be in my little house waiting for Aunt Dan . . ." (22). Lemon is a willing Red Riding Hood to Aunt Dan's wolf. Dan describes a professor as a "gigantic prince" (23); the two live for a week "like pigs" (24). Lemon is enchanted; her interjections are romantic frames for the women's evenings: "The light from the window—the purplish light of the dusk—would fall across her face" (24). Dan brings obscurity. By imperceptible degrees, like nightfall, her lessons of deception and brutality are learned. She is a carnivore and recollects crawling from a theatre "absolutely mad" and "dripping with blood" (27).

Lemon's most unsettling characteristic is the calm with which she proselytizes her audience. She exudes the peacefulness of one satisfied with both herself and her answers. She recalls she "used to read Mysteries—detective novels—to put myself to sleep, but I don't anymore"(2). Lemon has rejected the questioning spirit which causes Shawn to identify himself as detective. "Lately I've been reading about the Nazi killings of the Jew instead" 92). Solutions find their justification in Dan's impassioned politics, in the "honesty" of the Nazis in recognizing the necessity of murder for maintenance of class status quo. The existence of the Nazis soothes her, an effect accomplished by Dan's ideological relativism. Without question Dan is the play's most charming, intriguing character, just as Lemon is its surest speaker. Shawn admits evil's attractiveness. Friends who finally abandon morality, he writes, "begin to blossom, to flower, because they are no longer hiding" and "develop the charm and grace which shine out from all people who are truly comfortable with themselves, who are not worried, who are not ashamed of their own actions" (96). Such acceptance accounts for Lemon and Dan. If *The Fever* is a desperate confession of one still clinging to a tattered moral heritage, then *Aunt Dan and Lemon* is its opposite—an exuberant paean to corruption.

Shawn recalls tension during performances of *Aunt Dan and Lemon*, "a feeling that at any moment someone might speak out during the last speech" (Savran 215–16). His lengthy appendix essay "On the Context of the Play" addresses without dismissing, the dilemma of Lemon's undaunted confidence. The author considers the hazy concept of morality, its instillation and the absolute necessity of its unremitting maintenance. Comfort in his adult life comes increasingly in conflict with the "well-intentioned ethical training I received as a child." The analogy is telling: he has "caught a fever" and is "feeling sick" (89). The essay is cunningly organized; it agrees that morality is an aggravating guide to global responsibility and envies the assurance and vitality of those who have discarded such encumbrances to enjoy government protection and economic advantage. Shawn then introduces his reluctance: "But whenever I start dreaming about self-confident people I begin to get terribly nervous, because I always think of the marvelous self-confidence of Hitler" (97). Applicability to the play is unmistakable: "And meanwhile we're walking around in a daze, trying to remember whether we're still connected to morality or not. False arguments, rapidly expressed, confuse us, seduce us, corrupt us" (100). This is Dan's power. She says of herself, "with absolute confidence," that "I never, ever shout at a waiter" (24). What begins as espousal of labor and democracy rapidly shows itself to be a kindness to placate the poor. Their subservience is necessary to the smooth continuance of the leisure Dan and Lemon enjoy as aristocrats. The student naturally accepts the true tenor of her mentor's belief: preservation at any cost of a system controlled by money. As Lemon articulates in her closing statement, compassion "probably doesn't exist" (84). Like Wally and André, she has been moved by art, but not, in her recollection, by life. The similarity of Lemon's arguments to Wally's renders *Aunt Dan and Lemon* eerily familiar. The playwright reminds us that "just a few thoughts" separate "a perfectly decent person and a monster" (99).

For Shawn, personal morality is a taxing, almost scholarly, vigilance based on constant reexamination. The internal, self-monitoring voice is "a perpetual irritation" and "never stops denouncing" (92). In other words, morality, particularly its pertinence to actions beyond an immediate sphere of friends, leaves one stripped of Dan's charisma; such a life demands, instead, self-doubt, shame, uncertainty, continual revision. A great political, social, and historical burden is assigned the individual; "Privacy is an illusion. What I do is public, and what I think is public. The fragility of my own thoughts becomes the fragility of the world. The ease with which I become a swine is the ease with which the world could fall apart, like something rotten" (105). The proximity or distance of a character from moral health determines physical well-being. The predominance of sickness, rot, dizziness, and nausea in Shawn's plays literalize moral inadequacy.

In interviews, Shawn is customarily skeptical of the theatre's ability to educate and nurture. "Theatre is slow, it is unsexy, it's quiet." He adds that "people interested in the way the world is going don't go to the theatre." Yet he feels compelled in "confronting them as a playwright. It's quite embarrassing, it's quite unpleasant, it's quite awkward" (Savran 220). The author identifies himself as of the ruling class and sympathizes with the need to be pacified and entertained; still he is unable to supply the requested opiate. "Quite frankly, I feel that my life would be better spent if I were an entertainer or a clown. But it isn't my dream to be the guy who sings in the beer hall to entertain the Nazi generals" (Savran 221). As there is an absurdity as a struggling playwright in *My Dinner with André*, so to the author's growing success is problematic.[2] "Artists who create works of art that inspire sympathy and good values do not change the life of the poor," *The Fever*'s narrator insists (65–66). With this play the contradiction is most apparent—it attacks the foundation of the society enabling its commercial existence. *The Fever* was intended to be performed in the living rooms of the social class it scrutinizes but subsequently played in Europe and at Lincoln Center and won an Obie. Shawn considers the possible benefit of continuing on slippery ground:

> Theatre could have a political function in a very indirect way. It could have an artistic function that, I think, has political importance in that good works of art sharpen the awareness. That's part of what turns people into honest and sensitive observers of the world rather than complete fools. . . . Theoretically, a play can influence people for the better just by sharpening their sensibilities. (Savran 221)

He corroborates this belief in *Aunt Dan and Lemon*'s appendix. Theatre can serve as bulwark against alluring half-truths and evasions, against, in short, the sickness of moral delinquency and its distorting ideas. In this sense, a play's crucial element is its honesty in the exposition of socio-historic assumptions. "But if we look into the mirror, we just might observe a rapacious face. Perhaps the face will even show subtle traces, here and there, of hatred and savagery beneath the surface. And maybe most of us look a little like Hitler, that ever-present ghost" (106). Recall the mirrors surrounding the men's heads in *My Dinner with André*, odd angles in and out of view, reflections speaking, André's confession: "Because I think I am Speer. And I think it's time for me to be caught and tried the way he was" (57).

The Fever is the culmination of Shawn's work and the purification of his most important themes; yet it is his least theatrical play, as if its realization demonstrates the difficulty of Shawn's future in theatre. Fragmentary scenes, dramatic flashbacks and recollections, all are curtailed to a single voice of unspecified gender or age. The play contains no stage directions, sets, or physical action; when read, it is indistinguishable from a novella, the narrator perhaps akin to the speaker in *Notes from Underground*. "I am a sick man. . . . I am a spiteful man," Dostoyevsky's text begins (1). Shawn's story consists of one human's fevered anomie isolated, with each rationalization, by increasingly violent nausea. After a diatribe against a chambermaid, the narrator is immediately "seized by another fit of vomiting. My shoulders reach forward toward the toilet and pull me with them. My head drives toward the bowl of the toilet, and I vomit again and again and again" (40). Weales explains, "His fever is not physical; it is metaphysical" ("Degrees of Difference" 18). Wetzsteon adds that the narrator's "awakened conscience immobilizes as well as liberates him. His nausea is not so much purgative as inescapable. He has become his own Ancient Mariner . . ." (35).

Nearly every line of *The Fever* distills images, ideas, and themes of earlier work. The setting and situation are familiar: "I'm traveling—and I wake up suddenly in the silence before dawn in my strange hotel room, in a poor country where my language isn't spoken, and I'm shaking and shivering" (3). That morning the "cat-like" (3) man will be executed, recalling Wally's cat mask in *My Dinner with André*. The narrator recognizes himself in an insect on the bathroom floor, "big, like a water bug—it's flat, heavy—very tough legs, they look like metal—and it's waiting. Squatting, deciding which way to move' (5). More of these later invade his torture fantasy; eventually he ceases resistance and lies among them. He is the spiritual and geographic traveler, at last denied the exemption of responsibility customarily granted wealthy Americans. "Do you think this kind of thing is my normal life?" dismisses Jasper in *Aunt Dan and Lemon*. "I'm on vacation" (9).

The Fever takes to extremes Shawn's patterns of repetition and ironic undercutting, also further simplifying a dramatic device he uses very effectively: tension between ideas, between resignation and conviction. Rarely, an interior voice appears; "No, I'm trying to tell you that people hate you. I'm trying to explain to you about the people who hate you. Why do you think they all love you?" (55). Says Shawn: I wanted to find a form that would allow me to express the feelings and perceptions that underlie political opinions" (Wetzsteon 35). Ironically, *The Fever*, which has global behavior as its paramount concern, is Shawn's most private play—a haunted, searching, incomplete voice. One critic argues that the play "is in many ways a sonata version of his *Aunt Dan and Lemon* . . . with Shawn assuming the role of the diminutive Machiavelli. . . ." (Disch 24). The narrator does share Dan's propensity for discounting social inequities, defending privileged position, and belittling the poor.

The chief difference is that in *The Fever* such Machiavellian ethics fail. Confidence is insupportable. The narrator realizes that the chambermaid is born to a life sentence of labor for no just or justifiable reason: "The sentence says that she will serve, and then on the next day she will serve, and then she will, and she will, right up until her death" (66). The history of the ruling class, the legacy of democracy—"until the beautiful Christmas morning we woke up, and our proud parents showed us the gorgeous, shining, blood-soaked fields which now were ours" (48)—is founded in death and hatred and maintained by lies, paranoia, and oppression. "We can never forget the death of their families, those vows of revenge screamed out in those rooms that were running with gore. And the poor don't forget. They live on their rage. They eat rage" (49–50). It is no surprise the narrator tastes the "sour sort of lovelessness, a sort of horrible rotting lovelessness" (30) found in so much of Shawn's work. Daily enjoyment of comfort is uncontrollably, irrevocably interrupted by the character's experiences in "poor countries whose names were written on no T-shirts, where soldiers had strange expressions on their faces, where wealthy families sat in glittering restaurants eating plate after plate of multicolored ice cream . . ." (24).

Much of *The Fever* is dreamlike, a hallucinatory effect of its own illness; Shawn feels it is "obviously a fable or fairy tale" (Wetzsteon 36). Unlike the stories told by Aunt Dan, however, the narrative strived not to assure and comfort, but to nauseate, cripple, and stun—to begin to create, perhaps, Shawn's "uncomfortable and incompetent slaves of morality . . . who insist on believing in a standard which condemns them . . ." (*Aunt Dan and Lemon* 105). *The Fever* embraces no specific political agenda; its goal is to explore "the psychology of political indifference" (Wetzsteon 36) and the hollowing consequence of such apathy as traditional securities are drained of sustaining power to become "a sort of awful . . . blankness that was coming from somewhere inside me and filling me up, bit by bit. Things that would once have delighted or cheered me seemed to go dead on me, to spoil" (*The Fever* 26). "Spoil" is merely one of numerous recurrent words. In a sense, the monologue represents one of Shawn's somnambulant characters coming awake. Like the author in his preface to *My Dinner with André*, the narrator's expertise has been limited to internal life: "I've been a student of my feelings since I was nine years old! My feelings! My thoughts! . . . But the story of my life—my behavior, my actions—that's a slim volume, and I've never read it" (7). The reaction to forced inspection of his behavior is predictable: "And I vomit again. Dear God" (8). The sparse hotel room, lit by candles, reflects the ceremonial renaming of André Gregory. Unlike the comforting ride which ends *My Dinner with André*, the narrator stares, "frozen, out the taxi window" (27). The self-guarded prison camp of New York City returns as fantasy: a cell window "doesn't have bars" (45); a friend "sitting on my bunk, smoking quietly" is "that guard" (45–46).

While *The Fever* lacks *Aunt Dan and Lemon*'s political specificity, it shares an ambiguous, unresolved conclusion. No one except the audience may defend against *Lemon*'s final solutions, and *The Fever*'s viewers also must answer a narrator's enigmatic demands. "Forgive me. Forgive me. I know you forgive me. I'm still falling" (68). With these troubling words the play ends. Its success depends upon an audience recognizing in itself similar hypocrisy. The speaker's sureness that he will be forgiven is founded on the likelihood of the audience's desire to forgive itself; his insurance is others' guilt. This sort of reflection is the source of *The Fever*'s provocative power yet ultimately assures its failure. "For this play to truly succeed," writes Wetzsteon, "the world would have to be transformed." Moreover, "the energizing awareness of one's responsibility for injustice is often the genesis of radical politics" (37). Wetzsteon feels Shawn's importance as a playwright is the persistently audacious, shattering simplicity of his questions. "Certainly things cannot be questioned" (58), the narrator tries to convince himself, yet like Shawn he continues: "I kept trying to get her to talk about herself," he comments of a guerilla with whom he shares afternoon tea (25). Such incongruities destroy him.

The Fever fails to alleviate its character's suffering. Against the "dark wall of the sky: is found "a hint of dawn" (63), a mere suggestion of light. He extinguishes a candle and retreats to his bed. He will return home. Dawn brings both illumination and public execution. His insight is qualified, vitiated. Perhaps he is permanently altered in a way neither he nor the audience can anticipate. The values of comfort and class appear misplaced:

> On the table—what?—blood—death—a fragment of bone—a fragment—a piece—of a human brain—a severed hand.—Let everything filthy, everything vile. Sit by my bed, where once I had my lamp and clock, books, letters, presents for my birthday, and left over from the presents bright-colored ribbons. (68)

Within the virulence of the narrator's disease resides *The Fever*'s hope, a possibility of change. The play completes Shawn's journey to strip away the bestial selfishness of the living dead. *The Fever* ends over the abyss, its speaker falling. How or when he may land is indeterminable. It seems unlikely Shawn can further purify the monologue for the stage, an undertaking begun over a decade ago. He says of *The Fever*: "I didn't think this was actually a play and I was trying to get out of the theater" (Virshup 99). His commitment to truth is apparent; how he will continue his efforts is unclear. "I'd be delighted if I ever wrote anything in any form. . . . I'll do whatever I'm able to do" (Savran 222).

Recently Shawn has renewed his dialogue with Gregory, an encouraging reunion considering the fruitfulness of their previous collaborations. The two have staged an intimate reinterpretation of *Uncle Vanya*; a small audience is brought into the living room and to the dining table so that "the 'acting family' cannot distance itself from its watchful audience, nor can the audience 'behave' as outsiders" (Falk 21). Such a production increases the audience involvement always present in Shawn's work. In *My Dinner with André*, Wally comments to André, "And you know, you performed Chekhov in front of the patient, and it didn't work" (86). In *The Fever*, the narrator watches a performance of *The Cherry Orchard*; in his Marxist reaction to the play's aristocracy, he cannot recall "why I was supposed to be weeping" (27). Yet again Shawn and Gregory have returned to the physician and have assigned the audience a seat at the table. Gregory contends that this "Vanya is definitely not theatre. It is a sort of spiritual community" (Falk 21). That Shawn has forced his audience over the precipice is enough to thank him for; perhaps he still may prescribe some remedy for the fall.

Notes

1 Anyone interested in the assault on values so frequent in Shawn's plays would benefit from this translation. Even character descriptions are founded upon class and economic station. Callimaco is "wealthy and charming" (6); Madonna Sostrata "enjoys a frivolous life of gossip, parties, and social visiting" (7); elders instruct Madonna Lucrezia in morality "to obtain her subjugation and obedience" (8), then force her to abandon these ideals as it benefits them; Sirio, "servant," is the character "most capable of moral awareness" (6). The social assumptions and tone of *The Mandrake* argue, if not an enormous early influence of Shawn, at least a sympathetic literary ancestor in Machiavelli.

2 Shawn recognizes the frequent predicament of his success: "*Aunt Dan* has elements that are poisonous and frightening, so I feel that there's something distasteful about saying I'm having a great time because of it" (Clarke 105).

Works Cited

Atlas, James. "The Artistic Recipe for *My Dinner with André*." *New York Times* 28 Feb. 1982: D1+.

Barnes, Clive. "Stage: *Our Late Night*, at the Public Theater." *New York Times* 10 Jan. 1975: L20+.

Brustein, Robert. "Addressing a Hostile Audience." *New Republic* 9 Dec. 1985: 26–28.
——. "Two Couples." *New Republic* 5 Apr. 1980: 28–29.
Chaillet, Ned. "Wallace Shawn." *Contemporary Dramatists*. Ed. D. L. Kirkpatrick. Chicago: St. James, 1988. 478–80.
Disch, Thomas. "Theater." *Nation* 7–14 Jan. 1991: 24–26.
Dostoevsky, Fyodor. *Notes from Underground*. 1864. New York: Bantam, 1981.
Falk, Florence A. "Dangling Conversation." *American Theater* Dec. 1991: 20–21.
Gill, Brendan. "Out There and Down Here." *New Yorker* 11 Feb 1980: 64–65.
Hatch, Robert. "Films." *Nation* 7 Nov. 1981: 483–84.
Kael, Pauline. "Flag Nag." *New Yorker* 4 Jan. 1982: 81–83.
Kroll, Jack. "Cast of Thousands." *Newsweek* 7 Sept. 1981: 81.
——. "Conversation Piece." *Newsweek* 26 Oct. 1981: 78.
——. "I Love You/I Hate You." *Newsweek* 18 Feb. 1980: 117.
——. "That Nice Mr. Hitler." *Newsweek* 18 Nov. 1985: 90
Machiavelli, Niccoló. *The Mandrake*. Trans. Wallace Shawn. New York: Dramatists Play Service, 1978.
Rich, Frank. "Stage: Cast of 70 at La Mama." *New York Times* 28 Aug. 1981: C3.
Savran, David. "Wallace Shawn." *In Their Own Words*. New York: Theatre Communications Group, 1988. 207–22.
Schickel, Richard. "Small Bore." *Time* 26 Oct. 1981: 94.
Shawn, Wallace. *A Thought in Three Parts. Wordplays* 2. New York: Performing Arts Journal, 1982. 28–57.
——. *Aunt Dan and Lemon*. New York: Grove, 1985.
——. *The Fever*. New York: Noonday, 1997.
——. *The Hotel Play*. New York: Dramatists Play Service, 1982.
——. *Marie and Bruce*. New York: Grove, 1980.
——. "Notes in Justification of Putting the Audiences Through a Difficult Evening." *Famous American Plays of the 1980s*. Ed. Robert Marx. New York: Laurel, 1988. 189–94.
——. And André Gregory. *My Dinner with André*. New York: Grove, 1981.
Shewey, Don, & Susan Shacter. "Wallace Shawn." *Caught in the Act: New York Actors Face to Face*. New York: New American Library, 1986. 218–23.
Simon, John. "*Harold and Maude* and *Marie and Bruce* ." *New York* 18 Feb. 1986. 218–23.
——. "Real Lemon." *New York* 11 Nov. 1985: 129.
Virshup, Amy. "Sticking It Out: The 1990–91 Obie Awards." *Village Voice* 21 May 1991: 98–99.
Warrick, Camilla. "Play Inspires Social Thought on Home Tour." *Cincinnati Enquirer* 26 Jan. 1992: B1.
Weales, Gerald. "Bobbing & Invading." *Commonweal* 28 Mar. 1986: 179–80.
——. "Degrees of Difference." *Commonweal* 11 Jan 1991: 18.
Wetzsteon, Ross. "Wally Shawn: Holy Fool of the American Theater?" *Village Voice* 2 Apr. 1991: 35–37.

Chapter Fifteen

The Agoraphobic Imagination: The Protagonist Who Murders and the Critics Who Praise Her

Nancy L. Nester

Long lured by its captivating strains, female protagonists of literature have fled to the untenable space of madness. Feminist scholars who scrutinize such journeys strive to determine the extent to which these characters succeed or fail to cross the meridian of patriarchy into the uncharted waters of liberated female determinacy and discourse. After careful soundings, some critics issue warnings. Shoshana Felman in "The Critical Phallacy" cites Phyllis Chesler's caution that although the madwoman is often glorified as heroic, the state of madness must never be mistaken as "political or cultural revolution" (qtd. in Felman 2). Rather, Felman depicts madness as a rhetorical trope, the diametrical opposite of "rebellion" (2), ultimately, an "impasse" (2). Yet other critics, heedless of such warnings, habitually interpret the dramaturgical use of especially the mad murderess as the apparatus of rebellion (Barbara Ozieblo), liberation (Barbara Bywaters), and transformation (Helene Keyssar).

This study, however, is driven by the conviction that the mad murderess and the critical language that attends her—rather than inspiring female transformation (Helene Keyssar), sparking evolution (Lois Gottlieb), exposing cultural codes (Sue-Ellen Case), and challenging the ethos of hegemonic ideology (Judith Stephens) called for by some feminist drama critics—evidences, instead, the manifestations of an agoraphobic imagination capable of circumscribing both protagonist and critic. The mad protagonist who murders, rather than transgressing, remains fearfully confined within a familiar, traditional paradigm. Critics are similarly restricted conceptually whenever they are drawn to the trappings of subversion that the mad murderess's actions take on and mistake those actions as liberating. In the process, they allow the flaunting of the antediluvian criminal madwoman to upstage the truly liberating and thematically revolutionary moments of the plays. Such readings become complicit in shaping perceptions of the dramas and of the larger body of feminist literature of which they are a part.[1] The collapse of female agency into stereotype goes unnoticed by critics of Susan Glaspell's

The Verge (1922), Sophie Treadwell's *Machinal* (1928), and Wendy Kesselman's *My Sister In This House* (1980), three dramas acclaimed as innovative and feminist and important to any expansion of the traditional canon.[2]

Consider, for example, the actions of Claire Archer in *The Verge* by Susan Glaspell, an early-twentieth-century feminist writer. Written shortly after women became enfranchised by winning the right to vote, *The Verge* is a cerebral, expressionistic drama, centering on the neo-apotheosis of a New Woman, Claire Archer. The exposition reveals the living arrangement of a group of sophisticated and, even by present-day standards, quite tolerant individuals: Harry, Claire's husband; Dick, her lover; Tom, her soul mate; Anthony, her work mate; and Hattie, her maid. Though Claire draws the action to herself, at the heart of the plot is her philosophy, a blend of Platonic and Aristotelian ponderings. Glaspell cues the reader to this classicism in her stage directions. When describing the first set, a greenhouse, she writes: "The frost has made patterns on the glass as if—as Plato would have it—the patterns inherent in abstract nature and behind all life had to come out" (58). Throughout the play, Claire spars with the Platonic notion of forms and mimesis. She challenges, too, the Aristotelian conception of re-creation. Victory, for her, lies in forcing life forms to remain unique by undergoing an accelerated process of evolution.

Claire, though, fails to escape the patterning she attempts to flee. Her daughter, Elizabeth, is typical, and according to Claire, a failure. Tom, too, eventually disappoints her when he offers little more than a predictable retreat from a foreboding unknown. Her botanical projects also disillusion her. She destroys the Edge Vine when it appears to regress (78). The Breath of Life, another plant, though technically a success, fails in objective—to escape form, to remain other (96). Instead, Claire recognizes in these experiments, nature's inherent tendency to establish patterns (96).

Critics overlook this aspect of the denouement, opting to read Claire's efforts, especially her desire to control and transcend natural law, typically male prerogatives, as fracturing female stereotypes. Sharon Friedman claims it is Claire's acute awareness of her confinement and her desire to escape imminence that distinguish her and earn the play the feminist moniker (76). Christine Dymkowski interprets Claire's struggle to reorder nature as a method of revealing the potential of human nature (100). Barbara Ozieblo believes the play disseminates a general commentary on all human beings who, like the protagonist stifling within her marriage, are hopelessly constrained by societal norms (70). In the course of their analyses, these critics become increasingly infatuated with Claire's attempts and, in their opinion, eventual success at achieving otherness in exchange for her sanity. Within the play, Glaspell reveals the state of "otherness" to be Claire's passion. Claire refers to the Breath of Life as being "alive in its otherness" (62). Humans, she believes, may achieve a similar state. "But it can be done!" she proclaims, "We need not be held in forms molded for us. There is outness—and otherness" (64). To reach it, they must take a "sporting chance"; they must go mad (65).

Critics largely ignore the very contradictions in Claire's philosophy which Glaspell seems so clearly to reveal. There is no otherness. Otherness exists only in binary opposition to sameness, to which it is inextricably bound. Without repetition and constancy, otherness or difference ceases to exist. This is the insight Claire comes to when she breaks into poetic discourse on the topic of the Breath of Life: "Breath of the uncaptured? / You are a novelty. / Out? / You have been brought in" (96). Unwittingly, Claire desired a pattern be set when she hoped to add fragrance or "reminiscence" (62) to her creation. "What has gone out," she says, "should bring fragrance from what it has left" (63). The essence it carries, the traces become the tendons linking it to what it once was, despite Claire's claim she can make this essence something less than overpowering (64). Claire seems not to recognize the fissures in her logic, leading her to eventually languish in the "cave" from which she professes to have seen "immensity" (87). She, like the cave dwellers in Plato's allegory (*The Republic*, Book VII), gravitates toward shadows. When she murders her only convert, she, like the mythic cave dwellers, walks toward the fire rather than the sunlight.

Still, critics celebrate her deed. "Madness," Friedman writes of Claire, "may serve as an escape from her failure to fulfill an assigned role" (76). One must wonder which is the role the obliging characters *assign* to Claire. Granted, characters such as Adelaide and Harry suggest courses of behavior to her, but no one restricts Claire to one role. Perhaps Friedman mistakes the madness for a flare certifying the existence of a feminist ballistics rather than a "request for help," the latter a phrase Felman uses to label madness in general ("Women and Madness" 2). Friedman is not alone, though. Dymkowski explains that Claire's madness, because it meets the expectations Claire, herself, has placed upon it, becomes a "personal triumph" (101). Yet she does add a caution. It is a triumph to be "understood symbolically rather than realistically" (101). Claire has expected madness to free her to enter a space teeming with possibilities, especially for creative expression. Each life form, she believes, must contain within it the potential to create (76). She destroys the Edge Vine for lacking it (76). Yet, the space that madness opens for Claire is overgrown with destructive elements. The ascendancy "into the madness of the unknown" (76) that Friedman writes of is hopelessly encumbered with the violence of the murder. The reader/audience is likewise burdened by Dymkowski's expectation that she or he assume the responsibility of identifying what must be understood as didacticism and what must be interpreted as symbolism. This is especially important in that Dymkowski never explains *why* the characters' suggestion that Claire act more nurturing or thoughtfully be interpreted as representational—corresponding to a like situation in society—but her madness and attendant destructive impulse be regarded as metaphor, madness representing female potentiality. A reading dependent upon such ambiguity loses much of its feminist zing.

Critics feel equally compelled to guide the reader/viewer's understanding of the acts of Helen Jones, protagonist of Sophie Treadwell's *Machinal*, an expressionistic play presumably based on a love triangle murder (1927), in which Ruth Snyder and Judd Gray are accused and convicted of murdering Snyder's husband (Barlow xxviii). Helen, who has economic responsibility for herself and her mother, soon grows tired of the enervating drudgery of the work-a-day world. Relief, she mistakenly imagines, will come from a loveless marriage to George H. Jones, the wealthy vice president of the firm for which she works. This option appears as mechanically within the plot as the sounds surrounding her. That Helen, a product of an industrialized, capitalist society, a woman who physically reacts against confinement (Burke 77), chooses this traditional alternative does little to surprise the other characters within the play and the audience. Helen's response, however, to the banality of her life, in general, does surprise. Her rejections of not only her husband's touch but also of maternity subvert to the extent they are atypical. Certainly, frigidity is a stereotypical female response to sex. However, Helen's sexual relationship with her rebel lover, Richard Roe, belies her previous timidity and unresponsiveness, proving the initial response was acute rather than chronic. Interestingly, Roe, a fugitive and murderer, unwittingly inspires Helen to commit a copycat crime. She murders her husband by using a stone-filled vase, the type of weapon Roe used to commit murder in Mexico. As Barbara Bywaters points out, Helen becomes an "'every woman,' one who is neither politically motivated nor ambitious or creative" (100).

That this unexceptional woman would rather murder her husband than divorce him may shock those who in the final scenes stand in judgment of her, but in terms of plot patterns and characterization, her actions reproduce a standard dichotomy—the angel/monster. Helen's lover, in the nascent stages of their relationship, refers to her as an angel (217); and her husband has repeatedly remarked on her sexual innocence (199; 238). Her propensity to violence is suggested when she threatens to kill her mother (193). That these character traits inhabit the same body and not two separate individuals is a slight departure from the nineteenth century mad double or doppelgänger motif. Such shifts in one psyche might be regarded as a hallmark of feminist, even transformational theatre,[3] evidence of the psychological complexity of women and their ability to defy categories. Sandra Gilbert and Susan Gubar, in *War of the Words,* extol the militant madwomen's move from ancillary role to protagonist (67), and Gayle Austin applauds the madwoman who takes action *and* speaks ("The Madwoman in . . ." 76).

Yet, it is from an array of rigidly defined categories that Helen Jones chooses when she retreats into madness and resorts to murder in an effort to escape the suffocating expectations of her life as wife and mother. Marilyn French differentiates between two types of femininity—"in-law" and "outlaw"—the benevolent and the subversive (222); the latter "associated with darkness, chaos, flesh, the sinister, magic and above all, sexuality" (222). This woman, like the male, will kill (222). To pigeon-hole behavior in this manner is tantamount to essentializing what is feminine and masculine. However, French merely describes principles commonly associated with gender not sex. Still, the essentializing nature of these categories should not be erased. In *Machinal*, Helen Jones does recall the murder as her single moment of freedom. When confessing to the priest, she says: "I've been free, Father! For one moment—down here on earth—I have been free" (252).

Madness *is* essentialized because it is too often mistaken for the path to a female's liberation. Barbara Bywaters characterizes Jones's act as an example of a "strategy of resistance" (100). She builds on Sharon Friedman's identification of the "impulse toward resistance" (Friedman 71) in dramas by females, about females. Bywaters considers *Machinal* to be a social protest play. One cannot help wondering, though, what it is, specifically, that Jones resists when she occupies the space of criminal insanity. Certainly it is a space opened for her long ago in ancient dramas, a space into which she, like the agoraphobic, can too easily slip, never having to engage the struggle for access to the open marketplace of subject positions. I believe Friedman implies something quite different when she suggests that feminism in dramas written by females is felt when they express a certain freedom, a breaking free of tropes, in an effort to inspire social activism (71). One might ask of Bywaters, How does murder as problem resolution represent this type of *freedom* for women when the last image in Treadwell's play situates Jones in prison, about to be executed by males, according to the laws of males, alienated physically and spiritually from the other females in her life?

This is a conundrum, one which resurfaces when perusing the critical analyses of the murder of two women by two women in the drama *My Sister in This House.* Kesselman's drama is based on the lives of the Papin sisters who, in 1933, in Le Mans, France, murdered and then mutilated their employers, the Lancelins, mother and daughter (Flanner 98–104). This incident, much commented upon, inspired an earlier surrealistic drama, *The Maids* by Jean Genet. Kesselman, after meticulous research, achieves a remarkable degree of verisimilitude in her plotting, though she does take some liberties with the historical events. Although the action in Kesselman's drama unfolds within a patriarchal frame, males are absent from the stage. A male presence is achieved by the voices of the photographer and the judges, which are heard on stage. Other males are alluded to: Isabelle Danzard is said to be involved in a protracted engagement with an unnamed male, and we assume there at one time was a Monsieur Danzard. However, these males give little impetus to the action. The play's force comes from the interactions of the four women: the Madame and Isabelle Danzard (the employees) and Christine and Lea Lutton (domestic servants).

Kesselman allows the events to unfold chronologically; she offers glimpses of incidents which occurred in the course of several years, thereby mimicking closely the gradual escalation of oppression and concomitant frustration the historical maids experienced at the hands of their employers. She is daring, though, with point of view. Her juxtapositioned, simultaneous scenes afford the audience access to the actions of both the Luttons and the Danzards. The audience is brought to what in film theory is called the "impossible place,"[4] a point of view not motivated by the character or a vantage point beyond the natural realm of the viewer (Heath 410). By exposing the fluid boundaries between pockets of reality, Kesselman nudges the audience to see the gamut of emotions, from their insecurities to their machinations.

Also exposed is the confluence of eroticism and distrust. Lea's presence in the house disturbed, from the outset, some fragile calm Christine's guarded actions had created. As the relationship between the maids in the play becomes more sexual, the bonds of trust between servant and mistress and sister and sister fray. Gradually, Christine's early disappointment with Lea's ineptitude—Lea fails to ease the burden of servitude—(10) becomes transfigured by suspicion and jealousy; finally she obsesses about the growing affection of Isabelle for Lea. The tension of the play mounts as Kesselman gives the audience concrete evidence the relationship between the sisters now has a sexual dimension. Madame Danzard's own frustrated sensuality finds its only expression in her search for imperfections. She passes a white gloved hand across the treads of the stairs (Scene 4), seizes the scissors from Christine's hand, and shears the bodice of Isabelle's gown (Scene 12).

The climax of Kesselman's drama is driven by the Luttons' need to sustain their complex relationship. In the concluding scenes of the play, the sisters have fulfilled Mad Flower's prophecy: they are bound to each other for life (16). Lea, in particular, in the final moments, can no longer fathom an existence without her sister. The smoldering tensions ignite at Madame Danzard's claim that she will slander the sisters' reputation, thereby ruining their future prospects for dignified posts, especially together. The reaction of both sisters is feral. At the moment Lea poises a pewter pitcher above Isabelle's head, Christine leaps at Madame Danzard (69).

Characterizing the murder as a crime of passion is perhaps Kesselman's sharpest departure from the transcript of actual events. In actuality, this was a premeditated murder: the sisters, armed with a vase and knife, awaited their employers' return. Their action was prompted by the fear of yet one more reprimand after Lea burned Madame's blouse when the fuse had blown again (Kilkelly 28–29). However, during the court proceedings, concrete evidence of a sexual relationship—which was purported to be the motivation for the crime—never materialized beyond speculation (Hart 132–35).

In the hermeneutics critics use, the moral and allegorical significance of the events of the play carries the most import. In a world governed by patriarchal norms, peopled with women who are little more than cultural constructs, the very idea that the female *will* murder is consequential. Critics tend to focus on the murder as a transgression against the male-defined mores and traditional representation of the female. A cosmos where women are viewed primarily as "sources of good," Bette Mandl believes, must be systematically disrupted by representations which depict "female diversity" (Mandl 252). An important "variation" she sees in *My Sister* is that other females are now the target of the kind of violence which, if employed at all, would be typically directed toward a male or lover (Mandl 251). Lynda Hart, too, believes the Luttons break type, but do so by committing two important taboos. The maids kill violently, an action assumed beyond the "patriarchal prescription" of female as non-violent (136); and they react to oppressive homophobia by directing violence away from themselves. Typically, violence precipitated by enforced sexual repression is self-directed: martyrdom and suicide are the two most common options (136). The murder of the Danzards, Helene Keyssar claims, is "the only appropriate response" (181). The sisters act upon their sexual desires and against their social oppressors (181–82). Ann Kilkelly goes so far as to call the action revolutionary (33).

These critics, like those previously mentioned, are drawn to the wildness of the females' actions. Mandl's attack on essentializing female experience is grounded in an assumption that is no less restricting and essentialist: texts that depict women as *other than* guardians of the felicity of society or participants in a solid sisterhood always somehow afford glimpses of the complexity of female experience. She begs the question of whether the actions of the madwoman are in themselves liberating or transformative.

My Sister in This House depicts the maddened females' savage reaction to verbal abuse. In the end, the women are characterized as dangerous and presumably insane. It seems the denouement of this drama, like those of *The Verge* and *Machinal*, offers little that is unique in terms of subject positions nor does it multiply the number of positions women may occupy. The madwomen, again, become the alter egos of the angels of the house (see Gilbert, *Madwoman*). Hart, too, when commenting on *My Sister*, seems drawn to the stereotypical "female principles" (see French) metonymic of prescribed female roles. To see these occupations of traditional subject positions in drama as transforming or revolutionary is shortsighted. Perhaps in the confines of the plot, the "acting out" that the maids do may seem uncharacteristic. However, as these actions unfold within the larger frame, symbolized in this drama by the tableau motif, they fail to be novel. Though the women administer their own variety of justice by raging against their oppressors, their actions are ultimately judged by a vital, powerful disembodied male logos which decides their fate and eventually shrinks the circumference of their already limited sphere of action. They are imprisoned. The climax and denouement leave the maids, and by extension all women in an "impossible place." There is no relief to be found here. After the rage, there is nothing. The mad murderess, in each of these dramas, proves to be no disassembler of the patriarchy.

In the temporal world, murderesses are described by Florence Monahan, a prison warden, as often "futile, ineffectual women who could not think of a better solution than to shoot their way out of a bad situation" (qtd. in Jones 14). In the fictional world inhabited by the protagonists of these dramas, murder was not the only solution; none of the murders was mitigated by a verbal or physical threat to the women's physical well-being. In a civilized system, the backdrop for these dramas, humans may mete out harsh punishment only when confronted with such threats. The threat these protagonists perceived was to their spiritual vitality. For want of a better solution, they murdered. What is evidenced here is a fear of reaching into areas outside boundaries ostensibly outlined as the area of female agency. Carolyn Heilbrun, when commenting on the heroines of literature in general, charges that female writers have failed to imagine characters with the ability to move beyond suffering and pain, an agency which the writers have utilized but one not allowed their characters (71–72).

That dramatists continue to imagine women conditioned to believe they have few options is plausible and not the immediate issue. Barring falling victim to the intentional fallacy, we cannot assume to *know* how the playwrights intended the mad murderess to function in these dramas, whether she connotes hope or pessimism. The onus for positioning them as liberators, it seems, must shift from writer to audience/critic.

Barbara Bywaters suggests that in *Machinal*, Treadwell subverts and moves "against the patriarchal system" (100). Christine Dymkowski interprets the remark Claire makes in Glaspell's *The Verge*: "there is an outness—and otherness" (64), as implying "destruction of the old order" must precede the creation of the new (100). Ozieblo fixates on what she perceives to be Claire's "Nietzschean desire to overcome established patterns and to break into whatever lies beyond . . ." (71). Each implies that we may move against the patriarchal system and away from it. To get beyond it, we must destroy it. However, before we hastily embark on this path to a new order we must ask a crucial question: is it possible to get "beyond" this "system?" Ludwig Wittgenstein would answer "no." "Each thing," he writes, "is, as it were, in a space of possible states of affairs. This space I can imagine empty, but I cannot imagine the thing without the space" (9). Bertrand Russell clarifies Wittgenstein's pronouncements with commentary relevant to this proposition. Russell explains:

> According to this view we could only say things about the world as a whole if we could get outside the world, if, that is to say, it ceased to be for us the whole world. Our world may be bounded for some superior being who can survey it from above, but for us, however finite it may be, it cannot have a boundary, since it has nothing outside it. (xviii)

Wittgenstein's philosophy illuminates the impossibility of what Bywaters and Dymkowski suggest is happening in *The Verge* and *Machinal*. The protagonists in these plays can never move beyond the system they imagine oppresses them. They cannot get outside the system to comment on it. They are part *of* the system. They are complicit in creating the system. Men and women have lived on this earth, together, since the beginning of time. What is implied in these critical analyses is that women have played a negligible role in shaping their world. It is monolithic and patriarchal, haunted by the specter of the Foucauldian Panopticon (Foucault 106–17). Women have no choice but to whisper ineffectively, using the language of the oppressors, about the abuses; or if they can muster the courage, move against the central, concentrated power (e.g., *My Sister*).

Such a perception leaves them feeling trapped, yet fearful of escape. They see no other option than to assume the strongest role this limited sphere offers—the mad murderess. The mad murderess is perceived to have the ability to step "outside" the system, shunning even language as a tool. However, the space she moves into may be equated to the space one finds when emerging from a closet in a house. One realizes that the previous place of confinement was only one space within another, albeit larger one. The *madwoman* may find some autonomy here, in that she meanders unpredictably within the norms and mores of the society, but her power to share her "vision" is limited to the extent to which she still negotiates within the language system. The mad *murderess*, however, arrests future autonomy by transgressing a basic tenet of human law, that unless our life is threatened, we must not kill. In civilized culture, she is doubly doomed: silenced and imprisoned. Protagonists at this impasse leave no text to guide the reader/viewer to alternative paths.

That is unless we, as critics, retrace the journey and ferret out the text that was overlooked. Mary Jacobus, in responding to the attention given to the "monster woman" sired by history, suggests we attend to a more viable progeny, the "monster flux," inhered with that which was once ineluctable and unconscious (9). Rather than fetishizing the actions of the mad murderess, the critic might chart her linguistic maneuverings, especially those which disrupt a notion that the dominant discourse is an impermeable patriarchal discourse, Lacan's "law of the father" (Moi 100), a notion critics may have become complicit in perpetuating.

The reexamination I suggest is premised on two claims. The first is posited by Gayatri Chakravorty Spivak: "We know of no world that is not organized as a language, we operate with no other consciousness but one structured as a language (637). The second, is that, as many have proposed, the language system, the symbolic order is imbued as much with the mother tongue (the vernacular) as it is with the father (classical languages).[5] Gilbert and Gubar argue something even more basic, citing research that strongly suggests the "symbolic contract," the child's entry into the language system, is "signed" before the "social contract," the child's orientation to gender difference (*No Man's Land* 266). Therefore, females may not only make liberal use of the spaces in the ostensibly patriarchal discourse but also freely and cogently utilize the perceived dominant discourse. They, too, have been initiated into this language system, often by their mothers, and have vigorously and impressively shaped its form and its function.

It seems, then, that to foreground the female protagonist in the process of liberation, transformation, or even evolution, critics must select instances where she articulates and communicates what might otherwise, regrettably, remain ineluctable. If they fail to do so, the feminism conveyed (which is explained to us, ironically, by critics using language) is one at great risk, for it has no underpinnings in the language system. Glaspell, Treadwell, and Kesselman clearly depict women articulating radical messages. At times they identify oppressions, at other times, hopes. These messages, though, are conveyed in words not criminal actions. The words, not the murders, create the flux, shake up the discourse, and shift control to the protagonist.

Claire of Glaspell's *The Verge*, for example, practically breaks form by expressing her "philosophy" in poetic discourse. To Tom she says:

> My love, you're going away—
> Let me tell you how it is with me;
> I want to touch you—somehow touch you once before I die—
> Let me tell you how it is with me.
> I do not want to work,
> I want to be; . . . (88)

She creates flux by expressing her desire to break the rules of the Platonic relationships she once nurtured with Tom, who now must deflect her sexual advances.

Again in the last scene, preceding the murder and subsequent to the fruition of the Breath of Life experiment, she expresses her emotions in verse:

> A thousand years from now, when you are but a form too long repeated,
> Perhaps the madness that gave you birth will burst again,
> And from the prison that is you will leap into queerness
> To make a form that hasn't been—
> To make a person new.
> And this we call creation.
> Go away. (96)

She recognizes her inability to create a living organism resistant to natural patterns. Although she is dispirited in the final two lines of this "poem," she never seems fully cognizant of her contradictions. Her desire to shatter patterns ritualistically itself becomes a pattern. It is clear, however, that Claire takes command of the discourse. By doing so, she breaks type, once again.

In *Machinal*, Helen Jones rattles the dominant discourse—which in the play articulates the expectations the characters have of Helen—when she verbalizes a pastiche of emotions, maxims, theology, and conventional wisdom, in free association, mixing and yoking the sacred, the profane, the insightful, and the ordinary.

> Let me alone—let me alone . . . crawl off—crawl
> off in the dark—going up to be in heaven—heaven . . .
> St. Peter at the gate—you can't come in—it doesn't matter . . . a woman crawled under a bed . . . Let me rest—now I can rest—the weight is gone—inside the weight is gone . . . (205)

Her words shatter stereotypes and thwart the expectations of those who presume she will quietly accept the "natural" condition of maternity. Helen rejects motherhood and interrogates the logic of a God who determined it as woman's lot.

Even Christine and Lea Lutton, the maids of Kesselman's *My Sister in This House*, manage to express in song an unexpected optimism in the midst of their oppression.

> Dream my little sister, dream
> Dream I'm here now
> Dream your dreams
> All the things you want to be
> My little Sister
> Dream for me.
> Somewhere there are meadows . . . (82–83)

They use song, too, in the upstairs room where they articulate their affection and love for one another and engage in a sexual relationship ungoverned by the norms and codes of heterosexual conduct.

These variations in the discourse are not to be understood as essentially female. They are merely forms which interrupt the flow of the dominant discourse, revealing it as a shifting point of view which may be taken up by either sex at any given moment. The protagonists' words and their actions, up to the moment these are labeled as symptoms of "madness" and prior to the murders, delineate their femininity from the category "feminine." Still, Claire, Helen, Christine, and Lea fail to recognize their uniqueness. Or perhaps they fear it, for what is outlined is unfamiliar. Yet, all of them do suspect they have something to tell. The protagonists in each of the dramas attempt at least once to communicate their ideas or needs to other women. In their dialogue there is an urgency to make contact through language, a yearning to end the silence.[6] They succeed only to the point that they can resist the urge to retreat to the sterile space of "madness." This space becomes a refuge whenever the power of the flux causes them or the women around them, like the agoraphobic of real life, to panic.

Kesselman's maids attempt to tell their story in Scene 14 of the play. When the Danzards return home, after the fuse has blown and the blouse is burnt, Christine understands she must use language to communicate their innocence. They have committed no "crimes." She begins to explain to the mother and daughter the extenuating circumstances of the day. During the exchange, after Madame accuses Christine of lying about the day's events and their culpability in them, Christine speaks so boldly that Isabelle exclaims to her mother, "Are you going to let her speak to you like that? (63). Christine, undaunted, proposes a plan, an alternative to the imprisoning suspicion of the Danzard household. She claims she and her sister will seek another post (64). Aghast at Christine's audacity, Madame insinuates there is a sexual relationship between the sisters and forbids Christine to speak: "Not another word out of your mouth" (64). Christine, though, continues until Isabelle proclaims her mad (64). Isabelle at that moment subscribes to and represents the assumptions of a dominant discourse. Christine is mad if she is no longer stereotypically female (see Felman, "Critical Phallacy"). The voice of Christine, who now has regained command of the discourse, invites Lea to occupy the space of madness. When both Christine and Lea retreat to this confine, they are once again caged in type.

Treadwell, too, depicts the space of madness as initially having been opened to the protagonist after she controls the discourse. In "Episode Two: At Home," after Helen states she will not marry the vice president of the company, her mother asks, "Are you crazy?" (191). This question loses its idiomatic casualness when the mother insists Helen is talking "crazy" (192). As Helen continues to describe her panic and phobic reactions caused by her fears of entrapment in a society which mechanically reproduces products and wives, her mother identifies her language as nonsense and craziness (191–92). Helen, feebly resisting the trap, entreats her, "Ma—if you tell me that again I'll kill you! I'll kill you!" (193) Finally, enervated, she provisionally accepts her mother's characterization of her discourse: ". . . Maybe I am crazy—I don't know . . ." (192).

In the final scene, after remarking that her mother is a stranger who has never known her, Helen Jones comes to the realization that in order for her story to be told, she must rejoin the severed ties (253) and enter again the "conversation." "Oh mother! Mother!" she cries. "Wait! Mother, my child; my little strange child! I never knew her! She'll never know me! Let her live, Mother. Let her live! Tell her—" (253). She repeats the admonishment three more times, coming to the final insight: she would like to tell her daughter her story. Helen admits, "There's so much I want to tell her—Wait—" (253).

It is Claire Archer, though, who comes closest to sharing her story with another female. Glaspell creates a brilliant tripartite conversation among Claire, her sister Adelaide, and Harry Archer. Harry's comments are incidental to those of Adelaide, who functions here as much more than foil to Claire's rebellion. Imbedded in their repartee is an incisive examination of Claire's individualism. At times Adelaide enters the dialogue from the perspective of Claire's alter ego.

Adelaide, at Harry's invitation, has ascended to Claire's room in the uniquely designed tower. She requests that Claire make arrangements for Elizabeth, Claire's daughter. Adelaide has offered to care for the young woman. Adelaide initially represents the status quo. Towers should be round; familial ties should be honored. And mothers should care for their children (78–79). Those who will not, she claims, are monsters. Welcoming the charge, Claire shifts the focus to a discussion of imprisonment. Here the dialogue, though polemic, resists neat categorization. Nuggets of wisdom, often coexisting with folly in one exchange, are found in both camps. Claire speaks of her aversion to imprisoning roles and her chosen isolation. Adelaide speaks of her freedom to "go about in the world—free, busy, happy, among people . . ." (80). She invites Claire to enter other people's lives (80). Claire, as though acknowledging she has been "touched" by Adelaide, both intellectually and emotionally, becomes less resistant. Adelaide and Harry, sensing a vulnerability, plead with her to articulate her needs. Sensitive to a loss of power, Claire deigns once more to usurp it: "Adelaide came up here to lock me in. Well, she can't do it" (80). Adelaide appeals to religion from which Claire eventually recoils. Claire's emotional pain then becomes almost palpable. Adelaide invites her, again, to make emotional contact with other people: "There's something about being in that main body, having one's roots in the big common experiences, gives a calm which you have missed . . ." (82).

The tenuous links they had established dissolve as the emotion escalates and language, itself, becomes threatening to Claire. Claire labels her work madness and cites it as her only "sanity" (82). Adelaide accuses her of juggling words. Claire alleges Adelaide is a "whore with words" (82). As the conversation completely deteriorates, Adelaide once again demands conformity to the "natural" process of mothering (84). Before she exits, however, she comes to an interesting conclusion. ". . . I'm also beginning to suspect that—oddity may be just a way of shifting responsibility" (84).

Because threads of wisdom and folly quilt the entire discourse, to rip away one threatens the design of the other. Feminist sympathies may, in fact, be inclined to rest with Claire. However, one must wonder whether Adelaide has not leveled a charge to which all feminists must answer. Have feminists the responsibility to articulate their vision? Is it not that failure that inevitably becomes the undoing of each of these protagonists?

As each one, out of fear or anger, escapes that responsibility, they leave the stage devoid of female storytellers. In each of the final scenes, the women are surrounded by males, engulfed in their discourse. The last words the protagonists utter are tentative—songs shared with other women (*My Sister* and *The Verge*) and cries for "Someone, anyone" (*Machinal*). The murders they committed, rather than elevating their lives to higher ontological planes, led them only to the portals of their prisons and the virtual estrangement from language, imperiling the feminist message.

Critics must, perhaps, assume the responsibility of telling the stories. If the protagonists have failed to perceive the fault lines that they have created in what is thought of as presumably feminine, if they have lost sight of their uniqueness, the critics should not share their anxiety about leaving familiar territory. It is the ability to recognize when gendered behavior has been authentically challenged and what has caused the flux which will mark the remission of the agoraphobic imagination. It, and not the mad murderess, signifies that females have evolved beyond the angel or madwoman and now negotiate the open spaces.

Notes

1 Commenting on criticism, in general, Martha Nussbaum bemoans the dearth of "writing about literature that talks of human lives and choices as if they matter to us all" (171).

2 Sally Burke's *Feminist Playwrights: A Critical History* provides an insightful, feminist overview of a newly shaped canon of women playwrights.

3 See Megan Terry's definition of transformational theatre, in "Process and Problems" in Chinoy's and Jenkin's *Women in American Theatre.*

4 Stephen Heath quotes Edward Branigan in "Narrative Space," p. 401. This term refers to any shift in narration or camera angle which positions the viewer in a position not motivated by point of view or plausible angle of vision.

5 The vernacular, which replaced literary Latin and Greek as the written language, was widely used by women writers. The themes of their writings drew attention and were eventually co-opted by males. The writing women did was sporadically preserved after the tenth century (Kolb 1, 28).

6 Jonnie Guerra, in her analysis of Beth Henley's dramas, identifies storytelling as an important mode of sharing female experience, creating bonds and, most importantly, "breaking silence" (123).

Works Cited

Austin, Gayle. "Feminist Literary Criticism: The 'Resisting Reader.'" *Feminist Theories for Dramatic Criticism.* Ann Arbor: U of Michigan P, 1990. 21–37.

——. "The Madwoman in the Spotlight: Plays of Maria Irene Fornes." *Making a Spectacle.* Ed. Lynda Hart. Ann Arbor: U of Michigan P, 1989. 76–87.

Barlow, Judith, E. ed. *Plays by American Women: 1900–1930.* New York: Applause Theatre, 1988.

——. "Introduction." Barlow. ix–xxxiii.

Burke, Sally. *American Feminist Playwrights: A Critical History.* New York: Twayne, 1996.

Bywaters, Barbara. "Marriage, Madness, and Murder in Sophie Treadwell's *Machinal.*" Schlueter 97–109.

Case, Sue-Ellen. *Feminism and Theatre.* New York: Methuen, 1988.

Chinoy, Helen K., and Jenkins, Linda W. eds. *Women In American Theatre.* New York: Crown, 1981.

Dymkowski, Christine. "On the Edge: The Plays of Susan Glaspell." *Modern Drama* 31 (1988): 91–105.

Felman, Shoshana. "Women and Madness: The Critical Phallacy." *Diacritics* 5 (1975): 2–10.

——. *Writing and Madness.* Ithaca: Cornell UP, 1985.

Flanner, Janet. *Paris Was Yesterday: 1925–1939.* New York: Viking, 1972.

Foucault, Michel. "The Structures of Punishment." *Contemporary Critical Theory.* Ed. Dan Latimer. San Diego: Harcourt, 1989. 103–22.

French, Marilyn. "The Gender Principles." *Contexts For Criticism.* Ed. Donald Keesy. Palo Alto: Mayfield, 1993. 220–26.

Friedman, Sharon. "Feminism as Theme in Twentieth-Century American Women's Drama." *American Studies* 25 (1984): 69–89.

Gilbert, Sandra M. *The Madwoman in the Attic.* New Haven: Yale UP, 1988.

—— and Susan Gubar. *The War of The Words. Vol. 1 of No Man's Land.* 3 vols. New Haven: Yale UP, 1988.

Glaspell, Susan. *The Verge. Plays by Susan Glaspell.* Ed. C. W. E. Bigsby. Cambridge: Cambridge UP, 1987. 57–101.

Gottlieb, Lois. "Looking To Women: Rachel Crothers and The Feminist Heroine." Chinoy 138.

Guerra, Jonnie. "Beth Henley: Female Quest and the Family-Play Tradition." *Making A Spectacle.* Ann Arbor: U of Michigan P, 1989. 118–30.

Hart, Lynda. ed. *Making a Spectacle.* Ann Arbor: U of Michigan P, 1989.

——. "'They Don't Even Look Like Maids Anymore': Wendy Kesselman's *My Sister in This House.*" Hart 131–46.

Heath, Stephen. "Narrative Space." *Narrative, Apparatus, Ideology: A Film Theory Reader.* Ed. Philip Rosen. New York: Columbia UP, 1986. 379–420.

Heilbrun, Carolyn G. *Reinventing Womanhood.* New York: Norton, 1979.

Jacobus, Mary. *Reading Woman: Essays in Feminist Criticism.* New York: Columbia UP, 1986.

Jones, Ann. *Women Who Kill.* New York: Holt, 1980.

Kesselman, Wendy. *My Sister in This House.* New York: Samuel French, 1980.

Keyssar, Helene. "Nooks, Crannies, and New Directions." *Feminist Theatre.* Hong Kong: Macmillan, 1984. 180–84.

Kilkelly, Ann Gavere. "Who's In The House?" *Women and Performance* 3.1 (1986): 28–35.

Kolb, Elene. "When Women Finally Got the Word." *New York Times Book Review* 9 July 1989: 1, 28.

Mandl, Bette. "Disturbing Women: Wendy Kesselman's My Sister in This House." *Modern American Drama: The Female Canon.* Ed. June Schlueter. Rutherford: Association of U Presses, 1990. 246–53.

Moi, Toril. *Sexual/Textual Politics: Feminist Literary Theory.* London: Routledge, 1985.

Nussbaum, Martha C. *Love's Knowledge: Essays on Philosophy and Literature.* New York: Oxford UP, 1990.

Ozieblo, Barbara. "Rebellion and Rejection: The Plays of Susan Glaspell." Schlueter 66–76.

Plato. *The Republic. Great Dialogues of Plato.* Ed. Eric H. Warmington and Philip G. Rouse. New York: New American Library, 1956. 312–41.

Russell, Bertrand. "Introduction." *Tractatus Logico-Philosophicus.* By Ludwig Wittgenstein. Suffolk: Richard Clay, 1966. ix–xxii.

Schlueter, June. ed. *Modern American Drama: The Female Canon.* Rutherford: Association of U Presses, 1990.

Spivak, Gayatri Chakravorty. "Feminism and Critical Theory." *Contemporary Critical Theory.* Ed. Dan Latimer. San Diego: Harcourt, 1989. 635–58.

Stephens, Judith L. "Gender Ideology and Dramatic Convention In Progressive Era Plays, 1890–1920." *Performing Feminisms: Feminist Critical Theory and Theatre.* Ed. Sue-Ellen Case. Baltimore: Johns Hopkins UP, 1990. 283–93.

——. "Subverting the Demon-Angel Dichotomy: Innovation and Feminism in Twentieth-Century Drama." *Text and Performance Quarterly* 1 (1989): 53–64.

Treadwell, Sophie. *Machinal.* Barlow 171–255.

Wittgenstein, Ludwig. *Tractatus Logico-Philosophicus.* Trans. D. F. Pears and B. F. McGuinniss. Suffolk: Richard, 1966.

Chapter Sixteen

McLuhan, Perfect People, and the Media Plays of Jean-Claude van Itallie

Gene A. Plunka

In 1964, Marshall McLuhan wrote, "in a culture like ours, long accustomed to splitting and dividing all things as a means of control, it is sometimes a bit of a shock to be reminded that, in operational and practical fact, the medium is the message" (*Understanding Media* 7). McLuhan argued that the various media tend to channel private, isolated thoughts into communal consciousness. Instead of a mass audience that conceivably would be an engaging, creative, and actively participating force, the media have molded modern society into a passive body accepting stereotypes without question. The message, whether profound or trite, has become subsumed by the "narcotizing" power of the sender. McLuhan states, "Societies have always been shaped more by the nature of the media by which men communicate than by the content of the communication" (McLuhan 8). The power of the media to seduce humanity to collective viewpoints often created a soporific mentality, a lethargic society in which individuality is suppressed in favor of the fixed viewpoints of the mass. In particular, during the latter half of the twentieth century, humanity's archetypal state has been increasingly shaped by the media, molding the norms and values of society.[1] Several of American dramatist Jean-Claude van Itallie's plays depict McLuhan's nightmarish image that the media "narcotizes" individuals, sanitizing them into a Madison Avenue or Hollywood-type version of how American society ideally should function.

In September 1963, *Tulane Drama Review* associate editor Gordon Rogoff, former administrator of the Actors Studio, introduced van Itallie to Joseph Chaikin, founder of the Open Theatre. During the early years of the Open Theatre's development, van Itallie and three other playwrights (Marie Irene Fornes, Michael Smith, and Megan Terry) worked with Chaikin's cadre of four stage directors, two associate directors, sixteen actors, two advisors, three administrative personnel, and fifteen associate members mostly actors) who met twice a week to explore and develop theater exercises and improvisations.[2] Through improvised exercises and structured short plays, Chaikin and the Open Theatre members explored political and spiritual motifs without the encumbrances of commercial Broadway concerns that might restrict artistic freedom. The Open Theatre functioned as a laboratory in which actors performed in a well-knit ensemble that improvised without a star system that might otherwise inhibit creative response. At times, van Itallie would devise a short play that the actors would explore together, deleting segments with which they felt uncomfortable and improvising to insert new material; in other instances van Itallie would observe the improvisations (even participate occasionally) and would work up an outline for the structure of a play based upon the prevailing mood that he tried to capture during those specific workshops.

During the early phases of the workshops in 1963 and 1964, when McLuhan's research was initially being published, the Open Theatre explored the methods by which the media control and distort our lives. Chaikin developed a series of "perfect people" exercises designed to probe the stultifying effects of the media's influence on the American psyche—how Hollywood and Madison Avenue mold the image of the American personality. Chaikin explained to Richard Schechner the purpose of the "perfect people" improvisations:

> We ask the questions, "What kind of country is it that is populated by 'perfect people' talking about cigarettes, toilet paper, spaghetti sauce, detergents, and the thousands of other products that we consume?" and "Who are these 'consumers'? A night watching TV convinces us that they are "perfect people"—and if these are the images of our aspirations, God help us. (Schechner 194)

In his book *The Presence of the Actor*, Chaikin discussed how contemporary American society, confused and chaotic, idolizes movie and television personalities as icons for daily experiences (73). Our banal, mundane, everyday lives become warped and out of sync with the media types who portray perfect models of behavior. The images that we are inundated with become authentic, viable codes of behavior to be emulated by the unsuspecting, duped masses who are "narcotized" by the ever-pulsating underlying messages of the medium. Chaikin's "perfect people" exercises were satires in which Open Theatre members played television or advertising media personalities speaking in cliches and slogans. "Perfect people" were sarcastically ridiculed as sanitized, glamorous men and women depicted in commercials, advertisements, television programs, and movies. The actors improvised skits about the "perfect lives" such icons conceivably might lead.

Actors in the Open Theatre often would begin with a "perfect" person defined by the media and then act out forbidden responses to the ideal standard of behavior. For example, they might become physically abusive or perform an offensive sexual charade, all the while hiding behind the facade of a socially correct code of conduct or artificially polite conversation. Other skits placed "perfect people" within incongruous environments, such as funeral parlors, concentration camps, battlefields, prisons, or shipwrecks. Another improvisation was "The Party," in which "perfect people" at a soirée relied on advertising slogans (e.g., "It's what's up front that counts") to become the perfect guests, albeit satirically portrayed as impersonal, insipid, and obtuse. One actress stood apart from the group as sensitive and caring, imperfect because she did not rely upon advertising slogans; unable to relate to the other perfect guests, she was thrown into a swimming pool and drowned while the others sipped martinis. A similar satire on sanitized dinner guests, "Dinner with the Boss," appears as part of *Nightwalk*, a 1974 collaboration by members of the Open Theatre.

Van Itallie incorporated Chaikin's "perfect people" exercises into the plays that he wrote for the Open Theatre. Prior to joining the Open Theatre, van Itallie was a researcher for CBS in 1962 and had his first screenplay, "The Stepinac Case," aired on the CBS Sunday morning religious program *Look Up and Live*. Between 1963 and 1967, van Itallie continued to freelance as a writer for public affairs programs on CBS and NBC television. This rather unique combination of television writer and playwright for the Open Theatre's satirical explorations of media stereotypes as "perfect people" provided material to fuel van Itallie's own portrayal of the hypocrisy of contemporary American values. Indeed the Plastic Girl of *Where Is De Queen?* (1966), originally titled *Dream* (1965), derives from the Open Theatre's "perfect people." In addition, *The First Fool* (1965), a mime written during the early workshop explorations of the Open Theatre, examines, as van Itallie states, "one that was utterly guileless, newborn into the world, with the vision of an innocent" (*First Fool* 49). The Fool, untouched by the influence of modern media, has yet to receive the message and is therefore the antithesis of one of the "perfect people" who are inculcated with a constant bombardment from the purveyors of commercialization. In this sense, the Fool is similar to the imperfect actress who is so out of place in "The Party."

The first dramas that van Itallie wrote concerning the influence of the media on American society are the "Doris plays": *Almost Like Being* and *I'm Really Here*, both penned in 1964 and performed the following year. Both plays are one-act satires on the ersatz quality of the Doris Day movies of the 1960s in which Hollywood depicted Doris as the virginal, antiseptic girl next door—America's stereotypical sweetheart. Thus, in both dramas, van Itallie farcically probes our fascination with "perfect people" in the form of

Doris's sanitized sweetness and sentimentality. In addition, both plays have the same structure: boy meets girl, boy loses girl, boy gets girl—a parody of the trite Hollywood formulaic love stories so adored by the masses.

McLuhan has stated, "The movie is not only a supreme expression of mechanism, but paradoxically it offers as product the most magical of consumer commodities, namely dreams" (*Understanding Media* 291). In *Almost Like Being*, van Itallie satirizes the illusory, dreamlike quality of "perfect people," personified by Doris, in contrast to the real world, where one endlessly attempts to "play at Being." Humanity is forever at the mercy of the camera—life becomes a never-ending movie in which mankind is forced to play roles. Van Itallie's stage directions depict our deadpan existences in an eternal montage emulating the Doris Days created by the media:

> *This play is to be done as if it were a movie being shot by several cameras. When the individual actors are not, for a moment or two, on camera, their expression is deadpan and bored. They are "turned on" for their "bits." Often Doris will make a facial expression especially for the camera, or she will address it instead of another actor. The actors will always know exactly where the camera is at a given moment—sometimes a closeup, sometimes a two-shot, panning, etc. This technical device should serve as a comment on the action.* (3)

Doris's dreamlike world in *Almost Like Being* is inundated with cliches and smiles, the purity of an idyllic world that Hollywood offers to "narcotize" the masses into forgetting the mundane realities of their daily lives. Doris, described by the Narrator as "perfect, just perfect," realizing that "All America is waiting" for her performance, can only mouth trite palaver scripted by Hollywood: "I'm always on my tippytoes, always. But I can only do my best, and with God" help, I'll get by"(5). In the elevator, Doris explains to Rock (and to the viewing public) that she is not a star but is instead just your average girl next door who merely epitomizes "perfect people": "I'm really nothing but a television, radio, theatre, and motion picture actress doing her best. And really underneath, well, I'm just the girl from Dubuque" (7). When Doris momentarily rejects Rock to have cocktails (only lemonade for Doris) with wealthy Barry Knockefeller, the romantic triangle, glamorized by the movies, is in place. However, Doris refused a life of champagne and yachts, longing to return to her true love. The catharsis is as artificial as in any Hollywood soap opera, as Doris laments, "Sometimes life is like an angel-food cake that will never rise again" (10). Reinforcing her courage to return to her idyllic love affair with Rock because "thousands of pebbles don't make up for one Rock" (10), Doris is reunited with her sweetheart, and the movie ends with a song that *"should sound like every popular movie joyous ending"* (11).

I'm Really Here is a more successful play than *Almost Like Being*, which does not go beyond sterility of Hollywood movies. *I'm Really Here* more clearly depicts the dichotomy between the sanitized illusory world created by the media and the harsh realities of modern life. In a 1966 *New York Times* interview, van Itallie stated, "I think something is out of joint with American society. I think everybody is alienated . . . things are not what they seem and we all suffer from the disparity" (Novick 1). In *I'm Really Here*, van Itallie's satire on the way Hollywood's celluloid version of life conflicts with reality, coincides with his philosophical desire to portray "at least some vision of the contrast between how things are and how things should be" (Novick 1), the latter glamorized by the media.

The stage directions for *I'm Really Here* are virtually identical to the ones included in *Almost Like Being* except for two additional lines: *"At the end of the play it is as if the cameras were locked in place. Doris cannot get out of this movie now if she wanted to"* (42). Doris becomes trapped by her own image, a victim of Hollywood iconography. Van Itallie parodies the American-in-Paris movies in which the naive tourist coming right off the boat (in this instance, the tour bus) is swept off her feet by the suave European native à la Rossano Brazzi (now Brassy). The stereotyped idyllic relationships of the Doris Day movies coalesce into a quick succession of events. Rossano, the tour guide, provides Doris with an Edenic introduction to Paris. Rossano charms Doris by purchasing flowers for her and ordering drinks at an outdoor bistro; they *"break into a song and softshoe number"* (44) amidst the wonderful springtime weather in Paris. However, Doris's chastity precludes inviting Rossano up to her room, and they depart with Rossano's irresistible, "Au revoir, Miss Prettyasabutton" (45). Doris decides to take a bath in order to "wash that man right out of your hair" (46). Unfortunately, love has struck the starlet, whose remark, "He's out there somewhere. Somewhere in Paris" (46), forces her to gravitate to the balcony. Doris swoons, falls off the balcony, but is deftly caught by her savior, Rossano.

Rossano comes up to Doris's room. The love scene first goes awry when Doris farts for Rossano's edification. Phyllis Jane Wagner explains the incongruity: "It is certainly true that she [Doris] has never been taught to recognize and understand, let alone deal with and express, her personal feelings" (41). Rossano, excited by Doris's gesture, kisses her, then pulls out a knife. With phallic overtones, Rossano wields the knife to nick Doris repeatedly on the arm. Doris becomes confused, unable to understand how to react. At first, she is concerned that her image will be tarnished. "My father is a minister," Doris says to Rossano, but she is uncertain (48). Doris expected that such a scenario, like in the movies, would lead to a love scene, not to a rape. Stepping out of her synthetic celluloid environment, during this brief touch with reality is impossible for Doris: "I am pert. I am pretty. I am an American. I don't know anything about this" (48). Unable to rely upon the fairy-tale ending to which she has grown accustomed during her film career, Doris is lost. She can only babble platitudes and cliches from her tinsel world: "Everything's coming up roses, Doris. Doris. Doris, take hold of yourself. I'm going to wash that man right out of my hair. I'm going to—I'm alone. Doris. Some enchanted evening you will see? Meet? See? A stranger. But I'm Doris. I love Paris in the springtime when it drizzles" (49). Doris cannot comprehend that she is really dying—the ugly episode can only be make-believe to her. Her life has been artificial, "almost like being." She is trapped in one of her own movies, resulting in an inability to comprehend any real situation, which, in turn, will ultimately lead to her death. As McLuhan might say, she has been seduced by the "narcotizing power" of the media. Van Itallie has placed one of the media's "perfect people" in a disastrous, incongruous situation, demonstrating the sterility and parochialism of contemporary American society.

The next media drama that van Itallie wrote was *TV*, which was completed in the summer of 1966 as the third play of the *America Hurrah* triptych.[3] Van Itallie acknowledged that his work in television during the mid-1960s inspired the play (McColl 8). In the epigraph to *TV*, van Itallie cites McLuhan's quotation from *Understanding Media*: "The youth Narcissus mistook his own reflection in the water for another person. . . . He was numb. He had adapted to his extension of himself and had become a closed system" (57). "Narcissus" stems from the Greek "narcosis." Although van Itallie explained that *TV* is about "how television takes you over and how you become the thing that you watch on television" (55). Television numbs the viewer, anesthetizing the masses into a sanitized version of the Madison Avenue or Hollywood mentality. In a paper presented at the Texas-Stanford seminar on "The Meaning of Commercial Television," McLuhan stated,

> If I were to ask the television industry, "What is the business you are really in?" the answer would have to be, "We are in the business of reprogramming the sensory life of North America, changing the entire outlook and experience of the population." This has nothing to do with programs; it has everything to do with the medium. ("Television" 93)

In short, McLuhan acknowledges that the media potentially have the ability to make life into programmed behavior. McLuhan declares, "the photo and

TV seduce us from the *literate* and private 'point of view' to the complex and inclusive world of the group icon" (*Understanding Media* 230). The result is the "closed system" in which mankind's behavior is homogenized to a banal societal norm, described by van Itallie in his epigraph.

TV depicts Hal, Susan, and George as television researchers who spend all day evaluating programs. As the trio discuss their work and gossip about their social lives, a second group of actors, whose "*faces are made up with this horizontal black lines suggest the way they might appear to a viewer*" (64), play television characters acting in the programs that the evaluators are watching. During the course of the play, the performers playing television personalities begin to occupy more of the stage, slowly invading the viewing room. The action on television eventually encroaches on the lives of the reviewers (or viewers) watching the programs. In the stage directions, van Itallie cautions, "*The attention of the audience should be focused not on a parody of television, but on the relationship of the life that appears on television to the life that goes on in the viewing room*" (65). *TV* thus graphically depicts synonymy between the illusory world of television and the real world that is equally sterile.

The contrast between what is presented on television and the personal lives of the programmers is seen throughout the play, continually reinforcing the concept that the mass media control our social perceptions. Scientist Harry Fargis plans an experiment that will eliminate the need to be "hungry for love" (66) while sex-starved George and Hal make passes at Susan. Unable to control his experiment, Fargis turns into a monster; George, who must satiate his appetite for a cigarette, admits that he cannot "control myself for just another half hour" (69). When President Johnson's name is mentioned, Hal and Susan are provided with a subliminal stimulus and soon speak of their own company president. The sexuality of a commercial for Longford cigarettes is juxtaposed with George making a pass at Susan. A menage à trois shown in the TV Western *The Endless Frontier* parallels the romantic triangle in the viewing room. When Sally shoots Steve in the Western and is therefore free to have an affair with Bill, Susan simultaneously sides with George by revealing that Hal is searching for another job; a similar parallel occurs when we are reminded that Steve has been shot in the back while Hal plans to do some backstabbing of his own by leaving his job without providing adequate notice to his coworkers. A Defense Department report of a U.S. aircraft that errantly flew over Chinese territory prompts Susan to acknowledge that she is "upset" (90). A peace march initiates a discussion about politics between George and Hal. Richard and Sarah in *Billion Dollar Movie* discuss their apartment while Susan announces her plans for the evening: "I want to work on my apartment" (113). Luci Johnson extols the virtues of the family; meanwhile, George, who had lied to his wife about working the late shift in order to seduce Susan, now calls his wife and plans to spend the evening with her. Finally, *My Favorite Teenager*, a trivialized sex triangle gone awry, becomes the icon for the unrequited love in the viewing room. As the television world invades the viewing room, the canned laughter of the actors is shared by the viewers. The television actors now laugh at the real people. Gerald Weales aptly notes that the juxtaposition of both worlds suggests that our lives are situation comedies (236). We internalize the media's message all too well.

In *TV*, van Itallie demonstrates that the medium is our message—one that is synthetic, formulaic, and indifferent. Van Itallie writes, "the set is white and impersonal" (58). Gautam Dasgupta has astutely observed that the rectangular set is similar to a television box frame, uniting the vapid world of the television performers with the insipid lives of the observers (73). The constant barrage of messages from the media makes it difficult to distinguish palaver from serious, newsworthy events that affect our lives. Thus, the fictitious exploits of Wonder Boy are treated with the same sort of indifference as an announcement of the deaths of innocent Vietnamese civilians at the hands of U.S. servicemen who hit a "friendly village" by mistake. The messages, presented by performers playing roles, become so homogenized and sterile that the public becomes "narcotized"; the reviewers literally resort to tranquilizers, which only exacerbate the desensitizing effects of the media. Hal, who has learned to mouth inanities and cliches after watching television all day, is virtually drugged by the media's influence even after working hours; after eight hours of television viewing, he invites Susan to a movie, much like an automaton enslaved by the media's omnipotent control.

Over the years, Hal, Susan, and George have become inculcated with the hypocritical values that they see portrayed on television. The result is that they adopt indifferent, impervious attitudes themselves. When George chokes on a chicken bone, Susan and Hal demonstrate their lack of humanity as they self-servingly debate whether bread or water should be used to dislodge the bone, all the while being mocked by the television's droning of "Onward Christian Soldiers." The same type of news information that assuages the deaths of Vietnamese civilians is unconsciously absorbed by George, who lies to his wife in order to romance Susan. The hypocrisy that allows the television industry to sell bombs and cigarettes to a gullible public provides Hal with the gall to deceive his fellow workers about his employment prospects. And when the hostess of *Luncheon with Carol* ignores the fact that her guest, Ron Campbell of the Green Berets, vividly documents the atrocities he witnessed in Vietnam, we see how daily doses of his imperviousness impregnate the viewing room into its own brand of callousness. As C. W. E. Bigsby acknowledges, *TV* portrays a life without transcendent values, a sterile and impersonal society in which roles have replaced personal identities (109). Van Itallie's message is alarming: the media have used their tranquilizing effect to turn the public into insensitive role players modeled after the "perfect people" and their formulaic messages we see on television.

Eat Cake (1971), a hilarious satire on the magnetizing power of television, is van Itallie's first examination of the advertising industry. The setting is

> *A middle-class American interior, with emphasis on the furniture and the many appliances, gadgets and conveniences available from department stores—what we are looking at is like the inside of a beautiful magazine ad.* (7)

The anonymous female protagonist of the play "*is admiring her hair which is done and dyed to the exact softness shown in ads. She is comparing the image she sees in the mirror with an image she has seen on T.V.*" (7). The Woman is stereotyped as a typical American housewife with her vacuum cleaner in hand, staring at a television image that drones incessantly. The voice on the television socializes the Woman, channeling her thoughts into a homogenized version of "perfect people":

> You're one of the very lucky. Your skin is creamed, your hair is styled, you wear the latest. No product is the world is too good for you. You are an American. You may use your husband's credit card to vacation anywhere in the world. You may have two, even three, children, and keep your figure. You bend gracefully and empty the plastic garbage pail wearing white gloves and not getting a spot on them. (7)

The Woman, mesmerized by a television image that has virtually replaced the voice of God, admires her figure in the mirror, cups her breasts, and tosses her hair, "*posing as do models and actresses on television*" (7–8).

As the Woman loses herself in media fantasies, an intruder enters the house. The young man has the same voice that was heard coming from the television set. The Woman thinks he is one of the "perfect people": "*Indeed he might be a fantasy of hers or someone who stepped out of the T.V. screen. He might also be an ad executive indulging neat and attractively in a perverse little hobby*" (8). The Woman epitomizes the commercialized product of the television and advertising industries to the extent that she can only associate the intruder with show business personalities such as a game show host or a doctor in a soap opera:

> *In this first encounter with the Man in Black she tries to find the right manner, i.e. to feel out which T.V. show she is in. She is trying to figure out her role vis-à-vis him and the situation—which T.V. role she is playing.* (8)

The young man, revealing himself to be a rapist, forces the Woman to remove her clothing, open the refrigerator, and eat cake. Although on a diet, the Woman acquiesces to the Man's demands because she believes that he must be a game show host awarding some sort of prize for her compliance. The Man then forces her to order three cakes from various bakeries for each day remaining in the week. To subdue the Woman's initial reluctance to comply, the Man "*slaps her lightly across the face, and she is quieted, as she has seen hysterical women be quieted on soap operas*" (11). Each day the Woman eats the three cakes under the watchful eye of the intruder. Burping, crying, and vomiting through the eating binge, the Woman gains weight by the end of the ordeal; her diet, an individual goal, is subsumed by a more powerful collective authority. Finally, the intruder departs, and the Woman "*realizes she is alone. The moment she does realize this the voice and the music from the television, which have been going on in one way or another throughout the play, stop*" (13). Then horrible realization takes hold of her consciousness: "Rape! RAPE! RAPE!!!" (13).

In her desire to adhere to the demands that are subliminally conveyed by the "perfect people" of the media, the Woman is raped by the voice of advertising and television. McLuhan stated that advertising is "quite in accord with the procedures of brain-washing" (*Understanding Media* 227). The media, in their latent attempt to produce "perfect people" who will buy certain commodities, turn individuals into automatons. McLuhan warns, "Ideally, advertising aims at the goal of a programmed harmony among all human impulses and aspirations and endeavors. Using handicraft methods, it stretches out toward the ultimate electronic goal of a collective consciousness" (*Understanding Media* 227). The Woman believed that the intruder, the personification of an advertising representative or a media hawker, embodies the consensus of opinion for society. In this sense, *Eat Cake* is similar to *I'm Really Here*. Doris and the Woman are raped by a suave, sophisticated media appeal that affects their unconscious impulses. Both characters are lulled into passive acceptance of the media's subliminal messages. As a metaphor for the "narcotized state of contemporary society, *Eat Cake*, like its predecessor, *I'm Really Here*, turns individual violation into a statement about the rape of society by the media.

The last of the media plays, *Sunset Freeway* (1983), explores the effects of radio as another method of mass communication molding the individual into the collective psyche. *Sunset Freeway* is a panoramic look at contemporary

America, a caricature of how the media channel our dreams and aspiration. Former waitress Judy Jensen is careening down Sunset Freeway en route to a date with destiny—a 6:30 P.M. audition for Dick Darrin, which, if successful, may mean her big break into show business. Judy has dabbled in all of the media arts; she is Charm Girl Number One on *Million Dollar Door*, was a townsperson in the movie *Brontosaurus Returns*, took a commercials class taught by a dancer from *The Carol Burnett Show*, has played in musicals at community colleges, and now has received her audition through Starfinders. She has covered all the bases.

In fact, Judy has been so successful in emulating media icons that she cannot divorce herself from them. As she zooms in and out of rush-hour traffic on the freeway, she merges with the radio and billboard advertisements that inundate her consciousness en route to her screen test. She knows by heart the jingle sung by Philo Pennybaker and his dog Rover, advertising a car dealership. She changes her appointments for the week based upon the radio's projected crowd figures at Dodger Stadium on Tuesday. Her nutritional needs are regulated by the reputable book *Junk Food Diet*. Annuity plans are coordinated by the radio's advertisement for Western Savings's retirement package. Stevie Wonder's "Isn't She Lovely?" initiates a concern for her grooming. Soon, the radio advertisements and news broadcasts become an integral part of Judy's real life. When Judy spots a patrol car, the radio beams, "Speaking of alerts" (16). When American and Soviet computers create a national disaster by nearly deploying nuclear missiles, Judy, alerted to the potential debacle, asks, "So is there a problem or not," to which Colonel Firestone of NORAD on the radio responds, "No, there's nothing to worry about" (16). A radio jingle about riding fast horses ("Doo-dah, doo-dah") turns into a contemporary version of the rodeo as Judy passes cars expertly on the freeway, humming "Doo-dah, doo-dah" (17).

McLuhan has written about the ability of radio to titillate the unconscious into mass behavior. McLuhan asserts, "The subliminal depths of radio are charged with the resonating echoes of tribal horns and antique drums. This is inherent in the very nature of this medium, with its power to turn the psyche and society into a single echo chamber" (*Understanding Media* 299). Judy Jensen, on her way to glory through Starfinders and via her heavenly guardian angel cum agent Tommy Diangelo, is zooming down the highway with high expectations that she can translate her stereotyped behavior accrued from the media into stardom. Suddenly, she thinks that she has spotted Warren Beatty driving beside her. This icon of Hollywood, one of the "perfect people," energizes Judy: "Warren Beatty and I are driving neck and neck on the Sunset Freeway. Nobody in the world is closer to Warren than I am at this minute: I feel so alive!"

Listening to "Rhapsody in Blue" on the radio, Judy muses about Warren Beatty: "Isn't he wonderful? Right on Romertson, left under freeway, right on Venice to the Palms, and 'Heaven . . . I'm in Heaven . . .' (*She turns on her headlights which shine for an instant at the audience.*)" (18). Judy Jensen, product of her confidence training course, a former waitress whose telephone number is SER-VICE, has been reduced to automatonlike behavior as a charm girl trained to do "Not very much, really. Act pretty. Show the prizes" (11). Like the anonymous woman in *Eat Cake*, Judy Jensen, modern-day cipher, has been mesmerized by the media's "perfect people." She has been brainwashed into believing that the glamour and glitter of Hollywood is a highway to heaven open to any sycophant. Shining the headlights in the audience's faces is van Itallie's way of implicating the masses in Judy Jensen's macabre plight.

In the 1960s, when van Itallie began writing his media plays, McLuhan was viewed as a guru warning against an apocalyptic decline of imagination at the hands of the electronic age. McLuhan's proselytizing currently continues to be significant in assessing the influence of technology on the social and psychic conscience of American society. Today's electronic technology and mass communication systems have adversely affected our cognitive powers; we have become more like vegetables than creators. By reshaping and restructuring American society, Madison Avenue and Hollywood hawkers have transformed our individual sensibilities. What is perceived as programmed harmony for the good of society is actually the media "narcotizing" the masses into socially acceptable channels of behavior. As we watch America mesmerized by the power of Nintendo and video cassettes, we realize that McLuhan's insights are even more true in the high-technology age of the latter part of the twentieth century than they were thirty years ago.

Th inclusive dates of these dramas, beginning with the Doris plays in 1964 and continuing through to *Sunset Freeway* in 1983, depict van Itallie's twenty-year preoccupation with the benumbing power of the media on contemporary American society. Whether the focus of the play concerns television, cinema, or radio, van Itallie satirizes the media as an agent of inducement, "narcotizing" gullible, defenseless masses. From New York's Madison Avenue to Hollywood, van Itallie, who has lived on both coasts, sees American society in the middle, deceived by advertising companies lulling the plebeians into accepting "perfect people" as their models for behavior. Van Itallie's media plays reinforce McLuhan's research on the advertising medium:

> But ads are carefully designed by the Madison Avenue frogmen-of-the mind for semiconscious exposure. Their mere existence is a testimony, as well as a contribution, to the somnambulistic state of a tired metropolis. (*Understanding Media* 229)

Van Itallie can only warn us of the dangerous path we tread when, like a nation of automatons, we blindly accept the medium as the only message.

Notes

1 A good example of the media's ability to involve mass society in a ritual process is the assassination of President Kennedy. McLuhan notes, "It was the funeral of President Kennedy that most strongly proved the power of television to invest an occasion with the character of corporate participation" (McLuhan 125). In *The Serpent*, van Itallie used the Zapruder film of the Kennedy assassination as an illustration of the indelible imprint that the media can make on the archetypal consciousness of a nation. *The Serpent*, however, is not primarily concerned with the effects of the media on public consciousness and, therefore, is not discussed in this essay.

2 For a thorough examination of both historical development of the Open Theatre and an understanding of its goals and purposes, see Blumenthal and Pasolli.

3 *Motel*, the earliest play of the trilogy, was written in 1962, before van Itallie was associated with the Open Theatre. *Interview*, originally titled *Pavane*, premiered at the Academy Theater in Atlanta in 1965 and was presented shortly thereafter by the Open Theatre at the Sheridan Square Playhouse and Café La Mama. *TV* was written to accompany *Motel* and *Interview* for the premiere of the trilogy at the Off-Broadway Theater in 1966.

4 *Sunset Freeway* premiered with *Final Orders* and *Bag Lady* (the latter originally produced 11 November 1979) at the Manhattan Theatre Club in New York City, April 1983.

Works Cited

Bigsby, C. W. E. *A Critical Introduction to Twentieth-Century Drama*. Vol. 3. Cambridge; Cambridge UP, 1985.

Blumenthal, Eileen. *Joseph Chaikin: Exploring at the Boundaries of Theater.* Cambridge: Cambridge UP, 1984.

Chaikin, Joseph. *The Presence of the Actor.* New York: Atheneum, 1980.

Dasgupta, Guatam. "Jean-Claude van Itallie." *American Playwrights: A Critical Survey.* Ed. Bonnie Marranca and Guatam Dasgupta. Vol. 1. New York: Drama Book Specialists, 1981. 65–79.

McColl, Patricia. "Young Man in a Hurrah." *Women's Wear Daily* 8 Aug. 1967: 8.

McLuhan, Marshall. "Television in a New Light." *The Meaning of Commercial Television: The Texas-Stanford Seminar*, 1966. Ed. Stanley T. Donner. Austin: U of Texas P, 1967. 87–107.

——. *Understanding Media: The Extensions of Man.* New York and London: McGraw-Hill, 1965.

Novick, Julius. "About the One That Succeeds." *The New York Times* 27 Nov. 1966, sec. 2:1+.

Pasolli, Robert. *A Book on the Open Theatre.* Indianapolis: Bobbs-Merrill, 1970.

Schechner, Richard. "The Open Theatre: An Interview with Joseph Chaikin." *Tulane Drama Review* 9.2 (1964): 191-97.

Van Itallie, Jean-Claude. *Almost Like Being*. In *America Hurrah and Other Plays*. New York: Grove, 1978.
———. *Eat Cake*. In *Seven Short and Very Short Plays*. New York: Dramatists Play Service, 1973.
———. *The First Fool*. *Theatre Quarterly* 4.16 (Nov. 1974–Jan. 1975): 49.
———. *I'm Really Here*. *War and Four Other Plays*. New York: Dramatists Play Service, 1967.
———. *Sunset Freeway*. *Early Warnings*. New York: Dramatists Play Service, 1983.
———. *TV*. *America Hurrah and Other Plays*. New York: Grove, 1967.
Wagner, Phyllis Jane. "Jean-Claude van Itallie: Political Playwright." *Serif* 8.4 (1972): 19–74.
Weales, Gerald. *The Jumping-Off Place: American Drama in the 1960's*. London: Macmillan, 1969.

Chapter Seventeen

Desire, Death, and Laughter: Tragicomic Dramaturgy in *A Streetcar Named Desire*

Verna Foster

Tennessee Williams, like Ibsen, Chekhov, and O'Casey before him, understood that in modern drama tragic experience can be expressed only through tragicomedy.[1] In an interview in 1974 he remarked, "One can't write a tragedy today without putting humor into it. There has to be humor in it now; it's so hard for people to take tragedy seriously because people are so wary now" (Devlin 273). While working on *A Streetcar Named Desire* in 1945, he commented in a letter to his agent, Audrey Wood, that he was "writing it with as much lyrical and comedy relief as possible while preserving the essentially tragic atmosphere" (Qtd. in Burks 21). The comedy in *Streetcar*, however, does not simply provide relief from the play's tragic strain; rather the tragic and the comic function symbiotically, the comic modifies, and by subverting, also protects what is tragic from becoming either melodramatic or laughable and, indeed, renders the tragic more bitter. Lyle Leverich reports in his biography of the dramatist that while watching his own plays in the theatre, Williams would often choose moments of pathos or suffering to laugh out loud with his "mad cackle," which he has said was "only a substitute for weeping."[2] If a "mad cackle" is the equivalent of "weeping," then, as Shaw remarked of Ibsen in *The Wild Duck*, Williams presents tragicomedy as "a much deeper and grimmer entertainment" than tragedy (32).

Although many critics, especially in the earlier years of the play's reception, have read *A Streetcar Named Desire* as a tragedy, such a reading not only raises problems about Blanche as a tragic protagonist but also fails to account for the appeal that Stanley has for audiences and thus does not adequately comprehend how Williams' complex dramaturgy creates a peculiarly modern form of tragic experience that opens like an "abyss" out of comedy.[3] (Dürrenmatt 255). Unlike Arthur Miller, who contributed to the (problematic) definition of his own *Death of a Salesman* as a tragedy, Williams himself has commented in various interviews on both tragic and comic elements in *Streetcar*. In this essay, then, I propose to examine how Williams's subtle handling of the relations between weeping and cackling create *A Streetcar Named Desire* as tragicomedy, a genre that offers its audience a less cathartic, more ambiguous and disturbing kind of theatrical experience than tragedy might but also an experience better suited to the needs and tastes of audiences in mid- to late-twentieth-century America.

Streetcar's tragicomic genre, I would suggest, is one reason for the play's continuing vitality and contemporaneity in the theatre. The tragicomic opposition in *A Streetcar Named Desire* inheres most obviously in the conflict between Blanche and Stanley. Just as Blanche represents the soul, culture, and death (the moth drawn to the candle) and Stanley (the "*gaudy seed-bearer*" [29]) the body, the primitive, and life, so Blanche seems to embody the play's tragedy and Stanley its comedy. However, the tragic and the comic are related in a much more integral and complicated way than this rather diagrammatic account of the play suggests. Both Blanche and Stanley are tragicomic figures, and *Streetcar* is richly ambiguous: it presents a sensitive, tormented woman cast out from her final refuge, deprived of her last hope of happiness, and brutally destroyed by her crude brother-in-law and/or a down-to-earth working man defending his home and his masculinity from a neurotic, snobbish intruder who would destroy both and indeed almost succeeds. Williams has said that "the meaning of the play" is that Blanche, "potentially a superior person," is broken by the "falsities" of society and also that "the meaning of the play" is that Stanley "does go on" with Stella at the end (Devlin 81, 275). But it might equally be true to say that Stanley *has* to "go on," though his sexuality and his family life are forever tarnished, and that Blanche in some sense escapes, if only into madness, on the arm of her last kind stranger, the Doctor. Throughout the play Williams carefully balances the audience's sympathies between Blanche and Stanley by his orchestration of tragic and comic effects, producing finally not the catharsis of tragedy but instead the richly stimulating discomfort that is characteristic of the endings of tragicomedies.

Blanche is at the center of *Streetcar*'s tragic action and also the focal point for much of its comedy. She is tragic in her attempt to expiate her guilt over her young husband's death and to find consolation in "intimacies with strangers" (118), and in her self-destructive sexual game-playing with Stanley that leads him finally to rape her. I do not wish to suggest that anything Blanche does excuses Stanley for the crime of rape, but rather that her own complicity in bringing it about produces the tragic inevitability of her downfall ("We've had this date with each other from the beginning!" [130]) and makes Blanche a tragic figure rather than merely a victim.

Despite her tragic trajectory, however, Blanche is in many ways a comic character. Underscoring in various interviews the comedy of *Streetcar*, Williams has focused particularly on Blanche, describing her as "funny" (and as having a "comic side, her little vanities, and her little white lies"), as "a scream"; and as "really rather bright and witty" (Devlin 277, 285, 316). If we ignore the comic perspective created both by Williams's attitude to Blanche and by Blanche's ironic detachment from her own behavior, as a tragic persona Blanche is too febrile and too self-indulgent to evoke the kind of emotional identification that an audience typically feels with the sufferings of a tragic protagonist. But Williams's comedy cuts into and allows the audience to laugh at Blanche's fantasies, her vanity, her selfishness, her hypocrisy about her drinking, and even her aggressive sexuality. By presenting the weaknesses that contribute to her downfall in a comic light, Williams creates in the audience a degree of critical detachment from Blanche but also protects her from the audience's disapprobation by making her vanity and her role-playing endearing to us though annoying to Stanley. By also giving her an intelligent and even comic apprehension of her own tragic situation, Williams ensures that Blanche has the capacity to engage the audience's sympathetic understanding. Paradoxically, then, it is as a comic rather than as a tragic character that Blanche wins the audience's sympathy for her tragic situation.

One of the chief ways in which Williams creates almost simultaneous engagement with and detachment from Blanche is through her theatricality. As C. W. E. Bigsby has pointed out, Blanche "is self-consciously her own playwright, costume designer, lighting engineer, scenic designer and performer"; she enacts "southern belle, sensitive virgin, sensuous temptress, martyred daughter, wronged wife" (4). Since Blanche in some sense is all of these roles, she quite appropriately elicits the audience's sympathy for herself in each character. But the theatricality of her behavior also serves to block complete identification and create the critical distance needed for a comic response to the performance as well as a tragic response to the persona.

Today we tend to associate the blocking or partial blocking of empathy with Brecht. Brecht certainly has taught us to understand and appreciate the theatrical uses of detachment, and his own *Verfremdungseffekte* have contributed to the repertoire of distancing devices available in late-twentieth-century theatre. But the manipulation of dramatic engagement and detachment to create complicated audience responses long preoedes Brecht's work. It is a defining characteristic of both Renaissance and modern tragicomedy. Both Shakespeare and Beaumont and Fletcher in their tragicomedies often use a dramatic style that is at once moving and absurd: Leontes's expressions of jealousy in *The Winter's Tale*, for example, or Arbaces's internal conflict over committing, supposedly, incest in *A King and No King*. And, similarly, in a modern tragicomedy, *The Wild Duck*, Ibsen creates in Hjalmar Ekdal a comic character who sees himself as tragic. The audience is moved by the genuinely tragic nature of Hjalmar's plight, the death of his daughter, not because of his self-regarding, pseudo-tragic posturing, which is indeed comically alienating, but because his absurdity throughout the play has rendered him endearing and thus sympathetic.[4]

As a comic character Blanche is more complex than Hjalmar. She understands herself, as Hjalmar does not understand himself, and thus solicits as well as elicits laughter. We are wryly amused when she is being "bright and witty," in some of her turns of phrase ("epic fornications" [43]), for example, and in the way she plays up to and with Mitch. "I guess it is just that I have—old-fashioned ideals!" she tells Mitch, rolling her eyes to express the absurdity of any such sexual reticence on her part. Sometimes, seeing Blanche through Stella's eyes, we laugh in a good-natured way at her foibles. After she grandly orders Stella not to clean up after Stanley, Stella asks, "Then who's going to do it? Are you?" Blanche replies in comic shock, "I? I!" (66). The punctuation says it all.

Most often the audience both laughs at and pities Blanche's behavior. Her attempts to hide her drinking, for example, become a running joke, a comically obvious form of role-playing to save appearances. Blanche gushes to Stella in the first scene, "I know you must have some liquor on the place! Where could it be, I wonder? Oh, I spy, I spy" (19), even though she has already had a drink and carefully washed her glass. Later she tells Mitch, "I'm not accustomed to having more than one drink" (54). When we consider, however, that Blanche drinks to forget her past and to make living in Stanley's apartment bearable, that she hides her drinking because she needs to maintain a ladylike image if she is to persuade Mitch, whom she sees as her last hope of salvation, to marry her, then the behavior we have laughed at becomes pitiable. Pirandello's definition of "humor" (essentially tragicomedy) is helpful here. We move from the *perception of the opposite* (that Blanche's behavior is the opposite of what she pretends to be), which produces laughter, to the *feeling of the opposite* (recognizing the reasons for Blanche's behavior), which creates sympathy (Pirandello 113); our laughter at Blanche and our pity for her are thus inextricably bound together, producing a quintessentially tragicomic response. By scene nine when Mitch knows the truth (at least Stanley's truth) about her, Blanche's pretense of abstemiousness has become more painful than funny: "Here's something.

Southern Comfort! What is that, I wonder?" (115). The joke is the same, but the audience no longer laughs.

Another comic motif that turns tragic is Blanche's insistence on behaving like a southern lady in an environment ignorant of and even hostile to any such elegant manners. As she walks through the room where the men are playing poker in the play's last scene, Blanche says, "Please don't get up. I'm only passing through" (138). "Please don't get up" is an exact repetition of what she gaily says to the poker players in scene three when Stella and she return home before the game is over (48). On the earlier occasion Stanley's comeback emphasizes the comic inappropriateness of Blanche's expectation of gracious manners in his home: "Nobody's going to get up, so don't be worried" (48). Blanche's repetition of her earlier line underscores how she has been unwilling and unable to change her behavior to fit her new circumstances. Her inability to change, however, is not only an example of Bergsonian comic rigidity but also expresses a tragic commitment to values and traditions—art, poetry, and music (72), "beauty of the mind and richness of the spirit and tenderness of the heart" (126)—that are not relevant in Stanley's world but are finer than anything that might replace them. Blanche's repetition of "Please don't get up" (this time most of the men do stand) superimposes on the audience's memory of the earlier comic exchange between herself and Stanley a sense of sadness and loss, reinforced by her self-deprecating addition "I'm only passing through." This tragicomic use of repetition with variation is typically Chekhovian.[5]

The most overtly comic elements in *Streetcar* are the exchanges between Blanche and Stanley, such as the one I have just discussed, that underscore the oppositions between them and often take on the force of repartee. When Stanley asks Blanche how much longer she is going to be in the bathroom, she tells him, "Possess your soul in patience!"; Stanley quickly responds, "It's not my soul, it's my kidneys I'm worried about" (102). This exchange, little more than vulgar verbal humor in itself, here represents the classic conflict between soul and body, the sublime and the grotesque, whose union, Victor Hugo suggested, produces the modern genre of tragicomedy (Hugo 357–61). Stanley transforms Blanche's fine phrase and her spiritual, therapeutic use of the bathroom for cleansing that is symbolically regenerative (giving her "a brand new outlook on life" [105]) into a physical need to use the bathroom for purposes of evacuation. The spiritual sublime becomes the physical grotesque.

Since the sparring couple is a staple of romantic comedy, the relationship between Blanche and Stanley provokes both ready laughter and uneasy anticipation of their (quasi-incestuous) coupling. Their diverse comic styles, however, appropriate to the personality, attainments, and way of life represented by each, emphasize the unlikelihood of any rapprochement between them. Blanche's comedy is intellectual and playful, consisting in flirtation, conscious role-playing, and irony directed at others and also at herself, emphasising at once her resilience and her vulnerability. Stanley's humor, by contrast, is always self-aggrandizing; it consists of physical horseplay (smacking Stella on the thigh to assert his ownership of her [48]), crude jokes dealing with bodily functions that draw attention to his own body, or literal-minded sarcasm that can be as cruel as it is funny. Stanley's aggressive humor can, of course, be interpreted as a mark of his own vulnerability.

Early audiences sympathized with Stanley because they identified with a working man defending his home from an invader who despises him and everything he stands for and because of the charm and sensitivity that Marlon Brando brought to the part (Clurman 72–80; Spector). They were prepared to laugh with him at Blanche's expense, as Stanley repeatedly takes her down a peg or two. He refuses to accommodate her fine airs or to flirt with her or to allow her to gain any sexual advantage over him; he reduces her fantasies to sober facts, and he sees through all of her pretenses, often in a wry, humorous way: "Liquor goes fast in hot weather" (30). As the play progresses Stanley's humor at Blanche's expense becomes more cruel. When Blanche corrects Stanley, saying that her millionaire is from Dallas, not Miami, Stanley undercuts her fantasy with the retort "Well, just so he's from somewhere!" (124). Their repartee pungently expresses the opposition between Blanche's fantasy world and Stanley's world of facts. Sometimes Williams develops this tragicomic opposition throughout a whole scene, creating a counterpoint between reality and fantasy, death and life. In scene seven Stanley plans to give Blanche a one-way ticket out of town, while offstage Blanche, happy for once in anticipation of seeing Mitch, sings "Paper Moon," a song about the make-believe nature of love and happiness. In scene eleven Blanche, depending on the kindness of strangers, leaves for a kind of death in the asylum, while the community of men play a game of poker with its implications of raw male sexuality: "This game is seven-card stud" (142).

The most important tragicomic opposition in the play is that between desire and death. Desire, says Blanche, is the opposite of death (120). Rather than constructing any such simple dichotomy between desire and death in *Streetcar*, however, Williams renders desire tragicomic and makes desire and death identical as well as opposites. Stanley, the "*gaudy seed-bearer*" (29), who smashed the light bulbs on his wedding night, who is forever taking off his shirt, and who plans to wave his "brilliant pyjama coat . . . like a flag" when he hears that his son is born (125), possesses a comic satyr-like sexuality that is life-giving when he impregnates Stella but death-giving when he rapes Blanche. Blanche's sexuality seems to her an escape from death—from "the bloodstained pillow-slips" (119) of her dying relatives—but actually leads her to it. After a sexual encounter with a young male student, Blanche is sent away by her school principal, Mr. Graves. Arriving in New Orleans, she takes *A Streetcar Named Desire*, transfers to Cemeteries, and arrives at Elysian Fields. Both psychologically and symbolically, Blanche's sexual experiences lead her on a journey to death.[6]

According to Lyle Leverich, Williams "once said that desire is rooted in a longing for companionship, a release from the loneliness that haunts every individual" (347). So it is with Blanche. As Blanche describes her sexual promiscuity to the uncomprehending Mitch in scene nine, Williams powerfully elicits the audience's sympathy for the terrible loneliness and the need to forget the death of her husband and the grotesque, drawn-out deaths of her relations that drove Blanche into self-destructive "intimacies with strangers." Blanche's condition, to which her guilt for the death of her husband and her own desperate need have brought her, exemplifies a tragic boundary of the human spirit, worked out in psychosexual terms. However the need that drives Blanche is not to be explained simply in such terms. It is rather a more existential loneliness and a more metaphysical need that impel her and other Williams characters into self-destructive behavior. As Bigsby remarks, "The irony which governs the lives of his protagonists, whose needs are so patently at odds with their situation, is less a social fact than a metaphysical reality" (39). Bigsby finds in Williams's work a strong affinity with the "absurd."

Indeed, while the need that drives Blanche's sexual behavior retains its tragic and metaphysical force, Williams often presents the particular manifestations of her sexuality as comic and even mildly grotesque. The comedy of sex is most obvious in the scenes (three and six) in which Blanche plays with Mitch. The comedy of the two scenes arises out of the interplay between a knowing Blanche, who can flatter Mitch into believing in her "old-fashioned ideals" (91), and a fumbling Mitch, concerned about his jacket, his sweat, and his weight, who is easily dazzled by Blanche's charms. Some of Blanche's lines seem to convey a sophomoric wink at the audience, as when, knowing that Mitch cannot understand French, she asks him, "Voulez-vous coucher avec moi ce soir?" (88). In these scenes we laugh with Blanche. But in the scenes in which she tries unsuccessfully to play similar sexual games with Stanley, we are obliged to view her more objectively. Stanley induces the audience, if not quite to laugh at Blanche's expense, yet to become uncomfortably critical of her behavior. When Blanche sprays

Stanley with her perfume, for example, he responds, "If I didn't know that you was my wife's sister I'd get ideas about you!" (41).[7]

Williams evokes an even more complex response to Blanche's behavior with the Young Man, who calls to collect money for *The Evening Star* (scene five). This tense scene, a reenactment of Blanche's tragic attraction to boys that cost her her teaching job, exists at the border of the terrible and the farcical. Williams uses expressionist techniques both to convey the drama Blanche imagines occurring and to comment on it. The visual and aural imagery of the scene is intensely sexual: it is dusk and "*a little glimmer of lightning*" plays about the building (82); blues music is heard in the background; Blanche asks the young man to light her cigarette. Though literally only a shy, polite newspaper boy who is comically eager to leave, the unnamed Young Man symbolically takes on the sinister role of Blanche's nemesis. In the list of characters the Young Man is referred to as a Young Collector, reminding us perhaps that everything, even the evening star (as Blanche jokes), must eventually be paid for. Blanche's overt desire for the Young Man threatens to disrupt any future she might have with Mitch; she only just manages to control herself and let the boy go with one kiss.

Despite the scene's disturbing quality, there is, nonetheless, an element of comedy in Blanche's self-consciously predatory use of *double entendres*: "You make my mouth water" (84), referring both to the young man and his cherry soda. Blanche herself is able to adopt a comic stance towards her own sexuality, and it is this self-awareness that gives a tragic dignity to her sexual obsessions. She mocks even the horror of her life at the Flamingo and Mitch's disgust with her promiscuity by satirically calling the hotel where she brought her "victims" the "Tarantula Arms" (118), an allusion that is lost on Mitch. This scene (nine) is quintessentially tragicomic. Williams makes Mitch's sexual obtuseness, at which we have previously laughed, destroy any hope Blanche might have for a secure future when, unable to see her as anything other than a whore, Mitch rejects her as unfit to be his wife. Blanche is finally destroyed by both Mitch's sexual diffidence and Stanley's sexual predatoriness, both of which Williams initially presents as comic.

The play's last scene, depicting the consequences of Stanley's rape of Blanche, counterpoints life and death in an even more disturbing tragicomic mix.[8] Blanche's mental breakdown is not, of course, a literal death, but Williams evokes the idea of death as at once absurd, terrifying, and in Blanche's imagination at least a prelude to resurrection. Blanche imagines dying at sea from "eating an unwashed grape" (136). Her fantasy of being "buried at sea sewn up in a clean white sack and dropped overboard—at noon—in the blaze of summer—and into an ocean as blue as . . . my first lover's eyes!" (136), spoken against the sound of the cathedral chimes, suggests purification, peace, and resurrection: "That unwashed grape has transported her soul to heaven" (136). This echo in Blanche's fantasy of one of the defining features of Renaissance tragicomedy—the resurrection motif—is given a certain objective warrant by the sound of the cathedral chimes, but it is also countered by the appearance of the Doctor and especially the Matron—"*a peculiarly sinister figure*" (139)—who have come to take Blanche to the asylum and whom Williams presents expressionistically as death figures.[9]

The play's contrary ending, depicting the life that "has got to go on" (133), in Eunice's words, is at best problematic, at worst another kind of death in life. *Streetcar* allows its audience to experience neither tragic catharsis from Blanche's destruction nor comic satisfaction that Stanley "does go on" with Stella. In fact, the continuation of their life together is the most appalling thing about the play's ending and in that sense more truly moral than the ending (in which Stella says that she will never return to Stanley) imposed by the censors on the 1951 film version. Stella implicitly knows that Blanche was telling the truth about Stanley's raping her, even though she also knows that in order to go on living with Stanley, she must not believe it. At the end we see her crying "*luxurious*[*ly*]" (142) with Stanley's hand in her blouse, a prelude to sex. But now more than ever sex seems to be a narcotic.[10] The ending of *Streetcar* is as horrifying, as disturbingly tragicomic, for Stanley and Stella as it is for Blanche. Though Blanche has "lost" and Stanley has "won" whatever game they were playing, the outcome for each remains ambiguous. Blanche may have found a terrible release in fantasy; Stanley's relationship with Stella is forever tarnished.[11] For the audience, even Stella's baby, who should be a sign of new life and hope (like the children who are reunited with and reunite their parents in Shakespeare's late tragicomedies), is symbolically linked through his blue blanket with Blanche, whose final outfit is "the blue of the robe in the old Madonna pictures" (135).[12] Thus the baby reminds us of Blanche's essential innocence and vulnerability and that his birth coincided with her destruction, and Stanley's.

In *Streetcar* Williams entertains such conventional elements of comedy as marriage, birth, and reunion but gives them all a tragic twist. The wished-for marriage (between Blanche and Mitch) is abortive; the birth occasions rape, and the reunion (of Stanley and Stella) remains horrifyingly ambiguous. Through these distortions of comic conventions Williams creates the moral and aesthetic discomfort that is a defining characteristic of tragicomedy.

Apart from obviating the problems in writing tragedy in the modern age, tragicomedy provided Williams with the most effective way to explore the darker regions of human sexuality since tragicomedy allows for the expression of both the painful and the absurd in sexual experience as well as the creation of a peculiar relationship between sex (carnal, life-giving, and thus comic) and death (tragic). Desire may be the opposite of death, just as comedy is the opposite of tragedy, but in *A Streetcar Named Desire* tragicomedy fuses an emotionally charged and psychologically acute symbiosis between them.

Notes

A shorter version of this essay was given at MLA in Toronto in December 1997.

1 Williams's acknowledged master was Chekhov (Devlin 114). He was also impressed by the "quick interchange of comedy and tragedy" in O'Casey's *Juno and the Paycock* (Leverich 344).

2 On Williams's laughter, see Leverich 112, 202, 240, 562.

3 Adler discusses the early critical reception of *Streetcar* as tragedy (47–50). See also the essays by Harwood and Cardullo ("Drama of Intimacy and Tragedy of Incomprehension"). Roderick discusses the play as tragicomedy but focuses more on the juxtaposition than on the integration of tragic and comic elements.

4 See Foster, "Ibsen's Tragicomedy: *The Wild Duck*."

5 See Foster, "The Dramaturgy of Mood in *Twelfth Night* and *The Cherry Orchard*."

6 For a discussion of the play's symbolism, see Quirino.

7 For a good discussion of the sexual relationship between Blanche and Stanley, especially Blanche's sexual game-playing, see Davis (60–102).

8 Cardullo points to the importance throughout *Streetcar* of images of "birth and death, of rebirth and death-in-life" ("Birth and Death in *A Streetcar Named Desire*").

9 Schvey sees the end of the play as "an expression of spiritual purification through suffering" (109); Adler comments, "Blanche leaves the stage a violated Madonna, blessed by whatever saving grace insanity/illusion can provide" (46); and Schlueter points out that the John Erman film of *Streetcar* (1984), starring Ann-Margret and Treat Williams, ends with a view of the cathedral and the sound of its chimes, suggesting a "sacramental context for Blanche's wish for purification" (80). Leverich comments that Williams "used the passage from crucifixion to resurrection as a constant theme in his work" (582).

10 Williams describes Stella as exhibiting an "almost narcotized tranquility" (62) after a night of sex, following violence, with Stanley.

11 Bigsby comments, "Even Stanley now has to live a life hollowed out, attacked at its core" (46).

12 On color symbolism in *Streetcar*, see Schvey. Cardullo provides a good discussion of the baby.

Works Cited

Adler, Thomas P. *A Streetcar Named Desire: The Moth and the Lantern.* Boston: Twayne Publishers, 1990

Bigsby, C. W .E. *Modern American Drama, 1945–1990.* Cambridge: Cambridge UP, 1992

Burks, Deborah G. "Treatment Is Everything: The Creation and Casting of Blanche and Stanley in Tennessee Williams's '*Streetcar.*'" *Library Chronicle* 41 (1987): 17–39.

Cardullo, Bert."Drama of Intimacy and Tragedy of Incomprehension: *A Streetcar Named Desire* Reconsidered." Tharpe 137–53.

——. "Birth and Death in *A Streetcar Named Desire.*" Kolin 167–80.

Clurman, Harold. *Lies Like Truth.* New York: Grove, 1958.

Davis, Walter A. *Psychoanalysis, Modern American Drama, and the Audience.* Madison: U of Wisconsin P, 1994.

Devlin, Albert J. *Conversations with Tennessee Williams.* Jackson, MS: UP of Mississippi, 1986.

Dürrenmatt, Friedrich. "Problems of the Theater." *Plays and Essays.* Ed. Volkmar Sander. New York: Continuum, 1982. 231–62.

Foster, Verna A. "The Dramaturgy of Mood in Twelfth Night and The Cherry Orchard." *MLQ* 48 (June 1987): 162–85.

——. "Ibsen's Tragicomedy: *The Wild Duck.*" *Modern Drama* 38 (Fall 1995): 287–97.

Harwood, Britton J. "Tragedy as Habit: *A Streetcar Named Desire.*" Tharpe 104–15.

Hugo, Victor. "Preface to Cromwell." 1827. *European Theories of the Drama.* Ed. Barrett H. Clark, Rev. Henry Popkin. New York: Crown Publishers, 1965. 357–70.

Kolin, Philip C., ed. *Confronting Tennessee Williams's A Streetcar Named Desire.* Westport, CT: Greenwood P, 1993.

Leverich, Lyle. *Tom: The Unknown Tennessee Williams.* New York: Crown Publishers, 1995.

Pirandello, Luigi. *On Humor.* Introd. and trans. Antonio Illiano and Daniel P. Testa. Chapel Hill, NC: U of North Carolina P, 1960.

Quirino, Leonard. "The Cards Indicate a Voyage on *A Streetcar Named Desire.*" Tharpe 77–96.

Roderick, John M. "From 'Tarantula Arms' to 'Della Robbia Blue': The Tennessee Williams Tragicomic Transit Authority." Tharpe 116–25.

Schlueter, June. "'We've had this date with each other from the beginning': Reading Toward Closure in *A Streetcar Named Desire.*" Kolin 71–81.

Schvey, Henry I. "Madonna at the Poker Night: Pictorial Elements in Tennessee Williams's *A Streetcar Named Desire.*" Rpt. in Tennessee Williams's *A Streetcar Named Desire.* Ed. Harold Bloom. New York: Chelsea House Publishers, 1988. 103–9.

Shaw, Bernard. "Tolstoy: Tragedian or Comedian?" *The London Mercury* 4 (1921): 31–34.

Spector, Susan. "Alternative Visions of Blanche Dubois: Uta Hagen and Jessica Tandy in *A Streetcar Named Desire.*" *Modern Drama* 32 (1989): 545–60.

Tharpe, Jack, ed. *Tennessee Williams: A Tribute.* Jackson, MS: UP of Mississippi, 1977.

Williams, Tennessee. *A Streetcar Named Desire.* New York: New American Library, 1947.

Chapter Eighteen

Ma Rainey's Black Bottom: Singing Wilson's Blues

Harry J. Elam, Jr.

> Somewhere along the way it dawned on me that I was writing one play for each decade. Once I became conscious of that, I realized I was trying to focus on what I felt were the important issues confronting Black Americans for that decade, so ultimately they could stand as a record of Black experience over the past hundred years presented in the form of dramatic literature. What you end up with is a kind of review, or reexamination of history. . . . The importance of history to me is simply to find out who you are and where you've been. It becomes doubly important if someone else has been writing your history. I think Blacks in America need to reexamine their time spent here to see the choices that were made as a people.
>
> August Wilson

As indicated in the quote above, August Wilson's dramaturgical project is to review African American history in the twentieth century by writing a play for each decade. He re-creates and reevaluates the choices that blacks have made in the past by refracting them through the lens of the present. Wilson focuses on the experiences and daily lives of ordinary black people within particular socio-historical circumstances. Carefully situating each play at critical junctures in African American history, Wilson explores the pain and perseverance, the determination and dignity in these black lives. He has now written plays for the 1910s, 1920s, 1930s, 1950s, 1960s, and 1970s. Viewed together, these plays represent a decidedly proactive dramaturgy that not only reflects on the past but intends to empower the African American present and future.

Implicitly and explicitly, within his dramaturgy Wilson desires to recuperate the African in African American experiences. Wilson's plays talk to each other, repeating, revising, building upon narrative tropes. Images and concepts that are developed in one play are extended and reimagined in subsequent plays. A significant element in this process is Wilson's reconsideration of African American spirituality and faith. Dissatisfied with the relationship African Americans have historically shared with Christianity, Wilson works to establish a syncretic African and African American–based theology. At the center of this typology is music, in particular the blues. According to Wilson, the discovery of one's blues song is critical to reintegrating African Americans with their African spiritual and cultural roots. Repeatedly in his plays, Wilson imagines black people in a liminal space, displaced and disconnected from their history, their individual identity and in search of spiritual resurrection and socio-political reconnection. They search for and are in need of their blues song.

Ma Rainey's Black Bottom, Wilson's first critically acclaimed play and the most musical of his plays to date, establishes a foundation for Wilson's blues theology that he articulates further with each of his later plays. In *Ma Rainey*, the significance of finding one's cultural and spiritual regeneration through the blues song plays out principally through the conflicting views of the title character, Ma Rainey, and the spirited young trumpet player, Levee, the pivotal character, who fails to understand his relationship to the music and never realizes his blues song. Ma Rainey, on the other hand, recognizes that the blues can become both a self-accentuating song and a declaration of the collective, cultural memory of African Americans. Wilson's dramatic canon extends and expands on this exploration of this blues theology. In fact, close readings of his more recent plays provide insight into the early manifestations of Wilson's blues project revealed in *Ma Rainey*. Accordingly, in this essay, I will discuss the significance of Wilson's blues theology or "bluesology" in *Ma Rainey*, by reading this play on and through an understanding of his subsequent plays.

Historically the blues have been not only a site for black cultural production but a space for critical inquiry and considerable theoretical speculation as well. Ralph Ellison argues that the blues have the power of "transcendence;" the blues can transcend "those conditions created within the Negro community by the denial of social justice" (*Shadow and Act* 257). The fact that blues can act as a transcendent, oppositional location has brought both critics and artists to this space. In the 1960s, Amiri Baraka theorized that the emergence of the blues in slavery times marked "the beginning of the American Negro" (*Blues People* xii), the point where blacks ceased to be Africans and became consciously African Americans. Houston A. Baker, expanding and revising Baraka, sees the blues as the foundation for African American vernacular culture and as a critical element in his vernacular theory for African American literary criticism. He imagines himself as a "critique-as-blues singer" analyzing African American literary texts with an "invitation to inventive play" (*Blues, Ideology* 14). More recently, black feminist critics such as Hortense Spillers and Hazel Carby have recuperated the early blues and black women blues singers as examples of black feminist self-assertion.[1] In this theoretical context, Wilson's play emerges at a fertile text in which to examine the agency of the legendary black female blues singer Gertrude Pridgett, "Ma" Rainey, to explore blues theories in practice and to observe what Paul Carter Harrison refers to as Wilson's "blues poetics" (291–318).

Wilson discovered the blues in 1965 while listening to an old recording of Bessie Smith's "Nobody in Town Can Bake a Sweet Jellyroll Like Mine." This recording transformed his life and his cultural ideology. The blues not only became a guiding force in his writing but the foundation he found for African American expressive culture and for what he believes is a distinctly African American way of "being."

> I saw the blues as a cultural response of a nonliterate people whose history and culture were rooted in the oral tradition. The response to a world that was not of their making, in which the idea of themselves as a people of imminent worth that believed their recent history was continually assaulted. . . . In such an environment, the blues was a flag bearer of self-definition. . . . It was a spiritual conduit that gave spontaneous expression to the spirit that was locked in combat and devising new strategies for engaging life and enlarging itself. (*Three Plays by August Wilson*, ix–x)

According to Wilson, then, the cultural, social, political and spiritual all interact within the blues. Forged in and from the economics of slavery as a method of mediating the pains and dehumanization of that experience, the blues are purposefully duplicitous, containing a matrix of meanings. The blues are built upon the complexities and contradictions that comprise African American life. In *Ma Rainey*, Ma reminds her band leader and guitar player, Cutler, "The blues always been here" (*Ma Rainey* 500). Houston A. Baker similarly calls the blues "an economically determined and uniquely black "already-said" (*Blues, Ideology* 63). The blues for Wilson continue to offer a methodology for negotiating the difficult spaces of African American existence and achieving African American survival.

In *Ma Rainey*, as in Wilson's subsequent works, the dominant culture seeks to suppress, to control and to commodify the black blues song. *Ma Rainey* opens with two white characters: Ma Rainey's manager, Irvin, and Sturdyvant, the recording studio owner and a producer of "race records," on the stage. Together Irvin and Sturdyvant strategize on their plan for the recording session and for capturing Ma Rainey's blues voice. Sturdyvant reminds Irvin, "I just want to get her in here . . . record the songs on the list . . . and get her out. Just like clock work, huh"? (*Ma Rainey* 457). Wilson juxtaposes Irvin and Sturdyvant's plan to commercialize Ma Rainey's blues song with Ma's own resolve to protect the integrity of herself and her music. Ma testifies to Wilson's contention that the blues are a uniquely black voice that whites desire but cannot understand, "White folks don't understand about the blues. They hear it come out, but they don't know how it got there (*Ma Rainey* 499).

Throughout his historical cycle of plays, Wilson replays this theme, as whites repeatedly attempt to seize or possess black music, the black blues song. Early in *The Piano Lesson*, when the protagonist, Boy Willie, inquires about potential buyers for the family's heirloom, a carved piano, his uncle Doaker tells him that there is a white man going around trying to buy up black people's musical instruments. Even more significantly, the ghost of the recently deceased white southern landowner, Sutter, materializes in the Pittsburgh home of Doaker and Boy Willie's sister, Berniece, in an effort to reclaim the family's piano, the symbol of their African American struggle and survival. In *Joe Turner's Come and Gone*, the brooding central figure in the play, Herald Loomis, has lost his identity and his place in the world after being incarcerated by Joe Turner. The title character, Joe Turner, is an absent presence in the play. Mythologized in an old blues song, Joe Turne(y)r,[2] the brother of a former governor of Tennessee, kept black men in servitude for seven years. These indentured black men functioned as a personal chain gang performing menial labor throughout the state. Through the action of the play Joe Turner, Wilson reveals that Joe Turner imprisoned Herald Loomis and these other black men in an effort to capture their song. In Wilson's plays, music and song act as metaphors for African American identity, spirit, and soul. Through the invisible presence and symbolic activities of off-stage white characters, Wilson suggests that the dominant culture has continually sought to subjugate African American humanity and suppress the power and ability of African Americans to sing their song.

This musical metaphor has considerable contemporary significance. It reflects on the ways black cultural expression has been commercialized and exploited in today's mediatized culture. The raw, hard edge and social critique of black urban rap music, for example, has been commodified and softened to sell everything from soft drinks to hamburgers. In addition, Ma Rainey's obstinacy in the face of white hegemony parallels Wilson's own struggle against co-optation as a black artist and his desire to maintain his creative integrity and autonomy. Wilson's fierce resolve not to allow the film version of *Fences* to go forward without a black director evidences his determination to protect his agency as a black artist.[3]

Wilson's blues theology privileges the blues musician. He posits the blues musician as a potentially powerful site of black resistive agency. Too often, however, the musicians do not realize the power that they possess. As with any gift or power, the power of the blues musician exacts certain costs and expectations from the ones to whom it is given. Lyons in *Fences*, Jeremy in *Joe Turner's Come and Gone*, and Wining Boy in *The Piano Lesson*, all represent blues musicians who have not recognized the spiritual force of the blues song and the cultural responsibility inherent in their ability to play the blues. As a result they are exploited for their music and fall victim to those who wish to control their spirit and song. The band members in *Ma Rainey*, similarly, do not realize the power and privilege of their music, their blues voice. Toledo, the piano player, chastises his fellow band members, "You lucky they [white people] let you be an entertainer. They ain't got to accept your way of entertaining. You lucky and don't even know it" (*Ma Rainey* 507). Still it is on and through these musicians that Wilson positions himself as blues musician improvising on a theme (*Blues, Ideology* 17).

One theme that Wilson continually improvises on in his work is the struggle for African Americans to find connections, to reorient and reestablish themselves after the disorienting and dislocating experiences of the Middle Passage, slavery, and the northern migrations. Yet, Wilson's blues improvisations not only infuse the content of his plays but his form and structure as well. Ralph Ellison calls the blues a unique combination of the tragic and the comic, of poetry and ritual (*Shadow and Act* 256). The structure of *Ma Rainey* embodies this blues formula. The events that transpire—from Sylvester's stuttering rendition of the introduction to the recorded version of "*Ma Rainey's Black Bottom*" to Toledo's unfortunate death—combine the comic and the tragic, the poetic and the ritualistic. Ma Rainey plays out as an extended series of blues riffs providing each of the members of the band the opportunity to solo. Wilson sets the band interaction in the band room downstairs and separated from the recording studio above. The band room represents what Houston A. Baker terms a "blues matrix" (*Blues, Ideology* 3). Baker envisions the blues matrix is a "point of ceaseless input and output, a web of intersecting, crisscrossing impulses always in productive transit" (*Blues, Ideology* 3). For Baker the prototypical site of the blues matrix is a railroad crossing, "the juncture of multidirectionality," a place "betwixt and between" (*Blues, Ideology* 7). Situated at the blues matrix, the blues singer through blues song transcends spatial and socio-historical limitations. Positioned at the blues matrix, the blues singer is empowered with unlimited and ending possibilities. The band room as blues matrix is equally a site of power and potential. The band room is a space of unfinished business, where the band must rehearse its songs for the recording sessions. It is a metaphorical space where the band members enact rituals and tales of survival that replicate the patterns of black experiences in America. Like Seth's boarding house in *Joe Turner's Come and Gone*, the band room is a liminal space, a space that people pass through, a space where the band must await the arrival of Ma Rainey. The liminality of the space is subconsciously recognized by Levee, who comments upon entering into the room, "Damn! They done changed things around. Don't never leave well enough alone . . . That door! Nigger, you see that Door? That's what I'm talking about. That door wasn't here before" (*Ma Rainey* 460). The liminality of the band room makes it a location of great creative and destructive force. Within the storytelling riffs of the band members and the tragic demise of Toledo, both the creative and destructive potential of liminality are realized in Ma Rainey's band room.

> Down in the band room, the band members engage in a series of vernacular games, the dozens, and signifyin'. All are extensions of the blues, variations on a blues theme. Wilson adds, through the voice of Toledo, that these forms of blues games are also examples of African retentions. When the bass player, Slow Drag, signifies on Cutler in order to extract a reefer from him, Toledo explains that what he has performed is an "African conceptualization": That's what you call an African conceptualization. That's when you name the gods or call on the ancestors to achieve whatever your desires are. (*Ma Rainey* 466)

Correspondingly, in the climactic moment of *The Piano Lesson*, Wilson extends this blues riff and the concept of African conceptualizations through the actions of the character, Berniece. When Berniece sits at the piano to play, she employs an African conceptualization. Just as Toledo suggests in *Ma Rainey*, her song at the piano calls on the power of her ancestors to exorcise the ghost of the white landowner, Sutter, and to save her brother, Boy Willie.

Toledo's declarations of the need for African Americans to recognize their connections to Africa represent an important element of Wilson's blues theology. Wilson believes that in order for African Americans to be able to sing their own song, to feel truly liberated in the American context, they must rediscover their "African-ness." "One of the things I'm trying to say in my writing is that we can never begin to make a contribution to the society except as Africans" (Savran 296). Toledo, accordingly, reprimands the band and himself for not being an "African" and for being "imitation white men." In later plays, such as *The Piano Lesson*, Wilson further delineates the connections he sees between African cultural roots and contemporary African American identity. In *Joe Turner's Come and Gone*, Bynum's rituals of pigeons and blood, his story of the shiny man, as well as Herald Loomis' cleansing himself with his blood are all rooted in Yoruba religious practices and cosmology. Wilson's bluesology builds on African traditions, adapting them to an African American context. In fact, Wilson's valorization of music and the blues musician parallels the position that Wole Soyinka establishes for music in Yoruba cultural expression. According to Soyinka,

> The European concept of music does not fully illuminate the relationship of music to ritual and drama among the Yoruba. . . . The nature of Yoruba music is intensively the nature of its language and poetry, highly charged, symbolic, myth-embryonic. . . . The true tragic [Yoruban] music, unearths cosmic uncertainties which pervade human existence, reveals the power of creation, but above all creates a harrowing sense of omni-directional vastness where the creative Intelligence resides and prompts the soul to futile exploration. (147–48)

For Soyinka, music in Yoruba tragedy transcends the physical world and particularized meanings. Music expresses the cosmic, the spiritual, the metaphysical. Similarly, the blues are an integral component of Wilson's dramaturgy. They express and embody the African American soul. The blues inform both the content and form of Wilson's work enabling the spirituality and mythopoetic power of the works to emerge.

To further the blues mood in *Ma Rainey*, Wilson composes his blues musician characters to correspond with the instruments which they play. Slow Drag, the bass player, maintains the bass line in the play. He is a slow and deliberate voice who reinforces the action around him. Cutler, the bandleader and guitar player, strikes a practical tone. He is not one to improvise but has the power to embellish a theme as when he tells the involved story of Reverend Gates. Toledo, the piano player, is the only member of the group who can read. He is a philosopher who engages in monologues and storytelling riffs that are analogous to virtuoso, improvised piano solos. Toledo preaches a doctrine of Afrocentric nationalism. "As long as the colored man look to white folks to put a crown on what he say . . . as long as he looks to white folks for approval . . . then he ain't never gonna find out who he is and what he's about" (*Ma Rainey* 469). Toledo agitates for black nationalist consciousness. In the plays of the Black Arts Movement of the 1960s and 1970s, Toledo would have been the most prominent voice in the play. Toledo's voice in Wilson's drama, however, is muted. He is part of the ensemble, one instrument blending with the other blues sounds emanating from the blues matrix band room.

Still, in Wilson's bluesology, as in the 1960s and 1970s platforms of black cultural nationalism, the cultural and the spiritual are inextricably connected to the political. Wilson advocates and agitates for African American social consciousness and black nationalistic self-determination through his art. Accordingly, Toledo instructs the band members as to their status as products of the economics of slavery. These are lessons that Wilson wants all African Americans to understand. In his powerful, poetic, and humorous analogy of a stew, Toledo explains that African Americans are historical leftovers. "See we's the leftover. The colored man is the leftovers. Now what the colored man gonna do with himself? That's what we waiting to find out. But first we gotta know we the leftovers" (*Ma Rainey* 483). For Wilson, African American advancement can only come after African Americans recognize their leftover status, appreciate the legacies and lessons of slavery and realize and express their African-ness. In *Ma Rainey,* unfortunately, Toledo's words do not activate an increased social awareness in the brash young trumpeter, Levee, nor in the other band members.

Levee, the youngest member of the band, presents himself with a boldness that the others lack. His self-importance is both stubborn naivete and camouflage. Levee desires to fit in with the band, to be accepted, to achieve within a world that devalues African American spirit and accomplishment. Like a trumpet, Levee blares onto the stage. According to Wilson, "With the trumpet you have to force yourself out through the horn. Half-consciously I tried to make Levee's voice a trumpet . . . Levee is a brassy voice" (Savran 293). Levee with his brassy voice represents the forces of modernity in conflict with tradition. Significantly, Wilson has set the play in 1927, at a time when the country blues of Ma Rainey were fading in the taste of the black consuming public and being replaced by the more upbeat, danceable blues of Bessie Smith and the jazz sounds emerging from urban cities. Levee symbolizes this modern, urban blues landscape. Paul Carter Harrison writes that Levee's very name signifies, "possible kinship with the new music soundings of jazz being created along the Mississippi levees of New Orleans during the period" (307). Levee rejects and ridicules the "jug band" circus style songs of Ma Rainey. He desires to play music that makes people move and that he can "lay down in the peoples lap." Yet, Levee does not recognize nor understand that his new urban blues sound and jazz beats are deeply indebted to earlier African and African American sounds and socio-cultural traditions. One of the most significant and repeated messages in Wilson's historical project is that modernity cannot erase but must embrace tradition, that the past constantly and continually impacts on the present.

Tragically individualistic, Levee speaks of personal ownership and individual achievement. He wants to play "his" music, write "his" songs, and form "his" band. He is unable to heed Toledo's warning to embrace communality and to think collectively:

> It ain't just me, fool! It's everybody! What you think . . . I'm gonna solve the colored man's problems by myself? I said, we. You understand that? We. That's every living colored man in the world got to do his share. (*Ma Rainey* 473)

Levee does not think in terms of "we," but rather, isolates and alienates himself from the other band members and systems of African American communal empowerment. Rejecting communality, Levee believes that he is on a mission to sing his song. Yet, he does not understand the technologies of capitalism and white racism which constrict him and prevent such self-actualization.

> Levee does, however, have a profound aversion to black peoples' unquestioning acceptance of and devotion to the doctrine of Christianity. Waving a knife at Cutler and at the heavens, Levee decries Christ's lack of action in protecting his mother from being gang raped by a group of white men. He berates the traditionally Christian Cutler, "God don't pay niggers no mind. In fact . . . God hate niggers! Hate them with all the fury in his heart. Jesus don't love you nigger! Jesus hate your black ass!" (*Ma Rainey* 510)

Levee feels betrayed by the inability of a Christian god to act proactively on behalf of black people. He finds Christianity severely insufficient in meeting the spiritual and practical needs of black people. Wilson similarly comments on the impotence of Christianity in African American lives in his later plays. At the end of *Joe Turner's Come and Gone*, Herald Loomis, wielding a knife like Levee, bemoans the ineffectiveness of Christianity in his life. Ironically, Joe Turner captured Herald Loomis when he had stopped to preach the Christian gospel to some men who were gambling on a Memphis street corner. In *Piano Lesson*, Christianity again fails. Avery, called upon to perform a Christian ritual of exorcism to rid the house of Sutter's ghosts, loses his resolve when confronted with the powerful spiritual forces present within the house. The picture Wilson paints in these plays is of a Christianity that has not provided blacks with tangible support in the struggle for liberation.

Consequently, Wilson in his bluesology formulates alternative syncretic strategies for African American spirituality. In the final moment of *Fences*, Gabriel Maxson performs an atavistic dance that unites him with his African origins, his blues spirit, and serves to open the gates of heaven for his recently deceased brother Troy to enter. At the conclusion of *Joe Turner's Come and Gone*, Herald Loomis subverts the traditional Christian ritual of bloodletting in which Christ died for our sins. Loomis, instead, bleeds for himself. He cuts himself with his knife and then, in Yoruba fashion, cleanses himself with the blood. Through this symbolic process, Herald Loomis rediscovers his identity and his ability to sing his blues song. Berniece, after witnessing Avery's aborted exorcism in *The Piano Lesson*, turns to an African conceptualization and calls for the intervention of her ancestors. Her actions not only save her brother but also bring spiritual redemption to herself and her family. Significantly, all these moments infuse the Christian with the African and transpire on and through music.

Despite his protest against the inaction of Christ and the racism of Christianity, Levee has not yet found a recourse in the syncretic spirituality of the blues. Instead he turns to the devil. He is quite literally willing to sell his soul to the devil. Interestingly, the notions of the "devil" within *Ma Rainey* implicitly resurrect the black nationalist rhetoric of the 1960s and 1970s which referred to members of the dominant culture as "white devils." In *Ma Rainey*, the "white devil" to whom Levee is willing to sell his soul is Sturdyvant. Levee gives Sturdyvant his songs and expects that Sturdyvant will help him to form his own band. Levee naively believes that Sturdyvant will protect and serve his interests. Levee, however, is betrayed and undone by these actions, as Sturdyvant only desires to exploit him. Levee's deal with the devil signals his demise. Tragically, Levee disavows African American community and allows his music, his song, to be commodified and controlled by Sturdyvant.

Levee believes that his interactions with Sturdyvant build upon lessons he learned from his father on how to "deal with the white man." At the end of the play's first act, Levee tells of his father's act of retribution against the white men who gang raped his wife, Levee's mother. Levee explains that his father, Memphis Green, "acted like he done accepted the facts of what happened," while he gathered the names of the white men involved. Memphis even smiled in the face of one of these white men and sold that white man his farm. Later, after he had sold the land and moved his family, Memphis returned and managed to kill four of his wife's attackers before he himself was killed. Memphis's actions unite the power of the trickster with that of the revolutionary. Duplicitously, Memphis had smiled in the face of a white man who had wronged him and his family deeply, all the while plotting his revenge. Present in Memphis's response to his wife's rapists is the inherent irony of the blues. In effect, his performance is analogous to that of Baker's blues musician at the crossroads. Memphis, through his actions, negotiates and transcends the excruciating pain of his African American experience. Interestingly, in *Two Trains Running*, Wilson again features a character named Memphis who has also been abused and run off his land by a group of white men. Much like the earlier Memphis, this Memphis, a restaurant owner in *Two Trains Running*, has unfinished business that he must settle. After a conversation with Aunt Esther—a woman who, at over three hundred and twenty years of age, is as old as the black presence in America—Memphis reconnects with his past and discovers his blues voice and the power to sing it. At the end of the play, he will return south to reclaim his land.

Levee in *Ma Rainey*, however, misinterprets his father's legacy. While his father plotted revenge with cunning duplicity, Levee approaches Sturdyvant with romantic naivete. Levee defers to Sturdyvant because he believes that Sturdyvant has the power to make him a bandleader and a star. Levee does not recognize the authority of black people over the blues song. Cutler attempts to explain this reality to Levee citing Ma as an example: "The white man don't care nothing about Ma. The colored folks made Ma a star. White folks don't care nothing about who she is . . . what kind of music she make" (*Ma Rainey* 508). Levee does not listen to Cutler's explanation. Unlike his father, Memphis, Levee allows his blues voice to be bought and controlled by the mechanisms of institutionalized racism. Memphis sells his land but maintains his power of self-determination, his soul. Levee, on the other hand, internalizes his oppression and becomes both a victim and a victimizer.

Wilson establishes Levee's status as victim with his first entrance onto the stage. Levee enters the band room later than the rest of the band members because he has been delayed buying shoes. The shoes function as a symbol of his internalized oppression. Levee's sense of respect and identity are constructed around his sense of acquisition and property rather than an internal sense of self-worth and pride in his blues voice. This notion of "respect" being tied to external, material items is repeatedly played out on contemporary urban streets, where black young men battle fiercely with each other and without any recognition of their blues voices. Young black men kill each other over tennis shoes and issues of respect. Such battles for respect evidence the ultimate lack of respect for the black self. In his autobiographic memoir, *Makes Me Want to Holler*, Nathan McCall writes of this battle for respect:

> For as long as I can remember, black folks have had a serious thing about respect. I guess it's because white people disrespected them so blatantly for so long that blacks viciously protected what little morsel of self-respect they had left. . . . It's still that way today. Young dudes nowadays call it

> "dissin'." They'll kill a nigger for dissin' them. Won't touch a white person, but they'll kill a brother in a heartbeat over a perceived slight. The irony was that white folks constantly disrespected us in ways unseen and seen, and we tolerated it. (*Makes Me Want to Holler* 52)

Levee, as victim, suffers from a similarly impoverished self-image. When Sturdyvant exploits him for his songs, he is further diminished. Levee then encounters the ultimate frustration that many blacks experience under white oppression. At that moment, Levee the victim turns victimizer. His internalization of his oppression constricts him from acting out against Sturdyvant. Instead, he strikes out with fury against Toledo for the disrespect of stepping on his shoes. As Wilson explains, Levee transfers his "aggression to the wrong target" (Savran 300). The result reinforces the tragic implications of black-on-black violence: the senseless, self-destructive loss of black lives.

In contrast to Levee, Ma Rainey, the title character, realizes her blues song and understands her relationship to the music. Ma Rainey recognizes the power of the music to move through her. "You don't sing to feel better . . . You sing 'cause it's a way of understanding life" (*Ma Rainey* 499). Ma explains that singing the blues is not simply therapy but rather an engagement with a complex and enabling force that acts to understand and even to transform and to transcend life. Ma, unlike Levee, perceives her blues voice as a source of identity, collective African American empowerment and self-actualization. Her late entrance into the play is juxtaposed against Levee's tardy appearance in the band room. Levee is late because he falls victim to the seductive authority of American capitalism. Ma's tardiness is also due to her victimization. She, however, finds herself the victim of institutionalized racism when she refuses to be commodified. Ma struggles against the efforts of the policeman, who accosts her after a traffic incident, to treat her as just another "nigger." Repeatedly and insistently Ma shouts to her manager Irvin, as she enters the studio accompanied by the arresting officer, "Tell him who I am!" With her late, chaotic entrance, well into the play's first act, Wilson focuses the spectators' attention on Ma and further establishes her importance.

Ma remains a fiercely independent woman throughout the action of the play. Her interaction with all the men in the play is analogous to Baker's reading of the blues musician at the crossroads; she situates herself inventively and uses the resources she has at her disposal to control and mediate the world around her. Ma demonstrates a practical understanding of the material hierarchy of the record industry and her place within it.

Recognizing that the purpose of the recording session is to record her voice and her music, Ma does not allow herself to be objectified but uses her position as a desired musical commodity to legitimize her authority. She reminds Irvin, "What band? The band work for me! I say what goes!" After the recording session, Ma exercises her blues voice in one final act of defiance. She leaves the studio without signing the release forms that legally grant Irvin and Sturdyvant control over her recorded music. Through this act, she asserts the power of blues singer to transcend and overcome material limitations. She retains her artistic autonomy and rebuts the usurpations of others who wish to claim her song. Wilson maintains,

> The music [blues] is ours [African Americans], since it contains our soul, so to speak—it contains all our ideas and responses to the world. We need it to help us claim the African-ness and we would be a stronger people for it. It's presently in the hands of someone else who sits over it as custodian, without even allowing us its source. (Savran 305)

While Ma confronts the desires of the dominant culture to control and suppress her blues voice, she also must struggle against the patriarchal hegemony that seeks to commodify and objectify her as a woman. Ma must negotiate systems of oppression not only as an African American but as a woman. Interestingly, in *Ma Rainey*, Wilson uses his black male characters, rather than the white ones, to reveal attitudes of sexism and male privilege. In their band room bonding rituals and verbal games, the band members speak of women only as sexual objects. At one point Cutler admonishes Levee, "Slow Drag don't need you to find him no pussy. He can take care of himself" (*Ma Rainey* 481). Ma is well aware of the objectification of women as well as the exploitation of African American musicians. In fact, at one moment she uses the image of black-woman-as-sexual-property to emphasize her position as expendable commodity with the dominant culture's musical economy: "As soon as they [white folks] get my voice down on them recording machines, then it's just like if I'd be some whore and they roll over and put their pants on" (*Ma Rainey* 497).

In Wilson's character Ma Rainey, as well as in the real persona of the legendary blues singer Gertrude Pridgett "Ma" Rainey, issues of race and gender interact. The legendary Gertrude Pridgett "Ma" Rainey continually and purposefully challenged the limits placed on women. Through her music and its lyrical content, her public performances and stylistic flair, Ma Rainey developed an image that contradicted conventional representations of black female sexuality. By traditional standards of western beauty, Ma Rainey would have been perceived as an ugly woman. Yet, her body in performance signified not the limitations of stereotypes but the possibilities of self-definition. Ma Rainey became known for her flamboyance. She adorned herself in lavish gowns and extravagant gold jewelry. Through her performance the image of the heavy-set black woman as mammy figure was subverted and transformed into a symbol of sexuality and style. Her performance revealed traditional Western beauty standards to be a socially constructed means of oppressing black women. Since the horrors and inequities endured by slave women on the plantation, the American patriarchal system has denied or misrepresented black women's sexuality. Historically, mainstream American culture limited black female sexuality to two stereotypical images—the wanton black whore and the asexual black mammy. In *Sex and Racism in America,* Calvin Hernton argues that in American public discourse black women disappear as legitimate subjects of female sexuality (166). Michelle Russell posits the blues and black female blues singers as important historical sources of black women's sexual empowerment. Russell writes that the blues

> are the expression of a particular social process by which poor black women have commented on all the major theoretical, practical and political questions facing us and have created a mass audience who listens to what we say in that form. ("Slave Codes and Liner Notes" 131–32)

Through the activity of singing the blues, black women such as Ma Rainey positively acknowledged and represented black women's sexuality. Ma Rainey's songs displayed an earthy and forthright, crude and sassy sensuality. As she asserted control over the content and form of her songs, she equally declared control over her own sexuality. "She is in the moment of performance the primary subject of her own being. Her sexuality is precisely the physical expression of the highest self-regard and, often, the sheer pleasure she takes in her own powers" (Spillers 88–89). Present always in Ma Rainey's performance of her music was the concept of the black woman as empowered subject.

In her personal sex life as well as in her music and on stage performances, Ma Rainey refused to conform to traditional gender expectations. She was a bisexual with acknowledged lesbian relationships. According to Harrison, "Rainey's and Bessie Smith's episodes with women lovers are indicative of the independent stance they and other blues singers took on issues of personal choice" (*Black Pearls* 104). Her lesbianism and the public knowledge of it further testified to Ma Rainey's personal revolt against male hegemony and her ability to survive outside male domination and societal norms.

Paradoxically, while Ma Rainey's own activities in life attempted to subvert the male-dominated, heterosexual status quo, the events of Wilson's play appear to uphold it. Decidedly more overt than the physical exchanges between Ma and Dussie Mae, her younger lesbian or bisexual companion, is the sexual embrace shared by Dussie Mae and the young rebellious trumpet player, Levee. Protected by the privacy of the downstairs band room, they exchange a passionate kiss. Their stolen embrace emphasizes Levee's fateful defiance of Ma's authority. Significantly, Dussie Mae jeopardizes her financially stable—Ma has supplied her with money and clothing—but nontraditional lesbian relationship with Ma Rainey for an extremely tenuous but conventional heterosexual affair with Levee. Implicit is the message that relationships with men are more valuable.

Ma, a woman, is not the primary subject of Wilson's *Ma Rainey*. Although placing Ma Rainey's entrance late in the first act draws the audience's attention to her, it also provides Wilson with the time to establish interest and involvement in the lives of the band members who await Ma Rainey's arrival. The construction of the set further emphasizes the collective voice of the band, while silencing the presence and power of Ma Rainey. Ma Rainey remains above, on the surface, in the Recording Studio. In the band room below, the domain of the men, the drama simmers. In the stories and conflicts of these men, she is powerless. Significantly, Levee's murder of Toledo occurs after Ma has gathered her entourage and left the recording studio. Just as she does not determine the action at the outset of the play, she does not determine its conclusion. The play does not end with Ma's defiant exit from the recording studio but escalates into tragedy in the band room below. Despite her assertions of her blues voice and her powers of self-determination, Ma remains outside of the discourse of men and the decisive action of the play. While Gertrude Pridgett's own life and blues music represent examples of black women's sexual agency and strategies of feminist empowerment, black female sexuality and the politics of gender are neither the subjects of Wilson's play nor the focus of his bluesology. As evidenced in *Ma Rainey*, Wilson's bluesology is both a racialized and gendered ideology and practice.

The ending of *Ma Rainey* is a complex and confounding blues moment. It stands in stark contrast to endings of Wilson's later dramas in which characters reach moments of spiritual fulfillment, acknowledge their relationships to the African American past, and perform actions of self-actualization, self-determination, and communion. Present in the final scene is the ironic anguish of the blues wail. Levee's stabbing of Toledo, like all acts of black-on-black violence, strikes out against African American collectivity and cultural unity. The murder of Toledo represents a performance of tragic, unfulfilled promise, a loss of the black self that must be reclaimed through the triumph of the blues voice. The death of Toledo stands as a lesson that African Americans must learn from and that Wilson will build upon in his later plays. In African American life and Wilson's historical project of African American cultural expression, African Americans can and must overcome by acknowledging their blues voice and learning to sing their own blues song.

Notes

1 See Carby 238–249; Russell 129–140; Spillers 73–99.

2 The actual twenty-ninth governor of Tennessee (1893–1897) was Pete Turney and his brother was Joe Turney. However, as related in the autobiography of W. C. Handy, the name was changed to Joe Turner in the blues song which black women sung to lament his abuse and the capture of their husbands and loved ones.

3 See Wilson 200–204.

Works Cited

Baker, Houston A. *Blues, Ideology, and Afro-American Literature: A Vernacular Theory*. Chicago: U of Chicago P, 1984.

Baraka, Amiri. *Blues People.* New York: William Morrow, 1963.

Carby, Hazel V. "'It Just Be's Dat Way Sometime': The Sexual Politics of Women's Blues." *Unequal Sisters A Multicultural Reader in United States Women's History*. Eds. Elene Carol DuBois and Vicki L. Ruiz. New York: Routledge, 1990. 238–249.

Ellison, Ralph. *The Shadow and the Act.* New York: Random House, 1964.

Harrison, Daphne Duval. *Black Pearls.* New York: Rutgers UP, 1988.

Harrison, Paul Carter. "August Wilson's Blues Poetics." Wilson, *Three Plays*. Pittsburgh: U of Pittsburgh P, 1991. 291–318.

Hernton, Calvin. *Sex and Racism in America*. New York: Grove, 1965.

McCall, Nathan. *Makes Me Want to Holler*. New York: Random House, 1994.

Powers, Kim. "An Interview with August Wilson." *Theater* 16.1 (Fall/Winter, 1984): 52.

Russell, Michelle. "Slave Codes and Liner Notes." *All the Women Are White, All the Blacks Are Men: But Some of Us Are Brave*. Ed. Gloria T. Hull, Patricia Bell Scott, Barbara Smith. Old Westbury, NY: Feminist P, 1981. 129–140.

Savran, David. *In Their Own Words*. New York: Theatre Communications Group, 1988.

Soyinka, Wole. *Myth, Literature, and the African World View.* London: Cambridge UP, 1976.

Spillers, Hortense. "Interstices: A Small Drama of Words," *Pleasure and Danger.* Ed. Carol S. Vance. Boston: Routledge, 1984. 73–99.

Wilson August. *Three Plays by August Wilson*. Pittsburgh: U of Pittsburgh P, 1991.

——. "*Ma Rainey's Black Bottom.*" *Black Thunder.* Ed. William Branch. New York: Mentor P, 1992.

——. "I want a Black Director." *May All Your Fences Have Gates*. Ed. Alan Nadel. Iowa City: U of Iowa P, 1994. 200–204.

Chapter Nineteen

"Any Baggage You Don't Claim, We Trash": Living With(in) History in Wolfe's *The Colored Museum*

Marc Silverstein

Cornel West has defined a new cultural politics of difference emerging in African American aesthetic and theoretical practice based on the critique of

> the monolithic and homogeneous in the name of diversity, multiplicity and heterogeneity . . . reject[ing] the abstract, general and universal in light of the concrete, specific and particular . . . historiciz[ing], contextualiz[ing] and pluraliz[ing] by highlighting the contingent, provisional, variable, tentative, shifting and changing. (3)

Since this politics of difference involves contesting the dominant structures of authority and intelligibility governing the representation of African American experience and history, it is hardly surprising that West sees cultural institutions—"the academy, museum, mass media and gallery networks" (3)—as the terrain of ideological struggle. One aspect of this struggle takes the form of the demand for a voice from all those silenced by the reigning historical myths and social fantasies produced in these institutions. Spencer Crew and James Sims, both associated with the National Museum of American History, write that curators can no longer ignore the art and artifacts of "African Americans, women, ethnic communities, common laborers, and other groups, who in the past were seen as peripheral to the main currents of American history" (164) but must include such material in order to achieve as high a degree of authenticity as possible.

Such sentiments are laudable but when advanced in the name of inclusion and authenticity they tend to become, at best, stop-gap solutions to more systemic problems, since they do not challenge the fundamental structure or ideological work performed by the museum. Indeed, what initially seems a move to introduce heterogeneity into an homogeneous space could produce a new form of homogeneity if one form of cultural production becomes definitive of African American culture, women's culture, etc. Dramatist George C. Wolfe told *New York Times* reporter Jeremy Gerard that he encountered this kind of problem while working on *The Colored Museum*: "People kept asking for a 'black' play. I kept asking, 'What's a "black" play. Four walls, a couch and a mama?' I can't live within those old definitions" (16). Like West, Wolfe suggests that a new cultural politics of difference cannot simply revise and extend existing definitions and cultural institutions but must challenge their very essence as definitions and institutions. Wolfe has interest not in creating a new paradigm for black plays or colored museums but in exploring and critiquing how the representational practices and ideological operations of the theatre and the museum have systematically alienated African Americans from a viable engagement with their history—an history, as Wolfe's character Topsy asserts, consisting of "colored contradictions" (53) that demand acknowledgment as a prerequisite for empowerment.

While Harry Elam, Jr. has examined the play in relation to the representational strategies of African American theatre practice (291–303), in this essay I want to explore how Wolfe questions the ideological function of the other cultural institution at the heart of the play: the museum. To say that a concern with the museum lies "at the heart of the play" may initially appear puzzling. Certainly, based on the title alone, we enter the theatre expecting the play to have some connection with a museum. Reading our programs, we note that Wolfe labels the play's individual episodes as "exhibits" rather than "scenes." Viewing the performance space even before the play begins, we see a stage setting that Wolfe describes as follows: "White walls and recessed lighting. A starkness befitting a museum where the myths and madness of black/Negro/colored Americans are stored." When the performance concludes, however, we will have seen a play in which no character goes to a museum, in which no episode is set in a museum; indeed, in which no one ever utters the word "museum." What role, then, does the museum play in Wolfe's examination of the "colored contradictions" of African American experience—an examination that leads Topsy to affirm "there's a madness in me and that madness sets me free" (53)? To answer this question, I first want to consider the ideological work performed by the museum[1] before discussing Wolfe's sense that the acceptance of "madness" and "contradiction," the vital engagement with history rather than the retreat to an illusory trans- or extra-historical realm, can only occur (to borrow a phrase from Douglas Crimp) on the museum's ruins.

Initially, we might regard the museum as a fitting institutional backdrop for such an engagement, since, as Elam observes, "traditionally 'museum' connotes a place where treasures of the past, important artifacts of the present are housed and exhibited" (292). Elam's comment implicitly raises the fundamental issue at stake in the debate over the museum's cultural role: who sets the criteria for determining which art, artifacts, and cultural traditions count as "treasures" and "important?" This is precisely the kind of question that leads West and Wolfe, in their different ways, to see the museum as a site of intervention for the new cultural politics of difference. Traditionally, the museum presents itself as possessing a mimetic relation to the historical real, as constituting a space dedicated to the preservation and *transmission* of history. Yet, as Ivan Karp notes, "The consequence of putting objects into even the Spartan context of the art gallery makes the museum . . . into an apparatus of power" (14). This power consists in the ability to engage in the production of social fantasies under the guise of transmission, as the museum constructs an imaginary version of history (or, as Lacan and Althusser might phrase it, an historical imaginary) that replaces rather than represents the historical realm. That is, the museum *ideologizes* history in a manner illustrated by the following paean to the museum from Robert Rauschenberg's 1970 proclamation for the Metropolitan Museum's Centennial Certificate: "*Timeless in concept* the museum amasses to concretize a *moment* of pride serving to defend the dreams and ideals apolitically of mankind . . . while keeping history and love alive" (cited in Crimp 60; emphasis added).

Rauschenberg's words capture the essential contradiction of the museum, for it can only "keep history alive" by transforming history, that most temporal of concepts—the realm of contingency, variability, flux, rupture and discontinuity—into a "timeless moment," a transhistorical history whose modern institutional form, as Douglas Crimp argues, arises coextensively with and helps both to legitimize and draw its legitimization from idealist aesthetics (2–31). Such idealism becomes the means for suturing this contradiction, since it substitutes the internal history and dynamic of the development of art for history conceived as the sphere of socio-economic-political praxis, ultimately effacing all traces of the latter. Rather than the access to history it promises, the museum offers us the aestheticization of history, what Walter Benjamin calls "cultural history," in which the museum "may well increase the burden of the treasures that are piled up on humanity's back. But it does not give mankind the strength to shake them off, so as to get its hands on them" (356, 361). It is worth noting that Benjamin does *not* seek liberation from the "burden" of history like The Man in Wolfe's "exhibit" "Symbiosis" (to which I will return), but from the "burden" of the aesthetic fetishes that the museum offers under the sign of history. In short, he bases his critique of the museum on the call for a radical immersion within history that remains irreconcilable with the traditional function of a museum that separates its exhibits from the "worldliness" of both the historical periods of which they are products and our own historical period. For Benjamin, then, the traditional museum structure "presents an eternal image of the past" that denies the spectator "recourse to a consciousness of the present that shatters the continuum of [aestheticized] history" (352).

Since many of the most famous museums—the Louvre, the Metropolitan Museum of Art, etc.—are universal survey museums mixing exhibits from different eras and cultures, Benjamin's anxiety may strike us as counterintuitive. If, for example, one visits the Boston Museum of Fine Arts, she can view Egyptian mummies, "Third World" tribal artifacts, and such canonical "First World" works as the permanent Impressionism exhibition. Such cultural heterogeneity would seem to deny the charges Benjamin levels, since the museum apparently foregrounds rather than forecloses a spectatorial consciousness of difference and cultural pluralism. Yet, such cultural alterity primarily takes the form of the ideology of liberal pluralism in which difference is acknowledged only to be contained within the inexorable logic of the same, in which art as material praxis inextricably bound up with its specific historical moment becomes superseded by art as the changeless ontological essence uniting "primitive" craftsman and "civilized" artist. In these "pluralistic" museums, as André Malraux writes in their defense, "diverse as they are, all these objects . . . speak for the same endeavor; it is as though an unseen presence, the spirit of art, were urging all on the same quest" (44).

Rather than encourage the spectator to acknowledge what I would call, at the risk of tautology, the difference of difference, the Malrauxian museum becomes the last space in which the Hegelian Absolute Spirit—specifically defined here as "the spirit of art"—can manifest its temporal unfolding. Such an approach, however, *does* allow for an alternative reading of the survey museum, one in which "the spirit of art" invites us to emphasize difference rather than sameness but difference defined as progressive development. According to this narrative, our gaze may discern "the spirit of art" pervading both a Mijikenda memorial post and, for example, Manet's *Olympia*, but we will judge the Manet as superior, since his work represents a further stage on the "quest" than the Mijikenda tribesman could possibly attain. Thus, whether difference is assimilated to "the same endeavor" or defined within the strict limits of a teleological aesthetic, the "pluralism" of the museum depends upon constructing art as autonomous, organically unified, internalizing its own sharply circumscribed history. This veritable erasure of difference suggests the nature of the "quest" undertaken by Malraux's "spirit of art"—a quest for the aesthetic utopia in which art becomes absolutely self-referring, a *ding an sich* whose auratic presence ensures its freedom from the contamination of interest, ideology, politics, cultural contradictions and the vicissitudes of temporal discontinuity. As Douglas Crimp argues, the modern museum's ideological mission consists in its attempt to provide that utopian space: "The idealism of [the museum], in which the art object *in and of itself* was seen to have a fixed and transhistorical meaning, determined the object's placelessness, its belonging in no particular place, a no-place that was in reality the museum—the actual museum and the museum as a representation" of an idealized and idealist version of history (17).

Not only idealist but ideological: this utopianism casts the museum in the role of privileged site for the production of an ideological view of history which, as Althusser argues, "far from functioning as a (provisional) truth for the production of new knowledges . . . [presents itself] as the truth of History, as exhaustive, definitive and absolute knowledge of it, in short as a system closed in on itself" (cited in Bennett 78). Such a closed system, reducing the heterogeneity of history to the ceaseless activity of "the spirit of art," ultimately can only preserve its hermeticism through a kind of destruction in which art retains its freedom from the critical praxis of "the production of new knowledges" only by achieving a corpselike impermeability. As Adorno observes, museums, "where we put the art of the past to death . . . are bearers of a death symbolism" (177–78). Etymology affords him the chance to meditate upon this "symbolism": "The German word, '*museal*' [museumlike], has unpleasant overtones. It describes objects to which the observer no longer has a vital relationship and which are in the process of dying. . . . Museum and mausoleum are connected by more than phonetic association. Museums are like the family sepulchres of works of art. They testify to the neutralization of culture" and history (175), and it is through this "neutralization" that they accomplish their ideological work.

I have dwelt at such length on the nature of the museum in order to suggest why it has become a site of struggle for the new cultural politics of difference. At stake here is not only the museum as an institution but also, as Crimp points out, the museum as ideological representation, and it is this latter sense of the museum that Wolfe targets in *The Colored Museum*. The line from the play that I have chosen for my title—"any baggage you don't claim, we trash" (5, 53)—encapsulates the museum's function in its role as site of ideological production. As Benjamin and Crimp argue, it is precisely the "baggage" of an history conceptualized as "the production of new knowledges" and practices, as the terrain of cultural contradiction and cultural struggle, that the museum's idealist aesthetics disable us from "claiming." The museum "trashes" such historical "baggage," but, as Adorno implies, this effacement of history, which is also an effacement of the human, "trashes" and "neutralizes" the very objects it fetishizes.

Here we find the very crux of Wolfe's play, which challenges African Americans to learn to live with(in) history and resist the temptation of the "museum"—the temptation to succumb to the belief that one can jettison the historical experience which to some degree shapes us and occupy a space above and beyond the claims of history. Wolfe understands the difficulty of such an endeavor, for what begins as a vital engagement with the heritage of African American history can all too easily become a passive resignation to victimization—a resignation to the pain of slavery, racism, economic exploitation, political disenfranchisement and cultural marginalization that has marked the experience of African Americans. The problem for Wolfe and his characters is, how to acknowledge without surrendering to this history. As Topsy affirms in the play's final "exhibit," "Whereas I can't live inside yesterday's pain, I can't live without it" (52). Wolfe's characters may not want to "live inside yesterday's pain," but, unlike Topsy, many of them have yet to learn that they "can't live without it." Indeed, one response to this "pain" running throughout the play consists of the attempt to "become" a museum exhibit; that is, to become a coherent, unified, centered being, self-enclosed, self-referring and self-defining, "aestheticized" in its insulation from pain and vulnerability. Wolfe dramatizes and critiques this response in the two "exhibits," "The Photo Session" and "Symbiosis."

These "exhibits" reveal Wolfe's nuanced understanding of difference, for the new cultural politics of difference explores both the contradictions and differences between being African American and belonging to the dominant white culture in America and the contradictions and differences *among* African Americans. As Stuart Hall asserts, we must accept "the end of innocence or the end of the innocent notion of the essential Black subject . . . the recognition that 'Black' is essentially a politically and culturally *constructed* category" (cited in West 28). In his review of the play, Jack Kroll quotes Wolfe's remark that "Black American culture is a very fragmented thing. We're all trying to come up with some definition of what we are. My absolute definition of me is the schizophrenia, the contradiction" (85). As the play reveals, one source of this "schizophrenia" arises from our construction in terms of multiple categories, multiple markers of subjectivity. Not only are we ethnic subjects, but we are also ideologically interpellated into identity formations of gender, sexuality, class, etc., and the clash among these categories can create potentially irresolvable contradictions.

It is hardly surprising, then, that the Girl and Guy in "The Photo Session" and the Man in "Symbiosis"—those characters who most yearn for an aestheticized utopia to shelter them from the demands of history—are caught in the contradiction of identity categories, trapped between the Scylla of race and the Charybdis of class, specifically an affluent upper-middle class that, if not assimilationist, finds its interests tied to a dominant white culture. Wolfe highlights this "schizophrenia" in "The Photo Session" by utilizing lighting to create literal "colored contradictions." Against the backdrop of the "stark" white walls, we see the Girl and Guy, "*a very glamorous, gorgeous, black couple, wearing the best of everything and perfect smiles. The stage is bathed in . . . bright white light*" (9). This staging produces an highly ambiguous effect in the theatre, for it is impossible to decide if the white walls and light surrounding the couple emphasize their blackness or if their blackness makes the surrounding whiteness dominate the stage. My point is not that the new African American bourgeoisie are inherently ethnically inauthentic or that only among the working-class could we locate the mythical "essential Black subject." Rather, Wolfe reminds us that class, no less than race, "is essentially a politically and culturally constructed category"—constructed in terms of the desires, meanings, and values of a cultural order enjoying hegemonic control over representational systems and structures of ideological interpellation. As West remarks, the dominant cultural order denies African Americans "power to represent themselves to themselves and others as complex human beings, and thereby to contest" the particular mode of their construction (27).

For the young couple in "The Photo Session," caught between the privilege of their class construction and "the bombardment of negative, degrading stereotypes put forward by White supremacist ideologies" (27) that West describes as the process of "othering" through which "blackness" accedes to its dominant social meaning, resistance and contestation are foreclosed, and the only possibility is escape from an history whose cultural coding doubles the pain of its lived experience:

> GIRL: The world has become too much for us.
> GUY: We couldn't resolve the contradictions of our existence.
> GIRL: And we couldn't resolve yesterday's pain.
> GUY: So we gave our life away and now we live inside *Ebony Magazine*. (9)

Wolfe here dramatizes a classic Althusserian paradigm of ideological interpellation.[2] For Althusser, ideology manages potential social conflict by erasing contradictions between the various subject positions we inhabit—contradictions that, if left unattended, could be utilized as the launching site for cultural struggle. Denied this contestatory power, unable to formulate a nomadic subjectivity to form social allegiances and identifications provisionally around whatever subject position would allow them to oppose their disempowerment, the couple respond to their "hailing" by the class-specific images in *Ebony*, (mis)recognizing themselves in those images to such an extent that, in an inversion of the Lacanian/Althusserian paradigm, the images "introject" them, pulling them into the magazine rather than vice versa. Wolfe dramatizes the power of an image that allows the couple to identify themselves as "black and fabulous" (9); to identify themselves in terms of ethnicity and class, since the former has been ideologically neutralized by being assimilated to the latter, which itself has been constructed in terms valorized by the dominant white culture. In the glamorized images of *Ebony*, to be black means "looking fabulous while holding up a bottle of vodka" (9), a meaning that "guarantee[s] no contradictions . . . And no pain" (10), but that prevents the couple from constructing allegiances with those African Americans whose experience remains unacknowledged by the magazine—allegiances that could provide them with a different, "counterhegemonic" understanding of their lack of place in white culture.

Rather than pursue this course, they withdraw to the pages of *Ebony*, entering a museum-like text that reduces history to "a system closed in on itself," an eternal moment in which "everyone is beautiful, and wears fabulous clothes. And never says anything . . . contradictory" (9). Yet, as Adorno observes, the museum cannot entirely separate itself from the mausoleum. Insulating themselves within the world of dominant ideological images, purging and "aestheticizng" their lives of the economic and social reality of those African Americans whom the magazine refuses to include within the signifying field of "black," ultimately produces its own form of pain: "And at times it feels like we're suffocating, like we're not human anymore . . . [it's t]he kind of pain that comes from feeling no pain at all" (10).

"The pain that comes from feeling no pain"—the line perfectly captures the dialectic of preservation/destruction that defines the museum for Adorno, and that, for Wolfe, defines the futile efforts of African Americans to inhabit a place transcending historical contradictions from which they can say, with the Man in "Symbiosis," "I have no history. I have no past" (36). That the young couple can feel aesthetic painlessness as a form of pain reminds us of Adorno's remark that "*museal*" "describes objects . . . in the process of dying" rather than already dead. Despite the idealist aesthetics supporting the museum's attempts to exclude the materiality and heterogeneity of history, to say that the museum *succeeds* in erasing history would mean surrendering to the inevitable accomplishment of its ideological project. To be "in the process of dying" means to be still engaged in the process of living, no matter how attenuated that process has become, to be still marked with what Adorno calls "the hieroglyphics of history" (185), located *within* history rather than in a mythical "no-place" of "transhistorical meaning" to which both *Ebony* and the museum aspire but can never attain. In other words, claims to occupy a domain with "no history . . . no past" and "no contradictions . . . no pain," are themselves responses to an historical situation whose deeply felt phenomenological reality becomes unbearable, the situation of the Man in "Symbiosis."

In this "exhibit," as in "The Photo Session," Wolfe presents a character who, caught between the contradictions of class and ethnicity, attempts to attain the aesthetic purity of "an impersonal eye" (36), an eye detached from the body on whose surface the marks of otherness have been imposed not only through ideological operations, as the heritage of slavery, lynchings, the Tuskeegee experiments, etc., remind us. Again, Wolfe uses the stage to create a visual image of social contradiction; when the "exhibit" opens, we see the "MAN *in corporate dress*" confronted by "THE KID, *who is dressed in a late-sixties street style*" (33). If the two styles of dress signify different class identities, they also signify different cultural identities. That the Man's dress identifies him as part of the corporate elite suggests that, even more than the couple in *Ebony*, his social and economic status, his very "survival depends on" erasing all markers of ethnic subjectivity (34), and defining himself in terms of the dominant culture. Where the couple are allowed the ideological solace of proclaiming their "blackness," the Man declares that he can "have no stake" in any construction of race: "It's too much. It's much too much . . . Being black is too emotionally taxing; therefore I will be black only on weekends and holidays" (36), only when beyond the gaze of an overwhelmingly white corporate culture.

Similarly, the Kid's "street-style" clothing identify him as part of the African American "underclass," socially marginalized, economically exploited, and politically disempowered by both the dominant white culture and a newly affluent African American bourgeoisie. More is at stake here, however, than a simple center/periphery dichotomy, for the Kid transforms his clothing into what John Fiske calls a "producerly text" (103–6), refusing the dominant reading of his "style" as the visible sign of subordination by investing it with new social meaning as a sign of resistance and opposition. As the Man says, the Kid embodies "his own rage" (36), the rage he has had to suppress as he learned to succeed by "smil[ing] on cue. And watch[ing] the news with an impersonal eye" (36). Nor is the Man speaking metaphorically here, for Wolfe reveals that the Kid is the Man's younger self from the 1960s come to demand historical accountability from even those African Americans who have attempted to lose themselves in corporate America: "You may put all kinds of silk ties 'round your neck . . . but the Kid is here to stay. And regardless of how much of your past that you trash, I ain't goin' no damn where" (36).

In this "exhibit," Wolfe presents a literal trashing of the past as the Man throws a series of objects into a large trash can—not just any objects, but examples of material culture from which a provisional but historically specific cultural identity was constructed by militant African Americans in the 1960s. As we watch the Man "trash" "my first Afro-comb . . . My first dashiki . . . My autographed pictures of Stokely Carmichael . . . Eldridge Cleaver's *Soul on Ice*" (33), buttons reading "Free Angela! Free Bobby! . . . U.S. Out of Harlem, Detroit, Newark" (34), and recordings by Jimi Hendrix, Sly Stone, and The Temptations, we witness an attempt not so much to erase an historical period per se, but to destroy all traces of a specific African American subjectivity formulated in response to the contradictions and "pain" of that period. The Kid acknowledges as much when he equates the trashing of these historical/cultural artifacts with the murder of "what we are. Who we are . . . a way of life" (35)—a symbolic murder literalized when the Man chokes the Kid to death in a final bid to destroy "anything and everything that connects me . . . to who I was, to what we were . . . I have no history. I have no past" (34).

We should not read the Kid's charge that the Man murders "what we are, [w]ho we are" as racial essentialism on Wolfe's part; rather, the line anticipates Topsy's observation that African Americans "can't live without . . . yesterday's pain." The Kid does not argue for the content of a "real" cultural identity possessing the kind of authenticity and self-containment that the museum claims for its artifacts. On the contrary, he reminds us that cultural identity in the present finds itself related to the multiple identities that comprise the history of the cultural group in question. The relationship between past and present identities may take several forms, but the fundamental connection "to who I was, to what we were" cannot be erased, a point Wolfe underscores in the "exhibit's" final moment when the Kid rises from the dead, an historical "artifact" that refuses to submit to the process of "museumification."

As Benjamin noted, this process not only neutralizes the objects exhibited but forecloses any form of oppositional praxis or resistant subjectivity based on those objects. I have referred to his comment that the museum disables us from claiming the "baggage" of history—"it does not give mankind the strength . . . to get its hands on them"—but we might wonder what he means by "get[ting] its hands on them." Benjamin writes that we need access to these artifacts in order "to set to work an engagement with history original to every new present" (352). For Benjamin, oppositional practices involve appropriating the objects "trashed" within the museum not in order to reactivate their original meaning but to reinterpret and "reinvent" them in terms of the cultural and political needs of the present. In this sense, there is little difference between the museum's hermetic preservation of art and the Man's trash can, both filled with objects removed from cultural circulation. Neither the museum nor the trash can allow their "treasures" to aid in "the production of new knowledges," new subjectivities, new identity formations, new engagements with the history of "yesterday's pain." To the Man, the Kid remains "a sociological dinosaur" (34), but what the Man fears is less the past as a temporal category than a present engagement with that past—an engagement that one hopes will produce a future in which the social order will undergo fundamental cultural, ethical, and political transformation.

In "The Photo Session" and "Symbiosis," Wolfe dramatizes the utter impossibility of escaping the legacy of "yesterday's pain" through the purging of cultural specificity. The young couple and the Man hope that their obviously precarious insertion within dominant culture will save them from the claims of historical engagement and struggle. Yet, if they cannot achieve the "impersonal" aesthetic utopia of the museum, perhaps the "pain," the historical reality they would transcend, can lend itself to aestheticization. The danger of such aestheticization, as Adorno realized in his most pessimistic comments about the obscenity of continuing to produce art after Auschwitz, lies in art's ability to confer meaning on historical horror in such a way that the art thrives at the expense of the horror, becoming a form of compensation for the horror. Wolfe explores this problem in the play's first "exhibit," "Git on Board."

The play opens in "*blackness. Cut by drums pounding. Then slides, rapidly flashing before us. Images we've all seen before, of African slaves being captured, loaded on to ships, tortured. The images flash, flash, flash*" (1). Many museums featuring special exhibitions present slide shows or films, not so much to communicate information about the exhibit as to create the "proper" spectatorial consciousness for us to appreciate "the spirit of art." Wolfe's slides, however, reveal the underside of the reverence and awe such shows aim to produce, for these slides reduce their historical basis in violence and brutality to a cliché "we've all seen before," thus suggesting that when the history of "yesterday's pain" does enter the museum, its aesthetic form distances us from the content. Such aestheticization contributes its own version of what Hannah Arendt calls "the banality of evil," a banality embodied by the "exhibit's" lone character, Miss Pat, a stewardess for Celebrity Slaveship, who delivers her lines in a "*rehearsed manner, smiling and speaking as she has done so many times before*" (1), anaesthetizing us from the horrors of the Middle Passage.

When the reality of slavery does threaten to break through the barriers of the slides and Miss Pat's automaton-like delivery, when history intrudes through the angry and insistent "pounding" of the drums that refuse to be silenced, she acknowledges and subdues the threat through a strategy of aesthetic containment:

> (*She proceeds to single out individual passengers/audience members.*) Why the songs *you* are going to sing in the cotton fields, under the burning heat and stinging lash, will metamorphose and give birth to the likes of James Brown and the Fabulous Flames. And you, yes *you*, are going to come up with some of the best dances. The best dances! The Watusi! The Funky Chicken! And just think of what *you* are going to mean to William Faulkner. All right, so you're gonna have to suffer for a few hundred years, but from your pain will come a culture so complex. (3)

Here, Wolfe demonstrates how easily the kind of ethnomusicological accounts that trace the roots of soul and rhythm and blues back to the experience of slavery can slide into a teleological narrative of redemption in which historical suffering exists for and becomes "justified" by the complexity of the culture it produces. "Complexity," of course, has performed ideological service in its role as a criterion for inclusion—hence, necessarily, a criterion for exclusion—within the museum specifically and aesthetic canons in general. The irony of Miss Pat's comments lies in their implicit argument that the institution of slavery—an institution representing an extreme form of othering inscribed upon the body by the "stinging lash"; an institution whose violence and exploitation arose from a sense of the exclusionary limits of the human—allows African Americans to enter the universal aesthetic culture enshrined in the museum. Even as she sees aesthetic production as the vehicle through which African Americans can transcend their otherness and historical suffering, Miss Pat admits that, while as productive agents their main contribution will lie in the sphere of popular culture, the chief reason "we value you" is for providing the material from which Faulkner will create his high modernist canonical art (3). This "we"/"you" dichotomy undercuts Miss Pat's universalizing rhetoric, for it reminds us that any transformation of "yesterday's pain" through aesthetic stylization must receive cultural validation, must conform to the standards set by "we," the dominant institutional forces enjoying hegemonic control over the definition of what counts as art.

I have already mentioned Wolfe's own frustration with the power of these forces—the forces that demanded he write "a black play"—a frustration voiced in the "exhibit" "The Last Mama-on-the-Couch Play." Elam has discussed in detail how the "exhibit" constitutes "an explicit use of motivated signification [on] and parody" (299–302) of Lorraine Hansberry's *A Raisin in the Sun* and Ntozake Shange's *For Colored Girls Who Have Considered Suicide / When the Rainbow Is Enuf.* While the "exhibit" does parody these works, Wolfe's target is less the plays as self-existent texts which, as I have argued, is merely an ideological category generated by museums and other institutions of "high" culture, than the social use to which they are put. In his review of *The Colored Museum*, Jack Kroll quotes Wolfe's comments on *Raisin*: "It's a wonderful play, but every February all the regional theaters discover black people because it's Black History Month and they pull out 'Raisin in the Sun.' I want to remove these dead, stale, empty icons" (85).

Wolfe levels his objection not against Hansberry, but against a theatrical apparatus that produces what I have been discussing as "museumification." If Adorno views museums as "family sepulchres of works of art," Wolfe sees the network of regional theatres converting African American drama into "dead icons." If this appears to be an aesthetic lament for the evacuation of meaning that follows the constant and often unimaginative revivals of the "classics" of dramatic literature, then we need to consider Wolfe's comments more carefully. Like any aesthetic production, *Raisin* possesses a multifaceted relationship to the historical moment in which it first appears. That Hansberry's play has become the work of choice for Black History Month means that the work has been wrenched from its historical context and, in a sense, come to represent Black History—that this play about an African American mother's struggle to move her family into their own home in a white middle-class neighborhood has become paradigmatic of the "meaning" of Black History. In other words, the ideological effect of the circumstances under which *Raisin* typically receives a production reduces the diversity of African American experience to a single, defining and definitive experience: a version of the "American Dream" in which African Americans transcend their historical legacy and cultural specificity to become part of the "we," the dominant class and culture to which Miss Pat, the *Ebony* couple, and the Man have "escaped."

Once *Raisin* assumes this "transhistorical meaning," we are disabled from exploring the differences between at least the potential for challenging the status quo that Hansberry's Mama would have represented when the play first appeared, and the ideological interpellation into, hence validation of, the dominant culture Wolfe satirically attacks in his bourgeois characters.

Wolfe embodies this "museumification" of *Raisin*, with its attendant effacement of historical context, in Medea, the daughter in his "exhibit," who speaks a parodic version of tragic blank verse bearing no relation to the marginalized class, ethnic, and cultural position of her family. After bemusedly listening to one of her speeches, the Son asks, "Girl, what has gotten into you," to which she replies, "Juliard, good brother. For I am no / longer bound by rhythms of race or / region. Oh, no. My speech, like my / pain and suffering, have become / classical and therefore universal" (28). That its realistic style easily fits the conventions of mainstream American theatre, that it lends itself to being read in terms of the "classical" and "universal" tragic theme of the search for self-definition and self-affirmation in the face of an hostile universe, that *Raisin* can simultaneously epitomize Black History Month while being detached from its moorings in black history—such are the dangers of the "museumification" against which Wolfe levels his critique.

Balanced against this critique, however, Wolfe presents characters who resist incorporation within the dominant culture—an incorporation that, as the *Ebony* couple's "pain that comes from feeling no pain" and the Man's repressed but unextinguished rage demonstrate, can never resolve "colored contradictions" or eradicate the legacy of "yesterday's pain." We have already seen that the Kid rejects "museumification," since he realizes that books, recordings, and clothing are "who we are . . . a way of life;" that through investing these inert artifacts with meaning we formulate resistant social identities. It is perhaps not surprising that the most resistant characters in Wolfe's play are the most economically and culturally marginalized African Americans, since they remain at a distance from the "hailing frequency" of the dominant ideology, and since their "otherness" is, paradoxically, needed to legitimate the ideology of pluralistic inclusiveness by presenting the examples of the unredeemable, the "incorrigibles" who refuse to respond when told, as Miss Pat says, that "we value you."

Wolfe locates resistance in the culturally as well as economically marginalized, in figures such as the drag queen Miss Roj in the "exhibit" "The Gospel According to Miss Roj." As a transvestite, Miss Roj inhabits the periphery of both white and African American culture, but he "ain't just your regular oppressed American Negro . . . [because] I have the power" (14, 16)—the power of the Snap! The gesture of the Snap! emerged from the African American gay community and, indeed, is a gesture whose social meaning helps define an oppositional subculture within that community. It is the cultural specificity of this gesture—as opposed to the "classical . . . universal" speech to which Medea aspires—that allows the Snap! to act as a shared code, a sign of recognition among those who neither, like the Man, have a desire to become "Mr. Cream-of-the-Crop, Mr. Colored-Man-on-Top" (36) nor are content to accept their definition as perpetual victims, as nothing more than "a whole race of people . . . trashed and debased" (17). Indeed, the Snap! performs its own kind of ideological hailing, providing a point of reference around which to form a counter-hegemonic "we": "We don't ask for acceptance. We don't ask for approval. We know who we are and we move on it!" (17–18).

The inclusiveness of this "we" provides a positive counterpoint to the spurious inclusiveness of the liberal pluralistic "we" that ultimately subsumes the differences it claims to welcome. For Miss Roj extends the Snap! beyond its origins in a particular segment of the gay population to include all those of every class, race, gender or sexual preference who refuse to accept the economic exploitation, social asymmetry and cultural violence that mark the present disposition of power relations in America. Addressing the audience as a whole, he invites us to form a kind of "rainbow coalition" against injustice:

> A high-rise goes up. You can't get no job . . . Snap those fingers . . . Some sick bitch throws her baby out the window 'cause she thinks its the Devil. Everybody snap! . . . Snap for every time you walk past someone lying in the street, smelling like frozen piss and shit and you don't see it. Snap for every crazed bastard who kills himself so as to get the jump on being killed. And snap for every sick muthafucker who, bored with carrying around his fear, takes to shooting up other people. (17)

Unlike the artifacts the Man trashes, snapping will never be enshrined or, more to the point, entombed in the museum of "dead, stale, empty icons" since its power resides in the refusal to accept the "negative, degrading stereotypes [of otherness] put forward" by the dominant ideology, and to make visible the historical suffering and inequity that "museumification" disavows, to bring into focus that which we "walk past . . . and . . . don't see."

Standing at the furthest extreme from the museum, Topsy, in the play's final "exhibit," "The Party," extends the affirmation of Miss Roj's "we know who we are and we move on it." Quite literally, we perceive her as movement before fixing her as an identifiable character. As Wolfe's opening stage directions read, "*Before we know what's hit us, a hurricane of energy comes bounding into the space. It is* TOPSY WASHINGTON" (50). With this "exhibit," Wolfe draws an implicit contrast between the museum as secular shrine, aesthetic temple, "family sepulchre of works of art," and the party as communal celebration, charged with dionysian energy and life-affirming movement; between the museum as policed space, where spectators move cautiously, speaking in hushed tones, their bodies docile and disciplined, and the party as carnivalesque disruption of spatial order which sets the body free from all physical constraint and delimiting categories: "Everybody joined in . . . Dancing to the rhythm of their own definition. Celebrating in their cultural madness . . . Before anybody knew what was happening, the entire room lifted up off the ground. The whole place just took off and went flying through space—defying logic and limitations" (51).

With "*her hair and dress . . . a series of . . . contradictions*" (50), Topsy embodies the "schizophrenia" and "cultural madness" of an history that includes triumph as well as pain, empowering self-representations and social identities as well as "negative, degrading stereotypes," activists committed to cultural struggle like the Kid and those who have chosen the illusory safety of economic privilege over the demands of historical accountability like the Man. Indeed, Wolfe utilizes the party as a metaphor for the multiple strands and contradictions of African American history, an history whose heterogeneous experiences are represented by the inclusiveness of the party's guest list: "Over in one corner you got Nat Turner sippin' champagne out of Eartha Kitt's slipper. And over in another corner, Bert Williams and Malcolm X was discussing . . . Aunt Jemima and Angela Davis was in the kitchen sharing a plate of greens and just goin' off about South Africa" (50). The party celebrates "cultural madness," since Topsy and the other guests make no attempt to synthesize the disparate and conflicting elements of their history into a seamless totalizing narrative "closed in upon itself," nor do they attempt to escape these elements, searching for a realm where they can admit contradictions under the rubric of aesthetic "complexity." Rather, all the guests "danc[e] to the rhythm of their own definition[s]," rejecting the homogeneity of a rigid taxonomy for the "dancing" and "spinning" (51) of what Julia Kristeva terms, in another context, the "subject-in-process." As Topsy declares, "Don't waste your time trying to label or define me" (52).

Topsy's rejection of definition disables one of the simplest and yet most effective mechanisms through which the museum aestheticizes history—the exhibit label. In his critique of the traditional museum structure, Michael Baxandall notes that by usually restricting itself to discussing the materials used in a particular artwork, the label actually withholds information that the spectator needs for interpretation and evaluation. Even more to the point of Topsy's comments, Baxandall succinctly observes that the label "does not describe the object. It decries the exhibitor's thinking about the object" (38), a "thinking" that all too often deploys labels and definitions so as to ensure the construction of those "others" who must bear the social cost of the present. Rather than conform to the label affixed to her, Topsy, like the new cultural worker Cornel West imagines possessed "with [a] protean identit[y] who avoid[s] ethnic chauvinism and faceless universalism" (36), internalizes the party "inside of my head" (51), leaving her with a polyvocal self, acknowledging the entire range of her cultural heritage: "And everything I need . . . is inside here, connecting me to everybody and everything that's ever been. So, hunny, don't waste your time trying to label or define me . . . 'cause I'm not what I was ten years ago or ten minutes ago. I'm all of that and then some" (51–52).

Topsy acknowledges that only by living with the history of "yesterday's pain"—the brutality of slavery against which Nat Turner revolted, the debasing racial images of blackface (Bert Williams) and docile mammys (Aunt Jemima)—can she celebrate and learn from figures like Malcolm X and Angela Davis, who struggled to end that pain. By accepting that the struggle cannot exist without and constitutes an ethical response to the pain, and that both are part of the legacy from which her self emerges, Topsy can find empowerment within the cultural "schizophrenia" from which Miss Pat, the *Ebony* couple and the Man attempt to dissociate themselves. As she sings repeatedly at the scene's conclusion, "THERE'S A MADNESS IN ME / AND THAT MADNESS SETS ME FREE" (53). Such "madness" reveals that Topsy both lives with history and within history, or, to be more precise, that history lives *within* her, since her "protean identity" includes "everybody and everything that's ever been." Neither a form of historical determinism in which the past conditions the present nor a kind of "transhistorical history" in which every action repeats the fundamental "meaning" and "truth" of History, Topsy's view of the self represents an historical relationism in which past and present lose their spatio-temporal boundaries, flowing into and enriching each other without congealing into a closed synthesis. Whether "ten years ago or ten minutes ago," the pastness of the past yields to the presentness of the past, allowing for "the production of new knowledges" and the formation of new subjectivities—"I'm all of that and then some"—based on the reinterpretation, recoding and reappropriation of the past within the present.

Topsy has learned that, as Benjamin writes, "to set to work an engagement with history original to every new present" demands abandoning the museum, the mausoleum of history, and joining the party, the scene of social allegiances with which African Americans claim the "baggage" of history allowing them to negotiate and draw empowerment from the "madness" of their "colored contradictions." As Topsy is joined by Miss Pat, Miss Roj, the

Man and characters from other "exhibits" for her final affirmation, Wolfe reminds us that no matter how extensive the reach of the dominant culture, it is neither ultimately monolithic nor monologic, that what it labels as "madness" can be redeployed against the forces that would seek to marginalize such "madness" as a first step on the path of social transformation. And it is transformation, not simply survival, that is ultimately at stake for Wolfe—the creation of a vital future rather than accommodation to a stagnant present. It is this transformative vision and energy that Topsy, the Kid and Miss Roj possess, the vision and energy that Cornel West—and here he could be speaking for Wolfe—sees characterizing all those committed to the new cultural politics of difference: "We promote a prospective and prophetic vision with a sense of possibility and potential. . . . We look to the past for strength, not solace; we look at the present and see people perishing, not profits mounting; we look toward the future and vow to make it different and better" (31–32).

Notes

1 I realize that my use of the term "*the* museum" throughout this article obscures the differences between the various kinds of museums and the various agendas they set for themselves. As my argument will make clear, I employ this admittedly totalizing term in order to discuss the work the dominant traditional structure of the museum performs as a scene of ideological production—the production, as Theodor W. Adorno, Walter Benjamin, and Douglas Crimp argue, of an idealist (and ideological) vision of history.

2 For Althusser's conception of ideology, see the essays (especially "Ideology and Ideological State Apparatuses (Notes Towards an Investigation)" and "Freud and Lacan" in *Lenin and Philosophy*.

Works Cited

Adorno, Theodor W. *Prisms*. Trans. Samuel Weber and Sherry Weber. Cambridge: MIT Press, 1981.

Althusser, Louis. *Lenin and Philosophy and Other Essays*. Trans. Ben Brewster. New York: Monthly Review P, 1971.

Baxandall, Michael. "Exhibiting Intention: Some Preconditions of the Visual Display of Culturally Purposeful Objects." Karp and Lavine 33–41.

Benjamin, Walter. *One-Way Street and Other Writings*. Trans. Edmund Jephcott and Kingsley Shorter. London: New Left Books, 1979.

Bennett, Tony. "Texts in History: The Determination of Readings and Their Texts." *Post Structuralism and the Question of History*. Ed. Derek Attridge, Geoff Bennington and Robert Young. Cambridge: Cambridge UP, 1987. 63–81.

Crew, Spencer R., and James E. Sims. "Locating Authenticity: Fragments of a Dialogue." Karp and Lavine 159–75.

Crimp, Douglas. *On the Museum's Ruins*. Cambridge: MIT, 1993.

Elam, Jr., Harry. "Signifyin(g) on African American Theatre: *The Colored Museum* by George C. Wolfe." *Theatre Journal* 44 (1992): 291–303.

Fiske, John. *Understanding Popular Culture*. London: Routledge, 1991.

Gerard, Jeremy. "'Colored Museum' Is Author's Exorcism." *New York Times* 6 Nov. 1986, sec. 3: 16.
Karp, Ivan. "Culture and Representation." Karp and Lavine 11–24.
Karp, Ivan, and Steven D. Lavine, eds. *Exhibiting Cultures: The Poetics and Politics of Museum Displays.* Washington: Smithsonian Institution, 1991.
Kroll, Jack. "Theater: Zapping Black Stereotypes." *Newsweek* 17 Nov. 1986: 85.
Malraux, André. *The Voices of Silence.* Trans. Stuart Gilbert. Princeton: Princeton UP, 1978.
West, Cornel. *Keeping Faith: Philosophy and Race in America.* New York: Routledge, 1993.
Wolfe, George C. *The Colored Museum.* New York: Grove Weidenfeld, 1988.

Contributors

Granger Babcock is an Assistant to the Vice Chancellor and Dean in University College at Louisiana State University in Baton Rouge. He has published essays on Luis Valdez, Tennessee Williams, Arthur Miller, and Langston Hughes.

Gaylord Brewer is an Associate Professor at Middle Tennessee State University, where he edits the journal *Poems & Plays*. His most recent book is *Charles Bukowski*.

Harry J. Elam, Jr. is Professor of Drama, Director of Graduates Studies in Drama, and Director of the Committee on Black Performing Arts at Stanford University. He is author of *Taking It to the Streets: The Social Protest Theater of Luis Valdez and Amiri Baraka*, and has a forthcoming book on August Wilson. He has co-edited three volumes on African American drama, and his articles have appeared in *American Drama*, *Theatre Journal*, *Text and Performance Quarterly* as well as several critical anthologies.

Penny Farfan is Associate Professor of Drama at the University of Calgary and has published articles in such journals as *Text and Performance Quarterly*, *Theatre Journal*, *Canadian Theatre Review*, *Modern Drama*, *Woolf Studies Annual*, and *Inversions*.

Verna Foster teaches modern drama, Shakespeare, and dramatic theory at Loyola University Chicago. She has published essays on Shakespeare, Ford, Ibsen, Chekhov, Williams, Beckett, and Wertenbaker, among others, and has recently completed a book-length study of tragicomedy.

Deborah R. Geis has taught at Queens College of the City University of New York, the University of Tennessee, and Oberlin College. She is the author of *Postmodern Theatrick(s): Monologue in Contemporary American Drama* and co-editor, with Steven F. Kruger, of *Approaching the Millennium: Essays on "Angels in America*.

Jennifer Gillan is an Associate Professor of English at Bentley College in the Boston area. She has co-edited three multicultural anthologies, and her articles have appeared in *American Literature*, *Cinema Journal*, *American Drama*, *African American Review*, *North Dakota Quarterly*, and *Arizona Quarterly*.

John Gruesser is Professor of English and Acting Director of the Master of Arts in Liberal Studies Program at Kean University. He is the author of *White on Black: Contemporary Literature about Africa* and *Black on Black: Twentieth-Century African American Writing about Africa* as well as the editor of works by Pauline Elizabeth Hopkins and John Edward Bruce.

Janet V. Haedicke is a Professor of English at the University of Louisiana at Monroe, where she also serves as Director of the Performing Arts Series. She is President of the David Mamet Society and has published numerous articles and reviews, one of which won a Modern Drama Best Essay award.

Philip J. Hanson is an assistant professor of Interdisciplinary Studies at the University of San Francisco. He has published articles in *South Central Review*, *Clio*, and *Prospects: An Annual Journal of American Cultural Studies*, among others.

James Hurt teaches in the English department of the University of Illinois. His books include *Catiline's Dream: An Essay On Ibsen's Plays*, *Aelfric*, *Film and Theatre*, *Writing Illinois*, and several textbooks.

Norma Jenckes teaches dramatic literature and playwriting at the University of Cincinnati. She has published extensively on American, British and Irish drama, and she is editor of the journal *American Drama*.

Jeff Johnson is a scholar who lives in Indialantic, Florida.

Nancy L. Nester is an Associate Professor in the Department of Writing Studies and in the Interdisciplinary Core Program at Roger Williams University. She has written papers on American drama and images of family in contemporary American fiction.

Marcia Noe is Professor of English and Coordinator of Women's Studies at The University of Tennessee at Chattanooga. She is the author of *Susan Glaspell: Voice from the Heartland* and eleven other publications on Glaspell.

Gene A. Plunka is Professor of English at the University of Memphis. He has written books on Peter Shaffer, Jean Genet, Antonin Artaud, Jean-Claude van Itallie, and John Guare.

David Radavich is Professor of English at Eastern Illinois University. He has published essays on William Saroyan, Jean Giraudoux, David Mamet, and other dramatists.

Marc Silverstein is Associate Professor of English and teaches modern and contemporary drama at Auburn University. A past president of the Harold Pinter Society, he has authored a book on Harold Pinter and has published articles in *American Drama*, *Essays in Theatre*, *Journal of Dramatic Theory and Criticism*, *Modern Drama* and *Theatre Journal*.

Albert Wertheim is Professor of English and of Theatre & Drama at Indiana University, where he is also Associate Dean for Research in Humanities. His publications include a book on Athol Fugard and essays on Arthur Miller, Clifford Odets, Eugene O'Neill, and Mary Chase.

Barry Witham is Professor in the School of Drama at the University of Washington. His articles on American theatre have appeared in a variety of publications and he has recently completed a book on the Federal Theatre Project.

Index

A

Achebe, Chinua, 44–45

Achieve Greatness, 108

Adding Machine, 160

Adler, Thomas, 101

Adorno, Theodor, 102–103, 259–260, 262–263, 265, 267

Aeschylean, 133

Africa
- portrayal of, 38–46

African Americans
- Africanist depiction, 39–40, 41
- and the American Dream, 267
- and the blues, 239–254
- cultural schizophrenia, 260–261, 271
- depiction of, 39–46
- ennobling of, 133
- and Haiti, 131–143
- history, 260
- image, 40
- and loss of self, 253–254
- and museum ideology, 255–260
- and naturalist drama, 131–143
- non-Africanist depiction, 38–46
- searching for connections, 243–245
- and their African roots, 239–254
- and white society, 23–36, 256–267
- *See also* Slavery

Albee, Edward, 1–7

Alger, Horatio, 26

Alice Adams, 140

Alison's House, 9, 10, 13, 14, 15, 17, 18, 19

All the Dark and Beautiful Warriors, 40

Allen, Lewis, 126

Almost Like Being, 215–216

Althuser, Louis, 261–262

Althusserian paradigm, 257, 259, 261–262

America
- and Haiti, 131–143
- post WWII, 61, 124, 125
- and Russia, 159–169

American
- dream, 23, 26, 31–32, 51, 87–90, 98, 267
- identity, 26–27
- Imperialism, 111
- masculinity, 108–109
- society
  - and the media, 213–225
  - morality, 171–192
  - new definition, 23–36
  - and perfection, 214–215, 216, 218, 221–222, 224–225

American Buffalo, 150–151, 156

American Hurrah, 218

American Landscape, 168

Anderson, Sherwood, 18

Anti-feminist, 53, 56
- *See also* Feminist

Anti-Oedipus; Capitalism and Schizophrenia, 103–104

Antonia Saw the Oryx First, 46

Apollonian order, 65

Approaching Zanzibar, 49, 57

Arendt, Hannah, 265–266

Aristotle, 94, 128, 196

Art
- and society, 24, 31
- as Utopia, 258–259
- *See also* Museums

The Art of Dining, 57

Atkinson, Brooks, 164, 167

Auerbach, Doris, 73

Aunt Dan and Lemon, 171, 172, 173, 176–177, 179, 184, 185–188, 189
- compared to *The Fever*, 190–191
- compared to *My Dinner with André*, 179–188

Austin, Gayle, 199

Awake and Sing!, 119

"Awakening," 78, 80–83

Ayers, Edward L., 137

B

Backlash: The Undeclared War Against American Women, 57
Baker, Houston A., 243
Baraka, Amiri, 240
Barnes, Clive, 172
Baxandall, Michael, 270–271
Beckett, Samuel, 6, 55, 85, 90
The Belt, 168
Benjamin, Walter, 257–258, 259, 264–265, 271
Berlant, Lauren, 23, 25–26, 29–30
Bernice, 9, 10, 11–14, 15, 16–17, 19
Bernstein, Aline, 160, 164
Between Two Worlds, 160, 161, 162, 165–169
Bhabha, Homi, 26–27
The Big Knife, 120–128
Bigsby, C. W. E, 1–2, 3, 9, 18, 107, 221, 229, 232
Birth and After Birth, 49–53
  comparison to *One Shoe Off*, 54–57
  as a feminist play, 52–53
Birthright, 25–26
Black Arts Movement, 245
Black Power, 46
Blank Darkness: Africanist Discourse in French, 39–40
Blues, 239–254
  as African American expression, 242
  in historical context, 240–241
  matrix, 243–244, 245
  and politics, 246
  and spirituality, 247–248
Blues theology (bluesology), 240–254
Bly, Robert, 156
Box, 6–7
Brayshaw, Richard, 73
Brecht, Bertolt, 229
Brown, Janet, 52–53
Brown, John Mason, 121, 126–127, 167
Brucher, William T., 110
Brustein, Robert, 176, 185
Bunyan, John, 127
Bus Stop, 62–67
Bywaters, Barbara, 199, 203–204

C

Capitalism, 88, 105–108, 110, 111, 115–116, 119–124, 160, 163, 164
  and Communism, 160–169
  and Hollywood, 119–124
  and Russia, 160, 163–164, 167
Carby, Hazel, 240–241
Carter, Steven, 40
The Castle of Perseverance, 125
"Catastrophe," 78–79, 80, 84
The Catcher in the Rye, 33–34, 36
CBS, 215
Chaikin, Joseph, 213–214, 215
"Chains of Dew," 19
Cheney, Anne, 41
Chester, Phyllis, 195
Childbearing, 50–53
Churchill, Caryl, 10
Cixous, Hélène, 10
Class
  and race, 33–36, 261–263
Cloud Nine, 10
Clum, John, 29
Clurman, Harold, 122, 125–126
Coastal Disturbances, 57
Cohn, Ruby, 4, 101, 109
Cold War, 159, 160, 168
Color
  meaning of, 31–32
The Colored Museum, 256-267
Come Back, Little Sheba, 68–70
Comedy, 55–56, 148–149, 227–228, 229, 231–232, 234 , 235
Communist Party, 159, 163, 164, 167, 168–169
Conrad, Joseph, 41
Conwell, Russell, 108–109
Cook, George Cram, 17–18
Cook, Nilla, 18
Cooper, James Fenimore, 150
Courlander, Harold, 138
Crew, Spencer, 255
Crimp, Douglas, 256, 257, 259
"The Critical Phallacy," 195
Critique of the Dialtectical Reason, 116
The Cryptogram, 87, 90–98
Cultural schizophrenic, 260–261, 271

D

Daily Worker, 167
Dante, 64
The Dark at the Top of the Stairs, 70–71
Dasgupta, Gautam, 220
Day of the Locust, 121
de Lauretis, Teresa, 94
Death of a Salesman, 101, 104–116, 227
"Death of the boy," 147, 148
Decker, Jeffrey Louis, 26
Deleuze, Gilles, 103–104, 116
A Delicate Balance, 1
Dialectic of Enlightenment, 102, 103
Diamond, Elin, 15
Dieckman, Suzanne Burgoyne, 73
Dionysian, 68, 69
Doctor Faustus, 122–123
Dolan, Jill, 49, 57
Domestic realism, 87–98
"Doris plays," 215–218
Dramaturgy, 239
Dream, 215
Dreiser, Theodore, 18
Du Bois, Blanche
  comic behavior, 228–229, 230–231
  as a couple, 233–234
  sexuality, 233–234
  tragic behavior, 228, 234–235
DuBois, W. E. B., 41–42, 141
Duggan, William, 41, 46
Dymkowski, Christine, 196, 197–198, 203–204

E

East Along the Equator, 46
Eat Cake, 221–222
Ebony, 262, 263, 268
Elam, Harry Jr., 256–257, 267
Ellison, Ralph, 240, 243
The Emperor Jones, 131–143
  drum as a symbol, 138–139
  "haunts," 141–142
  religion, 137–138, 140–141, 142
  stealing, 133–134
"Explorations," 78, 83–85

F

Faludi, Susan, 57
Family
  as an icon, 50–53, 88–90
  and feminism, 49–54
  and power, 87–88
  realistic portrayal, 87–98
  and stereotype, 70–72
Felman, Shoshana, 195, 197
Female
  gender determined roles, 61–72
  as hostile, 49–50, 89–90
  and madness, 195–209
  portrayal of, 89–90, 148–149, 151, 152–153, 154
  unseen characters, 9–19
Feminine Focus: The New Women Playwrights, 49, 58
Feminist
  as hostile, 49–50, 89–90
  mantra, 23–24
  mimesis, 9–19
  portrayal, 57–58
  theatre, 9–19
  undermining of, 48–58
  See also Anti-feminist
Fences, 242, 243, 247–248
The Fever, 171, 172, 173, 176, 178, 179, 181, 186, 188–192
  compared to *Aunt Dan and Lemon*, 190–191
  and illness, 189
  need for commodities, 184
  theatre and its future, 189
  unresolved ending, 191–192
  use of questions, 181
Fiedler, Leslie, 150
The First Fool, 215
Fiske, John R., 263–264
Flanagan, Hallie, 160, 161
Flatley, Guy, 7
For Colored Girls Who Have Considered Suicide/When the Rainbow is Enuf, 267
Forte, Jeanne, 10, 15
Four Plays, 72
Franklin, Benjamin, 108–109
Freeman, Barbara, 10, 19
Freudian Theory, 102
Friedman, Sharon, 196, 197–198, 199
Funnyhouse of a Negro, 10

G

Gabriel, Gilbert, 167
Gardner, Howard, 75, 80, 81, 82–83, 85, 86
Garland, Robert, 167
Garvey, Marcus, 41
Gassner, John, 126
Gender roles, crossing of, 96–97
Gendermandering, 62–72
Genet, Jean, 44, 200
Gerard, Jeremy, 255–256
Gerrymandering, 61, 62
Getting Out, 15
Gilbert, Sandra, 199, 204
Glaspell, Susan, 9–19, 195–197, 203, 205, 208
 feminist or anti-feminist, 15–19
Gledhill, Christine, 29
"The Gospel According to Miss Roj," 268–269
The Great Thirst, 46
Greenblatt, Stephen, 135
Gregory, André, 172, 179, 180–182, 191, 192
Group Theatre, 119
Guanier, Lani, 62
Guare, John, 23–36
Guattari, Felix, 103–104, 116
Gubar, Susan, 199, 204
Guess Who's Coming to Dinner?, 33
Gussow, Mel, 57

H

Haiti
 and America, 134–137
Haley, Alex, 41, 46
Hall, Stuart, 260
Hansberry, Lorraine, 39–46, 267–268
 early influences, 41–42
Hansberry, William Leo, 41
Harrison, Paul Carter, 241, 246
Hart, Lynda, 201
"Haunts," 141–142
Heart of Darkness, 41, 42–45, 46
Hegelian Absolute Spirit, 258
The Heidi Chronicles, 57
Heilbrun, Carolyn, 202–203
Heller, Dana, 61–62
Hellman, Lillian, 160
Hernton, Calvin, 252
Hiss, Alger, 159
Hitler, 164, 184, 187, 188
Hoeveler, D.L., 115–116
Hollywood
 as an icon, 32–33, 125, 127, 128, 217
 as corporate capitalism, 119–124
 as corrupt, 121–122
 as a fable, 119–128
 types, 123
Homosexuality, 27, 28–29, 32, 68, 71, 90–91, 92–93, 124, 150, 151, 156, 268
Horkheimer, Max, 102–103
The Hotel Play, 171–173, 175
 foreign setting, 175–176
 and illness, 172–173
Howe, Irving, 159
Howe, Tina, 49–58
Huckleberry Finn, 150, 155
Huftel, Sheila, 101
Hurlyburly, 147–169
 and female characters, 148–149, 151, 152–153, 154
 and male friendship, 147–157

I

Ibsen, Henrik, 227, 230
Iconic citizenship, 23, 24, 25, 27, 28, 29, 32
I'm Really Here, 215, 217–218
Indians, 73
Inge, William, 61–72
Inheritors, 19
Interviews with Contemporary Women Playwrights, 49, 58
Isaacs, Harold, 41

J

Jacob's Ladder, 46
Jacobson, Roman, 73
Jacobus, Mary, 204
Jeffords, Susan, 23
Jim Crow laws, 134–135
Joe Turner's Come and Gone, 242, 243, 247, 248
Judd Rankin's Daughter, 9
Judgement Day, 164

K

Kael, Pauline, 182
Karp, Ivan, 257
Kelley, Margot Anne, 73
Kennedy, Adrienne, 10
Kesselman, Wendy, 15, 196, 200, 201, 205, 206–207
Keyssar, Helene, 201
Kierkegaard, 65, 66
Kilkelly, Ann, 201
Kopit, Arthur, 73–86
Kowalski, Stanley
  as a comic figure, 228, 231
  as a couple, 233–234
Kristeva, Julia, 270
Kroll, Jack, 170, 177, 179, 260, 267

L

La Mama, 171–172
Labor gang, 136–137, 141
Lacan, Jacques, 257
Lacanian model, 10–19, 262
Leatherstocking Tales, 150
Les Blancs, 40–41, 42–45, 46
Leverich, Lyle, 227, 233
Lewis, Allen, 120–121
Listening, 1
Lockridge, Richard, 167
Loman, Willy, 101–116
  and Biff, 112–114
  and Brooklyn, 109–110
  and capitalism, 105–108, 110, 111, 115–116
  desire for consumer products, 104–105
  and his father, 107–109, 110–111, 112
  masculine role models, 106–109, 110–113, 125
  and success, 101–102, 112
Look Up and Live, 215
Lovers of the African Night, 46
Lukacs, George, 132, 133, 140
Luken, Jim, 171
Luria, Aleksandr Romanovich, 75, 76–77, 78, 82–83
Lynching, 136
Lyotard, Jean-Francois, 3, 104

M

Ma Rainey's Black Bottom, 239–254
  blues theology, 240–254
  instrument representation, 245
  power of the musician, 242–243
  record industry, 250–251
  relationship with music, 250
  and religion, 247, 248
  and sexuality, 251–253
Machinal, 196, 202, 203, 205–209
Madness
  and the female character, 195–209
Mailer, Norman, 44
Makes Me Want to Holler, 249–250
Making A Spectacle: Feminist Essays on Contemporary Women's Theatre, 49, 58
Male
  friendship, 147–157
  patriarchal order, 155
  role models, 106–109, 110–113, 125, 179–180
  redefined, 23–36
  unconscious, 102
Malone Dies, 85
Malraux, André, 258–259
Mamet, David, 87–98, 147, 149, 150–151, 155, 156, 171
  portrayal of women, 89–90
The Man with a Shattered World: The History of a Brain Wound, 75, 76–77
Mandl, Bette, 201–202
The Mandrake, 182, 186
Mantle, Burns, 167
Marchand, Roland, 32
Marie and Bruce, 174, 176–179
  and illness, 178–179
  sexuality, 174–175
Marines, 134
Marlowe, Christopher, 122–123
Marriage
  portrayal of, 13–18, 49–50, 53–54, 64–65, 68–70, 176–179, 196
Marxist, 119, 127, 192
The Master and Margarita, 182
Matson, Norman, 18
McCall, Nathan, 249–250
McLuhan, Marshall, 213, 214, 216, 218–219, 223, 224
McMillen, Neil R., 135

Media
  and the theatre, 213–224
Metraux, Alfred, 139
Meyerowitz, Joanne, 61–62
Miller, Arthur, 7, 101–116, 159–160, 227
Miller, Christopher, 39–40
Mills, C. Wright, 111
Milton, John, 125
Minority Report, 161, 164
Modelski, Tania, 58
Monologue
  effective use, 1–7
Museumification, 267–268
Museums
  as an ideological function, 256
  as a cultural history, 256–258
  neutralization, 259
  special exhibitions, 265–266
  See also Art
My Dinner with André, 172, 179, 180–185, 187, 188, 190–191, 192
  compared to *Aunt Dan and Lemon*, 179–188
  need for commodities, 184
  use of questions, 180–181
  and the waiter, 183
My Sister in This House, 15, 196, 199–201, 202, 206, 207, 209

N

Nadel, Alan, 33–34
National Museum of American History, 255
Naturalism, 131–143, 160
Nazis, 160, 164, 184–185, 186, 187, 188
Nemiroff, Robert, 41
The Nest, 56–57
New Playwrights Theatre, 159–160
The New Women's Theatre, 57–58
"Nobody in Town Can Bake a Sweet Jellyroll Like Mine," 241
Norman, Marsha, 15
Not I, 6
Notes from Underground, 189

O

Odd Couple, 155
Odets, Clifford, 119–128
  and Hollywood, 119–122
Oedipal narrative, 90, 94–96, 97
  role of Woman, 96
Oh Dad, Poor Dad, 73
"Old Black Magic," 66
The Old Neighborhood, 87
One Shoe Off, 49–50, 53–56, 57
  as anti-feminist, 53, 56
  comparison to *Birth And After Birth*, 54–57
O'Neill, Eugene, 19, 131–143
Open Theatre, 213–215
Orr, John, 103
Other, 10, 88, 90, 93, 94, 96, 97–98, 116
Our Late Night, 172
The Outsiders, 9
The Owl Answers, 10
Ozieblo, Barbara, 196, 203

P

Painting Churches, 57
Paolucci, Anne, 3, 5
Paradise Lost, 119
Parker, Brian, 111
"The Party," 269–272
Perception
  the nature of, 88–89
Perfection, 214–215, 216, 221, 224–225
Philips, A., 137
"The Photo Session," 260–262, 263, 265
The Piano Lesson, 242, 243, 244, 247, 248
Picnic, 67–68
Pinter, Harold, 175
Pirandello, Luigi, 230
Plato, 196, 197, 205
Playwrights Company, 160
Poetic realism, 7
Poitier, Sidney, 33
Portrait of Dora, 10
"Prelude," 78
The Presence of the Actor, 214
Pridgett, Gertrude, 241, 251, 253
Provincetown Players, 11, 17, 19, 131
Public Theatre, 179

Q

Quinn, Arthur Hobson, 132–133
Quotations from Chairman Mao Tse-Tung, 6

R
Rabe, Dave, 147–157
Rabkin, Gerald, 127
Race
  and legitimacy, 23–36
  and style, 263–264
Radio, 222–224
A Raisin in the Sun, 40–41, 42, 267–268
Raphael, Ray, 147, 157
Rauschenberg, Robert, 257
Reagan, Ronald, 23, 29–30, 31
Reinelt, Janelle, 49
Religion, 137–139, 140–141, 142, 239–240, 247, 248
Renoir, Jean, 125–126
Reunion, 87
Rice, Elmer, 160–169
  background, 160–161
  defense of *Between Two Worlds*, 167–168
  and Russia, 161–163
Rich, Frank, 56, 156–157, 173
Rogin, Michael, 23
Roman, David, 29
Romeo and Juliet, 66
Roots, 46
Rosenberg, Harold, 73
Ross, Thomas, 30
Russell, Bertrand, 203
Russell, Michelle, 252
Russia
  and America, 159–169
Rutenberg, Michael E., 6

S
Sachs, Oliver, 76
The Safe and Sure Way to Amass a Fortune and Be a Benefactor, 108
Said, Edward, 140
Salinger, J.D., 33–34
Sam, Guillaume Vilbrun, 135–136
Samson Agonistes, 125
Sartre, Jean-Paul, 105, 116
Savran, David, 178
Schechner, Richard, 214
Schickel, Richard, 179
Schizophrenic
  See Cultural schizophrenic
Schmidt, Hans, 135–136, 143
Schroeder, Patricia, 15
Sedgwick, Eve, 152
Sex and Racism in America, 252
Sexual Perversity in Chicago, 156
Sexuality
  and beauty, 251–253
  brutal, 174–175
  and Hollywood, 125
  and role reversal, 61–72
Shakespeare, William, 66, 122, 229–230
Shange, Ntozake, 267
The Shattered Mind: The Person After Brain Damage, 75, 86
Shaw, George Bernard, 227
Shawn, Wallace, 171–192
  and morality, 186, 187–188
  political function, 188, 189–190
  and self-confidence, 187
  and success, 188, 189
  theatre as political, 188
Shepard, Sam, 2, 7, 147, 151, 156, 171
Sherwood, Robert, 160
Shuman, R. Baird, 125
Sifton, Paul, 168
Simon, John, 171
Simon, Neil, 155
Sims, James, 255
Six Degrees of Separation, 24–36
Slavery, 134–135, 141, 246, 266
  See also African Americans
Smith, Bessie, 241, 252
Souls of Black Folk, 141
Soyinka, Wole, 245
Speed-the-Plow, 155, 156
Spillers, Hortense, 240–241
Spindler, Michael, 103, 118
Spirituality, 247–248
Spivak, Gayatri Chakravorty, 204
Stansilavsky, Constatin, 94
"The Stepinac Case," 215
Stereotypes, 60, 62, 67, 70–72
  reversal of, 61–62
Street Scene, 160
A Streetcar Named Desire, 227–236
  as a comedy, 227–228, 235–236
  death and desire, 232–233

Stroke, 74–86
  affect on language and words, 79, 80
  affect psychologically, 80
  books about, 74–77
  clinical accuracy, 74–75, 77
Stuart, Jan, 55–56, 57
Style
  as identification, 263–264
Success
  as an ideology, 112
  and death, 115
Summer Evening, 173–176, 177, 180
  tropical settings, 173
Sunset Freeway, 222–224
"Symbiosis," 260–261, 262–265

T

Tarkington, Booth, 140
Television, 218–222
Terkel, Studs, 40
There Shall Be No Night, 160
Thomas, Maria, 46
Till the Day I Die, 119
Timebends, 103
Tiny Alice, 1, 4–6
"Tradition of the New," 73
Tragicomic, 147–157, 227–237
Treadwell, Sophie, 196, 198–199, 203, 205, 207
Trifles, 9, 10–11, 12, 13, 15, 18–19
Tulane Drama Review, 213
TV, 218–221
Two Trains Running, 249

U

Uncle Vanya, 192
Understanding Media, 213, 218–219, 222, 223
United States, *See* America
Unseen woman
  foils, 12
  personality, 12–13
  power struggle, 13–14
  presence, 10–11

V

van Itallie, Jean-Claude, 213–225
Verfremdungseffekte, 229
The Verge, 9, 17, 18, 19, 196–198, 202, 203–204, 205, 207, 208, 209
Vietnam, 220, 221
Vodoun (Voodoo), 138–139

W

Wagner, Phyllis Jane, 217
Waiting for Godot, 55
Waiting for Lefty, 119, 127, 128
War of the Worlds, 199
Wasserstein, Wendy, 57
Watch on the Rhine, 160
We, the People, 160, 163–164, 168
Weales, Gerald, 185, 220
Wernicke's aphasia, 75, 80, 81
West, Cornel, 255, 261, 271, 272
West, Nathaniel, 121
Wetzsteon, Ross, 171, 189, 191
Whan See, 51–52
Where is De Queen?, 215
White, Hayden, 109
"White Marines," 131
Who's Afraid of Virginia Woolf?, 1, 2–4, 5, 7
Wiegman, Robyn, 29
The Wild Duck, 227
Williams, John A., 46
Williams, Raymond, 103
Williams, Tennessee, 7, 227–236
Wilson, August, 239–254
  development of blues theology, 240–241
Wilson, Robert, 6
Winernitz, Helen, 46
Wings, 73–86
The Winter's Tale, 229–230
Wittgenstein, Ludwig, 203–204
Wolfe, George C., 255–272
Wright, Richard, 45–46

Y

Youth Hostel, 178

Z

Zola, Emile, 139–140
The Zoo Story, 1, 2, 7